WITHDRAWN

THE AMERICAN LIBRARY

10, RUE DU GÉNÉRAL CAMOU
75007 PARIS

American Library
in Paris
Book Award
2018 Submission

France's Long Reconstruction

France's Long Reconstruction

IN SEARCH OF THE MODERN REPUBLIC

Herrick Chapman

Harvard University Press

Cambridge, Massachusetts

London, England

2018

Library of Congress Cataloging-in-Publication Data
Names: Chapman, Herrick, author.
Title: France's long reconstruction : in search of the modern republic /
Herrick Chapman.
Description: Cambridge, Massachusetts : Harvard University Press,
2018. | Includes bibliographical references and index.
Identifiers: LCCN 2017015077 | ISBN 9780674976412 (alk. paper)
Subjects: LCSH: France—Politics and government—1945- | France—
Social conditions—1945–1995. | France—Economic conditions—1945–
Classification: LCC DC404 .C464 2018 | DDC 944.082—dc23
LC record available at https://lccn.loc.gov/2017015077

To Liz, Julia, and Natalie

Contents

Abbreviations

AMGOT	Allied Military Government of Occupied Territory
CADI	Centre d'action et de défense des immigrés
CCOS	Conseil central des oeuvres sociales
CDL	Comité départemental de la Libération
CE	Contrôle économique
CFDT	Confédération française démocratique du travail
CFTC	Confédération française des travailleurs chrétiens
CGC	Confédération générale des cadres
CGCM	Confédération générale des classes moyennes
CGE	Comité général d'études
CGPF	Confédération générale de la production française
CGPME	Confédération générale des petites et moyennes entreprises
CGT	Confédération générale du travail
CGTU	Confédération générale du travail unitaire
CNAF	Confédération nationale de l'artisanat français
CNE	Conseil national économique
CNPF	Conseil national du patronat français
CNR	Conseil national de la Résistance
CRS	Compagnies républicaines de sécurité
DGI	Direction générale des impôts
ECSC	European Coal and Steel Community
EDC	European Defense Community
EDF	Électricité de France
EEC	European Economic Community
ENA	École nationale d'administration
FAS	Fonds d'action sociale

FFI	Forces françaises de l'intérieur
FLN	Front de libération nationale
FNOSS	Fédération nationale des organisations de sécurité sociale
FO	Force ouvrière
GDF	Gaz de France
HCCPF	Haut Comité consultatif de la population et de la famille
HEC	Hautes études commerciales
IGAME	Inspecteur général de l'administration en mission extraordinaire
INED	Institut national des études démographiques
INSEE	Institut national de la statistique et des études économiques
MNA	Mouvement national algérien
MPF	Mouvement populaire des familles
MRP	Mouvement républicain populaire (Christian Democratic Party)
OAS	Organisation armée secrète
ONI	Office national d'immigration
PCF	Parti communiste français
PSU	Parti socialiste unifié
PTT	Postes, télégraphes et téléphones
RATP	Régie autonome des transports parisiens
SFIO	Section française de l'Internationale ouvrière (Socialist Party)
SNCF	Société nationale des chemins de fer
SNECMA	Société nationale d'études et de construction des moteurs d'avions
STO	Service du travail obligatoire
TVA	Taxe sur la valeur ajoutée
UDCA	Union de défense des commerçants et artisans
UFCS	Union féminine civique et sociale
UFF	Union des femmes françaises
UNAF	Union nationale des associations familiales
UNCAF	Union nationale des caisses d'allocations familiales
UNCM	Union nationale des cadres, techniciens et agents de maîtrise

Introduction

PEOPLE LIVING IN FRANCE at the end of World War II faced immense challenges, as did most Europeans who had survived Nazi conquest, genocide, and the ravages of total war. They had to repair the sinews of social solidarity and political community after Nazi occupation, Vichy autocracy, and a virtual civil war in 1943–1944 between collaborators and the Resistance had torn their country apart. Over two million former French prisoners of war, repatriated labor conscripts, and surviving deportees had to reintegrate into society. Although the death toll in France was half what it had been in World War I, the physical destruction was much larger: a quarter of all buildings were destroyed, compared to just 9 percent in 1914–1918. Seventy-four of the then ninety *départements* (administrative districts) in metropolitan France were touched by combat, in contrast to thirteen during the first war. A million families were homeless. Just 45 percent of the country's rail lines were serviceable, and then only in unconnected sections. One locomotive in six was useable.[1] As Pierre Mendès France, minister of national economy in de Gaulle's Liberation government, later encapsulated the complexity of recovery, "You had to repair rails to bring back the trains, but for that you needed steel from mills that could not be properly provisioned by trains."[2] Digging out of this war required tremendous collective ingenuity for a very long time. And the fortitude of an exhausted people. Catholic social activist Louisette Le Driand recalled the travails of living as a newlywed in makeshift cold-water barracks in her bombed-out Breton city of Lorient: "Rats were the masters."[3]

I

If people yearned most for a return to normalcy, French leaders across the full sweep of a fractured political landscape believed at the Liberation that reconstruction imposed an even bigger agenda. Many an ordinary citizen was more concerned with getting life back to a stable routine and rebuilding a home or a local school exactly as it had been—"à l'identique," as people put it.[4] But French leaders agreed that France had to "modernize." In Jean Monnet's much-quoted injunction, "We have no choice. The only alternative to modernization is decadence."[5] Defeat in 1940 had made this clear. To be sure, every country in Europe embraced an ethos of recovery, reconstruction, and rebirth. But no other nation's elite felt more humiliated or as convinced that a thoroughgoing economic transformation was essential for national renewal. "We will remake France," the Resistance exhorted in its underground press.[6] Just what this new France should be, however, was hardly self-evident, and as a consequence the question of reconstruction—what it should be and how to do it—remained at the heart of French political combat for more than a decade after the war, and as I will argue, until the end of the Algerian war in 1962.

One thing, though, seemed clear to nearly everyone in 1944, apart from a small market-liberal minority: the French state should serve as pilot and engine for the postwar reconstruction.[7] A heavy reliance on national government would be commonplace across the European continent in the late 1940s; wartime mobilization and public services had already expanded state capacities, and the Allied victory had reconfirmed the legitimacy of state authority. But in France, policy experts in the top levels of the civil service drew on a long history of state centralization to position themselves to play an especially big role in the reconstruction. In the post-Liberation era a wide range of specialists—economists, demographers, engineers, medical professionals, and a legion of policy experts trained in the law—acquired outsized authority in a nation whose leaders were hell-bent on "modernizing" their country.

At the same time, the autocratic rule of a collaborationist Vichy regime also left France with a complex *political* challenge for the reconstruction—reviving democracy. The defeat of 1940 had discredited the Third Republic (1870–1940), making it easier for Vichy and the far Right to cast aside France's democratic traditions. Without the subsequent failure of the Vichy regime (1940–1944) to adequately feed, shelter, and protect the nation from Nazi plundering, the renewed thirst for republican democracy might have been longer in coming. But come it did, as the call for democratic renewal soon became ubiquitous in Resistance tracts and crucial for uniting that movement's many factions. Leader of the Free French, General Charles de Gaulle, whose democratic credentials U.S. President Franklin Roosevelt doubted, proclaimed as early as 1941 in London's Albert Hall the desire of the Free French "to remain faithful to the democratic principles that our ancestors drew from the genius of our race and that are the very stakes of this life-and-death war."[8] For their part, Socialists in the Resistance like Jules Moch urged an expansion of democratic ambitions in a liberated France, insisting that "democracy must extend into the economic order." In that same spirit Albert Camus's Resistance newspaper, *Combat*, claimed it wanted "to institute a true people's and workers' democracy."[9] Not to be outbid, leaders of the Communist resistance sought to position their party as democracy's staunchest advocate, calling for such things as "a democratization of the structures of the state" and "a democratic army."[10] By 1944 nearly every Resistance tract and propaganda message emanating from London, Algiers, Lyon, and Paris in the months leading up to the Liberation called for a democratic revolution.

But the shape and form of a democratic rejuvenation was no more obvious than the formula for "modernization." A powerful parliament? Stronger parties? A greater role for the trade unions and other pressure groups? New opportunities for ordinary citizens to have their voices heard in factories, schools, trade unions, or chambers of commerce, to say nothing of the halls of government? The mere return to parliamentary government seemed to most Resistance leaders patently insufficient for a real democratic revolution. The Charter of the National Resistance Council, designed to give a cacophonous movement a common program to stand behind, kept the agenda for political reform vague by promising that the Resistance would "remain united after the Liberation . . . to ensure the establishment of the broadest possible democracy."[11]

In principle the dual objectives of reconstruction—"modernization" and democratic renewal—could go hand in hand. Indeed, modernization theorists of the 1950s such as Walter Rostow and Daniel Lerner would come to argue that industrial growth, the expansion of an urban middle class, and the consolidation of democratically run parties and governments were all mutually reinforcing processes.[12] But in practice a state-led, top-down modernization drive could all too easily threaten democratic renewal. Cabinet ministers and technical experts could insulate themselves from pressure groups, ignore dissent, and keep their own counsel for the sake of what they viewed as the national interest.

This inherent tension between administrative assertiveness and democratic participation worried contemporaries at the time. Writing in the grips of fury several months after the fall of France in 1940, the great medieval historian and later Resistance martyr, Marc Bloch, concluded his *Strange Defeat* with an appeal to the new generation of elites that he expected to emerge from the war and rebuild the country. "All I beg of them," Bloch wrote, "is that they should avoid the dry inhumanity of systems which, from rancor or from pride, set themselves to rule the mass of their countrymen without providing them with adequate instruction, without being in true communion with them. Our people deserve to be trusted, to be taken into the confidence of their leaders."[13] This anxiety about the destructive consequences for democracy if state leaders were to proceed with arrogant disregard for public participation found expression within official Resistance circles as the Occupation wore on. In 1943 an anonymous memorandum writer, working within the planning committees of the London-based wing of the Resistance, argued that in 1940 "democratic values" became "disassociated" from "technical values" and that postwar France must create a government "supported by scientific technique without abandoning power to the technicians."[14] Postwar reconstruction, then, posed a challenge fully discernable at the time: how to combine a state-led economic revolution with an expansion of democratic participation without the one undoing the other.

This book explores how the French expanded the role of the national state to spearhead the nation's recovery, how they clashed over the proper reach of state authority, and above all how they wrestled with the tension between administrative rule and democratic renewal in a country traumatized by defeat, occupation, and near civil war. I argue that from 1944 to 1962, during what I term the "long reconstruction," governing elites, parties, pressure groups, and grassroots citizens' movements failed to diminish, much less resolve, this tension between the democratic and the "technocratic"—to use the jargon of the time. On the contrary, the tension deepened and became more institutionalized, so much so that by the time of the first government of the Fifth Republic from 1959 to 1962 (with de Gaulle as president and Michel Debré as prime minister), the technocracy-democracy binary had become commonplace as a way of framing the problems of governance in the new republic. This preoccupation with "technocracy" stemmed not only from the concentration of executive authority that came with the new Constitution of the Fifth Republic and de Gaulle's statecraft. Nor was it simply the inevitable replaying of a long state tradition of relying on experts who provoked public resistance in turn. It emerged above all from the political dynamics of the long reconstruction.

At the same time, this book also shows how organized groups of people in French society fought for what they wanted in a polity where administrative power, pressure group politics, and grassroots mobilization went hand in hand. What emerged from the long reconstruction was not simply a single grand narrative of regime change and the expanding power of an administrative and "technocratic" elite. The long reconstruction also created a terrain in which interest groups and social movements learned to use an inherited repertoire of contention—resisting, cajoling, co-opting, and negotiating with state authorities—so as to give democratic politics a distinctive volatility in the Fourth and early Fifth Republics.[15]

To analyze these several dimensions of France's postwar reconstruction—the expansion of the state's functions, the rise of administrative power and the influence of experts, and the public's efforts to contest and negotiate with the state—I have focused much of this book on a set of policy domains. French people at the time, and historians since, have understood the reconstruction largely in terms of policies—efforts to consolidate a nascent welfare state, "modernize" industry, rebuild infrastructure, upgrade the training of high civil servants, redress a severe housing shortage, and so forth. Policies, however, involve domains—particular constellations of questions, choices, institutions, and networks of state and nonstate actors—all of which have histories that come into play as well and give those domains an enduring structure.[16] By investigating policy domains, not just policies, this book seeks to capture the social and political contestations—beyond the elite consensus supporting "modernization"—that shaped France's postwar recovery. And by teasing out the variations in the story that particular policy domains reveal, this book challenges established narratives that keep the spotlight on national politics, the Fourth Republic's chronic governmental instability, its collapse in 1958, and de Gaulle's triumph of consolidating a stable Fifth Republic. My approach illuminates more continuities across the 1958 divide than a stricter focus on national politics provides.

France's long reconstruction involved too large a range of policy domains for a single book to explore them all in the depth this approach demands. Every domain—from economic planning, agriculture, and housing, to health insurance, education, and more—embodied the tension between expert-driven, administrative rule and democratic participation. I have chosen to focus on four policy domains that dramatized how the state's role expanded after the Liberation and that capture most of the major forms of contestation and negotiation shaping policy-making in the reconstruction era: (a) manpower policy and immigration, (b) tax reform and the regulation of small enterprise, (c) family policy as a centerpiece of the postwar building of a welfare state, and (d) the nationalization of industry and banking as key to renovating the country's economic infrastructure. All four domains remained prominent in public debate throughout the period of the long reconstruction. And each activated different segments of French society: immigrants, shopkeepers, women, industrial and white-collar workers, and business entrepreneurs. These policy domains bring into the foreground as well many of the most influential politicians, policy experts, and social activists of the time—from Communists such as Marcel Paul and Madeleine Colin, or Social Catholics Germaine Poinso-Chapuis and Robert Prigent, or Pierre Poujade on the extreme Right, to the better-known architects of the reconstruction such as Pierre Laroque (the "father" of social security), financial expert François Bloch-Lainé, demographer Alfred Sauvy, and legal expert and politician Michel Debré.[17]

In addition to four core chapters on policy domains, this book also includes three chapters that explore the relationship between state administrative authority and democratic renewal through a broader perspective that transcends any single set of policies. Chapter 1 examines the Liberation period as a moment when de Gaulle and a host of other political actors, both national and local, sought to extend and legitimize anew the authority of the French state after the debacle of Vichy and the Occupation. This effort to reassert republican authority raised public expectations about the state's role as handmaiden to the economic and social renovation of the country. And when the constitutional struggles of 1945 and 1946 produced a Fourth Republic with many of the institutional weaknesses of the little-mourned Third, the pathway opened wider for top civil servants, government ministers, and policy experts to assert their leadership over the reconstruction. Following Chapters 2 through 5, on policy domains, Chapter 6 also looks at the broad national picture by analyzing how two key figures of the reconstruction era—Pierre Mendès France of the center Left and Michel Debré of the center Right—each struggled with the tension between state administrative authority and democratic renewal. These two men thought and wrote about this tension more than anyone else in political life at the time, revealing a great deal about how elite thinking on the matter evolved over the course of the Fourth and early Fifth Republics. Their disagreements about how best to blend a strong state with the public's democratic participation framed much of the mainstream political debate of the 1960s. Chapter 7 explores the final years of the long reconstruction by assessing the impact of the Algerian war on the state's role in metropolitan France and on the democratic process. France, unlike other countries in Europe, carried out its postwar reconstruction while fighting full-scale colonial wars, first in Indochina (1946–1954) and then in Algeria (1954–1962). The latter war in particular had the effect of consolidating much of the expansion and concentration of state authority that occurred through the long reconstruction. I conclude the book by showing how much the contestation between top-down leadership and bottom-up participation during the long reconstruction bequeathed to France's Fifth Republic its distinctive patterns of relations between state and society that in many ways still prevail to this day.

To comprehend the long reconstruction, we also need to understand its prehistory: state expansion and the tension between administrative power and democratic politics goes back a long way. In an address to public servants at the Conseil d'État (Council of State, a top juridical body) in 1970, two years after the upheavals of May 1968, President Georges Pompidou reminded his audience that "for more than a thousand years . . . there has been a France only because there was a state . . . to keep it together, to organize it, to make it grow, to defend it not only against external threats but also against collective egotism, the rivalry of groups."[18] De Gaulle had said very much the same thing to the Conseil d'État during the "week of the barricades," an army revolt in Algeria in January 1960: "There is a France only thanks to the state, and only by the state can France be maintained."[19] This conventional understanding of the centrality of the state in France rested on sound history and potent myth: history, insofar as by the eighteenth century the monarchs of France had indeed built a country outward from Paris to something close to its modern frontiers (in contrast to Germany, where, despite centuries of cultural integration, territorial unity under a single state came only in 1870); and myth, insofar as state authority in France depended on a widespread belief in the *idea* of the state as guarantor of order, justice, unity, and the common good. The rhetorical power of Pompidou's words also owed a great deal to a particularly *republican* conception of the state harking back to the French Revolution—the state as a rational actor giving direction to a conflict-ridden society in accord with the principles of liberty, equality, and fraternity. Revolutionaries from across a wide spectrum of opinion embraced the state as the chief instrument for forging "a one and indivisible Republic."

Alongside this rationalist view, however, the Revolution also produced another republican idea of the state, a more democratic idea that elevated citizens' voice and political representation as defining features of the Republic. Revolutionaries sanctified popular sovereignty, the principle that the state's authority derived not from God, the king's "divine right," but from "the people" and to the consent they lend to constitutional government. This tension—between a rationalist (often elite) view of the state's function, so evident in Pompidou's address, and a democratic (sometimes populist) view of how the state should be run and society governed—only deepened in the course of the Revolution and in the Napoleonic era that followed.[20] The revolutionaries of the First French Republic (1792–1795) radically expanded the coercive and bureaucratic power of the state, and Napoleon in turn more fully centralized authority, undermined representative institutions, and made rule by administration an everyday reality. The tension between administrative governance and democratic participation reinvigorated in the long reconstruction, then, had firm roots in France's prior history.[21]

If developments since Napoleon did little to resolve that tension, they did do a lot to shape the state that the nation's leaders were to inherit in 1945. As in other European countries, the French state grew slowly but inexorably in response to industrialization in the nineteenth century, expanding its personnel and authority in policing, tariff enforcement, and the regulation of mining, transport, and agriculture. The profession of engineering had especially tight links to the state in France via education and employment, and its avatars, often imbued with a near-utopian faith in their power to organize the good society, presided over the planning of canals, roads, and rails.[22] With the new Third Republic (1870–1940) the state vastly expanded its role in education, public health, and the regulation of the workplace. As important as expansion of state functions was, however, it was hardly exceptional in Europe. Indeed, France lagged behind Britain and Germany in the professionalization of its state bureaucracy.[23] Before 1914, moreover, French governments remained wedded to principles of economic liberalism that, apart from tariff protection, limited state intervention in the market. For all the much-touted centralization of political authority in France, local politicians and parliamentarians still had plenty of power to temper the authority of the ministries in Paris, even the Interior Ministry's locally based prefects.

The two world wars and the Great Depression changed this picture profoundly. During the First World War the colossal demands of total war put the state at the center of a command economy, much as had the French Revolution and the Napoleonic wars, only this time on a far greater scale. State officials conscripted soldiers and workers in staggering numbers, including from the colonies. They enforced wage and price ceilings, rationed supplies, and made major changes in business organization and labor relations. A similar story of state expansion and experimentation could be told about other belligerent countries in

World War I. What is striking about France, however, is how far its leaders went after 1918 to *dismantle* wartime innovations, more so than in Britain and Germany. Victory seemed to have redeemed the Republic, and it confirmed the conviction of many politicians, especially the conservatives who prevailed in the elections of 1919, that the conventional political and economic arrangements of pre-France were sufficient for the postwar world.

The more lasting breakthroughs in state expansion had to await the Depression and the Second World War and its aftermath. Though short-lived, socialist Léon Blum's left-wing Popular Front government of 1936 especially broke fresh ground. Social conflict, economic crisis, and war (or its imminence) had been pivotal occasions for state expansion in the past. The Popular Front now faced all three. To boost rearmament Blum nationalized much of the arms industry and a great deal of aviation. To aid a troubled farm sector he created the Wheat Board for stabilizing grain prices. To quell industrial unrest he brokered a nationwide wage deal, a forty-hour week, union rights, and compulsory arbitration. From the Popular Front, too, came new government programs for the arts, leisure, sports, and youth, as well as direct state involvement in radio—the beginnings of what historian Philip Nord has called the "culture state," later associated with the Fifth Republic cultural ministries of André Malraux and Jack Lang.[24] Meanwhile, some political elites in the 1930s, especially on the Right, became enamored with the idea that a strong state executive and a greater reliance on experts could rescue the nation from democratic excess and unfettered capitalism. Though "technocrat" and "technocracy" were not yet terms of common usage in France in the 1930s—that would come only after the war—many a Vichy and Fourth Republic policy expert came of age professionally during the Depression and acquired a sense of mission advocating planning and "rationalization."[25] Historian Jackie Clarke has aptly dubbed this period "the age of organization."[26]

Historians have, therefore, quite rightly emphasized continuities in state expansion and the reliance on technocratic styles of governance from the 1930s, through Vichy, and on into the Fourth Republic. Planning for the postwar began during the Occupation, and the men and women engaged in that project borrowed heavily from ideas and plans preceding the war. De Gaulle may have repudiated Vichy for its treasonous collaboration and its complicity in Nazi crimes, but his early postwar government built readily on many of Vichy's efforts to regulate scarcity, police the black market, promote childbirth, protect the nation's cultural patrimony, and innovate in economic planning and business coordination. As historians Richard Kuisel and Philip Nord have so effectively shown, a good many of the governmental elites in the postwar period managed to thread their careers through these regime changes and hold on to their outlooks and sensibilities—if not always their overt political convictions and loyalties—across the 1930s and 1940s.[27] It is possible, then, to construe the long reconstruction as even longer, as beginning in 1936 or 1940. And indeed, each of the following chapters on policy domains begins with a close look at how developments in the 1930s and during the Occupation influenced what happened after 1944.

That said, the Liberation also was a moment of rupture. It brought a seismic shift in political fortunes, with big consequences for the reconstruction. The Right all but collapsed, discredited by its wartime collaboration with Germany and by an immense groundswell of popular support for the Communists, Socialists, and left Catholic activists who had led the Resistance movement in occupied France. For the first time since its founding in 1920, the French Communist Party (the Parti communiste français, or PCF) became the dominant party of the Left. The Resistance had given it the stature and patriotic aura its leaders had long craved, and de Gaulle was astute enough to reward them with cabinet ministries in his Provisional Government of 1944–1946, even as he continued to regard the party as a danger to the country. Resistance work had enabled party activists to expand their influence in the rural districts, in the Parisian intelligentsia, and above all in the trade union federations of the leading labor organization in France, the Confédération générale du travail (the CGT). A PCF with a solid working-class base, a more disciplined membership cadre than any other party in the country, and a newfound willingness to function as a party of government shifted the political center of gravity in the country far to the left of where it had been before the war.

The Liberation also marked the arrival a major new political force in France, a Christian Democratic party calling itself the Mouvement républicain populaire (the MRP). Catholic resisters, most of them

"Social Catholics" with ties to the Catholic trade unions and youth organizations that grew in the 1930s, optimistically dubbed their party a "movement," and they sought to blend Christian values with progressive politics.[28] This mixture gave the MRP a prominent place in the left-leaning governments of the early post-Liberation years, as well as a large middle-class electoral constituency looking for an alternative to the Vichy-tainted conventional Right. It was a winning combination—the MRP won 28 percent of the vote in the 1946 parliamentary elections, in comparison to 26 percent for the Communists and 21 percent for the Socialists—until more unabashedly right-wing parties recovered their footing in the early 1950s. In the meantime, MRP leaders did much to shape the reconstruction, especially in family policy.

The Liberation also proved pivotal for the third major governing party of the immediate postwar years, the Socialist Party or SFIO (Section française de l'Internationale ouvrière). Socialists had rebuilt their party successfully enough after the crippling schism over Communism in 1920 to become the lead partner in Léon Blum's Popular Front government of 1936. But they fell victim to factionalism, fighting throughout the 1930s over whether to participate in government, break with capitalism, ally with rival parties, and jettison pacifism in the face of the fascist threat. Although Socialists were among the fiercest critics of the far Right, an astonishing three-quarters of the party's parliamentary deputies had voted Philippe Pétain full powers in July 1940, the vote that buried the Third Republic. The Resistance, then, became a crucial vehicle for resuscitating an ailing SFIO. André Philip, Jules Moch, Daniel Mayer, and many others in the Resistance restored the party's reputation as stalwarts of the republican tradition. They played a big role in postwar planning. And with the Liberation the party purged its ranks of the Pétain-enabling parliamentarians. Party membership shot up from a previous high of 285,000 in 1936 to 354,000 at the Liberation, attracting schoolteachers, postal workers, and other civil servants—the post-1920 occupational base of the party. Though still too anticlerical to join forces with leftist Catholics to create a unified non-Communist party along the lines of the British Labour Party—something Léon Blum hoped for—Socialists made their party the pivot point around which to build the tripartite governing coalition with the MRP and the Communist Party.[29]

This powerful left-wing coalition, allied with a network of Gaullist Resistance members loyal to the General himself (many of whom were, like him, conservative or military in their backgrounds), gave the dirigiste state of 1945 a patriotic republican legitimacy that would last well after this unique political moment had passed. As we shall see, the rupture of Liberation mattered more in some policy domains than others, but mattered it did and it changed the terms, the very vocabulary, with which people would talk about the challenges of combining a state-led, top-down modernization drive with new forms of democratic participation. The new political climate of the post-Liberation years, moreover, would continue to weigh heavily on those efforts, which is why the long reconstruction constituted its own era, a decisive chapter in the nation's history when administrative elites and policy experts exercised much greater power than they had under the Third Republic, even as they and a host of societal groups sought to revitalize France's democratic tradition.[30]

Although important scholarly work on reconstruction has relied on more conventional endpoints to the era in the early or mid-1950s, I insist on the *long* reconstruction stretching all the way to 1962, for a number of reasons.[31] True, France's period of impressive, sustained economic growth began in the mid-1950s, and by then price controls and prohibitions against collective bargaining had been dismantled, symbolically marking peacetime stability. But there were also signs aplenty in the mid-1950s that many people in France had hardly moved beyond "reconstruction" as a paradigm for thinking about the country's challenges. In his much-quoted investiture speeches before Parliament in 1953 and 1954, Pierre Mendès France called afresh for a policy of "recovery and national renovation," arguing that the reconstruction had stalled amid the competing budgetary demands of the Indochina war and government failures to make the tough choices a rebirth required.[32] And indeed, many of the key goals of the reconstruction—tax reform, housing growth, vast urban rebuilding projects, especially in devastated cities like Le Havre, and the renovation of much of the country's energy and transportation infrastructure—were just under way and would take many more years to accomplish. Not for nothing did the "modernizing," left-leaning wing of the Catholic labor movement continue to call itself the "Reconstruction" group on into the Fifth Republic in accord with its monthly publication of the same name.

The reconstruction paradigm also endured into the early 1960s because of Charles de Gaulle. When the General returned to power in 1958 and enlisted Michel Debré, first as his justice minister and Constitution drafter and then in January 1959 as the first prime minister of the new Fifth Republic, these two men understood their agenda as finishing the work they started at the Liberation. It was a politically convenient claim, a way to discredit the Fourth Republic they had replaced, but it also spoke to a commonsense view about what their policies represented. By incorporating the period of the de Gaulle–Debré government into a study of the reconstruction, we can assess anew how much the regime change of 1958 signified rupture and continuity. In constitutional terms the rupture is easy to see. But if we plunge back into policy domains, we can also take the measure of how much the Fifth Republic was built on the Fourth.

Finally, the notion of the long reconstruction enables us to see more clearly the links between the politics of national recovery and the struggles over both the Cold War and decolonization, the two crucial international contexts of the reconstruction era. Soviet-American rivalry had an enormous impact on the financial and political conditions of the French recovery. Not only did the Blum-Byrnes Accords of 1946 and then the Marshall Plan help the French restore financial stability in the late 1940s; the infusion of American dollars enabled French planners to structure the reconstruction as a modernization drive. The Cold War also helped precipitate the fissure between Communists and the rest of the French Left in 1947, with consequences for the reconstruction thereafter. American money made it possible for the French to pursue reconstruction and colonial war at the same time, and indeed French leaders in the early years of the reconstruction regarded the empire as an important economic asset for national renewal. North Africans, after all, came in large numbers to mainland France as migrant workers, and sub-Saharan Africa remained a valued source of raw materials, commercial markets, and foreign currency via its own export trade. Fourth Republic governments committed unprecedented sums to "development aid" in part because planners such as Jean Monnet regarded infrastructure projects and economic growth in the colonies as an indirect investment back into the reconstruction effort in the metropole. Indeed, a good deal of development aid did return to France as business profits from projects abroad and as salaries to French personnel.[33] But by the mid-1950s many government officials recoiled at the growing costs of holding on to empire. And colonial subjects, empowered with citizenship rights in 1946, became increasingly adept at making claims for greater equity in pensions, child allowances, and other provisions of a social security system that had extended into the empire. Achieving the goals of the French reconstruction, more leaders were coming to understand, became a matter of letting go of formal empire. It took until 1962 to work through what had become the conjoined efforts of consolidating executive authority in the new Fifth Republic, solidifying France's own "economic miracle," and negotiating an end to an Algerian war—and thereby finally enter into a post-reconstruction era in the 1960s.

To see the reconstruction as a single eighteen-year arc of policy-making and contestation is also to recognize France as something of an outlier in a larger Western European context. As historians David Feldman and Mark Mazower have argued, each country ended up with its own trajectory of reconstruction, and each with its own periodization, despite commonalities and interconnections across the continent. Some countries (the Netherlands, Belgium, and Norway) faced a simpler political task of restoring prewar regimes than did those that sought to replace collapsed democracies with something new, such as Greece and France. Some countries, such as Germany, Austria, and Italy, rebuilt under Allied occupation and others did not. The process went most quickly in Britain, with its regime intact and its physical damage, though significant, less extensive than the major battlefield countries of the war. For all this variation, however, in most cases reconstruction had given way, by the mid-1950s, to a sense of a new phase of national development.[34] Only in France did the politics of reconstruction and the rhetoric of national renewal get bound up so tightly to *two* rounds of regime change (1944 and 1958) and two large colonial wars.

Ever since Jean Fourastié coined the felicitous term "les Trente glorieuses" in 1979 to characterize 1945–1975 as "thirty glorious years" of sustained growth and national rejuvenation, in contrast to the troubled economic era unfolding afterward, the trials and turbulence of the early postwar period became harder to remember.[35] Historians and commentators have tended to read too much "glorieuses," consensus, and coherence back into the postwar French recovery. I have tried in this book to recapture the complexity, conflict, and open-endedness of the reconstruction era—to understand how people at the time saw their problems and options, how they fought with one another about the role of the state, how they absorbed their victories and defeats, and how they learned to defend their interests and convictions in an increasingly state-managed economy. They remade their country in the process. Over the long course of the reconstruction era they reshaped the economic and political landscape more radically than they could have foreseen in 1944.

I

Liberation Authorities

Legitimizing the State from Above and Below

To LIBERATE FRANCE in 1944, the Allies had to force the Wehrmacht from French soil. The French also had to create a new regime, a task that other occupied countries such as Belgium and the Netherlands were spared. Those countries had royal families and governments-in-exile empowered to restore the sovereignty of constitutional monarchies, once the Germans had gone. The French had no such recourse to a restoration. Parliament had effectively buried the Third Republic after the defeat of 1940 when it gave Philippe Pétain full powers to govern and to write a new constitution (which he chose to delay until peace returned to Europe). And the Vichy regime that he and Pierre Laval created lost all credibility by 1944 through its collaboration with the enemy, its own shadowy war against the Resistance, and its ineffectiveness in protecting, even properly feeding, the French people.[1] Liberation, then, gave de Gaulle and the Resistance the opportunity and the duty to start anew. They had a vast, centuries-old state apparatus to work with: a still-functioning tax and education system, an army reassembled in Africa and Britain to join the Allied campaign, and legions of civil servants prepared to adapt to regime change as their predecessors had done, so many times before, since 1789. What's more, many policemen, schoolteachers, and high-level public officials had become affiliated with the Resistance by the summer of 1944.

Still, if the rudimentary institutional continuity of government was one thing, the state's authority was another. That required efficacy—the capacity of a new regime to deliver justice, security, and material well-being after years of deprivation on all three counts. And it required legitimacy, both the formal kind conferred by elections and a new constitution, and the informal kind derived from the respect citizens accord their leaders and institutions. Efficacy had to be proven, and informal legitimacy earned. Neither came automatically in the summer and fall of 1944 when, after D-Day's Normandy invasion, the unified forces of de Gaulle's Free France and the internal Resistance sought to establish a new republic on the heels of the Allied advance. True, over the preceding year in Algiers, de Gaulle had gradually put together the rudiments of a government-in-the-making: the National Committee of French Liberation (Comité français de libération nationale or CFLN), with representatives of the many political tendencies within the Resistance, and with a coterie of potential ministers-in-waiting. While still headquartered in Algiers and London, the CFLN became the Provisional Government of the French Republic on 3 June 1944, three days before D-Day. But jockeying for power within this nascent governing group, especially between Gaullists and Communists, remained intense as the Liberation began. Nor was it clear to French leaders how much room their American and British allies would give them to carry out regime change as they wanted to. Roosevelt harbored doubts about de Gaulle's popularity and his commitment to democratic rule. Moreover, given the political wreckage Vichy officials were leaving behind and the tasks that lay ahead, no one could know at the Liberation exactly what kind of republican state—what new blend of democratic, paternalistic, technocratic, and even Bonapartist (authoritarian) qualities—would emerge from the long, practical business of repairing France's social fabric and reshaping its economy.

To see how public officials and societal groups navigated through these turbulent waters of regime change in 1944–1945, this chapter explores, first, how de Gaulle maneuvered to restore state authority "from above," and then how citizens' initiatives locally had the effect of expanding state authority "from below." The dual dynamic set the stage for politicians, civil servants, and policy experts to use a reinvigorated state to embark on postwar reconstruction, even as it also inaugurated a saga of contestation between public officials and societal groups that would continue through the Fourth Republic.

Renewing State Authority from Above

General de Gaulle, more single-mindedly than anyone else in the Resistance, regarded the Liberation as a task of restoring state authority. "The feebleness of the state," in his view, had made France ill-prepared for war in 1940. Putting "the state back on its feet," he later wrote in his war memoirs, would now be the *"sine qua non* of the country's recovery."[2] Most every major objective he pursued during the first months of the Liberation era—joining the continuing Allied military campaign against Germany, integrating Resistance fighters into the regular army, restoring civic order, rebuilding national unity across the Hexagon (mainland France), reasserting France's global standing via an empire—served the end of bolstering state authority. This statist way of looking at the Liberation came easily to a military professional such as de Gaulle, but it also drew on a venerable tradition of regarding France itself as being the creation of more than a millennium of statebuilding. De Gaulle also understood that reestablishing state legitimacy went hand in hand with restoring French sovereignty, something most citizens craved after the humiliation of the Occupation and amid the not so subtle sense of national embarrassment that it took the Allies, and not the Resistance alone, to liberate France. Hence, the willingness of so many of de Gaulle's compatriots to embrace the patriotic conceit that he articulated so movingly at the Hôtel de Ville on the night of August 25, 1944, proclaiming Paris liberated, "liberated by the people of Paris with help from the armies of France, with the help and support of the whole of France, of the France that is fighting, the only France, the real France, eternal France."[3]

But if most everyone at the Liberation shared the aspiration of restoring France's sovereignty, they disagreed about how strong or centralized or democratic a post-Liberation state should be. De Gaulle favored a presidential system with robust executive authority and centralized control. This view echoed what conservatives such as former prime minister André Tardieu had espoused during a rancorous, if in the end fruitless, national debate in the 1930s about what at the time was dubbed "state reform." But de Gaulle's well-known insistence on the primacy of state restoration and the need for a powerful executive evoked sharply differing views in the Resistance. Maxime Blocq-Mascart, for example, a businessman and leader of the conservative resistance group, OCM (Organisation civile et militaire, the Civilian and Military Organization), also wanted a strong executive, and he urged de Gaulle to promulgate a new constitution for that purpose immediately at the Liberation—an idea de Gaulle rejected.[4] The General knew the limits of his legitimacy in the summer of 1944. Socialists and Communists, though eager for an expanded, activist state to carry through the ambitious social and economic postwar agenda of the National Resistance Council, had deep reservations about a strong executive. Indeed, Communists were dead set against a presidential system that would almost surely concentrate power in a non-Communist executive.[5] In the constitutional debates to come in 1945 they would redeploy the old left-wing argument for a strong single-chamber Parliament. Still others in the Resistance had doubts about relying too much on the state. Leaders of the new Christian Democratic Party (the MRP) were still Catholic enough to fear an overweaning (and potentially anticlerical) republican state. They championed the associational life of civil society, Catholic and otherwise, as the necessary counterbalance to an expanding postwar government. And then there were a number of Resistance intellectuals, such as Albert Camus, Simone de Beauvoir, Jean-Paul Sartre, and Emmanuel Mounier, who regarded choice-making, risk-taking individuals—brought into their own in the Resistance and anchored more in society than in the state—as France's true propagators of national renewal. They believed the solidarities that resisters had built in the underground could give rise to new forms of national unity, transcending divisions of class and self-interest. German and Vichy repression had made them leery of expanding the state's power to police society. They had much less to say about the positive uses of state power than did the planners for the postwar reconstruction or the party activists of the National Council of the Resistance.[6]

Beneath this broad spectrum of views about the how much power the postwar state should exert and how its authority ought to be

concentrated lay a deeper distinction between de Gaulle and his lieu-
tenants, on the one hand, working in London and Algiers to plan the
establishment of the Provisional Government in the wake of the Allied
invasion, and the internal Resistance, on the other, surviving amid
Nazi terror and the Vichy militias and unsure what kind of republic de
Gaulle hoped to build. Both wings of the Resistance had worked hard
from 1942 to the summer of 1944 to become a unified force of national
liberation. Still, they harbored starkly different views of where the legitimacy for a new republic lay. For many members of the internal Resistance it resided in the moral rectitude and democratic qualities of a
new governing elite, created not by privilege or formal schooling but by
the Resistance experience itself. Jean-Paul Sartre would famously capture this vision in "The Republic of Silence," the brief essay he read
over the radio a few days after the liberation of Paris. "The Resistance
was a true democracy," he said, because the risks of resistance work,
taken under threat of imprisonment, deportation, and death, posed "for
the soldier as for the commander, the same danger, the same forsaken-
ness, the same total responsibility, the same absolute liberty within
discipline. Thus, in darkness and in blood, a Republic was established,
the strongest of Republics."[7] The internal Resistance counted on a
purge of collaborators and a proliferation of local liberation committees
to give this new moral elite its chance to govern in a new republic. This
outlook also dovetailed with Communist Party ambitions to be a
major force in postwar political life. By the eve of the Liberation, Communists held twenty-two of the thirty-eight highest posts in the internal Resistance.[8]

In de Gaulle's mind, by contrast, legitimacy still came from where
it always had in France, from its enduring institutions. He sought to
frame the Liberation as both political rupture and institutional continuity: he rejected the idea of restoring the Third Republic, which in
any event only a small minority advocated by 1944, and he reaffirmed
the obligation of the state administrative apparatus to carry on its duties. By restoring republican authority as quickly as he could and removing the most obvious of Vichy loyalists, he hoped to cut short the
work of the liberation committees. He feared them as a source of local
power for the Communist Party, especially in southern France where
the Resistance flourished most.

For all the political preparations de Gaulle had made in London and Algiers to assume power at the Liberation, he could not know in advance how the French people would receive him when he finally returned to France. In a country riven by division, he did not take their enthusiasm for him for granted. The chance to test his appeal came eight days after D-Day when he made an unannounced, carefully orchestrated visit to the just-liberated Norman town of Bayeux. "At the sight of General de Gaulle," he wrote later, "the inhabitants stood in a kind of daze then burst into bravos or else into tears. Rushing out of their houses they followed after me, all in the grip of an extraordinary emotion. . . . We walked on together, all overwhelmed by comradeship, feeling national joy, pride and hope rise again from the depths of the abyss."[9] He then rewarded the crowd with eloquence and mutual respect. Speaking from a makeshift platform and surrounded by Allied flags, he told the assembled "to continue the fight today as you have never ceased from fighting since the beginning of the war and since June 1940"—propagating his myth of an ever-resistant France. He then turned to the task of asserting control over local administration. He had brought along François Coulet, his newly appointed republican commissar (commissaire de la république, a kind of regional superprefect) to serve as the highest-ranking official in Normandy in the name of the new Provisional Government of the French Republic. Coulet immediately replaced Vichy's subprefect with Raymond Triboulet, the head of the local liberation committee, telling him to "establish French sovereignty at once; show the Allies we can administer ourselves competently."[10] Avoiding an Allied military occupation was as important as toppling Vichy. As the Allies liberated nearby towns, Coulet bicycled out to invest mayors with the authority of the Provisional Government. He took care to keep local policemen in their posts and co-opt local elites willing to submit to the new administration.[11]

De Gaulle's Bayeux baptism did its job. It confirmed his rapport with the public and kept the Allies at bay. British and American officials even acknowledged he could establish local order better than they.[12] Bayeux also validated the Provisional Government's strategy for taking over territory by installing a republican commissar, enlisting the help of local resistance committees, and keeping reprisals to a minimum and lower-level public servants on the job. Harmonizing with the local Resistance, however, would prove easier in Normandy, where it was weak, than in southern France, where it was strong. Many of de Gaulle's eighteen regional republican commissars would have a tougher time securing their authority over the internal Resistance.[13] In Marseille, Lyon, and Toulouse it would take a good deal longer than in Bayeux. For de Gaulle the biggest stakes were in Paris, where a Resistance-led popular insurrection liberated the city. In Bayeux de Gaulle sought to eliminate the threat of Allied administration of liberated territory. In Paris he aimed to secure the ascendency of a de Gaulle–led Provisional Government and subordinate the internal Resistance once and for all.

He achieved these goals by acquiring control over three key instruments of state authority: bureaucracy, the army, and public ceremony. To secure command over the state administration, he relied on Alexandre Parodi, a Gaullist loyalist and top civil servant from the Conseil d'État (Council of State) who, after the Gestapo had killed his brother for resisting, threw himself into the work of Libération-Sud, a major Resistance organization. By 1943 he had gone fully underground in Paris, served as a member of the secret Committee of Experts planning policy for the postwar, and by 1944, at age 43, was the Provisional Government's chief liaison to the Parisian internal Resistance. A fortnight before the insurrection, which Parodi was to help lead, de Gaulle telegraphed him to "always speak loudly and clearly in the name of the state."[14] De Gaulle counted on him to keep the insurrection short, lest it descend into chaos or empower the Communists to seize the levers of the Liberation.[15] Once the uprising began, Parodi swiftly replaced Vichy's general secretaries in each ministry—the executives within the bureaucracy—with the new men de Gaulle's people in Algiers had already approved. It was a sudden and efficient administrative coup—Coulet's Bayeux formula on a grand scale. The new general secretaries then assured most ministerial personnel they should continue in their work.[16] As de Gaulle had told the Consultative Assembly in Algiers the month before, his government had "no intention of suddenly making a clean sweep of the great majority of civil servants, most of whom during the terrible years of the Occupation and [Vichy] usurpation had done their best to serve the public interest."[17]

De Gaulle's preference for a restrained administrative purge prevailed in most ministries. In the huge bureaucracies for education, the
national railways (the SNCF), and the postal service, only about 11,000
were eventually sanctioned, and fewer than half of those lost their
jobs.[18] The purge cut deeper in the politically more sensitive ministries
of the Interior, Justice, and Information, but not so much in Finance,
Foreign Affairs, and Public Works. High-ranking civil servants in the
prestigious *grands corps*—the powerful state elite in the finance inspectorate *(inspecteurs des finances)*, the Council of State *(conseilliers
de l'État)*, the state auditors in the Cour des comptes, and state engineers in the Corps des mines or the Corps des ponts et chaussées
(bridges and roads)—tried to "wash the dirty linen within the family,"
as François Bloch-Lainé put it, rather than hurtle their members into
public trials.[19] All told, most of the state's administrative personnel
remained in place, more so than in 1940 or after the revolutions of the
nineteenth century.

De Gaulle's effort to establish predominance over the internal Resistance during the liberation of Paris also had a military dimension.
De Gaulle persuaded the Allied commander, General Eisenhower, to
allow General Leclerc to lead the French Second Armored Division into
Paris once the insurrection was under way. Leclerc, he hoped, would
help redeem French honor and signal the army's supremacy over the
FFI (Forces françaises de l'intérieur, the military wing of the internal
Resistance). The mission succeeded, though not without de Gaulle
scolding Leclerc for permitting FFI chief Rol-Tanguy to cosign the ac-
ceptance of Germany's surrender of the Paris garrison. De Gaulle orchestrated his own return to a liberated Paris on August 25 in the same
political key. He snubbed the National Council of the Resistance that
was awaiting him at the Hôtel de Ville and went instead to what he
called "the center"—the War Ministry—and to the very rooms he had
left in June 1940. In doing so he gestured to the military roots of his
own ascendancy, while avoiding what he feared might have turned out
to be an implicit investiture of authority by the Council. Parodi finally
convinced him by the end of the day to appear at the Hôtel de Ville,
where he then made his stirring "Paris liberated" speech. But he stopped
first at the Paris police prefecture to pay tribute to the police strike the
week before that had opened the door to the insurrection.[20] De Gaulle

made his symbolic priorities clear: restoring the state in the national capital, in his view, had to begin with reclaiming authority over the agents of national defense and public order.

The toughest challenge was still to come—absorbing the FFI into the regular army. On August 26 de Gaulle ordered the military high command to begin the process. Assimilation did not come easily. Some FFI units initially refused, though they soon figured out they had to comply. And then the clash of military cultures could be rough. Many a left-wing Resistance fighter found it hard to accept the authority of ex-Pétainist officers who themselves disdained the ethos of illegality in which the Resistance had been forged. FFI idealists who saw in the Resistance the makings of a people's army had to adjust to the rigid hierarchies and subordination of the professional military.[21] They had to make their way into an army that had recruited much of its infantry through colonial conscription. Few Resistance commanders, moreover, found in the regular army the respect and responsibility they believed they deserved. Political pressure enabled some FFI units to stay to-gether within larger battalions, but a great many Resistance fighters had to go it alone. By the end of 1944 the FFI had disappeared, and with it disappeared a power base for the Resistance Left.[22]

De Gaulle had one more task before he could claim that the state had restored its monopoly on legitimate violence—eliminating the "patriotic militias" that the Communist Party (the PCF) had created across the country in the final year of the Occupation. Party activists recruited men into these paramilitary units on into the autumn of 1944. They provided a place to go for FFI fighters who refused to join the regular army, and for "September resisters," who wanted to salvage their reputations for not having resisted before. Patriotic militias had an ambiguous legality: in principle they reported to local and depart-mental liberation committees, and they took upon themselves the au-thority to arrest collaborators and black marketers. In reality their leaders answered more to the Communist Party than to the state. In late October 1944 de Gaulle ordered them dissolved. Initially the party balked, and many militiamen held out stubbornly, but in January 1945 the party shut them down. PCF head Maurice Thorez had returned to France from wartime exile in Moscow with a pardon from de Gaulle for his desertion from the army in 1939. Now back at the helm of the party, Thorez also had Stalin's instructions to pursue a moderate, popular-front-style strategy of integrating into the political mainstream and serving as a governing party. Thorez told party members to accept "one state, one army, one police," an injunction that ended the PCF's contest with de Gaulle over military authority.[23] Militias disbanded, and members surrendered their weapons.

Essential as it was for de Gaulle to get control over the administration and military, he also needed to make visible the public's consent to his authority, especially in the absence of national elections. Hence the importance of the third instrument for consolidating power— public ceremony and oratory. If Bayeux had served him as a dress rehearsal, Paris at the moment of liberation was the main event. When on the night of August 25 he spoke at the Hôtel de Ville, he shrewdly paid homage, not to the Resistance, but to a Paris "liberated by its people." The next day he led the iconic grand processional down the Champs Elysées. Flanked by military men and Resistance leaders, at six feet five he towered over them all and sought to establish a kind of mystical communion with a crowd of perhaps up to two million people. In his memoirs he noted the focus he had maintained as he walked: "to look at every person in all that multitude in order that every eye might register my presence, raising and lowering my arms to reply to the acclamations; this was one of those miracles of national consciousness, one of these gestures which sometimes, in the course of centuries, illuminate the history of France." De Gaulle knew, too, that the moment was designed to create a feeling of unity in a fractious and traumatized country. "If you [only] knew how much alike you were [in that crowd]," he later wrote wistfully.[24] Just how much the crowd's jubilation expressed approval of de Gaulle as leader, or sheer joy at the Liberation, was impossible to say (see Figure 1.1). But there was no denying the implicit legitimacy it gave him. He used it the next day to convey to a distinguished group of Parisian Resistance leaders he had invited to the War Ministry that their medals would be duly forthcoming, but their principal work was done. They were stunned.[25]

Throughout the fall of 1944 de Gaulle repeated the processional ritual in the major cities of nearly every region of the France. There was ample precedence for inaugural provincial tours. Third Republic presidents had done this kind of thing after their elections since Sadi

FIGURE 1.1 Charles de Gaulle in Paris at the Liberation, August 1944. De Gaulle made skillful use of the street processional to legitimize his authority and galvanize enthusiasm for his Provisional Government. After the liberation of Paris he repeated this ritual in cities across the country. Popperfoto/Popperfoto/Getty Images.

Carnot did it in 1888, adopting what historians have sometimes called the republican reinvention of the royal entry.[26] But the provincial visit had a special urgency for de Gaulle. Normal communications between Paris and the hinterland were still in shambles: in fall 1944 even de Gaulle's interior minister, Adrien Tixier, had to use couriers to connect with his republican commissar and prefects around the country.[27] A visit by de Gaulle to Dijon or Bordeaux quite literally extended his personal authority beyond his isolation in Paris. The day's itinerary followed a simple protocol. De Gaulle would arrive with little public notice so as to short-circuit potential trouble and to demonstrate his capacity for surprise. After first meeting with local officials, especially the military commander and republican commissar of the region, reconfirming their authority, he would then move on to the prefecture where select guests awaited him to speak. In the politically volatile cities of Lyon, Marseille, and Toulouse he also used the parade-ground review of FFI units to assert his military superiority over their commanders. (For many years after, Toulouse leaders spoke bitterly of how de Gaulle had disrespected them.)[28] Then came the street processional through the thronging crowds of people eager to hail the first resister of France. The ritual culminated with de Gaulle's oratory from the balcony of the hotel de ville (city hall), where he exalted the nation's liberation, unity, and republican order. "Are we in agreement, then?" he asked 50,000 people in the Place du Capitole in Toulouse. "Yes!" they shouted in reply.[29] And all this was broadcast on the radio.[30]

By late winter 1945 de Gaulle had achieved his principal goals in restoring state authority and securing his government's legitimacy. Allied recognition of de Gaulle's government came, at last, in October 1944. As the internal Resistance had lost its unity and élan, political parties and the press had returned to the center of public affairs. Maurice Thorez's speech of January 1945 snuffed out any residual fantasies among Communists that Liberation augured a revolutionary turn. Meanwhile, the French army's participation in the imminent German defeat burnished de Gaulle's stature as commander in chief. Polls showed that the public applauded his dogged instance on restoring France as a global empire and an equal power among the Allies.

To be sure, restoring the state's authority was hardly de Gaulle's achievement alone. A legion of civilian and military officials, politicians, policy experts, and Resistance activists of many political stripes reestablished republican order in their respective spheres of governance. They used de Gaulle as their instrument as much as he used them. Still, de Gaulle's approach—his focus on administration and military control, the charismatic projection of his own marshal bearing, his relentless subordination of the Resistance after the liberation of Paris, and his continual invocations of "state," "nation," "France," and "republican order" with nary a word for the revolutionary tradition—gave state restoration a conservative thrust. He meant it to. With the established political Right in disgrace and with the Left in such public favor, de Gaulle relegitimized a tradition of centralized, hierarchical state authority to a degree no other conservative could have done in the wake of the Vichy debacle.

Renewing State Authority from Below

Leaders could not simply use the instruments of institutional and symbolic power to restore state authority on their own. Citizens, too, had to confer authority from below. They had to lend their consent, express their approval, allow—even oftentimes invite—state officials to assume new responsibilities for regulating everyday life. Citizens did this legitimizing work not only as individuals but even more so collectively through their unions, religious bodies, parties, business groups, and voluntary associations that all had lots to say about how government officials should use their power. Authority had to be negotiated, especially in moments of regime change such as the Liberation era.

Right from the start, at the Liberation, the Provisional Government's newly installed republican commissars and prefects had to establish the state's authority locally by working with local liberation committees who believed themselves endowed with state authority as well. As indeed they were: de Gaulle and the internal Resistance had agreed that liberation committees would assume local responsibilities was soon as territory was liberated. CDLs (Comités départementaux de la Libération) and CLLs (Comités locaux de la Libération) proliferated across the country, as did committees overseeing purges in professions and businesses, the confiscation of illicit profits, the enforcement of price controls, and the regional press. They had both a revolutionary air about them and an official sanction to fill the vacuum of authority that came with the collapse of the Vichy state. This blossoming of local committee governance had its demographic shortcomings. CDLs had few rural representatives (about 8 percent) and, not surprisingly after Vichy, few right-wing members (80 percent of these committees had left-wing majorities). Women constituted 7.5 percent of the members.[31] Still, these local institutions embodied a spirit of democratic renewal that stood in contrast to de Gaulle's more top-down administrative approach to restoring civic order.

Relations between de Gaulle's administrators and CDLs varied regionally. In the north, where Allied armies did most of the liberating and the Resistance had been weak, prefects and republican commissars established their authority quickly, as we saw with Coulet, and easily relegated CDLs to an advisory role—simply bimonthly meetings, for example, in the Breton department of Morbihan.[32] But in the south, the Resistance had played a bigger role in helping to drive out the Wehrmacht and had established deeper roots in local committees. CDLs there acquired greater power accordingly and then fiercely defended their authority. They took seriously the tasks of purging collaborators and tackling the black market. Republican commissars and prefects formally had the authority to override these committees. But in practice, with Paris far removed and the state still weak, they had to cultivate decent relationships with the local Resistance leaders who ran these committees. This kind of cooperation came easier in Lyon and Clermont-Ferrand—Commissars Yves Farge and Henri Ingrand were themselves local Resistance heroes—than in Limoges, Toulouse, Montpellier, or Marseille, where the bond with commissars was not so tight. The regional commissar in Nice, for instance, had a CDL revolt on his hands when the local prefect tried to run the department by ignoring the committee.[33] The commissar saw his way to finding a new prefect. Restoring state authority locally, then, especially in the south, forced the central government's chief agents and the committees to confront their conflicts, recognize their respective legitimacy, and negotiate their differences.

That practical reality came through in the local politics of the purge. In the weeks leading up to the liberation and in the early days following, local Resistance fighters (Figure 1.2) and other locals had taken the purge of collaborators into their own hands. FFI courts-martial and locally instigated tribunals meted out rough justice on an impressive scale. Likewise, in hundreds of small towns and cities, self-appointed local defenders of patriotic virtue (and perhaps, too, of a virility wounded by the Occupation, as historians have suggested) carried out an extraordinary wave of head-shearings, targeting women believed to be guilty of "horizontal collaboration" with German soldiers. (By 1946, about 20,000 women had fallen victim to this shaming ritual, some of them on the basis of false rumors.)[34] In the face of so much local initiative, republican commissars and prefects felt the urgency to channel purges into the proper halls of justice—established courts for serious cases and new special courts (chambres civiques) for lesser crimes of "national

unworthiness" *(indignité nationale)*.[35] They also interned thousands
of people who potentially were in the crosshairs of vigilante justice, so
that their cases could be properly adjudicated weeks or months later.
Not that internment always guaranteed protection. In the southern
town of Alès in January 1945, a crowd of 5,000 stormed the prison and
killed four prisoners awaiting trial. In many towns, smaller assaults
on prisons went on for nearly a year after the Liberation.[36] Republican
commissars learned that to tame local purges, they had to work with
liberation committees, not simply lay down the law. Henri Ingrand, for
instance, eventually succeeded in getting the CDL in the Allier (in central France) to condemn Resistance renegades who were assassinating
alleged collaborators. In Marseille the commissar, Raymond Aubrac,
learned to rein in his own inclination to commute the death sentences
of condemned collaborators, after violent protests against one such
commutation convinced him, as he later wrote, "to refuse clemency
whenever granting it would have in my opinion disturbed public
order."[37] Local left-wing activists often lobbied officials for harsher justice. Commissars and prefects found themselves mediating between
these sentiments and de Gaulle's preference for a moderate purge.

The politics of local purges had little long-term impact on the
structure and practices of the judiciary. But grassroots pressures did
shape the reach of state authority in three other areas. The first was
policing, because Vichy's brutal repression and deplorable complicity
in the deportations had compromised the police. The police strike in
Paris at the beginning of the August insurrection helped redeem the
police, as did the aid some policemen gave the Resistance elsewhere.
But the stain of Vichy went deep. Local prefects, with liberation committees looking over their shoulders, had to take seriously the need to
purge the worst elements in the force and recruit new policemen.

Patriotic militias provided a promising, if potentially risky, source
of police recruits. These men, after all, had firearms training and knew
the local territory. True, as former resistance fighters with likely loyalties to the Communist Party, they might still imagine themselves becoming the core of some future "people's police." But recruiting them
into the police would also co-opt the Resistance into the state apparatus, and besides, republican commissars were desperate in the fall of
1944 to get help arresting alleged collaborators, requisitioning illicit

FIGURE 1.2 Resisters in Marseille at the Liberation, August 1944. These fighters of
the FFI (Forces françaises de l'intérieur) played an important role in liberating
Marseille, giving them leverage to push for aggressive purges locally and for the requisition of enterprises that had worked closely with the Germans. De Gaulle's Provisional Government sought to integrate FFI fighters like these into the regular French
army for the continuing war against Germany. © Jacques BELIN/ECPAD/Défense.

property, taking on the black market, and aiding communities devastated by war. Lyon's commissar, Yves Farge, created a special police
unit under his command by recruiting 8,000 FFI fighters and 4,000
patriotic militiamen.[38] Commissar Jean Mairey in Burgundy felt he
had little choice but to accept a "republican civic guard" *(garde civique
républicaine)* that citizens in Besançon had recruited to supplement an
inadequate local police.[39] And most importantly, Commissar Raymond Aubrac, together with local resistance leaders, recruited 3,000
former members of the (mostly Communist) Resistance to join his new
Forces republicaines de sécurité (FRS or Republican Security Forces),
mobile police brigades for each of the departments in his region.

As Aubrac had hoped, the initial success of his FRS inspired the
Interior Ministry in Paris to try the idea on a national scale.[40] In December 1944 the Ministry launched the CRS (Compagnies républicaines de sûreté, or Republican Security Companies), mobile police

battalions—each under a regional commissar's command—to handle strikes, demonstrations, and other public security emergences. Unlike the FRS, CRS units amalgated left-wing militiamen *and* regular policemen, something Aubrac felt compromised the political integrity of the enterprise. Still, PCF head Maurice Thorez gave the CRS his stamp of approval in January 1945, an endorsement that helped integrate party members into the state's security apparatus and polished the PCF's image as a party of government. Until the beginning of France's domestic cold war in 1947, when Interior Minister Jules Moch purged the CRS of its Communists and then used CRS units to repress the big insurrectionary strikes of that year, this new institution had the image of being a "police in the service of the people."[41] The CRS helped the Provisional Government absorb local Resistance fighters into a state-run security service, and it gave the national police a left-wing grassroots dimension.

Industrial workers provoked a second key expansion of state authority locally—government involvement in requisitioning and regulating the management of business enterprises. This unplanned expansion arose from workplace rebellions that followed immediately on the heels of the liberation of coal mines in the northeast and towns in central and southern France. Outraged by mine operators' collaboration with the Nazis, miners refused to dig coal without the Provisional Government's promise to nationalize the mines of the Nord and Pas-de-Calais departments. This the government did in December 1944. Meanwhile, in dozens of factories to the south—at the Fouga plant in Bézier, for example, or Ratier in the town of Figeac—workers took over worksites to force a purge of owners and top management and put union-led employee committees in charge. West of Avignon in Alès, miners called on the republican commissar to nationalize seven companies. In the area around Montluçon, not far from Vichy, Socialist and Communist workers took over about twenty enterprises. This kind of pressure in Lyon led Republican Commissar Yves Farge to requisition a number of companies, most notably the big truck and car firm Berliet, and to turn over managerial responsibilities to employee committees. Marseille's republican commissar Aubrac requisitioned fifteen companies, a move his higher-ups in Paris thought went too far, and it eventually cost him his job. In Toulouse, a hotbed of labor radicalism at the Liberation, Republican Commissar Pierre Bertaux negotiated with striking workers to create the Accord de Toulouse, which brought the city's all-important airplane factories under the everyday oversight of employee-led management committees. The management committee movement spread further—to about a hundred companies around the country by early 1945.[42]

Labor's effort to force requisitions and install management committees did not weaken the state. On the contrary, it created opportunities for government officials to use their authority. Union activists fighting for requisitions and committees sought the help and endorsement of de Gaulle's commissars and prefects. They saw state officials as allies, not adversaries, in returning enterprises to the patriotic business of producing for a liberated France. Workers viewed their bosses as traitors, requisitions as part of the purge, and management committees as a way to give workers voice—a large but still advisory role in the enterprise—but not outright ownership or control. The Accord de Toulouse, for example, empowered a "qualified representative of the government" to step in to arbitrate when conflicts flared between management committees and factory directors.[43] Giving employees more voice meant expanding the supervisory role of the state.

Local publics encouraged state officials to expand their authority in a third area as well—in the pricing and distribution of supplies. If citizens thought the Liberation augured relief from food and coal shortages, they soon learned otherwise. Penury got worse. Renewed warfare on French soil in the summer and fall of 1944 took land out of cultivation, syphoned laborers into the army, and delayed the repair of bridges, roads, and rails. Scarcities fueled inflation, despite rationing and price controls, which were hard to enforce. The black market in ration cards and goods of all sorts got larger, not smaller, after the Liberation. Traffickers thrived, too, on selling to American and British soldiers, an expansion of the black market that the French government could do little about.[44] Price controls, moreover, notoriously pitted consumers against farmers and retailers who ached to have them removed. Predictably, prefects in rural departments advised the government to liberalize prices, while urban officials argued to the contrary.[45]

With government officials at loggerheads, the real action came from below. Working-class city dwellers took to the streets—in 221 demonstrations between October 1944 and the following May—to urge the state to toughen controls, boost supplies, raise rationing limits, and break the black market. Protesters typically marched to the local prefecture or town hall, as did 1,000 people did in the western town of Niort in November with signs reading "Heat for the old folks," "Sugar for our children," and "Against the black market."[46] Bigger towns had larger crowds—about 15,000 each in Saint-Étienne, Clermont-Ferrand, and Nancy. And some protests turned violent: in Denain (near Lille) 1,200 people busted into a mine to pilfer 150 tons of coal; in Toulouse women looted the open-air stalls and then the nearby stores.[47] Nantes had huge protests, first in January 1946 and then the following August when several thousand Nantais ravaged hotels, restaurants, and cabarets thought to be associated with the black market.[48]

All these protests revealed a public desperate to get the state to do more to regulate the market. Polls in April 1945 cited "supplies and transportation" as by far the public's top priority for government action.[49] To be sure, left-wing activists played a crucial role in mobilizing protest. Local militants in the Communist-leaning trade union confederation, the CGT, instigated about 15 percent of the demonstrations between October 1944 and May 1945. More important still were the organizing efforts of the two major women's organizations in working-class neighborhoods—the Communist-oriented Union des femmes françaises (UFF) and its Catholic counterpart, the Movement populaire des familles (MPF). The politics of these organizations mattered. Communists and Catholics mobilized urban workers with the municipal elections of May 1945 in mind. And Communists wanted to channel their constituents' energies into consumer issues rather than workplace ones—for the sake of the war effort and postwar recovery, the party's much-touted "battle for production."[50] Even so, activists were tapping into the heartfelt passions of angry local residents eager to pressure officials and troubled by inequities—real and imaginary—in getting supplies. (German POWs were rumored to be all too well fed.)[51] And consumers' targets could be quite precise, a cry for more wine supplies in Meurthe-et-Moselle or more vegetables and coal in Le Puy—and always striving to get a prefect's attention.[52] Protest organizers often found it difficult to control the protests they had begun, something Communists worried about especially, lest they jeopardize the ties they had worked hard to build with farming communities during the Occupation.[53] And food protests proliferated in part because they sometimes worked. Cherry prices in Bordeaux, for example, dropped by half after protests.[54]

The government certainly heard the message, as the voluminous memo traffic from republican commissars and prefects to Paris reveals. Even so, officials continued to try to balance the interests of producers and consumers, to the dissatisfaction of both. They tried to enforce controls but never scaled up the campaign against traffickers to break the back of the black market. They recoiled from the option of pursuing a genuinely serious anti-inflationary policy. When the minister of national economy, Pierre Mendès France, pushed the government, with support from most republican commissars, to avoid inflation by adopting a rigorous austerity plan and a new currency, de Gaulle refused. He choose instead to follow Finance Minister René Pleven's more politically palatable, but less anti-inflationary, strategy of issuing bonds to absorb the economy's liquidity.[55] By autumn 1945, with the country still awash in cash, inflation was becoming an endemic feature of the early postwar French economy. Three efforts to liberalize controls in the food sector in 1945 and 1946 brought soaring prices and a return to restrictions.[56] Price controls and rationing—and the black market that inevitably came in their wake—would continue to plague the first governments of the Fourth Republic. Rationing only ended in 1949, when the restoration of transport, boosts in supply, and currency stabilization were finally sufficient to bring something like normalcy back to the food market.

Popular pressures on the government to enforce controls and better manage the food supply right after the Liberation helped legitimize a form of state action that until the Liberation was associated with the Vichy regime. The effects of this expansion of state authority endured. Although the government would be able to lift most price controls by the early 1950s, some, such as those on bread, lingered, and remained popular long into the Fifth Republic. By the same token, however, had urban protest been even greater in 1945, de Gaulle might have seen tougher anti-inflationary measures as a means of restoring order, rather than the threat to political stability he thought them to be. Finance expert François Bloch-Lainé, who worked in the Treasury at the time, later suggested that de Gaulle might have been able to persuade the

French to follow the Mendès France plan, which resembled what the Belgian government managed to do in autumn 1944.[57] Nancy's republican commissar reported that locals in his region spoke well of the Belgian approach.[58] In the end, neither de Gaulle nor even the Communist Party wanted to challenge the beneficiaries of inflation in rural France. The PCF, too, opposed the austerity plan. Urban protest, then, both legitimized the state's role in regulating the food market and exposed the state's weakness in this domain.[59]

De Gaulle's rush to restore state authority from above and the efforts from below by liberation committees and local citizens to encourage state action in matters of justice, policing, and the economy combined to give the Provisional Government legitimacy. This dual dynamic expanded the state's authority to undertake the postwar reconstruction. Local Resistance groups, by integrating into departmental liberation committees, filtering into the army, or joining up for Aubrac's FRS in Marseille or the CRS nationwide, showed their willingness to work with, and not just against, the republican commissars and prefects who spoke for the Provisional Government. At least until the summer of 1945, when the nagging food and supply problems tarnished his reputation, de Gaulle himself was more popular at the local level, even in the south, than he was with national political leaders in Paris, who found him autocratic and hard to work with as the everyday business of governing the country returned. As historian Douglas Johnson has suggested, once de Gaulle, with his "grand view of history and his contempt for those who did not share it," had strode down the Champs Élysées on August 26, 1944, "contemplating the Tuileries, la Concorde, le Louvre," the politics of 1945 in Paris were hard for him to adapt to.[60]

But plenty of conflict also surfaced between the top-down and bottom-up efforts at restoring state authority. De Gaulle had clear goals for reconfirming the primacy of the state's traditional functions and institutions—its army, police, courts, and civil administration. And he understood the importance of putting the new republic on sound constitutional footings. But he lacked the same degree of ambition to use that state authority for the sake of social and economic reforms, despite all the planning that his Committee of Experts had done during the war.[61] The first nationalizations and requisitions—in the coalfields, at the Renault factories, in many towns in the south—came as a surprise, through grassroots pressure, not in accord with a plan. And then de Gaulle surprised his own government in January 1945 when he called for postponing the big nationalizations in the energy and finance sectors, which had been planned, until after national elections.[62] The hard legislative work that would shape the details of nationalizing gas, electricity, and coal took place after he resigned. Likewise, de Gaulle blocked Mendès France's effort to establish a strong planning capacity within the state in 1945, turning instead to Jean Monnet to create a weaker form of planning that would in 1946 become the Planning Commission.[63] He did authorize Pierre Laroque to chart the course of social security reform, something most everyone understood had to be done, and he created an atomic energy commission to work toward a nuclear bomb. In short, de Gaulle was most comfortable asserting the state's authority in its conventional realms, but was cautious about expanding the state's role in social and economic reform.

Local activists and citizens, by contrast, pushed the state into new social and economic territory, and they sought to revive democracy. The innovations and actions they supported—nationalizations and requisitions, management committees and republican security forces, price controls, purges, and the confiscation of illicit profits—all expressed the desire to build tighter connections between citizens and the state. Too be sure, these local efforts never coalesced into a single coherent movement for popular democracy, much less into a new political party. But the spirit of the Resistance that energized many of these local activists, and the public's appetite for a more reform-oriented government gave the Communist and Socialist Parties, and left-wing leaders in the new Christian Democratic Party, the MRP (Mouvement républicain populaire), impressive momentum going into the municipal elections of spring 1945 and the parliamentary elections the following fall.

Yet, if de Gaulle at the summit and local activists at the grassroots both played key roles in restoring—and enhancing—state authority after the Liberation, they also both saw their hopes dashed for transforming the state on their own terms. De Gaulle lost his bid to get a strong executive written into the Constitution of the Fourth Republic.

That defeat, along with Parliament's rejection of his budget for military modernization, contributed to his decision to resign in January 1946. Likewise, local activists and Resistance fighters had to adapt to the return of party politics in a Fourth Republic with a Constitution and a party system looking much like that of the Third Republic. Hopes for building a new big party on the left, whether by unifying Communists and Socialists or by amalgamating Socialists and left Catholics into a new Labour party, never got beyond wistful talk. By 1946 it was clear that the three big governing parties of the Liberation era—the PCF, SFIO, and MRP—had the fate of the postwar reconstruction in their hands, and with it what remained of the more utopian dreams of the Resistance that France could become more modern and democratic country. That tripartite coalition, however, had all the constraints that came with such a government: the need to work through Parliament and to bargain over differences and jockey for position, the cabinet shuffling that seemed endemic to fragile coalitions, and the need each party felt to answer to constituencies with conflicting interests. Socialists and Communists in particular had strong ambitions to use the state's newfound authority to carry forward the program of the National Council of the Resistance, but they also held back from going too far for fear of alienating farmers and other small producers who were eager to limit the state's reach.

This complex process of enhancing state authority in 1944–1945 without forging either the strong executive or the big, powerful catchall parties to make for stable government put high-level civil servants, policy experts, and creative politicians in an opportune position to shape the long reconstruction. Their ascendancy had already begun in the Third Republic, especially in the 1930s when government instability and the complexity of social and economic policy had already made cabinet ministers especially reliant on jurists in the Conseil d'État and engineers in the Corps des mines and Corps des ponts et chaussées to draft legislation, chart plans, and manage the rearmament drive. Policy experts and top-level civil servants in the *grands corps* played important roles in the wartime planning committees for the postwar. After the humiliation of the defeat and Occupation, however, the many economists, engineers, lawyers, and demographers working in ministries and in such bureaus as the National Statistics Office (Institut national des statistiques et des études économiques, or INSEE) and the National Demographic Institute (Institut national des études démographiques, or INED) were more open to new ideas than they or their predecessors had been in the 1930s, when many technical experts clung to policy orthodoxies as tightly as did the politicians.[64] Just as important, the peculiar dynamics of state-authority-making in 1944–1945 expanded the political space in which government experts could operate. De Gaulle's methods of state restoration had relegitimized the state administration, sheltered the *grands corps* from a potentially crippling purge, and revivified the myth of the state as guardian of the national destiny. Moreover, his refusal to create a Gaullist party helped perpetuate a weak party system, and hence unstable government, making parliamentary leaders dependent on high civil servants, policy experts, and interest-group spokespersons to provide knowledge and continuity in policymaking. De Gaulle enhanced the state's capacity to carry out ambitious plans for the postwar reconstruction, but he left a leadership vacuum in his wake. An emerging elite of policy specialists and innovative administrators were there to fill it—men like Alfred Sauvy (population and immigration policy), Paul Delouvrier and Maurice Lauré (taxation), Pierre Laroque (social security and family policy), François Bloch-Lainé (finance and industrial modernization), Jean Monnet (economic planning), and many others. They would, moreover, learn to team up with key men and women in Parliament to shape the postwar modernization drive.

Grassroots activism in 1944–1945 also opened up space for administrators, politicians, and interest-group spokespersons to expand the state's role in reconstruction. Liberation committees and urban protesters served as counterweights to conservatives and the many small property owners who had enjoyed great influence in the Third Republic. By the same token, if grassroots activism and the resurgence of the Left strengthened the hand of those who hoped to see the state renovate the economy, restore France's international standing, and improve the lives of its citizens, these popular pressures also raised people's expectations, especially in the labor movement, that they too would acquire greater voice in the polity. As the reconstruction got under way, it remained unclear whether expanding the role of the state would empower mainly the experts, administrators, and business elites or create new ways to democratize France.

2

Available Hands

From Manpower Crisis to Immigration Control

UPON THE LIBERATION of France, General de Gaulle's Provisional Government was faced with the challenge of restoring order and liberty to the world of labor: order, because war casualties, deportations, labor conscription to Germany, the absence of more than a million French prisoners of war, and the rapid growth of the Resistance in 1943–1944 had shattered the conventional workings of the labor market; liberty, because the Vichy government had shackled the unions, requisitioned laborers, rounded up foreigners into work brigades, and imposed employment restrictions on women, refugees, and Jews. As a result, few in a new post-Liberation government, even with its legions of civil servants continuing in their posts unpurged, could imagine replicating the authoritarian measures of Vichy that had given the very notion of state-controlled labor markets a bad name. Yet there seemed no going back to the more liberal, laissez-faire approach to overseeing the labor market that had prevailed before 1939. Too many leaders in French government and business circles found it easy to assume, as did labor expert Jacques Desmarest, that the "incoherence" of prewar France's liberal manpower policy had contributed to the defeat of 1940. Postwar recovery called for something new, an approach to labor market regulation that fell somewhere between the authoritarian and the liberal, or what Desmarest in 1946 called a *politique main-d'oeuvre dirigée* (a state-led manpower policy).[1] Just what that new dirigiste approach should be, however, was hardly self-evident. The state's role in the labor market remained an important source of contention among policymakers, employers, trade union leaders, and workers during the early years of the Fourth Republic.

Labor issues, by their very nature in a capitalist economy, brought to the surface the conflicting interests at play in the postwar reconstruction. Employers looked to a government's manpower policy to enhance the quantity and quality of labor as a factor of production, whereas trade unionists hoped to find in regulation a means to enhance wages, working conditions, and job security, perhaps even to give labor unions a role in regulation itself. Communists and other left-wing radicals eyed regulation with the same bifocal vision they brought to all matters of state intervention in the first postwar years: they saw it as a practical instrument in the short run to help workers, and as a way to secure a foothold for ascending to state power to advance socialism in a more distant future. As for government officials, they might sympathize with business or labor, but they also had aims of their own—goals for modernizing the economy, improving the country's international standing, and advancing their own reputations as "can-do" innovators sensitive to the quasi-revolutionary rhythms of the Liberation era.

What made labor market regulation all the more controversial after the war was its intimate connection to immigration policy. The French labor market had always had its cross-border flows of people into and out of the country, but never more so than in the twentieth century, when, during periods of sustained growth, demand for labor far exceeded its supply in the domestic workforce. After World War I the French had done more than anyone else in Europe to recruit foreign laborers to harvest crops, mine coal, and pound out steel—that is, until the Nazi regime showed Europe what a perversely ambitious foreign worker program could really look like, with its slave labor system, deportations, and coerced conscription, such as the Service du Travail Obligatoire (STO) in occupied France.

Any new postwar effort to recruit foreign workers to France, then, had plenty of precedent in the Third Republic to build upon, but also suffered from the extraordinary effects of Hitler's plundering. The war had left Europe's labor markets in shambles and created a refugee crisis of unprecedented proportions. Tensions between the Western powers and the Soviet-dominated East also began to alter the flow of peoples across borders almost immediately after the German surrender in May 1945. What's more, the French labor movement and the Communist Party, emerging from the Liberation with more political influence than ever before, had an unprecedented opportunity to shape manpower and immigration policies for the reconstruction era. With this combination of novel conditions—a disrupted continental and domestic economy, a powerful left-wing insurgency in national politics, and a Provisional Government ambitious for the country's postwar economic growth—public officials set out to give tangible form to a new kind of dirigisme in the labor market.

The Legacy of the Third Republic and Vichy

Although some key labor policymakers in the Provisional Government—such as de Gaulle's protégé Alexandre Parodi and Communist trade union leader Amboise Croizat, the first labor ministers—were unusually young, many others were old enough to have witnessed the revolution in labor regulation that the state carried out during the First World War. Until 1914, leaders of the Third Republic did little to intervene in the labor market, apart from some protective legislation (against child labor, for example). They upheld republican commitments to free labor markets going back to the French Revolution, when their revolutionary predecessors dismantled guild restrictions and other customary privileges that had made labor markets in the Old Regime heavily regulated. But faced with the staggering economic demands of the war of 1914–1918, Third Republic officials ventured into a brave new world of labor recruitment and workplace regulation. The government called back reservists from the front to staff the factory floor, and then created employment offices in each of the geographical departments in France to funnel workers into the war economy. As the war continued to grind on, the minister of munitions, Socialist Albert Thomas, used his authority to turn the arms industry into a vast laboratory of government regulation—setting wage scales, creating the country's first shop steward system and joint labor-employer arbitration committees, and introducing infant care services for the women workers, who by 1918 made up an astonishing 25 percent of the war factory workforce.[2] More dramatic still were new initiatives in recruiting labor abroad. The war and colonial ministries virtually conscripted 185,000 colonial subjects from North Africa, Madagascar, and Indochina, and engaged commercial labor contractors to bring over nearly 37,000 Chinese workers.[3] Almost all were sent home after the armistice. The government helped recruit workers from European countries, such as Greece, Italy, Portugal, and Spain, something that before the war had been left for entrepreneurs to do on their own. World War I, in short, radically changed the role of the state in shaping the workforce and the workplace.

Yet for all their reach, these wartime experiments left more enduring effects on the political imagination than on the realities of labor recruitment and factory management after the war. Conservative postwar governments in France staged a rapid retreat in this domain, as they did from most forms of wartime economic regulation. Only in immigration did the government continue to play a crucial role, albeit a diminished one. To encourage a continuing flow of immigrants to help with reconstruction and to fill a manpower gap created by nearly three million war casualties, the government negotiated bilateral immigration treaties with Poland, Czechoslovakia, Belgium, and Italy. The actual recruitment fell to business, especially to a new Société générale d'immigration, founded in 1924 by employers in mining and agriculture to bring immigrants by the trainful, mostly from Poland. The state focused its own efforts on policing. In contrast to the United States, where immigrants arrived as potential citizens and were free to find work where they could, in France immigrants were welcome only as workers under contract with an employer.[4] Foreigners who entered illegally could acquire the right to stay only if an employer succeeded in getting the worker's residency status "regularized." The system required constant police surveillance. As the immigrant population swelled to nearly three million by 1930, making France the leading immigrant destination in the industrial world, this policing and bureaucratic apparatus grew accordingly.[5]

In the 1930s, Third Republic governments faced new challenges in labor market regulation, first the unemployment crisis of the Great

Depression and then the remobilization for the Second World War. French leaders poured money into local unemployment funds and public works, but as in the 1920s made immigrants key targets of policy.[6] Amid a resurgence of xenophobia and anti-Semitism the government restricted the flow of foreigners to about a quarter of what it had been before 1930.[7] Companies slashing payroll usually cut immigrants first, and the government encouraged their repatriation by subsidizing train travel back to their countries of origin.[8] Such anti-immigrant zeal could not have come at a worse time for the many thousands of Jewish refugees flooding into France from central Europe after 1933, or for the 400,000 Spanish republicans who fled across the border after Generalissimo Franco's triumph in 1939.[9] Stepping up its policing over foreigners, French authorities started to force many of these refugees into internment camps, only to release them into war work or military service after the war began in late 1939.

In other respects manpower mobilization in 1939–1940 largely followed the playbook of First World War, though this time in a toxic political environment. The triumph of the Popular Front in 1936 and labor's subsequent achievements in collective bargaining had evoked a powerful right-wing backlash, signified by the Daladier government's crushing defeat of the general strike in late 1938. Labor repression, coupled with a wholesale attack on the French Communist Party after the stunning shock of the Nazi-Soviet pact, had poisoned industrial relations just when France headed into the war. Like his First World War predecessors, Armaments Minister Raoul Dautry requisitioned workers, set wages, and boosted the workweek to sixty hours, but he also felt compelled to police the factory floor with soldiers and threaten labor activists with transfer to the war front.[10] The Labor Ministry recruited women into war work even more rapidly than during the previous war (310,000 by June 1940, though shy of the 430,000 who were eventually put to work in World War I). A new Service de la main-d'oeuvre indigène within the Ministry aimed to bring 100,000 workers from North Africa, though France's quick defeat interrupted the process.[11] The war of 1939–1940, in short, provided authorities with a renewed opportunity to expand the role of the state in recruiting labor and overseeing its training, treatment, and pay, but state officials did little to repair the severe damage to social relations politics had wrought in the late 1930s.

After the defeat of June 1940, Pétain's new Vichy administration used this inheritance of expanded state power and labor's political isolation to steer employment policy into even more reactionary terrain. A law of October 11, 1940, prohibited women from taking jobs in the public sector. Women already so employed had to retire at age 50. Ministerial circulars encouraged private employers to lay off women and older male workers and to hire instead demobilized soldiers, former POWs, and fathers with three children or more.[12] Vichy laws excluded foreigners from the civil service, including teaching and the professions of medicine, dentistry, pharmacy, and law. The regime turned the former Daladier government's internment camps into a veritable concentration camp system for foreigners—especially Jewish refugees, who were put to work in labor brigades and after 1941 deported, under Vichy oversight, to Nazi death camps. Some 15,000 recent immigrants and refugees who had acquired citizenship in the late 1920s and 1930s saw their naturalizations revoked, and many of them were interned and deported as well.[13] With no prodding from the Germans, the Vichy regime used access to employment as its main weapon against Jews, French and foreign alike, excluding them from public service, teaching, cinema, the press, and by summer 1941 an expanding number of professions.[14] Labor market regulation became the principal—and grotesque—means for Vichy ideologues to remake France.

As the Occupation wore on, traditionalist goals gave way to practicality and the impact of Hitler's efforts to plunder the French economy. In September 1942 the Vichy government had to abandon its work restrictions on women as French factories geared up again to meet German demands and as the civil service went begging for new employees.[15] By 1944 the ratio of women to men in the aircraft industry had returned to what it had been in May 1940.[16] To help meet labor shortages the government sent foreigners, organized into compulsory work brigades, into the fields or into the German's "Todt organization" for building fortifications on the Atlantic coast.[17] Above all, Vichy complied in conscripting entire age cohorts of young men into the Compulsory Labor Service (Service du travail obligatoire, STO) to work in Germany, making France second only to Poland as a foreign source for Hitler's labor force. From mid-1943 until the Normandy invasion, men between the ages of 18 and 50 remained subject to compulsory labor laws, and starting in February 1944 so too did childless single and married women between the ages of 18 and 45.[18] Never before or since has the French state assumed such extensive formal administrative jurisdiction over the labor market, despite the fact that the actual administrative capacity of the Vichy state deteriorated steadily in 1944 as civil servants anticipated the Allied invasion. Indeed, STO recruitment suffered as young men escaped into the Resistance and employers, bureaucrats, and medical clinics found ways to slow the flow of laborers out of the country.[19]

Despite how pivotal the questions of manpower had become, policy planners in the Resistance had strikingly little to say about the subject in their planning for the postwar economy. To be sure, Jean Monnet, Pierre Mendès France, and other policy visionaries for Free France believed that the state, even in peacetime, ought do a great deal to influence the evolution of the nation's workforce—its mixture of natives and foreigners, its productivity and skill levels, its age and gender composition. And as labor specialist Jacques Desmarest would write soon after the war, "One of the essential tasks of the state is to overcome the consequences of labor shortages and unemployment crises."[20] But opinions differed widely over how much authority a postwar state should command over labor, especially given the burning desire of the trade unions to bring labor matters back into the domain of civil society, where they might assume a new commanding role of their own. The Communists put great store in the revival of the major trade union federation, the CGT (Confédération générale du travail), as a force independent of the state (if not, sub rosa, of the party), but they also had Jacobin ambitions to use state authority on behalf of the working class. Others in the Resistance toyed with varieties of corporatism, not altogether different from Vichy labor minister René Belin's stillborn plans in 1940–1941 to create new associations for business-labor cooperation. Christian Democrats, for example, spoke of new forms of cooperation between employers and unions to move beyond the country's deep divisions and to curb the power of the dirigiste state. Socialists like André Philip, by contrast, imagined such cooperation as complementary to robust state planning.[21] Three decades of state expansion in labor regulation had destroyed any illusions of going back to the laissez-faire labor markets of the nineteenth century.

But the experience since 1914 had failed to produce a common understanding of how best to regulate those markets and share the state's authority with business and labor. Neither the wartime mobilization of 1939–1940 nor Vichy's authoritarian interventions had left models for how to coordinate manpower policy with economic planning that state authorities, business, and labor were all itching to follow.

Confronting the Post-Liberation Labor Emergency

At first, then, de Gaulle's Provisional Government simply improvised, with powers inherited from Vichy and the mobilization of 1939, to cope with the crises of the post-Liberation economy. In the winter of 1944–1945, with France fully at war again with Germany, Gaullist labor minister Alexandre Parodi confronted the seeming paradox of labor shortage, on the one hand, and, on the other, a level of unemployment estimated to be as high as 600,000 people, of whom half were in the Paris region.[22] Workers sat idle after their factories had been bombed, while cities lay in ruins awaiting help to clear the rubble. A nation shivered for lack of labor to mine its coal. Parodi gave local employment offices authority to requisition available laborers to work where they were needed.[23] In Paris, authorities ordered many of the unemployed to cold, poorly provisioned worksites in the provinces, a fate not always welcomed by working-class Parisians who might otherwise have survived in the city on odd jobs and the dole.

The Labor Ministry also resorted to propaganda. In Parisian Métro stations, advertisements exhorted riders to contact their unions or their local state employment office: "Our country has a great need for the labor of all its children to bring about economic recovery and the victorious conduct of the war."[24] The ad implied, correctly, that the labor movement stood staunchly behind the government's effort to enlist workers into what the Communist Party dubbed the "battle for production," although the labor press also cautioned officials against perpetuating the wage inequities, work camps, and military discipline associated with Vichy.[25]

State employment offices also gave preference in job placements to demobilized soldiers and returning POWs and deportees.[26] This effort perpetuated a policy first promulgated by the Vichy regime, which had courted the loyalty of French POWs languishing in prison camps by guaranteeing returnees the right to resume their prewar jobs.[27] The post-Liberation government went one step further, delegating to the Labor Ministry the authority to approve all hiring and firing in a large number of business establishments. The Provisional Government hoped especially to relocate available skilled workers (POWs or otherwise) to key industries and hasten the hiring of citizens with compelling moral claims to a job. In May 1945 the government issued an ordinance requiring employers to rehire repatriated employees— that is, former POWs, demobilized soldiers, and deportees—or to assign them to positions equivalent to what they had had before, even if this meant laying off other workers to make this possible. POWs were given six months of immunity from any danger of being laid off. They also had special access to training programs.

Two conditions helped the government integrate repatriated citizens back into the labor force: the state's expanding control over the economy via nationalizations in banking, insurance, and industry; and the acute demand for workers in the construction sector, for rubble and mine-clearing operations, and for repairing thousands of miles of rails. To be sure, repatriated citizens had things to complain about: the modesty of the cash allowances and ration points they were given upon returning to France (along with an ill-fitting suit), and the lack of respect they sometimes encountered back home (some would associate them with the defeat of 1940, as POWs, or with the hated STO, as conscripted workers). In June 1945, 20,000 to 50,000 former POWs and deportees marched on the Ministry of Prisoners, Deportees, and Refugees to protest alleged broken promises about amenities such as extra points for clothing in the rationed market.[28] But a fear of chronic unemployment was not something most able-bodied returnees had to deal with by summer 1945.

Time, the enormous task of reconstruction, and the chronic shortage of labor played in their favor. Civil servants in the giant bureaucracies of education and the PTT, railroad employees in the SNCF, military personnel, and employees in such newly nationalized firms such as Renault and Électricité de France found it relatively easy to resume their prewar jobs. Employees in the private sector, though faced with the uncertain commitment of their employers to a policy of reintegration, had recourse to the Labor Ministry's local labor inspectors, who were charged with enforcing the rules. Reintegration was toughest in agriculture, petty commerce, and the liberal professions. Many farmers and farmworkers returned to fields and herds devastated by war. It would take time and government subsidies to restore them. Shopkeepers, doctors, and lawyers could return to discover their clients had left them for lucky competitors who had remained in town during the war. Government efforts to assist them mainly took the form of financial subsidies and training advantages to help people restart their businesses and careers.[29] In any event, by late 1945 most able-bodied male returnees had found their way back into the workforce one way or another and could hardly be regarded as a vast untapped reservoir of available manpower.

Faced with an acute demand for labor, authorities jumped to harness the half million German POWs the Allied victory had made available to France.[30] Most of these men arrived through transfers arranged by the American army starting in the spring of 1945, and a great many came via liberty ships from prison camps in the United States. The French had ample precedent from the First World War: by 1917 they had imprisoned 300,000 German POWs and put many of them to work in agriculture, mines, ports, and factories.[31] Now, the German prisoners of 1945 were sent out daily to mine coal, harvest crops, remove rubble (see Figure 2.1), labor in factories, and suffer the one job that Communist labor leader André Tollet told the Labor Ministry these men especially deserved: clearing mines. To Tollet it made little sense to displace French workers with German POWs in a town such as Provins, only to have a trade union leader blown up by a mine-clearing accident in Cherbourg.[32] The Labor Ministry's general director of manpower, Jacques Maillet, himself a distinguished Free French pilot and then intelligence and political operative in the Resistance, could only agree that the use of Germans in de-mining operations ought to be encouraged, though he also told Tollet that their French supervisors were nonetheless keen to assign themselves to the most dangerous work and hence could still be victims of accidents.[33] In any event, the government showed little hesitation in using German POWs for this, the most nerving-wracking job in reconstruction: nearly 25,000 German POWs served in de-mining details.

FIGURE 2.1 German POWs clearing rubble, circa 1946. French authorities got about a half-million German prisoners of war, mostly through transfers from American custody. Faced with an acute labor shortage, the French government put POWs to work, particularly in rubble removal, mine clearing, crop harvesting, and construction. ©Jean-Jacques TOURAND/ECPAD/Défense.

Most of the German prisoners worked elsewhere, especially in agriculture (200,000) and coal mines (50,000), and their employment called for the Labor Ministry to play an active role overseeing their use in the workforce. At first employers refrained from taking on German POWs in localities where, as one government report put it, people "suffered especially from German oppression."[34] To avoid having POWs languishing idle and ill in military depots, the government offered them to employers at a discount, so to speak, since companies were expected to cover the costs of feeding, clothing, and guarding the Germans and to pay them the wages, low though they were, that POW laborers were entitled to under the Geneva Convention.[35] This strategy seemed to work: by fall 1945, demand for POWs picked up, and soon POWs found their way into a wide gamut of job sites in construction, agriculture, and industry around the country. For the Labor Ministry the trick was to make the costs low enough to keep firms interested in using German prisoners but not so low as to incur the wrath of the

International Red Cross for turning POWs in virtual slave laborers. Indeed, American officials interrupted prisoner transfers from the United States to France between October 1945 and January 1946 after receiving Red Cross reports of the squalor POWs were made to suffer.

The Labor Ministry also sought to ensure that employers did not use POWs without first hiring unemployed French workers in their locality. Trade unions kept a watch on that front.[36] Union pressure mattered. Workers in Normandy, for example, by raising the specter of possible sabotage by German POWs at a local naval shipyard, managed to get some local French metalworkers shifted from rubble-clearing to shipbuilding.[37] Labor Ministry officials proved responsive to union requests of this kind, even as they remained eager to take full advantage of POW manpower, as demonstrated, for example, when they opposed the Foreign Ministry's effort to improve France's standing in the French-occupied Sarre distinct of Germany by getting Sarrois POWs repatriated.[38] Labor officials had no doubt about the economic utility of the POW workforce. They claimed it saved France 5 billion francs in 1945 and another 7 billion the next year, even after taking the costs of imprisonment into account.[39] In a different political climate critics might have regarded these figures as a measure of exploitation, but not so in a France still traumatized by the war and Occupation.

All these measures together—requisitioning workers, getting repatriated citizens into jobs, putting German POWs to work—plus the political achievement of getting trade union consent to boost the workweek to forty-eight hours, constituted what could be called "high voltage" dirigisme, resembling as it did the powerful role the government played during the labor mobilizations of the First World War and the war of 1939–1940. Perhaps due to the condition of the economy and the need to help people stabilize their lives, no one appears to have challenged outright the wisdom of expanding government authority to this extent. These measures, after all, fell far short of Vichy's authoritarian use of arrest, internment, and the STO. De Gaulle's government, moreover, had broad popular support after the Liberation to assert its authority in the interest of the national recovery effort. Labor Minister Alexandre Parodi, as a heroic figure from the liberation of Paris and a de Gaulle loyalist with impeccable credentials as a high-level civil servant, had the stature to use that authority in the realm of manpower policy.

Still, business and labor leaders could not help worrying about this expansion of state authority, even if they refrained from opposing it frontally. The business weekly *La Semaine Économique et Financière,* expressed concern over the *tendances dirigistes* manifest in the Labor Ministry's expanded authority—and this at a time when "dirigisme," despite its positive connotations to many government planners, was still an epithet to most employers.[40] Employers, of course, had a long history of jealously protecting their prerogative to hire and fire as they wished. Although many of them profited from contracts with the Germans during the Occupation, they also had deeply resented the state interference that the STO had represented.[41] After the Liberation, most employers tolerated the state's intervention in the labor market only as an emergency measure, and they counted on de Gaulle and his more conservative ministers, such as Finance Minister (and businessman) René Pleven, to keep the most eager interventionists in check.

Dirigisme in the labor market drew a more ambivalent response from trade union activists. Although they welcomed the Labor Ministry's initiative in abolishing private employment agencies, long a demand of the labor movement, they had reservations about the state's oversight of hiring and firing. Labor activists had not fought to free workers from Vichy's regimen of labor conscription only to see workers' renewed freedom of movement postponed further. When at the May 1945 meeting of the Labor Ministry's National Manpower Council a CGT representative urged that, with Germany's defeat, workers' freedom of movement should now be restored, Manpower Director Jacques Maillet defended continued controls to "guarantee employment to workers, proceed rapidly to the country's economic reconstruction of the country, and heed the job needs of the war's victims."[42] But the CGT kept up the friction. Henri Raynaud, the senior Communist and CGT leader on the National Manpower Council reminded the body at the August 1945 meeting that his confederation could sanction this "restriction" on the "liberté du travail" only as a temporary measure. He argued, too, that parity committees, that is, boards with equal labor and employer representation, should work alongside local Labor Ministry officials in exercising authority over employment.[43]

Raynaud's views reflected an ambivalence about dirigisme in the labor market that ran deep in the trade union movement, Communist and non-Communist alike. Militants valued the state's help in pressuring employers, but not to the point where it permanently compromised the freedom of workers to labor where they wished or postponed indefinitely the postwar return to collective bargaining.[44] *Liberté du travail* (the freedom of labor) had emerged from the French Revolution as a pillar in republican ideology, which even the Leninism of many CGT militants had not diminished.[45] And collective bargaining had been too hard won in the final decades of the Third Republic to see it wither away through the interventionism of even so labor-oriented a state as the Provisional Government of 1945. A moderate degree of dirigisme, then, could give trade unionists the twin advantage of exerting power over employers both indirectly through allies in the Labor Ministry and directly through the restoration of collection bargaining.

As for parity committees, moderates in the CGT had advocated them as a form of labor representation in their famous Minimum Program of 1918, inspired as they had been by Albert Thomas's experiment of labor-management committees in munitions plants during the First World War. Since then, parity committees with equal labor and management representation had remained a standard aspiration among trade union moderates, and by 1945 even Communist militants had come around to the idea, which had appeared too anodyne for them in the interwar years.[46] The parity committee appealed to labor activists partly because it could, potentially, give them genuine leverage over decision making and real legitimacy for the unions, and partly because it served to impede an excessive expansion of the state's administrative power. Henri Raynaud's call for the use of them in hiring and firing in 1945, however, fell on deaf ears with Labor Ministry officials, who, loath to dilute their own authority in the emergency climate of the post-Liberation period, had already decided to use labor and employer representatives in advisory roles, rather than in full-fledged decision making. Even so, advisory committees had real import. They kept Labor Ministry administrators better anchored in reality and they lent prestige to the unions and business groups represented around the table. Parity committees also gave an aura of democratic legitimacy to state regulation in the labor market. The Provisional Government thus established a large national network of manpower committees in 1944, which in 1948 the Fourth Republic were further institutionalized at the departmental level by decree. A similar network of committees, organized on the basis of occupations, took root in 1946 to offer advice on technical training and apprenticeship.[47]

If in 1945 Alexandre Parodi's Labor Ministry dealt with the immediate crisis of manning worksites and integrating returnees, more intractable problems with the nation's labor supply remained. Since the nineteenth century, French industrialists had grappled with chronic labor shortages, made worse by the demographic catastrophe of the First World War (1.3 million in battle deaths alone) and the further loss of over 1.4 million people to war, deportation, and migration between 1939 and 1945.[48] The physical reconstruction after 1945 created a daunting need for manpower, as did aims for longer-term industrial growth. Labor Ministry officials, therefore, sought ways to boost labor efficiency and enlarge the workforce.

The best methods for improving labor productivity took time and money. Investing in new plant and equipment, encouraging industrial concentration, raising the skill levels of the workforce, and experimenting with new manufacturing procedures all could potentially diminish the disadvantages of the country's chronic labor shortage. Economists associated with Jean Monnet's Planning Commission (the Commissariat général du Plan) and its first five-year plan (the Monnet Plan, 1946–1950) understood that investment, rationalization, and changes in the use of labor all went hand in hand, and this understanding became all the more widespread when the Marshall Plan began to sponsor "productivity missions" to the United States in the late 1940s. Labor Ministry officials also eyed techniques that could improve the fit between the labor needs of the French economy and what the French workforce had to offer. Jacques Desmarest, as labor expert at the Conseil d'État, called for the state to improve job placement services, subsidize professional training, and prod employers to sponsor apprenticeship programs suitable to the future needs of their industries. State incentives, too, he argued, could spawn the more widespread use of medical and social work services in companies striving to rationalize their production.[49] Boosting productivity and adapting the workforce for a changing economy: these would remain preoccupations in manpower policy planning at the Labor Ministry and the Commissariat général du Plan in the 1950s.[50]

However sound these measures appeared as long-term strategies for making the most of France's muscle and brainpower, they offered little as a short-term solution to the labor shortage. For this the government relied first of all on exhortation, or "Stakhanovism" to borrow the Soviet term, that is, patriotic invocations to inspire workers to apply themselves vigorously over long hours for the sake of the "battle for production." It was one thing, of course, to drive the workforce and encourage overtime when the country was still at war with Germany, and quite another when the goal was postwar recovery. Still, it made a difference that activists in the CGT and the Communist Party threw themselves wholeheartedly behind productivism, calling for hard work and long hours in the interests of national rejuvenation (and the stature of their unions), at least until the spring of 1947 when, amid a growing grassroots rebellion against wage constraints, the tripartite coalition of Communists, Socialists, and Christian Democrats running the government fell apart.[51]

It mattered, too, that the government refrained from launching an all-out campaign to push married working women back into the home. To be sure, Parodi's Labor Ministry did instruct employers to hire returning POWs rather than women, who, unless they were the sole breadwinner, were expected to step aside to make way for men. Women who lost jobs lost access to unemployment subsidies too, if their husbands were employed, a policy labor leaders on the National Manpower Council condemned as discriminatory.[52] War factories faced with demobilization typically shed women more readily than men. Women also lost jobs in textiles, traditionally a bastion of female employment, as that industry contracted in the late 1940s for lack of supplies.[53] Still, overall levels of female employment did not decline dramatically in the early postwar years, despite all the emphasis in the culture at large on returning to traditional gender roles and to what Antoine Prost has described as the postwar "romance of the couple."[54] Though data on female employment in this period are spotty, studies at the time by the Institut national des études démographiques (INED) and by the insurance expert qua economist, Jean Fourastié, pointed to an increase in the percentage of women working in 1946, in comparison to

1936.[55] The notion that women had a right to work may even have gained some legitimacy through the passage of a law in 1945 calling for equal pay for equal work, as well as through (poorly enforced) guarantees of equal rights for women written into the Constitution of 1946.[56] Although wage inequalities persisted, after the war women did make headway entering professions such as the law. As stewards of manpower policy, however, Alexandre Parodi and his associates at the Labor Ministry did not view women as a crucial, untapped resource in the postwar labor market in the way their counterparts during both world wars felt so compelled to.[57] Instead it was commonplace, even in the Communist Left, to view woman first and foremost as mothers capable of boosting the nation's birth rate. In the early postwar years, pronatalism trumped manpower policy all across the political spectrum.[58]

If cultural mores made it difficult to think of women as a major source of untapped labor, and if the most sophisticated ideas for improving productivity, training, and placement held promise only in the long term, where could government leaders and employers turn to supply the more urgent, short-term needs of an economy facing the challenges of reconstruction and modernization? De Gaulle's Provisional Government set its sights on the same source that employers had eyed in the 1920s: immigrants. Indeed, after the defeat of 1940 it was widely assumed in de Gaulle's entourage that immigration would have to be an important component of the country's postwar renaissance. In their influential Liberation-era tract *Refaire la France,* Gaullist policy planners Michel Debré and Emmanuel Monick called for "an immigration policy worthy of the name," that is, a tightly controlled recruitment strategy that assimilated immigrants into the regions and industries where they were needed.[59] De Gaulle himself made clear his own convictions on the matter in his speech of March 3, 1945, to the Consultative Assembly. Citing the "vital and sacred" need for the country to produce "twelve million beautiful babies" in the coming decade, he pointed not just to reducing infant mortality but also to introducing "good immigrant elements methodically and intelligently into the French nation."[60] Just what kind of immigrants were "good elements" was likely to be a matter of controversy. Nor were the experts of common mind about how optimistic to be about immigration after the Liberation. Jacques Desmarest thought that immigration offered some prospect for enlarging the workforce, but he doubted how robust the supply could be, now that Eastern Europe had reconstruction needs of its own and was falling under the dominion of governments that "perhaps will not authorize the immigration of their workers."[61] But most experts remained sanguine. Nothing rivaled immigration as an immediate remedy to labor shortage, and employers and public officials looked to the state to make it happen.

Immigration as a Strategy of National Rejuvenation

In 1945 several well-placed constituencies within the government—economic planners, populationists (proponents of demographic growth), and the high-level civil servants and politicians running ministries with a stake in labor supply (Agriculture, Industrial Production, and Labor)—concurred in their enthusiasm to promote immigration. Opinions differed, however, over who should be recruited and why, and with what degree of protection from the policing powers of the state. Jean Monnet and his team of economists at the new Commissariat général du Plan harbored some ambivalence about immigration. They recognized that some immigration was needed to fuel the recovery, but they worried that making too many foreign workers available to employers could weaken the drive to boost productivity. Some economists even went so far as to think a productivity campaign might be better served by avoiding immigration altogether—a view the undersecretary of state for population, Pierre Pflimlin, abhorred. "It could be very dangerous to lend credibility to the idea that France has a choice between two policies, the one of pursuing a technological solution, the other an immigration solution."[62] Officials at the Planning Commission understood the challenge and lent their support to an aggressive immigration policy by calling in 1946 for one million to 1.5 million new immigrants over a five-year period.[63]

This figure matched the ambitions of the leading populationists in the government: Georges Mauco, Robert Debré (father of aforementioned Michel), and Alfred Sauvy, who were the brain trust of the new Population Ministry (or more fully the Ministry of Public Health and Population). Bolstered by the pronatalist lobby and demographers at the new Institut national des études démographique (INED), the successor institution to Vichy's more avowedly eugenicist (and racist) Fondation Carrel, these men focused less on immediate manpower needs and more on the big demographic picture. They viewed immigration as essential for repopulating a country that would otherwise remain condemned to the ruinous effects of demographic decline and an aging population structure. "An immigrant is not only a worker," Debré and Sauvy wrote in their well-circulated post-Liberation book *Des Français pour la France*, "he is a man. . . . [T]he ultimate goal of immigration in France is to maintain the population, with a suitable choice of contributions from abroad."[64] When populationists imagined immigrants, they envisioned couples and their offspring. Sauvy believed that restoring a normal age distribution pyramid to France required bringing a whopping five million newcomers into the Hexagon.[65]

This vision, however, potentially contradicted the xenophobia that had long been a part of the pronatalist movement and the conservative family lobby—nationalists of the old school who viewed immigration itself as a sign of national decline. For this reason, particularly Georges Mauco, a key policy insider steeped in these same ethnocentric anxieties, invested enormous energy, from the 1930s on, promoting a notion of ethnic hierarchy that ranked nationalities on the basis of what he believed were their inherent capacities to assimilate into French society. Northern and Germanic Europeans, he argued, held pride of place, followed in descending order by southern Europeans, Slavic peoples, and last and only reluctantly, non-Europeans. As a Vichy official he published explicitly anti-Semitic views on assimilation. Despite a brief Resistance record in 1944 that salvaged his career, nothing about the war and Nazi racism had changed his views on immigration.[66] Mauco's ideas, though hardly official doctrine in the government, lent quasi-scientific legitimacy to prejudices held by a great many people in France.

Because the populationists set such store in welcoming some immigrants and excluding others, they also viewed the state's role expansively to include an ample range of police powers and social services designed to help anchor the coveted newcomers to France, monitor their whereabouts, and limit the stay and mobility of the unwanted. Mauco, whom de Gaulle named in 1945 to be general secretary of the government's prestigious Haut Comité consultatif de la population et de la famille (the HCCPF), tended to stress the state's role in screening newcomers and seeing to it that they found housing and jobs. Sauvy, named at the same time as general secretary for family and population in the new Population Ministry (in addition to serving as the intellectual steward of INED), was less obsessed by ethnicity and more convinced that assimilation was more a matter of individual traits rather than group characteristics.[67] He cared most about persuading the French of the need to boost overall immigration to levels beyond what they had previously contemplated, and he argued for enlarging immigrants' access to social services.[68] Still, his and Robert Debré's international map of immigration nationality was much the same as Mauco's—casting the greatest aspersions at non-Europeans and the inhabitants of Eastern Europe as essentially unassimilable, though with reserved openness to Poles, Czechs, Serbs, and Hungarians.[69] Together Sauvy and Mauco played a big role in drafting the ordinance of November 2, 1945, that accorded basic civil and social rights to immigrants and established the legal foundation for the state's revolutionary new role in overseeing immigration in a peacetime economy. The ordinance also authorized three types of residency permits—"temporary" for a year, "ordinary" for three years, and "privileged" for ten years with the additional freedom to reside anywhere in the country and pursue an occupation of one's choosing.[70] This framework created a hybrid approach to immigration that preserved the flexibility (and the precariousness, from the immigrants' point of view) of a guest worker system, while providing paths to permanent residence.

However, Mauco and Sauvy's efforts to have the ordinance also empower the state to discriminate by nationality in screening immigrants fell afoul of a ruling by the Conseil d'État that struck such a provision from the law.[71] This ruling marked a sharp rupture with the Vichy past. It secured the principle at the heart of the new postwar immigration regime in France that all immigrants had equal rights as individuals regardless of national origin. When they applied for permits, they were to be assessed only as individuals with their own particular abilities and suitability for employment or family settlement. The Conseil d'État also issued a ruling that extended the same principle to refugees. Were it not for the peculiarities of French legal procedure that gave this body authority to modify the ordinance, such a departure from legally inscribed ethnocentrism might not have happened in 1945.

Political will, too, played a role in blocking Mauco's drive for legalizing nationality selection. For one thing, René Cassin, who was to become a leading proponent (and principal author) of the Universal Declaration of Human Rights (1948), presided over the Conseil d'État. His stature and leadership weighed heavily in rulings of immigration, refugee, and naturalization laws. For another, immigrant advocates themselves had gained a voice in the Liberation era. This was a new development. Immigrant advocacy associations, many with links to the Left and the unions, had originated in the Third Republic but had little influence. Only with the Resistance did they begin to galvanize politically, principally in the form of the Centre d'action et de défense des immigrés (CADI).[72] This organization, created during the Popular Front era, served as an umbrella for a host of smaller nationality-based (and in many cases Communist-affiliated) associations. It had a seat at the table of the National Resistance Council. Its general secretary and animating influence, Edouard Kowalski, a Jewish refugee and Communist resister, led an effort in 1945 and 1946 to lobby against nationality selection and to enlarge the rights of immigrants under the November 1945 ordinance, liberalize naturalization and refugee laws, and limit the power of the police to harass foreigners. Interior Minister Adrien Tixier, a Socialist with a strong republican commitment to individual rights, proved receptive to CADI's advocacy—not only out of conviction but also because by issuing decrees and circulars responding to this pressure he sought successfully to avoid exposing the new immigration regime to renewed parliamentary debate.[73] For all the continuity in the ethnocentric thinking about nationality differences and assimilability and in the personnel involved in immigration matters in the Population, Labor, and Interior Ministries—and there was plenty of it—the new legal regime of 1945 and 1946, and the power of new voices like Kowalski's making a positive case for immigrant rights, marked a shift in this policy domain.[74]

The Labor Ministry embodied this mixture of change and continuity as much as any organ of the government. The first post-Liberation labor minister, Alexandre Parodi, embodied it too as both an innovator and a paragon of the high civil service establishment of the 1930s, where he rose to prominence as a conseiller d'État writing social and labor legislation and serving in top staff posts. He was something of an administrative godfather figure to Michel Debré, Pierre Laroque, and other rising starts in the Conseil d'État (and then, after the Liberation, the Provisional Government). His views on immigration were very much in the mainstream—the ambivalence about it, the ethnocentrism, the tolerance of the internment of foreigners in 1939, when he became the Labor Ministry's director of work and manpower in 1939. But the Vichy government soon fired him in 1940 for criticizing the regime, and he spent the rest of the war with ever greater administrative responsibility serving the underground as a key figure in the internal Resistance with strong ties to de Gaulle's inner circle. By the Liberation he had become more critical of tough policies such as internment, more skeptical of men like Mauco, and better equipped to work with labor and the Left. Like Tixier at Interior, Parodi made his ministry receptive to ideas for liberalizing the rights of immigrants and refugees. When Amboise Croizat, a leading figure in the French Communist Party (PCF) and head of the CGT's metalworking federation, replaced Parodi in October 1945, the same ethos prevailed, especially on account of CADI's links to the party.

At the same time, the Labor Ministry had a pragmatic, union-influenced approach to manpower regulation, and in this respect there was plenty of continuity with the interwar years. Parodi and then Croizat both had more modest goals for immigration than their counterparts at the Population Ministry. They argued forcefully against establishing nationality quotas, and they hoped to welcome into the country not so much the young families that the populationists yearned for, but instead the individual foreigners, especially skilled workers, who could be hired by contract to fill known vacancies in the French labor market.[75] This approach appealed to trade union leaders who advocated a new regime of immigration that was truly *dirigé* and *organisé*, that is, managed by the state to ensure that immigrants enjoyed the rights and wages of French workers and were not being used to deprive the latter of jobs and decent pay.[76] Some labor leaders no doubt embraced these principles of equity in the hopes that they would effectively preclude immigration altogether. This kind of labor protectionism had a long tradition, made all the more robust by the experience of unemployment in the 1930s. Indeed, the unions supported the Labor Ministry's decision in 1949 to revive the use of the 1932 law that authorized the imposition of quotas on immigrant hiring if unemployment were to spike in a given industry at the local level.[77]

Disagreements, then, festered beneath the surface of what appeared to be a great deal of consensus within the government that immigration was essential for reconstruction and a key instrument for rejuvenating the country. Apart from trade unionists and economists at the Planning Commission, few voices in public life dissented from this conviction, so thoroughly had national leaders from Pétain to de Gaulle and even the Communists hammered home the idea after 1940 that France had a population problem that had to be solved.[78] Agreement on this basic idea, however, did little to resolve the conflict within the government over the primary goals of its emerging immigration policy. The Labor Ministry viewed the new approach, embodied in the ordinance of November 2, 1945, as essentially the nationalization of the guest-worker system that employers and government officials had put into place after the First World War, a system that could treat foreigners as temporary or permanent residents depending on the needs of the economy. Populationists accepted this formulation, but saw alongside it a second, more important need to bring large numbers of young families-in-the-making with suitable prospects of assimilating into France. What both ministries underestimated were the difficulties involved in actually recruiting foreigners to come to France.

The Battle over the ONI

The struggle to define the state's role in recruiting foreigners to France soon found a focal point in the new Office national d'immigration (National Immigration Office, or ONI), a public agency established by the November 1945 ordinance to recruit foreigners into the workforce. Its invention marked a sea change in the history of state economic intervention. Never before had the government played so direct a role in the recruitment of foreign labor, apart from the conscription of colonial subjects and Chinese laborers during the First World War. Until the ONI the state's chief peacetime role in immigration, as manifest in the interwar years, had been, first, negotiating bilateral accords over the terms and conditions of labor migration with Italy and other countries, and second, policing. But with the creation of the ONI the state suddenly acquired an official monopoly over labor recruitment abroad. It replaced the old Société générale d'immigration that private employers had established in 1924 to recruit mostly Polish workers into farmwork and the mining and metal industries of the northeast.[79] The ONI's eclipse of the SGI testified to postwar disenchantment with the *patronat* (employers as a collectivity), with its stigma of collaboration, as well as to the new prestige of the trade unions, whose leaders had long argued that the SGI had profited excessively from serving its patrons with little regard for the needs of the immigrants it recruited. The newly founded ONI also had the virtue of financial transparency: it charged employers a flat fee of 6,000 francs for each of its recruits the employers hired. In contrast to the SGI, it enjoyed the legitimating aura of its association with the Resistance, the unions, and the Left, much as did the new nationalized companies and social security system in 1945–1946.

For all these virtues, the ONI had an ambiguous mandate. It came under the supervision of the Labor Ministry, with its commitment to matching immigrants to jobs, but it was also accountable to the broader lines of immigration policy established by the Population Ministry. By 1947 the latter ministry explicitly stepped up the pressure on ONI also to introduce whole families into the country. With a staff of 900 employees, the ONI had widespread operations—headquarters in Paris, eleven regional offices around the country for transferring immigrants into jobs, and recruiting centers in Milan, London, Copenhagen, and several cities in Germany, where medical staff and teams made up of ONI field officers and trade union and employer representatives screened recruits.[80] In this respect nationality preference crept back into the French immigration regime, not by violating the prescriptions against screening newcomers by national origin, but by setting up recruitment centers in some countries and not others.[81]

The ONI soon encountered serious obstacles to recruiting the Monnet Plan's annual target of over a quarter-million foreign workers, a goal made more compelling by the scheduled release of all German POWs by the end of 1948. The agency's most fervent hopes lay with Italy, long a key source of foreign workers for France and a favored site in the eyes of the CGT because many Italian workers, especially in the North, could be counted on to have Communist or at least trade union sympathies (see Figure 2.2). Two bilateral agreements between French and Italian governments, one signed in November 1946, the other the following March, established terms especially designed to make immigration to France appeal to an Italian workforce plagued with high levels of chronic unemployment at home. Italian immigrants, for example, were authorized to receive the same kind of family allowances in their wage package as their native French counterparts, monies that they could then send back to Italy to support their children.[82] Migration to France, however, proved slow and burdensome for many aspiring Italian immigrants, in part because Italian authorities created bureaucratic delays, in part because of ONI screening. The CGT militants attached to the ONI office in Milan acquired a reputation for judging recruits politically; it was even said they painted for many applicants a discouraging picture of what France had to offer.[83] Word was, too, that the Italian government favored Argentine immigration over the French program, and many migrants opted for the more prosperous climes of Switzerland.[84] Italians who nonetheless were determined to cross the Alps into France as illegal immigrants ran a good chance of being refused at the border.

In the summer of 1946 officials from the Labor and Population Ministries, frustrated by the slow pace of Italian immigration, took the remarkable step of ordering ONI director Bernard Auffray to begin regularizing the status of clandestine Italian migrants, and even to create more processing centers to aid them once they crossed the Franco-Italian frontier.[85] These steps helped, but still, from late 1945 to the end of 1947, the ONI managed to bring only 80,000 Italians to France, of whom 36,000 had entered illegally, far short of initial targets of 200,000 for the year 1947 alone.[86] Nothing frustrated the government's enthusiasts for immigration more than the desultory level of recruitment in Italy: virtually every French commentator on immigration in this period regarded Italians as superb recruits by dint of their reputation for assimilating easily, and Italy offered by far the most promising source of European labor in the late 1940s.

ONI efforts in occupied Germany, the other major focus of the recruitment program, proved even more disappointing. The Population

FIGURE 2.2 Italian migrants in Piedmont walking to the French border, 1946. French officials favored Italians over other nationalities as labor recruits. They came to France both legally, in accord with bilateral government agreements, and illegally, in hopes of finding jobs and getting their status "regularized." Never before in peacetime had the French government played so direct a role in recruiting foreign labor. © L'Illustration. Reproduction prohibited without the expressed agreement of Financière L'Illustration.

Ministry, true to its ethnic priorities, had hoped to attract Germans, Danes, Swedes, and Dutch (Sauvy had a particular hankering for the Dutch), but these so-called Nordics had little incentive to move to a France beset with a terrible housing shortage and little extra government cash to cover resettlement costs. Remarkably enough, the search for German recruits brought some results. Over the course of 1946 and 1947 ONI managed to introduce 9,600 German into France, and as many as 40,000 German POWs chose to stay in the country upon release and screening, rather than return to a Germany where poverty, family tragedy, or the Soviet authorities may have awaited them.[87] This latter figure represented about 20 percent of German POWs still laboring in France in 1948.[88]

In the wake of the war, however, many people in France took a dim view of German immigration. As a secret government report put it, settling Germans in France had to be carried out with "a thousand precautions" (mille précautions).[89] Alfred Sauvy and Robert Debré had anticipated this kind of reaction in their treatise on immigration, and they tried to make the case for overcoming an anti-German reflex, especially given the fact that forced repatriation of millions of Germans from Eastern European countries was bounded to create at least a temporary surplus of population in occupied Germany and hence an opportunity for France. "Recall," Sauvy and Debré wrote, "that there isn't any racial opposition [between Germans and French]: between the large and blond man of the North and the brown and stocky southerner, there are all kinds of intermediary types, especially between the Seine and the Rhine." Germans' faults, they went on to argue, such as "collective cruelty" and "passive obedience," can "disappear through contact with other populations. . . . The contribution of German blood in a reasonable quantity can be especially valuable . . . to compensate too great an influx of Latins and Slavs."[90] A certain ethnic, even racial, affinity between French and Germans, Sauvy and Debré seemed to be implying, ought to soften the hostility French citizens might feel. Ministry reports through the late 1940s continued to remark on local hostility to Germany migrants. Many young German women came to work as domestics, for example, including quite well educated but economically desperate frauleins who sometimes annoyed their employers for lacking the expected demeanor of class deference.[91] Even some Population Ministry officials, though eager for Germans, harbored some worry about bringing in Germans originally from Silesia and East Prussia whom they associated with the "vanguard" of pan-German nationalism.[92]

ONI's main role in Germany lay elsewhere, however, in the refugee camps where hundreds of thousands of displaced persons, or DPs, from Central and Eastern Europe awaited resettlement. The Population Ministry regarded these Europeans as potential demographic assets, of which the Foreign Ministry, for its part, was eager to deprive Germany. Foreign Ministry officials worried that the astonishing presence in an "already overpopulated" Germany of more than ten million refugees from Poland, Czechoslovakia, Yugoslavia, and elsewhere, many of them ethnic Germans, posed a danger to France, especially because their "precarious life" would make them "easy prey for nationalist propaganda of all kinds." Better they should be brought to France where their labor was needed, and all the more so because France had little choice but to honor the schedule for releasing German POWs that it had worked out with the Americans.[93]

But there were obstacles aplenty to getting DPs to France. For one thing, many of them, if given the chance, preferred to settle where wages, housing, and life's opportunities looked better, especially in Britain, Belgium, or the United States. ONI recruitment teams, for another, often took poor health, a "lost taste for work" as one labor official put it, and in the case of CGT screeners a fear of a refugee's presumed anticommunism as ample reason to refuse applicants. Polish DPs bore the heaviest brunt of these assumptions.[94] And then there was the odd case of the "Banatais," German-speaking refugees from Banat, a small border region straddling Rumania, Yugoslavia, and Hungary. This ethnic group had origins in Alsace-Lorraine, Swabia, and Bavaria in the eighteenth century when the Hapsburg Empire recruited settlers into Banat once it had been wrested from the Ottoman Empire. This historic connection to Alsace-Lorraine, however attenuated, made Foreign Minister Robert Schuman and others in the MRP enthusiastic promoters of Banatais DPs as promising future Frenchman, a view echoed in Alsace-Lorraine itself, where many people for their own reasons were eager to affirm the French bona fides of German speakers regarded by some people as all too closely associated with the Third Reich. CGT screeners, by contrast, viewed Banatais as *Volksdeuschte* and hence as Nazi collaborators, as some certainly were. Only a small number Banatais ended up getting to France.[95] Overall, DP recruitment fell flat, as the numbers show: over the course of 1947, the ONI had introduced only 6,625 DPs to France.[96] This outcome did little to improve the larger picture of the ONI's efforts. In 1947 employers had registered with ONI 140,000 job openings available to foreigners, for which the agency provided only 65,000 workers.[97] The mining and agricultural sectors felt the burdens of labor shortages most acutely.[98]

The ONI's failure to deliver foreigners in numbers equal to the available jobs, much less to the ambitious targets of planners and demographers, had, as we have seen, a number of sources: competition from other countries as sites of immigration, the behavior of foreign governments, bureaucratic bottlenecks, the housing shortage, and not least, the CGT's efforts to filter recruits stringently, whether for their political views or the threat they posed to French workers' leverage in the labor market. A deeper flaw in immigration policy was at work as well: the government's sharply contradictory approach to labor migration from North Africa. Alongside Italy, North Africa and especially Algeria would become the indispensable source of foreign workers during the boom years of the late 1950s and 1960s. Yet the French government did little in the early Fourth Republic to prepare for it. On the contrary, Algeria lay outside ONI's official purview in 1946–1947, and conventional assumptions about North Africans—their poor health and skill levels, their disinclination to assimilate in France—pervaded discussions in the Labor and Population Ministries on into the 1950s.[99] But if these ministries remained reluctant to do so, others in government did see Algerian migration as an opportunity,. The Ministry of Urban Reconstruction, desperate for construction workers, saw Algerians as essential for rebuilding the country. More important still, the governor general of Algeria itself, and officials in the Interior Ministry responsible for running this linchpin of the empire, viewed labor migration to the metropole as essential for relieving the poverty and demographic pressures building up—and fueling the anticolonial movement—in Algeria itself. A few visionaries of empire in the interwar period had already come to this conclusion. Albert Sarraut, for instance, viewed the French labor market as an arena where Algerian migrants would learn to become more French and hence to tie Algeria more firmly to the Hexagon.[100] But this was hardly a majority view in the social ministries in the late 1940s.

The incoherence of the government's approach to Algerian migration became apparent in late 1946 and early 1947, when new citizenship rights for Algerians and the resumption of transport between Algiers and Marseille brought an influx of travelers to the metropole. Many of them stayed to look for work, catching the Labor Ministry unprepared to provide the screening, health facilities, placement services, and housing that the situation called for. Officials scurried to reopen two abandoned internment camps near Marseille to house on an emergency basis hundreds of the many thousand new arrivals.[101] Rather than recognize these events as harbingers of opportunity, Labor Ministry officials lashed out at the governor general in Algeria for encouraging the migration.[102] Until the early 1950s and even more so the onset of the Algerian war, most immigration officials would continue

to see North Africans as a menace to be contained rather than a resource to be cultivated like the Italians.

Meanwhile, ONI's recruitment record by early 1948 made the
agency vulnerable to the kind of political shakeup that rocked many
state institutions—the nationalized firms, the Planning Commission,
the social security bureaucracy—with the onset of the Cold War and the
collapse of the tripartite coalition of the Left that had governed
France since the Liberation. Once Prime Minister Paul Ramadier had
expelled Communists from his cabinet in May 1947 and Amboise
Croizat lost the Labor Ministry, CGT militants working in the field
stations and on the administrative board of the ONI no longer enjoyed
the political protection that had given them the chance to shape the
day-to-day practices of the agency. And the Communist Party's hard-
ening line only made matters worse. CGT militants refused, for example, to participate in an international conference on immigration
that brought together delegations from the sixteen signatory countries
of the Marshall Plan.[103] Polarization deepened as authorities inside and
outside France contributed to the exclusion of the CGT from the entire apparatus of immigration management and policymaking. American and British officials cut off contact with ONI field offices in their
own German zones of occupation, and the CGT's leading representative in the ONI's Milan operation found himself expelled from the
country. The ax fell too on ONI director Bernard Auffray, who, though
a Catholic and a journalist and not in the CGT, had certainly hired
many trade unionists to the staff and had tried to include labor and
business in the agency's operations.[104] Predictably, the number two
person in the office, Julien Racamond, a Communist and major figure
in the CGT, was fired as well. Auffray's replacement, populationist
Pierre Bideberry, strengthened the hand at ONI of the Population Ministry, where he had been rising in the ranks of the civil service.[105]

The reorganization of the ONI went far beyond the effort to exclude
the Communists. Following a stinging critique of the ONI's shortcomings by inspectors of the Cour des comptes (the state's accounting
agency), Prime Minister Robert Schuman approved a thorough recasting of the decision-making structure for immigration policy. The
ONI's board of twenty-four members was cut to twelve, a move designed to eliminate all representatives from business, agriculture, and

labor and to convert the board into a governing body of civil servants. Interest group representatives lost their posts in the foreign field stations as well. The national organization representing employers (the Conseil national du patronat français, or CNPF), its agricultural counterpart (the Confédération générale de l'agriculture, or CGA), and the two non-Communist labor confederations (Force ouvrière, or FO, and the Confédération française des travailleurs chrétiens, or CFTC) had to settle for seats on a new National Council for Immigration, a purely advisory body. The CGT had no place at that table. The nerve center of immigration policymaking now shifted to the Interministerial Council for Immigration, which was composed of high-level civil servants and designed to resolve the competing objectives of the Labor and Population Ministries in particular. Populationists like Georges Mauco regarded this new council, which reported directly to the prime minister, as a boon to their agenda.[106] Foreign Minister Georges Bidault, a founder of the Christian Democratic Party (the MRP) and strong anticommunist, encouraged these moves and saw them as a way to position the top civil servants of the Foreign Ministry and the Population Ministry as preponderant authorities in immigration policy.[107] Many of ONI's administrative functions, such as the regularizing of the status of clandestine immigrants, were absorbed into other divisions of the Labor Ministry bureaucracy.[108] Staff reductions came accordingly: by early 1949 ONI's ranks fell to 800 (down from 900), and then to an astonishing 214 one year later, and all the way down to 135 in 1951.[109]

Cold War polarization transformed the politics of immigration in another way as well: it diminished the capacity, and the inclination, of the Communist Party to serve as what up to then had been the most important political force advocating on behalf of immigrants. The party's approach to immigration had long been contradictory: Immigrant activists had served the party, and the party in return had provided an umbrella for immigrant organizations, language groups, and press organs; and yet at the same time the party looked askance at immigration as a threat to French workers' bargaining power. When sectors of the labor market slackened briefly in 1948–1950, the PCF used the press and its presence on the Commission nationale de main-d'oeuvre, to call, in vain, for a halt to "all new immigration."[110] But it was government repression of the party in 1947–1948 that especially crippled it as an advocate for immigrants. The government shut down the CADI, along with a number of smaller immigrant associations and newspapers. It jailed and deported hundreds of Polish, Italian, Russian, and Spanish activists. And repression continued for years: from 1950 to 1953, anywhere from 1,000 to more than 1,700 foreign-born activists were expelled annually.[111] Police repression and popular xenophobia took an especially cruel toll on Spanish republican refugees in the French southwest. To protect themselves, activists of many nationalities scurried to take advantage of naturalization procedures they might be eligible for, and in so doing tended to retreat from the front lines of immigrant advocacy. Though some effort was made to revive the CADI under a different name, the Communist Party of the 1950s had become far less equipped to serve as supporters of not only European immigrants but also the Algerian migrants who would become so important to labor market expansion for the next two decades.[112]

Did the tumult of 1948, especially at the ONI, transform the state's role in immigration? CGT leaders certainly believed so, because in their view their exclusion from ONI operations called into question the agency's commitment to the principle of immigration *dirigé*. And many big industrialists certainly hoped so, sensing a new opportunity to more actively recruit workers abroad themselves, not by reviving the SGI but by working together informally to recruit abroad. In 1949 the powerful metalworking and mining federation, the Union des industries métallurgiques et minières (UIMM), gathered leaders from the chemical, sugar, and construction industries precisely to consider such a strategy.[113] Government officials, however, regarded the reorganization of 1948 as a way to manage immigration more effectively; they saw a continuity in dirigisme where business and labor, for different reasons, saw change. The key civil servants who masterminded the shakeup, and the politicians who sanctioned it, remained convinced that the Labor Ministry had acquired an enduring responsibility for "the movement of manpower," and the same conviction about the state's role in demographic planning and social services continued to inform thinking at the Population Ministry.[114]

What emerged by the end of the 1940s in immigration policymaking was what we might call "low voltage" dirigisme. State administrators had created laws and institutions to promote immigration, but not the elite consensus and interest group support to take full advantage of them. In this respect, immigration policy stood in contrast to several other domains of public policy—nationalization of industry, economic planning, and social security and family benefits—where an inventive phase of institution building in 1945–1946 was also followed by the political upheaval of anticommunist purge and conservative backlash in 1948. State elites in these domains came out of the crisis all the stronger as dirigiste overseers of public policy—usually in close alliance with business interests and conservative advocacy groups, and yet still with enough continuing involvement by trade unions and left-wing activists to help further legitimize the nationalized enterprises, planning commissariat, and vast network of social security and family benefit bureaus as arenas of democratic experimentation. In the case of immigration, dirigistes emerged from the turmoil of the late 1940s uncertain about the place of immigration, and not least the role of North Africans, in the drive to modernize the country. Immigrants themselves lacked vehicles of representation in policy debate, much less in the oversight of immigration administration. Moreover, the basic choices in immigration policy between labor market priorities and demographic goals still divided civil servants, policy intellectuals, and politicians in the early 1950s as much as they had in 1945. Ethnic prejudices still distorted their understanding of the demographic realities they had to work with. And by converting the ONI into little more than a bureaucratic arm of the Labor Ministry, they chose, for the purpose of anticommunism, to enfeeble the best instrument they had available to them for keeping business and labor invested in the process of supporting immigration through state action.

If in 1945–1946 the policy domain of immigration appeared to offer fertile ground for cultivation of new forms of interaction between expert leadership and democratic participation by interest groups, it had turned barren by the early 1950s. The ONI would continue to function in a much reduced and routinized fashion, and immigration continued apace, though still at a much lower level than planners had hoped for in 1946. As the 1950s unfolded, Italian and Spanish immigrants made up the overwhelming majority of European newcomers to France. But they settled in increasingly through the mechanism of "regularization," entering the country not through ONI-affiliated recruitment missions but either clandestinely or by overstaying tourist visas. Then, often with an employer's endorsement, they acquired work and residency papers that regularized their status. By the late 1950s and on through the 1960s well over half of France's new permanent residents (not including Algerians) took this route.[115] Employers, moreover, came to prefer regularization to recruitment missions because it enabled them to hire immigrants standing at the company's doorstep rather than to commit to the future employment of unseen foreigners often long delayed in the recruitment pipeline.[116] After 1956, regularization also helped offset the loss of labor to conscription for the Algerian war. Prejudice continued to play a role as well. Many an employer and government official saw the liberal use of regularization for European immigrants as an ethnic counterbalance to the Algerian migrants who were becoming an important segment of the workforce. With the new Common Market in 1957, expectations grew, too, that an intra-European labor market would begin to emerge. Regularization, then, was taking hold as the immigration procedure of choice. It made the state less the active manager of a deliberately planned immigration regime and more the validator, downstream, of decisions immigrants and employers had made on their own—a process historian Gérard Noiriel has called the "privatization" of the recruitment of foreign labor.[117]

Meanwhile, the real center of the dirigiste action in the 1950s and early 1960s, the major focus of innovation and conflict in the policy domain of immigration, shifted to Algerian migrants and their families. To some degree this was a consequence of the numbers: between 1946 and 1954 the Algerian population in the metropole shot up from 22,000 to 210,000, whereas in the same period the number of Belgians, Poles, and Spaniards in France actually declined (though Spaniards would pick up again, markedly, later in the 1950s and 1960s), and Italians increased only 10 percent.[118] But what mattered more were the political stakes of the Algerian migration, the need government officials felt to make the migration work as an antidote to anticolonial nationalism, indeed the need to make it work in the tumultuous context of the Algerian war. If the ONI faded as an arena of dirigiste experimentation, the state's efforts to manage migrants from Algeria kept this policy domain central to the long reconstruction straight through to the early Fifth Republic.[119]

3

Shopkeeper Turmoil

Tax Rebels and State Reformers
in the Postwar Marketplace

SHOPKEEPERS IN FRANCE found themselves in an ambiguous position in the reconstruction era. From the vantage point of the ordinary citizen, the local grocer, butcher, and baker enjoyed the status of local potentates who presided over the neighborhood nerve center of the everyday economy. Customers curried their favor. Decent cuts of meat and a couple of robust eggs above the ration quota could matter hugely to a family living with the kind of dearth that was commonplace in Europe after the war. Not for nothing, then, had the conditions of war and occupation, including rising prices, rationing, and the black market, inspired many people to venture into the retail business if they had the extra cash to do so. Owning a shop had its advantages in the 1940s: shopkeepers enjoyed their own access to suppliers plus the satisfaction of a social standing unusually elevated by the circumstances of economic scarcity. In an era of rising prices, a small property and an inventory of tangible goods provided security, and usually profit.

Yet shopkeepers also had their demons. Government inspectors could come calling to check on compliance with a host of regulations about rationing, prices, and product standards. Something might trigger irate customers to vent frustration on the man or woman across the counter. Some shopkeepers also imagined even larger hazards lurking over the horizon: big-time retail operations, the chains and the department stores, hoping to squeeze out the mom and pop shops; and a government, seemingly hell-bent on modernizing everything else in France, that might finally get round to "rationalizing" the retail sector itself.

In the immediate post-Liberation period it was difficult for shopkeepers to tell how vulnerable they were to future changes in the retail business. The sector got little attention in the postwar planning of de Gaulle's entourage or the National Council of the Resistance. The latter called for "the development and support of artisanal and agricultural cooperatives for production, purchasing, and sales," something that many shopkeepers would have objected to as an attack on the individual retail proprietor, an effort to avoid the middleman.[1] But little came of this idea after the Liberation. De Gaulle's provision government, with its hands full simply trying to administer rationing and price controls, made scant effort to rethink the structure of the future of the shopkeepers' world.

By the mid-1950s, however, the political landscape of shopkeeping in France had utterly changed. The thunderous march of Pierre Poujade's taxpayers' revolt had swept across much of the country, drawing small-town and lower-middle-class citizens, above all shopkeepers, into its ranks. The conditions of the retail business, its organization, travails, and taxes, found their way onto the front pages of the press and into parliamentary debate. Poujade's upstart extremist movement would go on to win an astonishing 12 percent of the votes and 51 seats in the legislative elections of 1956.[2]

This remarkable appearance of shopkeeper politics at the center of French political life is often viewed as the first of several reactionary campaigns by the "losers" of France's postwar economic transformation to cling to the protections they had enjoyed during Third Republic. One can certainly trace continuities of influence and ideas between Poujade's movement and Gérard Nicoud's shopkeeper protests after 1968 and Jean-Marie Le Pen's Front National of more recent vintage.[3] Indeed, Poujadism acquired, soon after its decline, a legendary aura as the quintessential grassroots reaction in defense of self-interest against the force of social and economic change.[4] What's missing in this retrospective picture, however, is an appreciation how much the shopkeeper politics of the 1950s grew out of the experiences of state regulation of the retail marketplace during and after the war. The shopkeeper revolt of the 1950s was first and foremost a battle with state authorities, and its origins lay less with the small-time proprietors' fear of the imagined supermarkets of the future and more with their palpable struggles in the 1940s and early 1950s over how the government should regulate prices, administer rationing, and restructure taxes in the interests of the country's postwar reconstruction. These areas of public policy shaped a volatile relationship between the vast sea of small-time merchants and an elite corps of government officials seeking to steer the economy out of a period of acute shortage and rising prices and onto an ambitious trajectory of industry-led economic growth. If in 1945 it was the food riot, not shopkeeper protest, that threatened social peace, by 1947 government officials would begin to get a taste of what would challenge their authority to tax petty commerce on an unprecedented scale in the 1950s. The shopkeeper rebellion that exploded a decade after the Liberation, then, had its primary origins in the festering politics of the regulation of retail and in the question that no one had faced up to in 1945: How would the bills of the country's postwar drive to modernize the economy be paid? The struggle to answer that question would make the small retail sector an unexpectedly fraught arena for witnessing the postwar difficulties of combining democratic renewal with state-led economic change. Conservative though shopkeepers were in wanting to preserve their familiar economic landscape, in battling the state they became political innovators in expanding the repertoire of democratic advocacy to emerge from the reconstruction era.

Shopkeepers in a Regulated Marketplace

The Second World War brought government into the retail market on an extraordinary scale. With the law of October 23, 1938, Parliament authorized Edouard Daladier's government to organize the economy for an impending war by regulating the importation, taxing, sale, and rationing of goods.[5] By October 1939 the government imposed wage and price controls to stem inflation, though it was only after the defeat of

France in 1940 that a new Vichy government began to administer rationing. In September 1940 the new Vichy government issued ration coupons for bread, along with personalized ration cards, which consumers had to show to retailers when making purchases of rationed goods. By the following fall, rationing extended to tobacco, clothing, and food, including wine, which became subject to occasional "jours sans" when it could not be legally sold.[6] Market controls, generally, had plenty of precedent. Control over grain prices had been commonplace during the Old Regime and legendary during the French Revolution. During the final two years of the First World War the French government had imposed rationing, which was quickly dismantled after the armistice. Grain prices had become subject again to regulation in 1936 through the Popular Front's new Wheat Office. But if price controls and rationing during the Second World War were not entirely new, they were unprecedented in their scale and duration. Their imposition during a lengthy enemy occupation, moreover, undermined their very legitimacy in public opinion and increasingly so during the second half of the war when the Germans sought to exploit French resources as much as possible. Despite legions of police, gendarmes, and agents from a host of bureaus in the ministries of Finance and National Economy, the Vichy government lacked the means to bring the vast world of buying and selling under its full surveillance. A black market flourished in food, drink, cigarettes, clothing, and virtually everything else a beleaguered, hungry population wanted to buy, including the very ration cards and coupons people needed to survive in a controlled economy.[7]

Price controls and rationing put shopkeepers (meaning, here, small-time retailers of all sorts) in the awkward position of enforcing among their customers the same regulations that they were constantly tempted to violate themselves.[8] The authorities counted on retailers to honor the prices set monthly by prefects in consultation with departmental review boards, and to collect the requisite coupons from their customers. Retailers also had coupons of their own, distributed to them monthly to authorize their own purchases from wholesalers, who in turn had to use their own rationed coupons to buy from suppliers. This method of policing the next lower rung on the ladder of distribution had an impeccable logic to it, but risk-takers easily found ways to get around it. Farmers who could exceed the quotas they were required by the government to meet could find ready buyers of the produce, milk, and meat they quietly sold on the side at black market prices. Wholesalers and retailers alike could play a similar game with goods they either acquired unofficially or held back for off-hour, backroom bargaining. The theft of cards and coupons from town halls was rampant. Not that the French or German authorities suffered these crimes lightly; punishments, though varying enormously by location and the circumstances of the guilty, could be severe.[9] But consumers' desperation, the illicit profits to be made, and patriotic connotations of subverting the system made the dual economy—controlled and black market—a reality every shopkeeper had to navigate as he or she (and often a married couple together) saw fit. If the black market exposed them to temptation, rationing empowered them with their customers, and scarcities gave them the chance to do a great deal better than their neighbors or than they themselves had done before the war. Despite, and because of, the shortages of the occupation, an astonishing 100,000 new shops opened annually in France during the war.[10]

If the occupation created economic conditions favoring entry into the business of small-scale retailing, political circumstances did little to strengthen the hand of small business as a pressure group. The interwar years had been a creative period of growth for organizations that sought to defend the interests of small business, such as the Confédération nationale de l'artisanat français (CNAF, founded in 1924), the Taxpayers League, or the Comité d'organisation de la Confédération générale des classes moyennes (CGCM). Small business people began to develop organizations that gave them a degree of independence from the powerful CNPF, which was geared to serve big enterprises.[11] But Vichy failed to provide shopkeepers the kind of advantages the regime's rhetorical celebrations of small-town France would have led them to expect. The Comité générale d'organisation de commerce (the General Organization Committee for Commerce), which Vichy ideologues hoped would pave the way to a corporatist organization of the sector, utterly failed in that endeavor and was even unsuccessful as a traditional pressure group.[12] Léon Gingembre, the key spokesman for small business who had emerged by the late 1930s, had a very limited impact on Vichy economic policy, which quickly became controlled by big industrialists and the technocrats associated with Jean Bichelonne, the minister of industrial production. Only with the Liberation in 1944 was Gingembre able to launch the new Confédération générale des petites et moyennes entreprises (CGPME), which soon became the leading national pressure group that had significant ties across the many branches of the retail sector.

What's striking, then, about the relationship between shopkeepers and the state in the early postwar period after 1944 is how little the political organization of the former had changed since the interwar years. Shopkeepers had proliferated during and after the war, but they had not used this growth to build pressure-group power. As political actors they remained dependent on local ties to men of influence— mayors, deputies, lawyers, bankers, leaders in local chambers of commerce—more than to powerful representatives in Paris. To be sure, butchers, bakers, bar and restaurant owners, and many other retailers and artisans had their syndicates, but they were scarcely much stronger than they had been in the interwar period. Gingembre's new organization, with which most of the syndicates were affiliated, aimed to represent a vast middle-class constituency that went well beyond the world of petty commerce. The CGPME had difficulty expanding its scope and mobilizing its myriad constituencies at the same time. Indeed, the Confédération served more as a political base for its founder than as a vehicle for nurturing its occupational constituencies as pressure groups.[13] This relatively weak organizational structure for pressure-group politics in petty commerce had scarcely mattered much during the Third Republic, when the very tenor of the regime and its parliamentary foundations in small-town republicanism had largely served to protect the interests of small property owners, who cared above all about keeping taxes modest and markets stable. Whether a Fourth Republic would similarly serve them, however, proved to be another matter once a modernizing elite in the state administration turned its attention to tax reform as an essential condition for financing a more competitive economy.

But in the immediate postwar years, between 1944 and 1948, price regulation and rationing, not taxes, tested how well shopkeepers could defend themselves in an economic environment where state officials asserted their authority more forcibly that had been customary during the Third Republic. When war ended in spring 1945, consumers and shopkeepers expected that rigid controls and severe shortages would begin to abate. But shortages endured until nearly the end of the decade. In November 1945 the government tried to lift price controls on bread, only to find itself forced to restore them when demand swiftly overran supply and prices soared. With Vichy and the Wehrmacht now gone, consumers now protested more freely, and the Communist Party proved particularly adept at galvanizing a growing wave of working-class discontent over shortages in coal and food.[14] A steady sequence of protests, sometimes quite violent, in 1944 and 1945 disabused de Gaulle's Provisional Government of any illusions it could liberalize the price regime promptly. A newly restored civic culture of parties, associations, and debate exposed the rationing and price administration more fully than during the war to the conflicting demands of buyers and sellers, shopkeepers and customers, city and country. The survival of the system of price controls, though in many ways dictated by the sheer severity of the shortages France faced after the war, was made all the easier politically by the strength of the Communist Party and public sentiment in cities and towns that the government had to keep in check the presumed price-gouging proclivities of farmer and shop-keepers. These early postwar circumstances—a shopkeeper sector economically empowered but lacking strong pressure-group representation, and working-class consumers emboldened by a resurgent post-Liberation Left and a desire for strong state direction in a potentially anarchic economy—made conflict between state officials and shopkeepers an endemic feature of the price administration system. It also made it more likely that clashes would flare up at the local level rather than get resolved in talks around the felt-covered tables in the Paris ministries.

Rehearsal for Revolt

Archives from the criminal division of the Justice Ministry can now tell us a lot about the tensions building up between shopkeepers and state officials, for these records reveal an extraordinary outbreak of local protests against inspectors and market regulation in 1947 that has largely gone unnoticed in the literature on the Fourth Republic. This wave of shopkeeper protest certainly stunned a government already reeling from a multitude of troubles in 1947—from the breakup of the tripartite governing coalition of Communists, Socialists, and the MRP and the bitter labor conflicts that followed, to the rapid unfolding of the Cold War and anticolonial rebellion overseas. These larger events may have driven the shopkeeper revolt of 1947 off the front pages of the national press, but it preoccupied the tax administrators, prefects, prosecutors, and cabinet ministers who sought to contain the movement. The shopkeeper revolt also brought into the vortex of conflict a key branch of the Ministry of the Economy, the Contrôle économique, which had been established in 1940 and had come to dominate the enforcement bureaucracy of the price control and rationing system.

The first clear signs of trouble appeared on April 30, 1947, in Agen, the capital of the department Lot-et-Garonne on the road between Bordeaux and Toulouse. Around seven in the evening a demonstration of 6,000 to 7,000 people assembled in front of the prefecture under the leadership of an organization called the Comité d'action et de liaison des commerçants, industriels, artisans et membres des professions libérales. They called for the "abolition of dirigisme and the return to economic liberty." After moving on to the Chamber of Commerce to present their resolution, a group of about forty demonstrators went on to the building of the Contrôle économique, where they roughed up the director, wrecked his bicycle, and then broke into the offices. There they rummaged through the files. What records they did not steal, they threw into the street.[15]

Two weeks later a rather different incident erupted in Millau, a town in the southern Massif Central famous for its glove-making industry. A crowd of about 2,000 people, including a great many workers and children, demonstrated at the subprefecture to protest the meagerness of the bread ration in the town. The crowd broke into the building and burned records, then moved on to the town hall to sack the offices of the food supply administration and burn its records, finally ending up at the offices of the Contrôle économique, where they likewise set materials ablaze. By this time the crowd had grown to 3,000. Prosecutors eventually determined that several shopkeepers, including a butcher, a barber, two leather goods retailers, and a 72-year-old grocer, had played the principal roles in steering the crowd. Only a month earlier, the butcher in question had run-ins with the local director of the price administration.[16]

The first incident at Agen, with its crowd drawn mainly from petty commerce rather than from a more mixed population as in Millau, proved to be the more typical in the wave of protests that then moved across much of the country. On May 19 and 20, events in La Roche-sur-Yon (near Poitier) and in Dijon echoed the Agen revolt. In La Roche-sur-Yon, 7,000 people responded to the call of the Union départemental d'action des classes moyennes de la Vendée. They marched from the municipal stadium to the prefecture, and then a rump group of forty stormed the offices of Contrôle économique and burned the records. Another group similarly raided the offices of the tax bureau. In Dijon demonstrators from a crowd of 6,000 eventually pillaged the food supply administration, the flour distribution office, and the Illicit Profit and Confiscation Service.[17] Two weeks later 15,000 demonstrators from commerce and the liberal professions came out in Nantes to protest *dirigisme économique* and the new social security laws.[18]

No less remarkable than these large, usually violent demonstrations was the proliferation of highly individualized attacks on inspectors. Take, for example, the incident on September 12, 1947, at Campel, a small town near Rennes. Two inspectors from Contrôle économique entered a bakery to determine if the baker had violated restrictions against using white flour. While the inspectors went about their work, someone rang the church bell. A crowd of 200 men, women, and children gathered in front of the shop. Several demonstrators then physically assaulted the inspectors, emptied their briefcases, and forced one of them to write a report exonerating the baker of any wrongdoing. One woman who figured prominently in the attack made the inspector show his identity card to be sure he had not falsified his signature. The crowd then pushed the two injured men into their car and sent them packing.[19]

Between May and November of 1947 this kind of event erupted in a number of other cities and towns around the country. Shopkeepers and their customers closed ranks to defend a shop from the government's effort to prosecute rationing violations. Many other cases were clearly more strictly shopkeeper affairs without much involvement from customers. In Meaux, for example, a crowd of 70 to 200 retailers and their friends (accounts varied) chased away three inspectors before they so much as entered a shop.[20] Many inspectors were not so lucky. At Saint-Aignan-sur-Cher, near Orléans, a group of shopkeepers tracked down three inspectors lunching in a local hotel after a morning's work in the shops of the town. The shopkeepers assaulted them, stole their papers, threatened to hang them, and then let them flee.[21]

Exactly how many inspections shopkeepers were able to prevent or subvert is not clear. The files of the criminal division describe incidents that produced some kind of formal correspondence between local prosecutors and their superiors in the Justice Ministry, which probably included all or most of the cases of illegal interference with inspections. According to this source some fifty-eight incidents occurred between late 1946 and the late fall of 1947, most of which were protests at the time of inspections rather than larger, highly orchestrated demonstrations along the lines of the riots at Agen and Dijon. Of these fifty-eight events, the overwhelming majority occurred in the more impoverished regions of the west, the southwest, and the Massif Central—in short, the heartland of Poujadism a few years later. The main exceptions were five events in the greater Paris region (though none in the city itself), and five in Burgundy. No cases appear in the files from the north, northeast, or the southeast. Moreover, the shopkeeper rebellion of 1947 was largely a small-town phenomenon. Few large cities appear in the files, apart from the bigger demonstrations. Some villages appear, mostly around protests over grain and flour inspections. Shopkeepers in towns large enough to sustain a tight network of retailers and artisans, especially towns in regions troubled by chronic underdevelopment and gradual depopulation, typified the settings of the 1947 revolt.

If this wave of shopkeeper resistance to government regulation had a distinct social and economic geography, it also had an important organizational and ideological dimension. Efforts to stop inspections, intimidate inspectors, sack offices, and burn official records obviously spoke to the immediate self-interest of shopkeepers eager to cover up illicit profits, black market transactions, and rationing violations. But it was easy in the context of postwar impatience with a regulated economy to construe these interests in the language of a higher cause, the struggle against dirigisme. Many leading figures in the shopkeeper community had links to middle-class pressure groups that provided just such a vision of an anti-tax and anti-dirigiste movement. In several of the judicial cases that emerged from these incidents, prosecutors identified key instigators as members of anti-dirigiste organizations, such as the Comité d'action et de Liaison des commerçants, industriels, artisans et membres des professions libérales at work in Agen, or a group called "Auto-défense contre le dirigisme" in the Stéphanois valley around Saint-Étienne. Prosecutors spent considerable energy trying to build a case against one key activist in these networks on the grounds that his speeches were inflammatory to a murderous degree. This man, a sugar merchant and the president of the Ligue pour la liberté de la production, du commerce et de la consommation, told a crowd of 4,000 at Dax, near Bordeaux, "In 1916 when I was at Verdun, five gendarmes were hung from a butcher stall for harassing the *poulus* instead of being at the front with us. . . . Contrôleurs économiques, watch out, watch out. . . . Remember the gendarmes of Verdun. . . . This is not a threat but a warning." He went on to suggest that since 1945 the government was giving inspectors paid bonuses for every errant shopkeeper that they nabbed. "These people," he said "are paid by the state and should not be enriched on the impoverishment of merchants and their children."[22]

On the basis of the judicial files it is difficult to tell how wide and deep these organizational networks ran in 1947. They likely built on old foundations, such as the artisanal and shopkeeper organizations of the interwar years, the taxpayers' league, perhaps even right-wing outfits of a shadier sort. (One prosecutor reported rumors in one case that an antirepublican gang called the "maquis noir" was involved.) Whatever the real reach of these networks, the judicial files show that the language of anti-dirigisme found its way into the slogans and catcalls of the rebellion. Crowds commonly insulted inspectors with epithets suggesting they were "lazy loafers" *(fainéants)* feeding off the hardship of others. People in an angry crowd in Rosières in the Haute Loire repeated the reference to Verdun when they threatened to hang three inspectors at a local mill.[23] To be sure, much of this hostility to inspectors and tax agents had roots in customary forms of tax resistance and local resentments toward Paris that went back to the Old Regime before the French Revolution. But regulatory conditions of the

1940s gave these sentiments renewed relevance, and war trauma intensified them. The sheer brutality, for example, of an attack on two tax
agents in the Burgundian commune of Genouilly—they were beaten
badly and one of them was paraded into town in a pig cart—arose from
one man's wish to punish the agent for reporting on his violations in
1943.[24] Vengeance against tax agents no doubt had precedents, but in
1947 it conformed to a larger pattern of settling scores that followed the
Liberation. And the longer the government kept wartime regulations in
place, the more likely it was that such accumulated resentments would
trigger violence.

Public officials disagreed on how to handle this grassroots rebellion.
Paul Ramadier's government had little desire to unleash the repressive force of the CRS (riot police) on a middle-class constituency, to
say nothing of men and women with considerable standing in their
towns. Still, ministers in Paris believed that the state's authority was
at stake. Moreover, high officials in the Justice Ministry likely had
little sympathy for the shopkeepers who had fared better than most
during the war and postwar inflation. Marginal comments on prosecutorial reports betrayed this view. When one report described a banner
that demonstrators carried as having the slogan "Dirigisme: Famine—
Liberté: Prospérité" (state regulation makes for famine, deregulation
makes for prosperity), a Justice official blue penciled alongside "pour
qui? [for whom?]."[25]

Despite the sentiment for repression, prefects and prosecutors sometimes argued for lenient sentences for fear harsh punishment would
trigger further unrest. In a number of cases Justice officials sent prosecutors back into the courts to appeal for tougher sentences, which in
most instances were limited to modest fines. Paul Ramadier himself
seemed to recognize the need to blend leniency and firmness, on the
one hand issuing firm instructions to repress the resistance rapidly in
the interests of maintaining "republican legality," while on the other
endorsing (against the advice of the justice minister) one prefect's efforts to placate a rebellious commune with additional food supplies.[26]
Overall, the farther removed officials were from the scene, first at the
regional level of the prosecutorial hierarchy, then in the Justice Ministry itself, the less inclined they were to appease shopkeepers and the

more they worried that locals would see in leniency, as one Parisian official put it, "an admission of government weakness."[27]

As for inspectors, the rebellion against them took its toll. Prosecutors sometimes found it difficult to secure accurate depositions from inspectors who feared further reprisals.[28] One inspector acquired the habit of using an assumed name, until his superiors scolded him.[29] But the best indication that shopkeepers had terrified more than one inspector surfaced when the trade union representing most auditors in the national bureau for indirect taxation pleaded with the government that its inspectors be armed.[30]

Just what happened to this wave of resistance to state regulation after the autumn of 1947 remains unclear. The trail peters out in the judicial archives. Although there may still have been scattered incidents into the late 1940s, the major wave apparently subsided. What changed, of course, was dirigisme itself. In December 1947 the new finance minister, René Mayer, introduced a plan to tame inflation by reducing liquidity and gradually taking the administrative lid off prices. With price deregulation the investigation of illicit black market profits lost its priority.[31]

Tax Reform

Soon after this wave of contention over market regulation and illicit profits receded, tax reform emerged to dominate shopkeeper politics. No one at the time of the Liberation could have predicted how important tax issues were to become in the new postwar republic. True, France had a long history of tax revolts, reaching back into the Old Regime, and many politicians in the 1940s were old enough to recall how volatile the long battle had been to establish an income tax in 1914. And even then, only when confronted with the monumental fiscal burdens of the First World War did the French government implement that tax, in 1917, and then in 1920 enact a second major reform—a sweeping national sales tax (converted in 1936 to a production tax).[32] Few things came harder in the politics of the Third Republic than changing the tax system, and everybody knew it. For one thing, in contrast to the United Kingdom, where ministries could go over the head of Parliament to alter tax programs, in France the parliamentarians held sway.[33] A legion of lobbyists, taxpayer leagues, and entrenched politicians used the legislature to defend their constituents' stake in the tax status quo. Once the country had navigated the torturous path in the 1920s of liquidating most of the financial costs of the war—through German reparations, debilitating inflation, and above all, currency devaluation—politicians lost their sense of urgency about restructuring public finance. Even after the defeat of 1940, a Vichy government ambitious to remake France in other respects had little stomach for altering the tax system. Nor did the Resistance. Its visionaries of the economic reconstruction, from the Socialist Party's dirigiste André Philip to the more neoliberal economist René Courtin, kept tax matters in the background, apart from calling for a tax on war profiting and the confiscation of illicit profits.[34]

The first post-Liberation governments, then, embarked on the nation's modernization drive with a Third Republic tax system that had not changed much since the nineteenth century. Within Europe, the French and Italian governments relied most heavily on indirect taxes—levies on the production of goods and services and on business transactions, charges that producers often evaded or passed on to consumers.[35] The direct taxation of income and wealth in France accounted for only about 30 percent of state revenues, and in 1950 only 15 percent of households were subject to it.[36] Likewise, farmers and small businesses retained their Third Republic advantages, especially the *forfait* system—the much abused option of estimating (usually underestimating) taxable income on the basis of simple indicators such as number of employees, volume of purchases, or average profit per unit of land, rather than on the basis of detailed disclosures.[37] Tax evasion, long rampant, had gained a patina of patriotism during the German occupation that made breaking shady habits that much harder. And the tax code's complexity—the twenty-five different taxes, for example, that a café owner had to worry about—impeded compliance.[38] All this inertia took its toll: a 1952 report estimated that unpaid taxes deprived the state of 20 to 25 percent of its revenue.[39] Inertia also made it tougher for government leaders at the time of the Liberation to make tax reform a priority for the reconstruction agenda. And de Gaulle made it less tempting still when in early 1945 he sided with Finance Minister

René Pleven (and not Minister of National Economy Pierre Mendès France) in opting for easy money and inflation, rather than austerity, as the path forward for national recovery.[40]

By 1948, however, the government could no longer ignore the gap between its reconstruction agenda and its tax revenues. Paul Delouvrier, Jean Monnet's chief of the financial division at the Planning Commission, first tried to focus the government's attention on this problem in 1947, without great success. But Delouvrier's views mattered. Though just 33 years old, he already had a reputation for brilliance and reliability, and he had the right profile for a rising star in the post-Liberation civil service: as an *inspecteur des finances* he was a member of the state's most elite bureaucratic corps, he was a Social (i.e., progressive) Catholic, he had fought the Germans in May 1940, and like a number of major postwar figures, he had attended Vichy's prestigious leadership training school at Uriage, near Grenoble, before eventually making his way into the Resistance, where he led a maquis unit in the Paris region in the summer of 1944.[41] After the Liberation he became Finance Minister Pleven's chief of staff before Monnet snapped him up for the Planning Commission. By 1948 not only had Monnet's Planning Commission and the Finance Ministry come to agree with Delouvrier's sense of urgency about taxes, but he himself moved to the number two post in the tax administration, where he could transform his convictions about reform into practical proposals that had a chance of being implemented. He arrived at the right time. In 1948 the Finance Ministry reorganized the state's vast tax bureaucracy into a single, concentrated new General Tax Administration (the Direction générale des impôts, or DGI), the better to position the government to rethink taxes and tax enforcement.

Political pressure from two quite divergent sources also strengthened the case for reform. In April 1947 the CGT (still unified as a trade union federation before its Communist / anti-Communist schism later that year) enlisted the expertise of economist Pierre Uri to produce an extensive report on taxes. Uri, an independent leftist intellectual with connections to Monnet and Mendès France, put together a stinging indictment of the tax system and a corresponding set of sophisticated reforms to fix it, including an early formulation of a value-added tax. Delouvrier and other finance officials could not afford to dismiss the

CGT's voice on these questions: the vast majority of tax inspectors and other employees in the tax administration's division for indirect taxes affiliated with the CGT.[42] The second source of political pressure came from Washington. David Bruce, the American administrator of the Marshall Plan in France, told his French counterparts in 1948 that release of funds to France would henceforth depend on initiating serious tax reform.[43] These stakes could hardly be higher. Major portions of the Monnet Plan for reconstruction and modernization depended on Marshall Plan money, which was slated to end in 1952. After that the French would have to finance reconstruction themselves, and more effective taxation offered the most anti-inflationary way to do it.

Key cabinet ministers and top tax administration officials collaborated for almost a decade to reform taxation. The first big effort came in 1948 when Parliament, at last persuaded of the need to do something, granted the government decree powers to make modest reforms within the existing structure. Delouvrier coordinated the effort, which, in accord with Parliament's wishes, did nothing to change the balance between direct and indirect taxation overall, but did raise the production tax by 25 percent and other indirect taxes by 15 percent.[44] By 1950, however, officials realized how inadequate these efforts had been, especially given the rising costs of the Indochina and Korean wars and the looming completion of the Marshall Plan. In the national parliamentary elections of 1951, the first since 1946, most parties offered their own tax reform plans. When the election results shifted Parliament rightward, the Left's hopes to boost direct taxation were dashed, but the new and decidedly conservative prime minister, Antoine Pinay, launched the second major effort to reform the system. He created the Loriot Commission, made up mostly of high-level civil servants from the Conseil d'État and the Inspection générale des finances, to craft legislation that would widen the tax base, crack down on fraud, and boost compliance by trimming back on rates.[45]

Once interest-group lobbying and parliamentary horse-trading did their customary work of watering down these proposals, this second reform effort might well have drowned there. But this time the Finance Ministry kept up the momentum on its own steam. Delouvrier and his superior, Pierre Allix, director of the General Tax Administration, used their authority to fortify the tax service's methods of tax enforcement.

Having centralized the tax administration in 1948, they were now in a position to reorganize their armies of tax auditors into local "brigades"— teams of inspectors from all three tax services (direct, indirect, and the transaction fee registry) who could coordinate their efforts to investigate particular taxpayers and firms. In some locales the administration also began to experiment with *polyvalents,* tax inspectors trained to audit small shops and businesses on behalf of all three tax services. In short, the focal point of inspection became the taxpayer rather than the tax category. Many auditors learned to specialize in an occupation or business sector.[46] Pierre Allix also sought to enhance the ethos of professionalism in the service by sending new auditors from Paris into the provinces and reassigning men and women in the inspectorate to new locales. Allix also created a new École nationale des impôts (National Tax School) to boost the competence and prestige of new recruits to the service. Altogether these changes signaled a big change in the culture of the tax system, because France depended more heavily than other countries in Europe on tax inspectors at the local level to enforce compliance.[47] And there was more. In 1952 Prime Minister Pinay took the further step, not without some grumbling from the tax administration, of granting an amnesty for past tax fraud. Large businesses welcomed this reprieve from further disclosures of their wartime violations, but shopkeepers detested it for enabling investigators to turn their attention to the endemic indiscretions that plagued the retail sector.[48] They could hardly have been appeased by Pinay's comments: "The counterpart of amnesty for the past is rigorous sanctions on the fraud to come."[49]

In addition to beefing up enforcement, the tax administration also embarked on a two-year struggle to establish the value-added tax (*taxe sur la valeur ajoutée,* or TVA). Though Paul Delouvrier played an important role in the effort, the key figure here was another young *inspecteur des finances,* Maurice Lauré. Born and raised in Morocco and Indochina as the son of a French military official, Lauré trained as an engineer at the École polytechnique. After surviving the war as a POW, he graduated from the new École nationale d'administration, served initially in the PTT (post, telegraph, and telephone administration), and then in 1952 moved into the tax administration to work closely with Allix and Delouvrier. He had a stronger interest in tax theory than they did, and as an engineer by training rather than a lawyer he had a keen interest in industrial problems and business productivity.[50] He also had the single-mindedness of a crusader—first convincing an ambivalent Pierre Allix of the superiority of the TVA over the production and transaction taxes, and then campaigning doggedly through a welter of committees and public speaking engagements to win support for the tax. Although he did not invent out of whole cloth the idea of a value-added tax—the CGT and the CFTC (the Catholic labor confederation) had proposed it in 1947 and 1951, respectively—Lauré crafted a version of it that encouraged investment and thereby stood a chance of winning enough business support to get it through Parliament.[51] Unlike the production and transaction taxes, which in effect double-taxed companies for investing in equipment (once when they bought it and again when the goods this equipment produced were taxed), Lauré's tax allowed each successive firm in the production chain of a given product to deduct from its tax bill the taxes paid by the previous suppliers. Firms could also deduct the costs of equipment. This scheme had two big virtues: it was "neutral" insofar as a firm paid tax only for the value it added to a product, and it made tax evasion more difficult because firms sought to document the taxes their suppliers had paid.

Despite these advantages it still took immense political effort to get the TVA through Parliament. The Socialist and Communist Parties opposed it for granting such clear benefits to big business. Léon Gingembre's small-business lobby, the CGPME, fought to preserve the old production tax. Big business itself was divided. Labor-intensive industries such as textiles fought to stick with the production tax, while capital-intensive firms at the heart of the modernizing drive, such as steel and chemicals, supported the TVA. When Joseph Laniel, a conservative and a textile firm owner and former head of the Textile trade Association, became prime minister, his counterintuitive commitment to the new tax began to turn the parliamentary tide in its favor. Paul Delouvrier's success in winning the backing of Georges Villey, head of the employers' peak organization (the Conseil National du Patronat Français, or CNPF), helped as well.[52] After the government yielded to requests for a few privileged rates and a delay to extend TVA to retail, the bill passed in April 1954. It applied to about 300,000 industrial firms

and wholesalers, or 15 percent of businesses registered with the tax administration.[53] (It was eventually extended to retail in 1968.) With the
adoption of the TVA, France, long an international laggard in tax reform, suddenly became a pioneer. TVA spread through the Common
Market in the 1960s and on across the global in the decades that
followed.

The Poujadist Revolt

With the TVA, the government created a more solid future for France's
public finance. But with the attack on fraud and the revamping of the
tax inspection service, public officials unwittingly set the table for the
biggest tax rebellion in the history of modern France.[54] The troubles
began, obscurely enough, in a southern town of 3,000 inhabitants,
Saint-Céré. There in July 1953 Pierre Poujade, a local stationery store
owner and member of the municipal council, rallied local shopkeepers
to resist a team of tax inspectors when they arrived in town (see
Figure 3.1). This initial success inspired others, but above all it inspired
Poujade and a growing entourage of colleagues to campaign for anti-
inspection disruptions in nearby towns and then in neighboring
départements (administrative districts). Their methods were simple:
assemble a crowd of local shopkeepers, artisans, bar and café proprietors,
and their friends to prevent tax inspectors from entering shops, or, if
they made it in, rough them up after a tax audit. If tax officials arrived
to auction off the goods or property of a local shopkeeper deep in tax
arrears, "Poujadists" would conspire to block the event or convince the
assembled to bid absurdly low on the goods on behalf of the owner.[55]
Soon Poujade's men were organizing rallies in small towns across the
countryside south of the Massif Central urging small businesses to join
what quickly became a movement. By autumn Poujade had created the
Union de défense des commerçants et artisans (UDCA), and through
this rapidly growing organization the tax rebellion spread across south-
western and western France and on into the heavily European-settled
cities and towns of Algeria. By 1955 the UDCA claimed over 350,000
dues-paying members and had become a political force.[56]

   In its obstructionist methods Poujade's movement echoed the 1947
protests against the Contrôle économique. Tax officials themselves

FIGURE 3.1 Poujadists in action, 1955. This crowd prevents a tax inspector (in the doorway) from entering a bakery in Joinville-le-Pont near Paris. The tidal wave of Poujadist protests sweeping across France in 1954 and 1955 created the biggest tax revolt in French history, forcing governments of the Fourth and early Fifth Republics to adjust their plans for tax reform and take shopkeeper interests more into account. Keystone France / Gamma Keystone / Getty Images.

certainly saw a link between the two waves of protest. They under-stood that the state's struggle to combat illicit profits had diverted enforcement personnel into Contrôle économique in the early postwar years and focused the government's attention on price regulation, leaving the tax administrations understaffed and ill-equipped to tackle fraud. Only with the end of rationing, in their view, had the state re-centered its resources and attention on the tax problem.[57] In short, shopkeepers and tax officials from quite different perspectives experienced the shift from the enforcement of rationing and price controls to the enforcement of tax collecting as part of the same era of postwar combat over surveillance and authority in the retail sector.

But the Poujadist revolt differed from the 1947 rebellion against price controls in two crucial respects. It was more political, and it was far larger in scale and impact. Its political valence owed a lot to Pierre Poujade himself. Although he liked to cast himself apolitically as a *modeste personne* and *fils d'une vieille terre* (a modest local boy and salt of the earth), he had a far-right political past: his father had supported Action française, and in his teens in the 1930s he himself became a local activist for the Union populaire des jeunesse française, a youth group affiliated with Jacques Doriot's far-right Parti populaire français, and then in 1940 he became a local leader of the Vichy government's youth arm, the Compagnons de France. During the war Poujade also became attached to the European settler world of Algeria. Once the German army occupied southern France in November 1942, he fled to Spain, where Franco's government interned him for several months, and then he made his way to Algiers to serve as an airman for the Allies. He eventually got to Britain and flew for the Royal Air Force, but not before marrying Yvette Seva, a European Algerian nurse he met in Algiers—a marriage that was to lash him tightly to the colonialist cause of Algérie française during the Algerian war (see Figure 3.2). The UDCA was to hold its first national congress in Algiers in November 1954, at the very moment that war began.[58] Conveniently, Yvette Seva also gave him a link to the French Communist tradition; her father had been a Communist in Algeria, something Poujade was keen to mention in the early days of the Poujadist revolt when it was trying to woo Communist sympathy.[59] Indeed, the French Communist Party did not come out unambiguously against the movement until 1955. The UDCA's leadership leaned unmistakably to the right. With the passage of national amnesty laws in 1951 and 1953 for wartime crimes and indiscretions, former Pétainists, collaborators, and extremists of the far right became more active in politics in the 1950s, and a number of them found the Poujadist movement a congenial home.

Poujade's UDCA proved adept at shaping shopkeeper discontent into a movement. With its membership dues, a newspaper *(Fraternité française)*, an indefatigable leader, and a growing network of activists

FIGURE 3.2 Pierre and Yvette Poujade at a Poujadist party congress in Paris, 1956. They are taking pleasure in a newspaper report of Poujadist success in winning seats in the National Assembly. The paper also reports on "The French Empire under Threat" with the escalating war in Algeria. Yvette was an Algerian of European descent. She and her husband became fierce supporters of the campaign to keep Algeria French. Bettmann/Getty Images.

who knew their local territory and could flit about it in cars, the UDCA built an organizational capacity that had been missing in the 1947 protest wave. And the results showed. By October 1954, tax-collection disruptions had proliferated into thirty *départements*, mostly in small and medium-sized towns rather than major municipalities, and by the following spring the contagion had grown to forty-six "incidents" a week. A year later, Finance Ministry officials determined that in 1955 only 60,000 tax inspections had taken place, down from 170,000 in 1953 and far short of the 100,000 that tax experts believed the tax administration's credibility required.[60] Normal auditing, tax agents reported, was occurring in only forty of metropolitan France's ninety-six *départements.*[61] The tax administration knew better than anyone how lethal a threat the Poujadist revolt was posing to public finance.

Although Poujade and his UDCA could take credit for much of the movement's momentum, it was economic trends, more than anything, that gave them their chance. By the early 1950s the petty retail sector began to feel the competitive consequences of its extraordinary wartime and early postwar expansion. As postwar shortages eased and inflation declined, shopkeepers watched their profits fall. A stabilizing franc also robbed them of the magic of covering last year's tax assessment with this year's inflated currency. Pressures like these made shopkeepers all the more alarmed by the government's newfound determination to tackle tax fraud and professionalize the tax inspection service with its specialized "brigades" and *polyvalents.* Hence the appeal of Poujade's message: it gave the shopkeepers a way to respond to the structural crisis in small-town commerce and the crackdown on tax evasion.

Given the scale of the revolt and Poujade's own history of political enthusiasms, it is easy to see why he and his entourage heard the siren call of political opportunity. And answer it they did. They turned the UDCA into a vote-getting machine for an electoral list they called Union et fraternité française. The gambit initially worked. In the 1956 parliamentary elections Poujadists surprised even themselves by winning two and a half million votes and fifty-two seats in Parliament on the strength of a populist campaign against MRP "Judases," Socialist "fossils," and Gaullist "magots." They sought not to topple but to "purify" the Republic of its "vultures" *(charognards)*—the parliamentarians, technocrats, academic cosmopolitans, and fat cats in Paris who they thought were selling off the empire (Indochina, Tunisia, Morocco, and maybe Algeria next?) and, as modernizers, were leaving the little man behind. "Sortez let sortants" (throw the bums out), they railed.[62] And they spared no venom in their anti-Semitic attacks on Pierre Mendès France, the reform-minded prime minister in 1954 and major aspirant for a return to power in the 1956 elections, whom they derided for serving the "stateless trusts" *(trusts apatride)* and big retailers and whom they mocked for taking on the alcohol lobby and championing milk. "If you had a drop of Gallic blood in your veins," Poujade taunted, "you would never have dared, as a representative of our France, the world's producer of wine and champagne, to serve milk at an international reception!"[63] Talk like this no doubt won votes from wine-growers and distillers, and the vilification of Paris, politicians, and the business and civil service elite played well in much of small-town France and in some declining textile communities. But the map of electoral victory largely matched the geography of the tax revolt and the shopkeeper movement.

Adept though they were at winning votes in 1956, Poujade and his fellow deputies soon proved inept in Parliament. Torn between obstructionism and alliance building on the right, they lost group discipline and Poujade lost control over his troops. Poujadist deputies had little inclination, and too little expertise, to draft bills, even on taxes.[64] They had waged a campaign to condemn their foes and to restore the Republic to its role of protecting small property, not to promote a carefully worked out policy agenda. Designing detailed proposals for change, Poujade said, was the job of government specialists.[65] As a political movement, then, Poujadism floundered in the real politics of the National Assembly, and by the late 1950s it nearly dissolved altogether in the rising tide of Gaullism.

But as a tax revolt Poujadism succeeded far beyond its founders' expectations, with lasting consequences for taxes, shopkeepers, and the state. The archives of the tax administration reveal how embattled public authorities felt and how eagerly they sought an exit from the tax crisis. The government first tried repression. Tax administration head Pierre Allix quietly encouraged the inspectorate to target UDCA leaders for audits.[66] The internal security police (Renseignements généraux) tapped phones and worked hard to infiltrate the UDCA with informants—so much so that Poujadist leaders learned to filter out protest planning from their speeches in public rallies.[67] In August 1954 Parliament passed the notorious Dorey amendment authorizing the arrest of anyone obstructing the work of a tax inspector. This legal initiative only fueled the revolt further, giving Poujadists a new symbol of oppression and a way to focus shopkeepers' anger not just on the tax man but also on Parliament. And many tax inspectors were hesitant to ask for much help from the police, as that could expose them to greater hostility in communities where they had to work and reside.[68]

Officials soon saw the futility of simple repression, because the movement continued to grow. Alert to the dangers the movement posed, Finance Minister Edgar Faure admitted in a secret memorandum that "a wind of insurrection against the state is blowing in the affected departments." He urged conciliation: "The repressive measures that have just been voted on, if they are used in isolation, will be powerless to dissipate these strong feelings and break the psychosis of rebellion. There has to be recourse at the same time to the psychological shock that a vast plan of tax relaxation will provoke." He called for lowering shopkeepers' tax rates, lightening their penalties for infractions, and boosting taxpayer representation on local boards of appeal. He advocated, too, new guarantees against arbitrary rulings and excessive zeal by the tax inspectorate.[69] These policies of détente guided the government's approach to the revolt thereafter. Top tax officials in Paris also felt a new sense of urgency about getting the new TVA tax in place. In November 1954, after Poujadists mounted especially big protests in Toulouse and nearby Castelsarrazin, the chief of the indirect tax administration wrote that "because of the undeniable appeal the Poujadist movement has with the mass of shopkeepers and artisans, we fear that the agitation fomented by this group can only be significantly reduced by dropping the transaction tax and the local tax and replacing it by raising the rates of the value-added tax and other indirect taxes whose collection and oversight does not create difficulties."[70]

The tax administration also went on a public-relations offensive. Director Allix urged tax inspectors to reach out to local chambers of commerce and to make house calls to taxpayers to offer free and friendly advice.[71] *Réalités*, the sophisticated coffee-table monthly, featured a long, sympathetic interview with a tax inspector in its February 1955 feature, "Talking to Your Tax Collector."[72] Finance Minister Faure used a speech at the National Assembly to refute the claim that the *polyvalent* were "la police volante" (flying police) or the "CRS" (riot squads) of the tax service.[73] Most of all the tax administration sought to cut back on complicated audits by expanding the use, in small retail, of the *forfait*, those multiyear assessments based on crude indicators of income.[74]

Though conciliation hardly put a stop to the revolt, tax officials claimed in their internal reporting in 1955 that it was making a difference. And the effort was obvious enough to draw its critics. The left-center newspaper *Combat* accused the Finance Ministry of sacking Maurice Lauré to placate Poujade. (Years later Edgar Faure admitted he replaced Allix and Lauré to calm the waters.)[75] Big business felt aggrieved that it was having to pick up the shopkeepers' tax burden. The government in fact raised the corporate profit tax to 38 percent and the average TVA levy to 19.5 percent, up from 36 percent and 17 percent respectively.[76] Business advocate Roger Priouret acknowledged that this shifting of the burden away from shopkeepers and artisans made "electoral" and "democratic" sense but at the cost of favoring "the static over the dynamic, the archaic over the modern."[77] What likely worried the government was criticism from within the state. A number of local prefects and subprefects grappling with Poujadism in their localities wrote their superiors in Paris to stress how much the movement resembled the far Right of the interwar years—the Croix de feu, even the Nazis—and conveyed that more should be done to repress its leaders.[78] The government's conciliation also drew criticism from the tax administration's own rank-and-file employees, whose trade union representatives (FO in the direct tax service and the CGT in the indirect tax service) condemned the revolt as an affront to republican principles of solidarity and equality.[79] They spoke out bitterly when local judges sentenced audit obstructionists leniently.[80] When employee morale hit a low, these personnel unions took the radical step of calling off inspections on their own initiative in seven *départements*.[81]

The government nonetheless stuck to its conciliatory strategy and its efforts to professionalize and reform the tax structure. Trends after 1956 appeared to vindicate the approach.[82] Business leaders acclimated to the TVA, even if some owners in labor-intensive industries such as textiles continued to complain about it. It also gratified top tax officials to see center-Left leader Pierre Mendès France endorse the state's growing reliance on TVA rather than insist on the need to boost the income tax.[83] The tax revolt, moreover, went into steep decline, no doubt in part because of the government's care in handling it and Poujade's faltering on the national political stage, but above all because inflation returned in 1957, and with it shopkeepers' improved capacity to pay their taxes.[84]

What does this story of tax reform and the Poujadist revolt reveal about the postwar challenge of blending a democratic renewal with a top-down, state-led modernization drive? Certainly in the policy domain of taxation, initiative came from above. Leading civil servants like Paul Delouvrier, Maurice Lauré, and Pierre Allix put TVA and the attack on fraud at the summit of the policy agenda, and they kept it there for years. They did so in partnership with a few key politicians—René Mayer, Antoine Pinay, Joseph Laniel, Edgar Faure—and this political support, combined with their own expertise, American pressure to modernize the tax system, and the urgency in financing reconstruction after the Marshall Plan, gave these men extraordinary authority.[85] In pursuing reform and then managing the Poujadist crisis, they enjoyed a notable degree of autonomy from the everyday pressures of parties, lobbyists, and unions. They benefited, too, from decree powers Parliament granted the government on matters of public finance in 1948 and 1955. Parliament did, of course, weigh in crucially on the founding legislation of the TVA and the Dorey amendment. High-level civil servants and ministers had to win the support of the peak business organization, the CNPF. But it was the leading professionals within the Finance Ministry who steered the ship of reform, so much so that some parliamentary opponents criticized the government for abdicating authority to the administrators. Finance Minister Edgar Faure repudiated the charge, but not without crediting the top tax officials with sustaining the TVA campaign amid considerable government instability.[86]

Their very success made the state's tax experts vulnerable to Poujade's charge that they had conspired with big business, America, and the department stores to modernize the country at the expense of small-town France. Poujade found it easy to cast his fellow tax rebels as true-France Davids battling the technocratic Goliaths of Paris. What is remarkable, however, is how quickly the experts responded to political pressures from below once the scale of revolt threatened, as Edgar Faure put it, "the authority and force of the state."[87] Finance ministers and top tax officials reduced the tax burden on small commerce, reined in the tax agents, and made local appeals procedures more democratic. In doing so they still managed to keep the core of their tax modernization drive—TVA and professionalization—on track, but they also implicitly acknowledged the legitimacy, and practicality, of popular protest.

For all of its grotesque features—its demagoguery, rowdy thuggery, anti-Semitism, and anti-parliamentarism—the Poujadist movement had the ironic effect of making tax reform experts more responsive to the pressures of a democratic polity. Shopkeepers and artisans did what hard-pressed interest groups had long done in France: they turned to the state for relief, and the state responded. Revolt reminded government leaders they needed to make tax reform more palatable to the retailers and artisans, even as conciliation made it harder afterward to imagine a radical restructuring of the tax system away from indirect taxes.[88] The lesson would not be lost on Gaullists, who in continuing to renovate the economy worked within the basic tax framework of the Fourth Republic and built in new protections for shopkeeper France.

Shopkeeper Politics into the Early Fifth Republic

When Charles de Gaulle returned to power in 1958, won the public's approval of a new constitutional republic, and then in January 1959 established his first Fifth Republic cabinet with Michel Debré as his prime minister, he inherited an ethos of caution about tax reform and shopkeeper politics. The Poujadist revolt had made its mark. As historian Frédéric Tristram has shown, Poujadism not only brought to a halt the tax administration's efforts in the Fourth Republic to continue to reform the tax system beyond the basic breakthrough to the TVA in 1954, it made the tax experts in the de Gaulle-Debré government jittery about initiatives that might trigger another revolt.[89] It took someone outside the tax administration, a young, ambitious, and talented Valéry Giscard d'Estaing (and future president of the Republic) to be willing to give tax reform a try in 1959 as the government's state secretary of finance. He sought especially to extend the TVA into retail, beyond its boundaries within the wholesale sector, only to learn the lesson that he could not ram such a big change through Parliament over the widespread objections of pressure groups. (He would eventually succeed in this effort in 1966 by negotiating carefully with the lobbies beforehand.)[90] Prime Minister Debré understood that his government had to navigate the small-business world gingerly. For example, he instructed his minister of industry, Jean-Marcel Jean-neney, to negotiate an improved statute for artisans in hopes of pre-venting local leaders in agriculture from "working in cahoots with artisans and shopkeepers toward a new Poujadist-style operation."[91] As much as Gaullists liked to claim their new republic had made a radical break with the past, they feared the revival of a tax rebellion that they knew had exceeded the state's capacity to quash it.

If the Poujadist revolt made government officials cautious, it also made Léon Gingembre and his small- and medium-sized business pressure-group organization—the Confédération générale des petites et moyennes entreprises (CGPME)—more aggressive and competitive than it had been before. Pierre Poujade had taken advantage of the CGPME's failure to build strong ties to small-town shopkeepers in the economic backwaters of France in the early 1950s. The CGPME had certainly been active in that period, but it focused on Paris and its national lobbying efforts. It was thin on the ground in the provinces. Gingembre himself took greater interest in the more dynamic, export-oriented sectors of small business.[92] He had a background, after all, in law and manufacturing, not petty retail. His family had a century-old enterprise with 120 employees making needles and hooks. By 1944, when he created the CGPME, he had long since moved on to the poli-tics of business advocacy, working in the late 1930s to build a voice for small- and medium-sized enterprise within the big-business-dominated Confédération génerale de la production française and then later doing much the same within Jean Bichelonne's Ministry of Industrial Pro-duction in the Vichy government. The financial straits of butchers and bakers in places like Saint-Céré had not shaped his vision of the CGPME.[93] Poujadists, by contrast, had grabbed pressure-group turf in languishing localities, and even after the tax rebellion died down, they still managed to hold on to seats in local chambers of commerce, es-pecially in areas south of the Loire. In 1957 they won the presidencies of nineteen chambers.[94] The Poujadist revolt and continuing influence stung Gingembre into action. By the late 1950s the CGPME stepped up their efforts to compete for the votes and confidence of shopkeepers and artisans across the country, borrowing some of the rhetoric and militancy of their Poujadist rivals along the way. In some towns, such as Dijon in 1957, they even managed to work out electoral alliances with Poujadists for chamber seats so as to better keep them out of the hands of the big-business CNPF (the postwar successor organization to the CGPF).[95] Poujade's provocation had inspired Gingembre to make the CGPME a credible advocate for shopkeepers in the early Fifth Republic.

The trick for Gingembre was to capture some of the populist militancy of the shopkeeper cause without jeopardizing the CGPME's respectability, a hard-won asset when negotiating with the government. He and his team used the organization's newspaper, *La Volonté du Commerce et de l'Industrie,* to thread that needle. They talked tough about taxes: "Whereas taxes are diminishing in neighboring countries . . . [the French tax system] is archaic, pettifogging, ruthless, and embodies in its essence the idea of punishment, of submitting to castigation."[96] Longtime anti-dirigistes, Gingembre's writers joined in the anti-technocratic rhetoric that had been a staple in the Poujadist movement and that was becoming even more commonplace in the first years of the Fifth Republic—castigating the new "technocratic era" and "the presence within the Debré government of a majority of technicians who are out of touch with everyday reality and hence with the country."[97] Gingembre took care, however, to counterbalance the critique by applauding the Debré government's tough new monetary policy and the new franc. In an implicit affirmation of the government, he called on the state to find "the authority, energy and courage necessary to carry out reforms."[98]

De Gaulle and the Debré government faced their own balancing act of placating shopkeepers and artisans while advancing what they viewed as the "modernization of distribution."[99] They hoped to make the commercial sector more competitive by lowering tariff barriers, opening France to Europe, and resuming the campaign of tax reform that had stalled in the mid-1950s. These goals put them in harness with the new breed of retail pioneers, men like Édouard Leclerc, villains in the Poujadist script, who sought to use low profit margins, high volume, big chains, discounting, and giant stores to concentrate the retail business—something many visionaries of the postwar modernization felt had been too long delayed. These retailers, moreover, recognized the advantages the TVA offered them: as a tax calculated on the difference between a retailer's purchasing price and his or her sales price, it rewarded high-volume, low-margin operators. Hence Debré's disappointment when Valéry Giscard d'Estaing's effort to extend TVA to retail ran aground in 1959.[100] Still, the Debré government found another way to support the big retailers when Joseph Fontanet, the state secretary for domestic commerce, issued a circular in 1960 forbidding suppliers to refuse to sell goods to any retailer who undercut the prices of local shopkeepers.[101] The so-called Fontanet decree was the Debré government's bare-knuckled response to Poujadist-inspired campaigns to make wholesalers boycott the big chains. The government struck another blow at small commerce in 1962 when it permitted the Belgian-American firm Bernheim to create a huge food emporium in the heart of Paris.[102]

At the same time, Debré and his government knew they could scarcely afford to turn their backs on petty commerce. The specter of Poujadist revolt felt too real, and Gingembre's CGPME too invested in proving its mettle to belittle shopkeepers' right to an economic future. Nor were Gaullists prepared to discard deep-seated convictions that social stability and the Frenchness of France depended on the viability of small property and small business. When Gingembre attacked the Fontanet decree, Debré wrote him a letter rebuking him for instigating "demonstrations of the kind that disrupt public order." But he then professed his government's support for small commerce: "We do think it desirable to expand self-service, supermarkets, and even the integration of farmers into distribution networks, but we also favor the organization of independent shopkeepers who make up the most important, distinctive, and indispensable part of our commercial system." It was not enough, he went on, for the government to make itself "a kind of arbiter of competition; it regards its mission as providing leadership and oversight [une tutelle] " by subsidizing management training and funding investment for small and medium-sized enterprises.[103] Other officials associated with Debré's government backed up this approach of helping small firms adapt to, rather than simply try to fend off, change in the retail landscape. Joseph Fontanet urged shopkeepers to adopt some of the big retailers' methods of purchasing, selling, and managing inventory.[104] The much celebrated Rueff-Armand report on breaking down barriers to economic growth made a similar plea, pushing shopkeepers to adopt "voluntary chains, retailer associations,

centralized purchasing, consumer cooperatives, and integrated enterprises."[105] And to press the case further that the Debré government, for
all of its modernizing zeal, wished to be seen as serving small retailers
well, Finance Minister Wilfrid Baumgartner told the General Assembly
of the CGPME: "The government wants to help prepare free enterprise
for changes in the modern world, but the old banker that I am knows
what commercial property means. And we won't demolish it. Your
efforts are useful for the future of France and important to us. Neither
Monsieur Fontanet nor I will go too far."[106]

As Baumgartner implied, the Debré government found a middle
ground in commerce between unleashing the potential of big retail (via
less-restricted markets and a more neutral form of taxation) and helping
the small fry survive. Debré and Fontanet's approach had a basis in
yoking a post-Poujade pragmatism to their modernizing ambitions. But
it also harked back to the kind of dirigiste confidence in the state's capacity to reshape the economy that he had expressed at the Liberation
in his programmatic text for the reconstruction, *Refaire la France*.[107]
Now as prime minister in de Gaulle's Fifth Republic, he sought to steer
the evolution of retail via government support for investment, training,
and technical assistance. Commerce had to modernize, much like agriculture, he told a radio audience in 1959, implying the need for government to help shopkeepers adapt as it was doing for the family farm. In
this respect Debré's government was writing a final chapter in the
long story of postwar reconstruction, even if in relationship to big retailers it was beginning a new chapter in the history of a more liberal
Gaullist state. The economist and demographer Alfred Sauvy thought
the government should make this pivot more decisively. He criticized
Debré's commercial policy as too dirigiste, too concerned for the survival of the family retail enterprise, when shopkeepers' children would
be wiser to train for other occupations.[108]

A shift from what one might call Debré's dirigiste liberalism to
more unambiguous support for big commercial enterprises did indeed
take place in the Pompidou governments of the 1960s. The state made
growth easier for big retail through land-use planning, commercial li-
censing, and the issuing of building permits. Between 1966 and 1971,
20,000 small shops disappeared whereas 1,887 supermarkets and 143
hypermarchés (giant box stores) opened.[109] Gingembre and his CGPME

continued to advocate on shopkeepers' behalf, as they did, for example, in the successful negotiations Giscard d'Estaing held in 1966 over extension of the TVA into retail. But in 1969, the challenges of adjusting to the new tax, new pressures arising from the reform of social security, the alarming expansion of big-store firms such as Carrefour, and the example students and workers set for protest in 1968, all helped to trigger a new huge wave of shopkeeper revolt, this time led by the firebrand Gérard Nicoud. Once again the state and the CGPME found themselves outflanked by a grassroots movement, and once again the government made concessions. The resulting Royer law of 1973 gave small business the power to slow down the advance of big retailers.[110]

The Debré government of 1959–1962, then, left a complex legacy. Neoliberals like Giscard d'Estaing would see in the Debré period the beginning of a reform effort that would lead to the final triumph of the TVA and the opening up of competitive conditions for the emergence of low-price, high-volume marketing. Political activists in the world of small retail, whether more mainstream in the Gingembre mold or neo-Poujadists on the right or left, would see in the same government the crystallization of a more top-down, technocratic style of governance that became so ridiculed in 1968. Yet at the same time, the Debré government also reinforced the idea that the state should protect small business and shepherd it into a more competitive, increasingly internationalized economy. Key leaders of the early Fifth Republic, then, did not make a sharp break from the dirigisme of the reconstruction era; they sustained it and even kept alive the older interwar principle that France could modernize by having both big and small firms and by balancing the old and new. That latter continuity, state officials' commitment to France as a balanced economy, came as something of a surprise at the end of the long reconstruction, given that the modernizers of 1945, men like Pierre Mendès France and Jean Monnet, had argued so forcefully against that kind of thinking. But the Poujadists forced a midcourse correction, a recognition that small business interests also had to be served. Continuity, ironically, required the upheaval of a shopkeeper insurgency.

The story of shopkeeper protest from the Liberation period to the early Fifth Republic reveals how seriously government leaders had to adapt their top-down reform efforts to the bracing realities of a potent social movement. From the localized rebellions against price control enforcement in 1947, through the Poujadist revolt of the mid-1950s and on into the era of tempered, negotiated reform in the early 1960s, "modernizing" elites such as Paul Delouvrier and Maurice Laure, tax administrators such as Pierre Allix, and their key ministerial allies like Edgar Faure and Michel Debré, learned that they ignored public protest at their peril. They reshaped plans and co-opted pressure-group spokesmen, even Poujadists, accordingly. Likewise, the more mainstream advocates of small and medium-sized business, most notably Léon Gingembre, scrambled over the course of decade to catch up with the small-fry brethren they had too long ignored. Not least of the lessons of Poujadism, however, was what it taught citizen-activists in small business and beyond: that if carried out on a grand enough scale, coordinated protest could bring a powerful state bureaucracy—the tax administration itself—to heel. Among the many factors spurring the shopkeeper revolts of the 1940s and 1950s, none was more important than the government's efforts to rationalize the auditing system for the purpose of boosting the tax revenues of a major occupational swathe of French society. To obstruct that top-down project to the extent that Poujadists did would be object lesson for others—farmers, workers, students, *pieds noirs* Algerians, and many others—in the Fifth Republic.

4

Family Matters

Expertise, Gender, and Voice
in the Social Security State

MANY A POLITICIAN and policy expert in France believed that the road to national renewal passed through the family. When Charles de Gaulle's Provisional Government ushered in its sweeping reforms of social insurance in 1945 to establish a social security system for postwar France, it also set about revamping *allocations familiales*—the provision of child allowances first established on a national basis for wage earners in business in 1932 and then further expanded to the rest of the country through Édouard Daladier's degree laws of 1938 and the Family Code of 1939. Now, with the Liberation, an ambitious array of family benefits—crafted even more aggressively than before to support motherhood and to encourage couples nationwide to have three or more children—became a centerpiece of the postwar welfare state. Governments all over Europe came out of World War II endowed with public mandates to make social security a keystone of the postwar state, but nowhere did pronatalist subsidies become as central to the new welfare edifice as they did in France.[1] Indeed, if there was one realm of public affairs that inspired consensus in France after the Liberation, one domain where state administrative elites, policy experts, and citizens' groups stood a good chance of working in harmony, it was family policy.

Or so it seemed at first. Every political party, from the Communists to the conservative Right, had come to embrace the prevailing prona-talist logic that the country's recovery and security required population growth. This consensus had already congealed in the 1930s.[2] The very notion of "family policy"—of using the state's regulatory, policing, taxing, and redistributive capacity to support childrearing—hardly existed as a practical notion in the nineteenth century. It had become a mainstream idea by the 1920s, when, after the Great War's devasta-tion, pronatalists and Catholic advocates of a family-centered polity found the public more receptive to proposals they had been promoting since the late nineteenth century.[3] The defeat of 1940 solidified this commitment to family policy and pronatalism all the more. Even the disgrace of the Vichy regime, which had embraced "the family" as the symbolic center of its National Revolution ("Travail, Famille, Patrie"), did little to discredit population growth as a cornerstone of the postwar recovery. As pediatrician Robert Debré and economist Alfred Sauvy put it in their influential book of 1946, *Des Français pour la France,* "For France, population is the essential problem, in reality the only problem. To be free, to look the future in the face, France has to be rich in children."[4] And this sentiment was broadly shared. The Institut na-tional d'études démographiques (INED; the new National Demo-graphic Institute established under Alfred Sauvy's leadership in 1945) published a survey in 1947 showing that 73 percent of the respondents regarded population growth as important for the nation.[5] De Gaulle's widely quoted exhortation after the Liberation, calling for twelve mil-lion "beaux bébés" (beautiful babies) in ten years, simply set an ambi-tious numerical target for something most citizens accepted as a commonsense aspiration for the postwar reconstruction.[6] Indeed, by 1945 France's baby boom was well under way.

Family policy had another thing going for it as an arena for poten-tially harmonious interaction between citizens and the state in the postwar reconstruction—its administrative structure. De Gaulle's chief architect of the new social security system, the widely trusted high-level civil servant Pierre Laroque, pushed successfully to organize both the new social security system and the new family allowance system into a huge network of geographically based local *caisses,* or fund offices, administered by citizen boards. This structure put considerable decision-making authority in the hands of the contributors to these caisses—the salaried employees and their employers who funded both systems via the payroll tax and who consequently elected representatives to the caisses boards. And these local boards had power: to select top caisse administrators and oversee the application of regulations and the distribution of allowances. Not least, they decided on the use of considerable discretionary funds for everything from summer camps to day care and family aides. To be sure, Parliament, the state bureaucracy, and the ministers overseeing social provisioning—especially the three key ministers of Labor and Social Security, Public Health and Population , and not least, Finance—still retained ultimate authority over the system, and they had an army of policy experts in their employ. The state, in the vocabulary of French administration, still maintained a *tutelle* (guiding and oversight authority) over the caisses. The structure nonetheless created the opportunity for citizens' groups and state officials to establish habits of mutual consultation in the development of the welfare state. And all the more so because trade unions, feminist organizations, and a network of hundreds of family associations—mostly Catholic and some with origins in the nineteenth century—provided a bedrock of activism in this domain. Here in the family policy domain, in contrast to tax reform, immigration, and even the nationalization of enterprise, it looked like state officials and societal groups of many kinds might be able to work well together.

Before long, however, family policy too, like so many other dimensions of the postwar reconstruction, became contested terrain. Although all major political parties applauded the expansion and consolidation of family subsidies, they disagreed sharply over how this sector of the new social security state ought to be structured and run. This question especially brought the Communist Party (PCF) and the Christian Democrats (MRP) to blows, because these two parties each had their own grand vision of what the family's role should be in a new postwar France. No less contentious was the long-standing question of what role the state ought to play in shaping norms and regulating behavior in families. Many Catholic family associations that for decades had lobbied for family subsidies harbored deep hostility to an expansion of state authority in matters that in their view were better left to the heads of families (i.e., fathers) or the Church. Political parties, advocacy groups, feminists, social workers, and policy experts disagreed too over whether family policy ought to enable or impede women's participation in the workforce, especially in the case of mothers with children at home. Issues of class proved divisive as well, with many participants in the debates wondering: Should family policy be used to diminish inequality?

Over the course of the long reconstruction, then, from the Liberation to the early years of the Fifth Republic, these key questions—how far to expand the state's regulatory authority over the family, whether to steer mothers toward or away from the workforce, and whether to use family subsidies to redress inequality—made family policy a source of conflict as strong as the consensus it had inspired in 1945. Likewise, as rival parties and advocacy groups clashed over family policy, state administrative officials tended to assert their authority over the caisses. This dynamic, combined with broader changes in societal values in the 1950s, the rise of new claimants to expertise in family matters, and growing conflict among state experts about policy priorities, eroded the pronatalist consensus that appeared to be so solid in 1945. By the late 1950s the populationist logic that seemed obvious at the Liberation as a basis for family policymaking gave way to new rationales for policy. State officials and policy experts became more focused on the labor market needs of an expanding economy, even as women were becoming more vocal in expressing their own views about child rearing, work, and the family. The "golden age of family policy," as historian Antoine Prost described the first three postwar decades, began to lose its luster almost from the start.[7]

Interwar Breakthroughs

Family policy at the Liberation built on sturdy interwar foundations. When Pierre Laroque drafted the ordinances of October 4 and 19, 1945, that created the postwar social security system, he expanded provisions for social insurance that employers, mutual aid societies, family associations, and the government had already invented. A national scheme for work accident insurance, for example, went all the way back to a landmark 1898 law. The 1928 and 1930 social insurance laws had already brought millions of French employees into a Bismarckian-style system providing medical insurance, maternity benefits, pensions, and disability benefits, all funded through a payroll tax. Likewise, the big breakthroughs in family allowances came during the twilight years of the Third Republic. The 1932 family allowance law obligated employers in commerce and industry to contribute to one of many approved "equalization funds" *(caisses de compensation)* that gave salaried employees with children a wage supplement to subsidize their households. Up until then child subsidies had developed piecemeal through voluntary employer initiatives—chiefly in the textile industry in the northeast and in the metalworking sector around Paris as a strategy to bind workers to their companies and to mitigate demands for across-the-board wage hikes. The new national law required all employers to share the burden by contributing to and affiliating with one of the many private equalization funds.[8] The Daladier government's decree laws of November 12 and 13, 1938, and its Family Code of 1939 then expanded and modified the family allowance system in three crucial ways: they made these benefits available only to families with at least two children (making the system more pronatalist); they extended the system to farm families, liberal professions, and the self-employed via state-financed funds (rather than the usual employer-funded and -managed *caisses de compensation* that still prevailed in commerce and industry), and they created a new state-funded *allocation de la femme au foyer,* a benefit for stay-at-home mothers (except in agriculture) fixed at 10 percent of the average laborer's wage in metalworking.[9]

The Family Code marked the beginning of a fully nationwide program to boost the birthrate. Catholic pro-family activists (familialists) claimed it as a huge symbolic victory, because they regarded the family as society's most fundamental and sacred institution and as a bulwark against moral laxity and social scourges of all kinds. Secular republican pronatalists—an influential nebula of doctors, demographers, business leaders, civil servants, and politicians, many of them members of the Alliance nationale contre la dépopulation—celebrated this breakthrough too.[10] Though familialists and pronatalists could differ in outlook over such matters as church-state questions, how intrusive government should be in private life, or whether to frame family policy and anti-abortion in terms of morality or national interest, they shared a firm commitment to family allowances as the best method to lower the cost of having children and hence to boost the size of families.[11] National panic after the Munich Crisis of 1938 and the subsequent rightward lurch of the Daladier government gave pronatalists their chance to push through the Code, which continued to serve as the central core of family policy from Vichy to the Fifth Republic.

Vichy's "Family State"

The path, however, from the Family Code to Laroque's reforms of 1945 was far from straight, given that the Vichy regime both sustained and diverged from Third Republic precedents. In family policy, as in much else, 1940 and 1944 were moments of *both* continuity *and* rupture.[12] Pétain's government extended family allowances to new groups, notably to families with dependent children whose principal breadwinner was disabled, sick, unemployed, widowed, or even pensioned.[13] It converted the Code's *allocation de la femme au foyer* into a new single-wage allowance *(allocation de salaire unique)*, available to either a husband or a wife and hence most importantly to working wives whose husbands languished for the duration of the war in Stalags or factories in Germany. For the first time, too, families in agriculture became eligible for this form of state benefit.[14] Continuity also prevailed in personnel. Many of Vichy's top officials in matters of family policy, or the experts they relied upon, had wielded similar influence in the Daladier and Reynaud governments of 1938–1940. Vichy's new Secrétariat d'État à la famille created a top advisory group, the Comité consultative de la famille, which included several key members of the Daladier government's previous Haut Comité consultatif de la population—policy experts Alfred Sauvy and Jacques Doublet, as well as Georges Pernot, the longtime head of the (Catholic) Alliance nationale des Associations des familles nombreuses. Even Pierre Laroque himself, who had participated in writing the 1939 Code, served a few months drafting social policy for Pétain's administration until the regime fired him for being Jewish and he began his sojourn to the Resistance and eventually London.[15]

Vichy officials, however, also took "family" as a concept and "family policy" as an instrument of social reordering in new directions. Indeed, by celebrating the family, rather than the individual, as the "initial

cell" of French society, Vichy propagandists used the family as its
sharpest weapon *against* the republican tradition. Pétain himself made
this clear. "The right of families," he proclaimed, "is, in fact, older and
higher than the right of the state, just like the right of individuals. . . .
[I]t is on the family that we must build; if it gives way, all is lost; as
long as it holds, all can be saved."[16] Building on the family meant embracing hierarchy and patriarchy as the natural order of things, and
taking succor in the idea of Pétain as a father figure, a notion he reinforced time and again with his demeanor, his words, and his iconic
image in propaganda.[17]

Family, in short, came first in the Vichy worldview. "You who want
to rebuild France," Vichy propagandists declaimed in brochures and al-
manacs, "first give it children."[18] To elevate the family and repudiate
the "individualism" associated with 1789 also made it easier to castigate self-assertion, dissent, and nonconformity—especially by women.
"The coquette without children," the Commissariat général à la
famille insisted, "was useless."[19] Vichy authorities, assailing female
employment as a cause of national decline, sought to return women to
the home.[20] The laws of October 8 and 11, 1940, gave hiring and promotion preferences to men, especially fathers of larger families, and
pushed married women with employed husbands and women over age
50 out of state employment.[21] Mother's Day, largely ignored since it was
first established in 1920, became something serious: the government
prodded family associations to orchestrate and fund public celebrations
in communes throughout the country.[22] The regime also outlawed
divorce during the first three years of marriage and made abortion a
crime against the state, subject to capital punishment. Anti-Semitism
permeated Vichy's family policy as well: "mixed marriages" were prohibited, Jews who were removed from their jobs in accord with the
regime's "Jewish statutes" lost their eligibility for family allowances,
and the notorious Carrel Foundation—a Vichy-supported think tank—
sponsored eugenicist research in harmony with the prejudices of
many of the government's social policy leaders.[23] In all these respects,
Vichy made its break from the family policy of the Third Republic.

The same could be said of the regime's attempt to create what
Philippe Renaudin, the head of the Commissariat général à la famille,
called the "family state."[24] Authorities began this effort modestly by

simply requiring municipal councils to include among their members
a father with a large family and a representative from the family associations.[25] A new national Centre de coordination et d'action des
mouvements familiaux gave family associations a quasi-official status
in the regime.[26] The government then accelerated: it issued the Gounot
law of December 29, 1942, creating a pyramidal structure of family
representation. Family organizations were expected to affiliate with
(and eventually dissolve into) a new official network of local and regional associations that in turn came under the umbrella of a new national family federation.[27] The latter would advise the government on
family matters. All these semigovernmental bodies were to elect their
steering committees via the "family vote" whereby members had one
vote per minor child (plus an extra vote per group of three children who
lived to the age of 21). Familialists had being clambering for the "family
vote" since the 1870s, and even feminists at the conservative end of
the feminist spectrum had come to advocate it in 1930s.[28] Vichy finally
made it a reality, along with the notion that family associations—again
in contrast to individuals—should serve as the basis of popular representation. The new national family federation thereby took its place
alongside other corporatist bodies—the Peasant Corporation, official
unions of the Labor Charter, and the Comités d'organisation of business enterprise—to give this antidemocratic regime some connection
to civil society. Still, this "family state" also had a statist quality that
could trouble otherwise ardent familialist supporters of the regime.
Renaudin insisted that this elevation of the family movement into
semigovernmental status did not imply its *étatisation* (bureaucratic
co-optation by the state).[29] But many family movement leaders were
not so sure.[30]

    For all this attention to the primacy of family, Vichy's ambitions
far outstripped what it actually achieved. Renaudin's Commissariat
général à la famille, for one thing, lacked the money and influence
to impose its will. Key ministries had the power to compromise its
priorities, be it Finance, which oversaw its modest budget, or Labor,
which administered the allowance programs.[31] With little money or administrative capacity of its own, the Commissariat depended heavily
on the cooperation of family associations to provide family aid and assistance, as well as on the vast network of employer-run *caisses de*

compensation that still were the source of family allowances in industry and commerce. This public-private partnership at the heart of Vichy's "family state" frayed under the strain of the Occupation and the government's shortcomings. Once the Obligatory Labor Service (STO) took hold in 1943, employers came to resent funding the family allowances of employees sent to work in Germany. The Family Commissariat faced a growing cascade of local complaints about the inadequacy of the allowances as living conditions declined. For all its moralizing, Vichy disappointed Catholic familialists dismayed by the weak enforcement of the anti-abortion laws (despite the guillotining of two abortionists), the failure to abolish prostitution, and decisions—made largely on populationist grounds—to grant divorced parents and unwed mothers the single wage allowance.[32] Pushing women into the home faded too as an objective as labor shortages forced the government to abandon its restrictions on female employment. By the eve of the Liberation, four years of economic deprivation, the absence of over a million POWs and over 700,000 forced laborers, not to mention the mass deportation of Jews young and old, had made a mockery of Vichy's claim to remake the nation in the interest and image of the family.[33]

Continuity and Rupture in the Liberation Era

The Liberation, then, presented de Gaulle's Provisional Government with an opportunity both to make a fresh start in family policy and to build selectively on what had come before. Policy planners in the Resistance gave thought to the mix, but stopped short of working up serious blueprints for reform. In London, left-wing Gaullist Henry Hauck headed up the planning team that Pierre Laroque was to join in April 1943, and they put their minds to work on how they might apply ideas from Britain's Beveridge Report, Belgian reforms, and other foreign models.[34] Meanwhile within the internal Resistance in France, the centrist, expert-dominated Comité général d'études (CGE) sought to strengthen the pronatalist impact of the 1939 Code by recommending a new interministerial commission after the Liberation that would coordinate population policy and be backed up by a Conseil supérieur de la population of experts and an Haut-commissariat à la population run by a high-level civil servant.[35] These steps, it was hoped, would give post-Liberation pronatalism greater administrative and scientific heft. Several key figures in the CGE, especially Michel Debré, Pierre-Henri Teitgen, and François de Menthon, were not just pronatalists; they were committed familialists as well, and they called for building the family vote, along with woman's suffrage, into the workings of a new republic. This blend of familialism and natalism was nothing new, of course, and it certainly reflected de Gaulle's perspective as well, combining as it did a conservative social outlook and a "modernizing" ambition.

Still, Resistance planners were hesitant to hammer out detailed plans. As an internal planning memorandum warned, Vichy had given "family" a pejorative connotation and any new organizations and policies in this domain should sport "Population" in their label.[36] "Family" as a focus of policy was hardly mentioned in the fiercely fought-over postwar agenda of the Resistance, the CNR's Charter of March 1944. The Charter did commit to a "complete social security plan . . . administered by representatives of the interested parties and the state."[37] But beyond these broad goals, Resistance planners pushed the serious planning down the road, in part because the choices divided them, especially Communists and Catholics in the Resistance coalition, and in part because Resistance thinkers placed greater priority on planning for full employment, workplace democracy, and nationalizations.[38] De Gaulle's Provisional Government came to power, then, potentially at odds over the policy choices it had postponed.

Indeed, finally deciding the details of social security and family policy became one of the new government's most divisive challenges in the early reconstruction period of 1945–1946. The effort began tranquilly enough. De Gaulle's new labor minister at the Liberation, Alexandre Parodi, tapped Pierre Laroque as his directeur générale de la sécurité sociale and charged him with drafting a proposal. Laroque was superbly equipped to do it. He had de Gaulle's confidence, a team in Paris of over 400 experts and support staff, and an insider's knowledge of the system. As a young lawyer in the Conseil d'État, he had worked closely in the early 1930s with then labor minister Adolph Landry, a towering figure in the populationist movement, to put the new social insurance laws into place, and he stayed intimately involved with the crafting of social legislation until his dismissal in

1940.[39] He knew the territory. By 1944 he also knew his own mind, which had evolved on these matters in accord with the times. Like a number of young policy thinkers on the elite schooling track in Paris coming of age in the early 1930s, he had flirted with the undemocratic, technocratic utopianism of anti-liberal groups such as X-Crise or the Plan du 9 juillet. But by the late 1930s he had left much of that behind.[40] Though no Marxist in 1944, and somewhat patronizing in his view of workers as burdened by an "inferiority complex" deriving from their material insecurity, Laroque nonetheless believed strongly in working-class empowerment as a basis for social integration and national renewal, a "new social order" whereby workers would no longer be subject to "state and business paternalism."[41] This view gave him credibility with Socialists, Communists, and the unions. Likewise, though nonreligious and avidly secularist *(laïc)* with regard to the church-state boundary, "not belonging to any religion," as he put it, he shared with the Catholic Left a solidaristic view of society that privileged obligations to others over individual self-interest.[42] He could, in short, speak in the idioms of both major sides in the social policy debate, without being captive to either. In this respect he personified the *serviteur de l'État,* the high-level civil servant and policy expert, so long idealized in France. "In my orientation I leaned toward the Left. But I never for an instant saw myself affiliated with a party. . . . I believe I have a duty to take positions only if I can take into account the full scope of a problem and the interests involved."[43] While prizing this independence, he also embraced the Resistance ambition of seeking to usher in via the state's stewardship "a true social democracy."[44]

The proposal Laroque created—an ambitious attempt to unify, universalize, and democratize the system—reflected this blend of administrative rationality and Liberation-era solidarity. For all its reach, the plan was also realistic. Laroque had admired William Beveridge's plan for Britain of a universal system of social welfare financed by the state through general revenues and capitalized funds. But he knew the French state was much too poor to attempt it. He opted instead to aim for Beveridge's universalistic goals by expanding and rationalizing France's Bismarckian, pay-as-you-go social insurance system hitherto corseted by the hidebound conservatism of big business and private insurers.[45] Laroque's proposal made into a single national fund, or *régime général,* what had been a congeries of separate insurance programs for death, disability, old age, health, work injuries, maternity, and family allowances. Payroll taxes would be doubled. Employees now would contribute 6 percent of their salaries, matched by 10 percent from employers, with the latter also paying an additional 14 percent to fund family allowances. And in fact, what eventually did come to pass, once much of Laroque's proposal was adopted, significantly expanded social provisioning in France. The social insurance system became available to 20 million employees by the late 1940s, up from 7 million in 1944.[46]

Laroque also proposed a "revolution" in the system's structure and governance.[47] Though a *conseiller d'État* with the strong "sense of the state" that came with such a career, Laroque had a keen understanding of how jealously mutual aid societies had long defended the principle of self-governance of their funds and how allergic both left-wing trade unionists and right-wing Catholics had long been to any hint of *étatisation* in social welfare. "French tradition in the domain of social security," he told an audience at the École nationale d'organisation économique et sociale in 1945, "is not a tradition of bureaucratic statism; it is a tradition of voluntary mutual aid, . . . of the syndicalism of [mid-nineteenth-century radicals] Fourier, Louis Blanc, and Proudhon, and it's this tradition whose name is inscribed on our national currency. It is the tradition of fraternity."[48] With this principle in mind, Laroque structured the *régime général* into a large network of local caisses (or *caisses primaires*), each with a self-governing board in which two-thirds of its members would come from unions to represent workers and one-third would include employer and family association representatives and people known for their relevant expertise. In Laroque's initial design the government would appoint members from the "most representative organization," which for workers in most parts of the country meant the CGT.[49] In addition to local caisses, Laroque's plan also provided for eighteen regional caisses, governed through a similar board structure, to provide for benefits and services beyond the capacity of local caisses. A Caisse nationale des allocations familiales replicated this pattern of representation at the national level. This decentralized structure of self-governance mattered a great deal to Laroque because in his view it provide a way to keep the system from becoming "a huge and forbidding administrative machine"[50] and also a way to transform the polity through "the creation of a new order in which workers are fully responsible."[51]

Make no mistake: this shift to democratically governed caisses marked a dramatic rupture with the past by striking a crippling blow to the employer paternalism that for so long made social insurance and family allowances an element of employee subordination in the workplace. Laroque himself described it as "clearly breaking with previously established principles" as embodied in the Family Code.[52] If, at the Liberation, business elites not been as marginalized as they were by the stain of collaboration, and if Communists, left-wing Catholics, and their trade union allies had not become so powerfully insurgent through the Resistance, this break with employer paternalism would not have occurred. As Laroque remarked later, of all the changes he proposed, it was the loss of control over family allowances that especially irked employers, who regarded these benefits as part and parcel of the wages they offered workers and hence functioned as a cost-cutting device and means of control.[53] This leveraging of family allowances in the wage bargain had soured the CGT and the Communists on family allowances since the 1930s. With Laroque's plan that linkage disappeared, along with the ability of employers to call the shots in the caisses. Though trade union worries about allowances did not disappear entirely after 1945, the Left could now embrace this segment of the welfare state more wholeheartedly than before.[54] Ironically enough, then, it was not Vichy's "family state" but instead the left-leaning government of the early post-Liberation period—armed with Laroque's rationalizing ambitions and the political will of the Provisional Government to break the *patronat*'s parochial grip on family policy—that made "the family" more broadly accepted as central to a vision of national renewal.

Had Laroque's notion of single caisse—the *caisse unique*—prevailed, the rupture with the past would have been even greater, because this idea would have further altered the balance of forces contending over family policy in favor of the Socialist and Communist Left. Much of what came under the social security system had as much bearing on families as did the family allowances, and therefore Laroque felt it an illogical encumbrance to maintain a system of separate caisses for family allowances, as had been the case since their invention in the interwar years. The *caisse unique,* in his view, offered the obvious advantages of simplicity, staffing efficiency, and coordination.[55]

The *caisse unique,* however, did not survive the process of official deliberation that made Laroque's plan a national policy. An advisory panel convened by Labor Minister Parodi rejected the *caisse unique* by a 9–8 vote, the Haut Comité consultatif de la population et de la famille rejected it 7–2, and the same choice prevailed soon thereafter in de Gaulle's cabinet, where most ministers agreed that some accommodation to Catholics on this question was politically wise.[56] Officially, the government decided to postpone indefinitely the merging of family caisses into *caisses uniques,* but delay was a decisive blow. The autonomy of the family caisse would be enshrined permanently in law in 1949, long after the issue had lost its bite and the political balance had shifted to the center.[57] These separate, autonomous family caisses, moreover, unlike the social security caisses, would have their managing boards structured on the basis of parity—half the members representing beneficiaries (mostly workers), a quarter their employers, and another quarter the self-employed.

This important alteration in Laroque's plan was hardly preordained in 1945, given that the CGT, the PCF, most Socialists, and initially Labor Minister Parodi himself supported the *caisse unique.* But a hefty coalition of interests fiercely opposed it, for the stakes were high: all that authority local family caisse boards could have over personnel, administrative oversight, and the doling out of discretionary funds. The Paris Chamber of Commerce condemned the idea of the *caisse unique* as a barely disguised scheme for the *étatisation* of the family caisses that would thereby "injure" *(léser)* the family.[58] The MRP had staked out family and population policy as a domain through which to assert its leadership as a party of government, its anchorage in civil society, its claim to policy expertise, and its ability to deliver patronage to its members. A separate nationwide network of family caisses provided lots of fertile terrain in which to do so. It also gave the Catholic trade union federation, the CFTC, with its strong ties to the Catholic family movement, a better chance of competing with the CGT for influence in the new welfare state apparatus. CFTC leader Gaston Tessier pulled no punches to make the case, condemning the *caisse unique* as a "perilous adventure along the route toward totalitarianism" and hence, in his view, reminiscent of Vichy.[59] Support for separate family caisses also came from another influential quarter, the Ministry of Public Health (notably rechristened Public Health and Population in November 1945). Here many of the state's demographic experts and familialist enthusiasts from the last years of the Third Republic or from the Vichy regime found new postwar perches of influence, including Alfred Sauvy, who for several months in 1945 directed the ministry's Secrétariat général à la famille before eventually taking up the directorship of the new Institut national des études demographiques (INED) near the end of the year.[60] All these diverse supporters of separate family caisses worried, not irrationally, that in a *caisse unique* the board members would be less inclined to make a priority of the needs of mothers and children when faced with competing welfare claims of men, older workers, and pensioners. "We are facing a real generational conflict," MRP spokesman Robert Prigent said, "a conflict all the more tragic given our country's demographic situation, what with single or married workers without children so largely prevailing."[61]

One other key development helped tip the balance in favor of maintaining the family allowance caisse as a separate autonomous wing of the new French social security state—the successful reemergence of the family associations as an integral part of the new postwar republic. Here lay a crucial element of continuity with the past to offset the ruptures that Laroque's plans represented. A law of March 3, 1945, drafted within the Ministry of Public Health and Population in part by the same official who had drafted the Gounot law of 1942, Georges Desmottes, gave official standing and independence to all family associations, including those created through the Gounot law of 1942, thereby instantly "republicanizing" the family movement.[62] The new law took the coercive element out of the Gounot apparatus: family associations were allowed to continue to exist in perpetuity, rather than dissolve into an state-corporatist hierarchy, and they were to be free to affiliate, or not, with a new republican reincarnation of Vichy's official associational network—now the Unions départementales des associations familiales (UDAFs) in each *département* of France, which were to be coordinated in turn by a new Union nationale des associations familiales (UNAF). Internal governance in the UDAFs and the UNAF would employ the family vote. The UNAF was headquartered what had been the site of Vichy's Centre de coordination et d'action des mouvements familiaux.[63] Like many institutions in early postwar France, the family associations benefited from the Provisional Government's willingness, in the name of national renewal, to make an easy transition to a post-Vichy era; purges in the family sector of the administration and in the associations were notably light.[64] And something more political was involved here as well: de Gaulle, MRP leaders, and some Socialists too in the government saw the family associations (and the over 400,000 people who were estimated to belong to them in 1946) as firmly rooted counterweights to the CGT and the Communist Party.[65] Separate family caisses would give the associations a focal point for their activism. The UDAFs and UNAF would in fact go on to play an important role identifying possible members of caisse boards, government committees, and other venues of consultation in family policy. And they also lobbied the government on behalf of family associations and provided a range of quasi-official family services, much like the Gounot associational network was intended to do.[66]

By the end of 1945, then, de Gaulle's government had put into place as a set of family policies and institutions that both drew on and broke from the achievements of the 1930s and the Vichy era. No one embodied this mixture of rupture and continuity more visibly than Robert Prigent. Having just turned 35 years old when de Gaulle named him minister of population in November 1945, he would go on to serve as minister of public health and population for most of the next two years and would remain a major figure in family policy circles into the early Fifth Republic. At one level he was agent and exemplar of the transition from Vichy to the Fourth Republic. He had risen rapidly through the ranks of Catholic Action in the early 1930s to become a founding leader in 1935 of the new Ligue ouvrière chrétienne (the Christian Workers League, or LOC), a family-focused branch of the movement, which in 1942 was rechristened the Mouvement populaire des familles (MPF) in the hopes of broadening its appeal. Leadership of the LOC/MPF catapulted Prigent into the engine room of Vichy's familialist entreprise, the Centre de coordination et d'action des mouvements familiaux. There he became acquainted with Sauvy, Doublet, Desmottes, and other key policy experts, and he learned the ropes of the new Gounot family networks. Before long, however, he had also joined the Resistance (via the Organisation civile et militaire with its strong roots in the north of the country and in the state bureaucracy) to emerge in Algiers in autumn 1943 as a Christian Democratic representative in the Assemblée consultative provisoire and de Gaulle's postwar government-in-the-making. There he became the principal, determined advocate for bringing family policy squarely onto the postwar legislative agenda and the family and population administrative bureaucracy into the postwar republic.[67] It was Prigent, more than anyone, who masterminded the republicanization of the Gounot law through the ordinance of March 3, 1945. Prigent, in short, had enough standing in both the Catholic familialist movement and the Resistance to orchestrate the former's re-anointment as a legitimate force in the new republican France.

But there is another side to the Prigent story that makes him emblematic also of rupture. Though clearly a talented political tactician and policy thinker who could work the corridors of the Provisional Government, he was also a militant of the Catholic working class. Like a number of the youngest leaders of the new MRP (future labor minister Paul Bacon, for example, and Jules Catoire, who was prominent in the nationalization debates), Prigent came of age during the interwar years in the industrial heartland of the Nord and Pas-de-Calais—in his case in Dunkerque—where his father had been a sailor, an anticlerical, and an activist in the CGT when the syndicalist movement was gathering steam before the First World War. Though his father died when he was only 12, Robert Prigent knew him well enough to see him as a model for his own labor militancy in the Catholic CFTC. Prigent's devotion to Catholicism he owed initially to his mother, who had insisted on his catechism lessons and confirmation. From there he gravitated as an adolescent into the local orbit of Catholic Action with its network of dynamic priests and lay activists who in the interwar years were making the parishes of northern France a hotbed of the Jeunesse ouvrière chrétienne (JOC; Christian Worker Youth) and its female counterpart, the Jeunesse ouvrière chrétienne féminine (JOCF). They recognized Prigent's potential for leadership in this movement for a socially committed Catholicism. After several years working as an electrician in a local steel mill, he became a full-time organizer and official for the CFTC, the JOC, and most importantly, the brand new Ligue ouvriére chrétienne (LOC). The latter, alongside the women's Ligue ouvrière chrétienne féminine (LOCF), built bridges at the local parish level between the Catholic labor movement and family associations that in this region had a distinctly working-class feel. Its national periodical, *Monde Ouvrier*, became an instrument for furthering the spiritual mission of Catholic Action via the family movement, as well as for giving the familialist cause a wider constituency by addressing the concerns of working-class women and men alike. The LOC led Prigent to his future wife—she was an LOCF leader—and to the national stage that the Vichy regime offered when it sought ways to harness the blessings and resources of the family movement.[68]

Prigent therefore represented something new, a distinctly working-class, left-leaning type of Catholic activist who came to questions of social policymaking with serious religious convictions about the sanctity of the family, preferably large ones (he was to have four children), but without an investment in the business paternalism or ethos of bourgeois uplift that had long animated the familialist cause. Unlike many familialists, he had grave doubts about the democratic propriety of the family vote: on that issue he was in the dissenting minority on the Haut Comité consultatif de la population et de la famille when that body voted for it in June 1945.[69] If by 1945 he had become a policy expert and MRP politician (as deputy from the Nord), and then indeed a minister, his background as a militant gave him a different outlook and basis of authority from that of Laroque, Sauvy, Landry, and other policy luminaries of the Liberation period. And to that extent, ironically enough, he had something in common with his Communist rivals who also had found their way into positions of power in the Provisional Government not through the *grandes écoles* and the *grands corps* but through a social movement. The novelty of this path to power equipped Prigent all the more to be an agent of both change and continuity.

In leading the opposition to Pierre Laroque's plan, then, Prigent took care to endorse its radical break from employer control over social insurance and family allowances. He, like most of his MRP colleagues, embraced the fundamentals of the new social security state. What he and they objected to was, above all, any effort to undercut the separate identity and autonomy of the family caisses. They also attacked the plan's statism, and here they won an early victory, in a rare alliance with the CGT, by beating back a notion of Laroque's to put a ministerial representative on every caisse board.[70] A former Catholic trade unionist, Prigent continued to fight doggedly along with his CFTC colleagues, despite initial setbacks on this score, for elected rather than appointed boards, so as to have a better chance of chipping away at the CGT's prominence in the new system.

National shifts in political fortune from late 1945 to mid-1947 proved decisive in settling debates about the institutional shape of social security and family allowances. When elections for the first Constituent Assembly in October 1945 strengthened the hand of the Communists in the governing tripartite coalition, the Communist trade unionist Amboise Croizat took over the Labor Ministry from Parodi. Croizat supported Laroque in the continuing effort to implement the social security reform, and the two of them worked effectively together until Premier Paul Ramadier's fateful dismissal of Communist ministers in June 1947.[71] Because Croizat was such a revered figure in the CGT and PCF—as a longtime leader in the metal-working sector, a parliamentary deputy in the Popular Front era, a Resistance figure who saw time in seventeen Vichy prisons during the war—his relatively long stint (twenty-eight months) at the helm of the Labor Ministry helped to consolidate the support of the working-class Left for the new social security system, including family allowances.[72] He came to regard the latter as essential to the whole edifice of the new welfare state, and he understood how to make that case to his Communist colleagues.[73] "We can't have competition between children and the elderly," he said in the National Assembly in 1946, "since these are the very children who will one day become the workers who provide for the pensions of the old."[74] Under Croizat's watch at Labor, the Communist Party made its political investment in social security and family allowances abundantly clear, and the notion took hold that the Laroque reforms were a "workers' conquest."[75]

A second shift in the political wind had even bigger consequences. Elections for the second Constituent Assembly in June 1946 diminished the power of the Socialists and proved a boon to the MRP, which was now in a position to stand down the Communists and the CGT in what up to then had been the latter's dominant role in social policy debate. Prigent and his allies pressed their newfound advantage: they virtually removed from any further serious debate the question of keeping the family caisses separate, they won the battle to make caisse boards elected, not appointed,[76] and they succeeded in keeping family policy itself on its pronatalist track. A law of August 22, 1946, boosted allowances sharply and structured them to reward couples for spacing the births of their children closely. A birth benefit continued to be available with the arrival of the first child, provided it came within the first two years of marriage—a provision designed so that newlyweds would be less inclined to, as state demographer Jacques Doublet put it, "settle down in a sort of shared bachelor life."[77] Subsequent children also came with birth bonuses, provided they arrived within three years of their predecessor. Allowances for the second child were raised to 20 percent (up from 12 percent) of the average metalworking wage in the *département,* and for the third child it rose to 24 percent. The existing rate of 30 percent for each subsequent child remained unchanged. The new law also introduced a new prenatal benefit, given out at three stages of pregnancy to women who registered within the first three months and came to the required prenatal medical exam—a plan designed to support motherhood, reward women for using prenatal services, and discourage abortion.[78] The single-wage allowance, now extended to unmarried parents and foreigners, rose sharply as well— up from 25 percent to 40 percent in families with two children, and from 30 percent to 50 percent for three.[79] All this, in addition to a generous schedule of income tax deductions for dependents *(quotients familiales)* that the government had established at the end of 1945, gave metropolitan France Europe's most pronatalist policy package of the postwar era, and one firmly geared to keep women with children at home.[80] (As we will see in Chapter 7, in exploring the Algerian war's impact on the long reconstruction, French authorities had quite different approaches to family policy outside the metropole.)

With these Catholic-led modifications to Laroque's plan in place, the new Liberation-era regime for family policy solidified by 1947 into what would prove to be a durable set of institutions and policy commitments.[81] But *within* this settled landscape, fierce partisan conflict, especially between Communists and Catholics, continued over new policy directions, the use of large sums of discretionary funds, the provision of patronage in the social welfare bureaucracy, and the balance of political power at every level of the new family policy regime, from local caisses to the ministries. The first caisse elections, held in April 1947 for both the social security and the family allowance boards, put this competitive reality on display. The CGT, along with the dominant Communist majority within it, won nearly 60 percent of the votes for beneficiary representatives, and secured a majority of seats on 109 of the country's 124 caisses for the social security *régime general.* It won a majority of seats in 101 of the 111 family allowance caisses. The CFTC won 26 percent of the votes, not all that bad considering the minority status of confederation in most of the country. Indeed, these elections proved crucial for the CFTC because it displayed the limits to the CGT's hegemony in the labor movement.[82] With the Cold War–fueled schism of the CGT in 1947–1948, the new non-Communist CGT-FO (Force Ouvrière) would weaken the Communist dominance in the caisses considerably, and proportionally strengthen the CFTC's hand, as made manifest in the next set of caisse elections in 1950.[83] Caisse elections would henceforth remain a vehicle for keeping family policy and social security a matter of political combat and debate in a most localities and enterprises, even as they also served as a means for trade union confederations to measure their strength.

The struggle for predominance in social welfare also played out in the invention of two new institutions in the winter of 1946–1947—the Fédération nationale des organisations de sécurité sociale (FNOSS) and the Union nationale des caisses d'allocations familiales (UNCAF). This episode began months earlier when the CGT's leading spokesmen in social policy, the former postal worker and influential Communist militant Henri Raynaud, called for the founding of the FNOSS to represent the many local and regional caisses. Each caisse, at Raynaud's invitation, designated three board members to become a part of this new body, which swiftly became yet another site of CGT influence in the new social welfare regime and the agency for the caisses to negotiate collectively with doctors over fees. The FNOSS also acquired authority over the hiring, firing, and contractual terms of personnel in the caisses. Raynaud became its first president.

Although Laroque had anticipated that something like FNOSS would emerge to provide greater coordination to what was a highly decentralized system of caisses, the CGT's firm leadership in the endeavor seems to have come as a surprise. Even so, Laroque and others in the Labor Ministry welcomed this new invention as a valuable link between the caisses and the state. Laroque discovered too that Raynaud lent an ethos of professionalism to the CGT's dominion in social security system.[84] Once established, the FNOSS became a political arena in its own right, a place where rival factions of the labor movement, employers, and mutual aid societies jockeyed for influence, much like the caisses had become. The FNOSS also replicated the struggle over autonomy for the family allowance caisses. Raynaud intended the FNOSS to represent family and social security caisses alike. But leaders of family associations, the CFTC, and what would soon be FO feared that matters of family welfare would be subordinated in a CGT-dominated FNOSS. In December 1946 they won the argument, convincing enough of the FNOSS delegates to endorse the creation of an autonomous, parallel body—the UNCAF—to serve the same function as the FNOSS for the family caisses.[85] Laroque, for his part, was relieved by this outcome, "having suffered too long," he told the UNCAF at their first general assembly, "from not having a body to work with me that could speak in the name of all the family caisses."[86] The UNCAF, as was to be expected, took on a more moderate cast than the FNOSS: Catholic familialist Roger Monnin and FO's Roland Lebel provided its core leadership for another two decades.[87] Still, it too became a focal point for partisanship in the family domain, especially as a growing diversity of interest groups were taking up the family as their cause.

Indeed, the "family movement" itself had changed its profile by 1947. Formerly an almost exclusively Catholic phenomenon rooted in cities and towns, the family association became a more appealing and viable form of civic engagement and political mobilization once the law of March 22, 1946, made it an unambiguously republican institution available to any group of like-minded citizens in any locale. From the end of 1946 to November 1947 the number of registered family associations grew to 8,887, up from 4,966. Much of this remarkable spurt came from two sources: new rural associations (2,834) and associations created by the Union des femmes françaises (1,322), a women's organization closely linked to the Communist Party. Even new CGT-affiliated family associations numbered in the hundreds, a mark of how far the labor Left had traveled beyond its allergies to family allowances in the 1930s.[88]

"Family," then, had become a watchword across the political spectrum after 1944 to a greater degree than before. By embracing "the family" as a cornerstone of reconstruction strategy (in continuity with Vichy) and by decoupling it from a tradition of workplace paternalism (rupture), the Provisional Government made "the family" more available for everyone—Left, Right, and center—to define anew as a focal point for political action. Pronatalist experts and the familialist Right no longer monopolized policy planning in this domain. The institutional revolution of the early postwar years, moreover, empowered a broader range of societal groups to take part in caisse elections, local family associations, and the pyramidal structures that brought local voices to the attention of policymaking elites in Paris. These linkages to local constituencies, be they Catholic, Communist, or otherwise, gave leaders such as Prigent, Croizat, and Laroque greater legitimacy in the postwar republic. But linkages also carried the potential to make state direction in the family policy domain more subject to discordant pressures from below.

Gender in Question

Debate over family policy put the spotlight on women—their fertility, maternity, and patriotic duty to be homemakers and mothers. Yet nearly all the major protagonists mentioned so far, the reader will have noticed, were men. Indeed, the chief architects of family policy from the 1930s through the Liberation period operated in a man's world, be it the pronatalist lobby centered around the Alliance nationale contre la dépopulation, Parliament and its committees, or even the family association movement, which was mostly a men's movement, and for men with three or more children at that. When the Conseil national des associations familiales (CNAF; National Council of Family Associations) came into being in 1945, it was principally a body of men. What's more, an inordinate number of the state's heavy hitters in social policy in the Liberation era—Alexandre Parodi, Pierre Laroque, Jacques

Doublet, and Emmanuel Rain—had risen to prominence through the *grands corps d'État* (most commonly as *conseillers de l'État*), the clubby, male, elite tracks of the high-level civil service.[89] Here, careers advanced not just through training, talent, and drive, but also through comradeship, loyalty, and a tradition of mentorship that had long made state service a man's world. Alexandre Parodi had in the 1930s become a mentor to Pierre Laroque, Michel Debré, and other new-comers to the Conseil d'État, and these bonds tightened through the shared travails of the Resistance and Liberation. In the postwar era, state expertise still carried a masculine valence. As Remi Lenoir observed in analyzing the language of Alfred Sauvy's obituary of Adophe Landry, a key mentor in his own right in populationist circles, to have been a "great man" or *grand seigneur* in this modern-day state nobility was to have displayed "courage and obstinacy," "fidelity," and "competence," and to have been "a man who rises to the occasion whenever necessary."[90] These qualities, of course, were not intrinsically masculine, but they were deemed to be so at the time, and especially when military combat, the Resistance, and heroic plans for national renewal were commonly regarded as tests of collective manhood.[91]

Indeed, as focused as policymakers were on women and children, concerns about fatherhood also attracted their attention after the Liberation. Defeat and the Occupation had taken its toll, with over a million husbands separated from their families as POWs, deportees, or conscript laborers.[92] Many of these men felt diminished by their ordeal or even displaced when families had managed to cope without them.[93] The great majority of couples reunited successfully after the absent spouse returned. Still, divorce rates spiked in the first years after the war,[94] and as Kristin Childers has shown, the Vichy regime had had a way of marginalizing fathers, even if it had unambiguously reaffirmed fathers' legal and moral sovereignty in the family. Pétain's propagandists had glorified mothers more than fathers, and because the fatherless family had become such a commonplace after the defeat, the deficient father became a focal point for Vichy policy: a 1942 law criminalizing family abandonment targeted wayward fathers. Welfare agencies were given greater leeway to channel family allowances directly to mothers when fathers were derelict.[95] And then there were the real and imagined insults to collective claims to manhood that came with the country's prolonged occupation by the German army. Not for nothing have historians interpreted the extraordinary tsunami of ritualized head-shearings of women thought to be "horizontal collaborators"—with a first wave in 1944 and a second when POWs and deportees returned in 1945—as a misogynist reassertion of the prewar gendered order.

After the Liberation, then, familialist leaders sought ways to restore confidence and authority to fathers as *chefs de famille* at a time when many mothers had had to assume that role. MRP leaders Robert Prigent and Fernand Bouxom advocated a proposal long cherished by Catholic familialists, the *prêts au marriage* (marriage loans for newlyweds), on the grounds that it would help solidify the position of the husband as a family provider.[96] Many women, especially if as POW wives they had carried the burdens of fending for their families alone, concurred.[97] At the same time, experts such as Pierre Laroque worried about getting the balance right between subsidy and self-sufficiency. "The head of the family," Laroque pointed out in a 1950 lecture on family responsibility, "the person who has the real and permanent responsibility for the child, must be the recipient of family allowances. The latter must be calibrated so as to reinforce, not undermine, this sense of responsibility."[98] The trick, then, was to provide aid in such a way as to reinforce the conventional notion of the father as *chef de famille.*

But if men presided over the family policy establishment and sought to fortify fatherhood, women were by no means passive bystanders in the politics of making family policy. On the contrary, women's organizations across the political spectrum, a number of them avowedly feminist and suffragette, had for decades weighed in on family policy issues. After the Liberation, women became more influential still in the politics of making family policy. Three institutional avenues either opened up or widened to women to make this possible. The first was state appointments. Under pressure to acknowledge women as authoritative participants in the nation's renewal, de Gaulle named two women to his prestigious Haut Comité consultatif de la population et de la famille (HCCPF)—family association veteran Simone Collet and left-wing trade union militant Jeanne Marcelle Delabit.[99] Women, moreover, having broken into the middle and upper ranks of the central state administration during the interwar years, advanced further still after the Liberation, especially in ministries critical to social policy—such as Labor, and Public Health and Population.[100] Indeed, in 1947 Premier Robert Schuman named Germaine Poinso-Chapuis of the MRP as his minister of public health and population, making her the country's first woman to hold a full-rank cabinet ministry.[101]

With the achievement of women's suffrage in 1944 a second major avenue opened up as well: political office and party politics. Six percent of the National Assembly of 1946 were women: twenty-three Communists, three Socialists, and nine MRP members—no stampede into the Palais Bourbon, but a stunning break nonetheless with past exclusion from Parliament.[102] And these party numbers were telling: Communists and Catholics, far more than Socialists and Radical Republicans, had actively recruited young women into their respective youth movements in the 1930s and Resistance organizations during the war. For many women, service as party activists in the MRP and PCF grew directly out of their involvement in the Resistance.[103] The MRP and the PCF, the two parties with the most totalizing visions of how politics ought to transform society, would consequently become key arenas in the late 1940s and 1950s where men and women debated women's rights and the future direction of family policy.

Alongside these parties a third avenue widened to give women greater opportunity after the war to voice their views—the many associations in civil society, be they independent, party-affiliated, trade-union-based, or religious, that provided services to families or lobbied for social policy during the Fourth Republic. This "parapolitical space" of voluntary and professional work in social services, as historian Laura Downs has described it, had already expanded considerably in the interwar years, and it grew apace after the Liberation.[104] Likewise, a great variety of women's advocacy organizations had already established firm roots by the 1930s, and however much they differed politically from one another, they nearly all combined an advocacy of individual rights for women, most notably suffrage, with a desire to see state policy improve women's condition as mothers and wives. For most feminists, the "liberation of women," a phrase widely used in the late 1940s, meant not the gender-blind equality more commonly espoused later in the 1960s and 1970s, but the freedom of women to flourish as wives, mothers, and maternal authorities in a gendered order where women and men respected one another in their complementarity and difference.[105]

After the Liberation two women's organizations assumed a special prominence by virtue of mirroring so accurately the Right-Left divide of social policy debate. The Union féminine civique et sociale (UFCS), with about 70,000 members after the war, flourished as a conservative, mostly bourgeois, Catholic association under the continuing leadership of Andrée Butillard, who had founded it in 1925 to advocate both women's suffrage and a "return of mothers to the home."[106] The UFCS had strong ties to the two-million-strong Ligue féminine action catholique (LFAC), and it had paid but a small political price for its close association with the Vichy regime, in part because a number of its leaders had distinguished themselves in the Resistance. UFCS militants hit all the right notes of conservative Catholic familialism, but they did so in a feminist key that implicitly challenged the male leadership of the MRP and the familialist movement to the share the platform with women.

The UFCS's strongest counterpart on the Left, by far, was the Union des femmes françaises (UFF). Although not every one of the UFF's purported 600,000 to a million members supported the PCF, a majority surely did, and most of the organization's local leaders emerged either from the Communist youth movement of the 1930s or from (often harrowing) experience organizing protests against food and fuel restrictions during the Occupation.[107] Officially formed through a merger of Communist-led Resistance organizations for women in the autumn of 1944, the UFF solidified its prominence after the Liberation by orchestrating demonstrations against shortages and price hikes in cities and towns across the country. It was not altogether rare for some local activists in the UFCS and the UFF to have acquired a mutual respect for one another through the Resistance, and they shared a certain sense of feminist common purpose. Still, UFCS and UFF militants inhabited different worlds in terms of class and politics, and the two organizations squared off on issues of family policy very much in tandem with the MRP and the PCF, respectively, be it over the question of the autonomy of the family caisses, the importance of the *salaire unique*, or improving conditions for working women. Though adamantly pronatalist and family-centered, as the Communist line had been since 1935, the UFF made more of the need for *crèches* (day nurseries), breast-feeding time, and equal pay in the workplace than did the UFCS, which sought every means of encouraging mothers to be full-time homemakers.[108] The UFF, by contrast, like the PCF and the CGT, utterly rejected the notion that women's employment threatened the pronatalist goals of the reconstruction. As a CGT pamphlet promoting female employment in metalworking was keen to point out, the Soviets, Americans, British, and Canadians had all boosted female employment and fertility at the same time during the war. Enabling women to work would likewise serve the "grandeur and radiance" of France.[109]

One other organization played a big role in nurturing women's activism, the Mouvement populaire des familles (MPF). As a predominantly working-class Catholic organization, the MPF occupied the political middle ground between the conservative UFCS and the Communist-leaning UFF. Most of the first MPF activists came from Catholic Action in the industrial districts of the Paris region, the Nord, and the Pas-de-Calais, and they won respect for the assistance they gave POW families during the Occupation. They helped POW wives send packages to their husbands, organized cooperatives to cope with shortages, trained home service aides *(travailleuses familiales)*, and relocated children to the countryside, especially in 1944 when families feared that combat might overwhelm Paris.[110] After the Liberation the MPF organized local collectives to share household appliances, especially washing machines, and this activity led the MPF to spearhead consumer advocacy in the 1950s.[111] The MPF also ran candidates for the caisses. Through all this work, the MPF trained women to live lives of public advocacy.

As a crucible for working-class activism, the MPF also became a site of sharpening political tensions over family policy. For one thing, some MPF activists defended women's desire to combine work and motherhood, which conservative Catholics opposed. Simone Rollin, for example, who rose to top leadership of the MPF during the war and in 1945 won election as an MPR deputy from the Paris region, supported working mothers, and she was hardly alone. As historian Arthur Plaza has shown, she and other women on the MPF national council in 1945 promoted the principle that women have the freedom to exercise their "rights to labor and to the home." They embraced maternity as women's primary role, but in tune with the teachings of Catholic personalism they regarded life outside the home, whether in service, advocacy, or work, as valuable for the fulfillment of "the human person."[112]

Dissidence within the MPF took another form as well: a drift leftward by many of its members in the late 1940s away from the Christian Democratic Party (the MRP), even from the Church itself. With the onset of the Cold War and the collapse of the tripartite governmental alliance of the Christian Democrats, Communists, and Socialists in 1947, divisions widened between left-leaning and moderate Catholic activists. The MPF supported the miners' strike of 1948, just when the MRP (the Christian Democratic Party) was drifting rightward and when the Church was becoming more stridently anticommunist. Many MPF activists found they had less in common with MRP party barons than with the Communist and UFF militants they competed against, but also often allied with, in the neighborhoods of towns like Roubaix and Dunkerque and in the Paris suburbs. The bitterness of class politics in the strike-ridden late-1940s took a corrosive toll on Catholic unity, as leftist Catholic activists increasingly adopted an approach to family policy issues akin to that of their Communist rivals. They became more insistent in demanding the much-needed and much-lacking material supports—from employers, local institutions, and the state—that would make it possible for mothers to raise their families. A small incident in Villeurbanne in 1950 speaks volumes: when MPF member Denise Brocard was invited by the mayor and municipal council to receive a Mother's Day medal for her fertility, she took the occasion, "having been influenced by UFF women in the neighborhood," to make a speech about the "inhuman work" mothers had to do at home and that making washing machines available would do more good than would handing out medals."[113] The stunned gathering at town hall went silent. This was hardly the tone of a Catholic consensus about the family.

By the early 1950s the attenuating connections between the Church and the MPF broke altogether as the latter spun into its own schismatic crisis. MPF's most left-leaning activists had by the late 1940s redubbed the organization the Mouvement de libération du peuple (MLP) and withdrew from the CNAF. Militants renounced the latter as too bourgeois, too dominated by fathers at the expense of mothers, and too removed from the everyday concerns of much of the family movement. Church officials and a newly insurgent Gaullist party on the Right now regarded the MLP as dangerously infiltrated with "Communists and their progressive Catholic sympathizers" who had become all too comfortable working in tandem with the UFF and joining the CGT.[114] Many members of the now-former MPF had in fact resisted this rapprochement with the Communist Party—one militant said later that whenever she heard the Internationale she wanted to break out singing the Magnificat—and in 1951 the more moderate militants in the MLP split off to form the Mouvement de la libération ouvrière (MLO).[115] In the divisive politics of Cold War France, "family"—the word and the cause—was no longer enough to hold together the fracturing loyalties of the working-class Catholic Left.

Even the MRP (the Christian Democratic Party) began to see cracks in its consensus on family policy. Take, for example, Germaine Poinso-Chapuis (Figure 4.1), one of the party's brightest lights and one of many MRP women who challenged the male leadership to think more liberally about women's rights and conditions. She spent her entire professional life as lawyer and politician striving to harmonize a Catholic devotion to child rearing with a feminist conviction that women had an obligation use their talents fully in the world. "The family," she wrote in 1950, ". . . is not an end but a means: it enables everyone who is a part of it to fully blossom and realize their potential."[116] An advocate of state-supported daycare and of professional careers for women, she threw her weight behind a law to open up the ranks of the magistrature to women. Half the professional staff in her ministerial cabinet in 1947–1948 were women.[117] Though no outright opponent of the MRP's sacrosanct *salaire unique* (the subsidy intended to enable wives to stay home), she warned openly against confining women's lives to the *foyer*, because "the need to expand and escape grows more and more as women become aware of themselves."[118] These views put her at odds with key allies in the party like Robert Prigent, who in the 1950s continued to write of homemaking as the fulfillment of women's "proper nature" and of the virtue of women who, though trained for top careers in science and administration, freely abandoned these pursuits "to devote themselves totally to their tasks as spouse and

FIGURE 4.1 Germaine Poinso-Chapuis, minister of public health and population in the Schuman government of 1947–1948. Building her career first as a lawyer in the Marseille region, then elected to the National Assembly in 1945, Poinso-Chapuis became the first woman in France to be named a full-rank cabinet minister. She sought to blend a feminist advocacy for the interests of working women with the conservative social vision of her Christian Democratic party, the MRP. AGIP—Rue des Archives/Granger, NYC. All rights reserved.

mother."[119] As minister, Poinso-Chapuis sought to expand the rights of unwed or abandoned married mothers, and later, as a member of Parliament in the 1950s, she championed divorce reform and efforts to overturn the inequalities in marriage long inscribed in the civil code—a cause that finally prevailed in the 1965 law that gave wives control over their own material assets.[120] If her feminism was never sufficiently radical to satisfy the Ligue française pour le droit des femmes or vanguard activists in the 1950s, such as the women in the Mouvement jeunes femmes who campaigned for contraception and abortion rights, Poinso-Chapuis and other feminists in the MRP did vocally dissent from the orthodox familialism of the party.[121]

As Catholic France was becoming more divided over questions of family and gender, so was the Communist Party. For several years after the Liberation, PCF leaders, male and female, stuck vigilantly to a position of advocating with equal force the pursuit of salary equality and better conditions for working women, on the one hand, and robust support for conventional family values, child allowances, and high fertility, on the other. This "double optic," as Jane Jensen has aptly described it, envisaged gender equality for the workplace (in the interests of working-class unity) but not in the family (which, it was thought, could only be transformed with the end of bourgeois capitalism).[122] Leading party figure Claudine Chomat's exhortation at the national congress of the UFF in 1945 harmonized perfectly with the predominant melodies of the moment: "Give children to France, establish a home, give children a moral upbringing, and inculcate in them an appetite for work, filial respect, a love of country, and a civic sense."[123] When the Cold War and the collapse of the tripartite governing coalition in 1947 pushed the PCF back to the sidelines of state power, party leaders chose to embrace motherhood and family even more to minimize the PCF's isolation.[124] To reach out to Catholics and blunt the Church's anticommunism, Jeannette Vermeersch, wife of party chief Maurice Thorez, even called on party supporters to join a Church-inspired parade to honor Joan of Arc, heroine of the Catholic Right. Many UFF *militantes* recoiled at this ecumenical gesture.[125] The PCF put invocations of motherhood and children to the service of its political program—the pro-Soviet, anti-American "peace campaign" of that began in 1949 ("to spare children from war"), the opposition to German rearmament and the Indochina war ("negotiate with Ho Chi Minh, mothers demand it"), and in 1955, calls for solidarity between French and Algerian women.[126] Mother's Days became much-publicized occasions to hale the CGT's ongoing fight for higher wages, day care, better family allowances, and longer vacations for mothers: "The best way to celebrate us is to give us the means to raise our children decently."[127]

FIGURE 4.2 Madeleine Colin at the 34th congress of the Confédération générale du travail (CGT). Born in Paris in 1905, as a young woman Colin worked in the postal service before joining the Resistance and the Communist Party during the war. In 1955 she became a high-ranking CGT official, as well as editor of *Antoinette*, the CGT's women's magazine. A feminist, she criticized misogyny inside the party. Photo © Gerald Bloncourt / Bridgeman Images.

For all the appearances of party—and gender—unity behind this approach to family, a number of women in the UFF and CGT resented their subordination in the PCF and the strictures of party discipline. After 1947 the strains began to show. As the UFF became more narrowly focused on motherhood than on the full range of women's concerns, the gulf some activists felt widening between the revolutionary hopes of 1945 and the familialist preoccupations of party practice become harder to bear.[128] An unconventional and free-speaking *militante* such as writer Marguerite Duras could find herself marginalized in the party, or even expelled, as was the case for Duras in 1950.[129] Revealing, too, was what longtime party loyalist Madeleine Colin (Figure 4.2) had to say years later about the misogyny she encountered in the party and the CGT. Raised in a modest middle-class family in Paris, in the late 1920s Colin became a career telephone employee in the PTT (Postes, télégraphes et téléphones), migrated leftward in her politics during the Popular Front, and then through her work in the Resistance became a PCF and CGT activist after the Liberation. She rose rapidly in the CGT to become, by the mid-1950s, its leading official responsible for women's issues and an editor of the CGT's monthly women's magazine *Antoinette*.[130] Though much respected for her success in organizing women and in leading strikes in the PTT, she still had to endure the indignities of second-class treatment in the movement's hierarchy—of men tuning her out when she spoke in committees, of having to share her editorship of *Antoinette* with party heavyweight Gaston Monmousseau, of women getting to write editorials in *La Vie Ouvrière* only in August when no one read them, of being given a dumpy little Renault 4 CV when her male counterparts on the CGT's governing bureau got impressive, chauffeured sedans.[131] "Activist men in the labor movement," she wrote years later, "are not fundamentally different from other men."[132] The party's patronizing of its own *militantes* and its resolute stance toward women and the family—crusading faithfully for workplace rights while extolling a conventional familialism with a Communist accent—squandered the political capital the PCF had acquired at the Liberation to remain at the vanguard in matters of family and women's rights in the postwar reconstruction.

Party leaders had their chance to recover that role in 1956, and they rejected it. Their opportunity: the chance to throw the PCF's support behind a law proposed in Parliament to legalize birth control. A long, beleaguered campaign to overturn the 1920 and 1923 laws banning abortion and contraception had finally acquired traction in the mid-1950s. French birth control advocates—many of them doctors and feminists with Protestant, Socialist, Communist, or Freemason affiliations—drew inspiration from the American family planning movement, and they got a fillip too from the publication of Simone de Beauvoir's immensely controversial *Second Sex* (1949). But to the astonishment of many party members, the PCF's principal female leaders, notably Vermeersch, Chomat, and Marie-Claude Vaillant-Couturier, came down thunderously against the reform. They condemned birth control as a "bourgeois vice" whose legalization would deprive the working class of its "right to maternity." Maurice Thorez raised the specter that such a reform "risks leading to the elimination of family allowances and the gains that the working class has won for mothers and children."[133] Why such obstinate rigidity on this question? As Sylvie Chaperon has argued, party leaders had grown too wedded to their conservative convictions about the family to give them up so quickly, and too invested in a rapprochement with Catholics, especially in 1956 when it looked as if a loosening of Cold War tensions might bring the party out of the cold.[134] Meanwhile, party dissenters, including a number of doctors, wrote letters of dismay to the independent left-wing newspaper *Liberation*. The UFF's press (*Femmes Françaises* and *Heures Claires*) maintained a stony silence on the subject, a remarkable display of protest under the circumstances, and even some Communist deputies admitted to having to vote the party line against their conscience.[135] Jacques Derogy, a Communist deputy who had initially introduced a birth control bill in Parliament, quit the party after a public scolding in the press by Thorez. In the end, Communist and Catholic opposition in the Assembly ensured the bill's defeat.

How many party supporters quit the PCF as a result is impossible to say. It was a year, after all, when Khrushchev's speech at the Twentieth Party Congress and the Soviet's obliteration of the Hungarian uprising drove many people from the party. Still, defections, silences, and adherence to party discipline made the PCF a less hospitable place to talk about women's rights, family planning, and questions of power within the couple—just when rising living standards and changing public mores were making these issues more salient in France. If the PCF and the CGT still remained the most stalwart defenders of women in the key bastions of female employment—the PTT and civil service, textiles and metalworking—the Catholic and Communist establishments had become more similar in their defense of conventional norms about gender and family. The Catholic-Communist divide in the Liberation period about family and gender had gradually given way by the late 1950s to new cleavages over these matters. The Catholic and Communist camps had become more riven within, more challenged by their own feminist dissidents, than at odds with each other. This fracturing of views about the family within Catholic and Communist France would give government authorities greater room to think afresh about policy in this domain in the late 1950s.

Expanding Realms of Expertise

As we have seen, political and administrative elites who had taken a special interest in family policy in the 1930s continued to exert much influence in the Fourth Republic, whether their expertise was anchored in medicine (Robert Debré) or law (Pierre Laroque, Jacques Doublet, Michel Debré, and many others). Legal experience also rewarded a newcomer to top leadership in this field such as Germaine Poinso-Chapuis. The medical or legal background of major authorities in this field was hardly surprising. But family and population policymaking also lent itself to the rising influence of demographers, statisticians, sociologists, psychologists, and economists who made their arguments with large doses of data. Alfred Sauvy, from his command post at INED and its journal *Population*, served as both exemplar and facilitator of this kind of expertise. Sophistication in these disciplines was advancing apace by the late 1940s. Fernand Boverat, a kingpin in the family movement, had been able to keep up with the major statistical studies of population in the 1930s, but he could no longer follow the technical mathematics of the young *polytechniciens* such as Louis Henry at INED, a trend that made someone like Sauvy—a highly trained expert who could also function effectively as a policy generalist—all the more important in the policymaking game.[136] He could translate the numbers and had a gift as a writer for getting economics and demography across to the general public. Advances in data analysis also enabled policymakers to ask more complex questions. INED's studies of the changing cost of child rearing as children aged, for example, sparked debate about how family allocations might be calibrated accordingly.[137] More than ever, experts made much of the *science* of their social sciences. As Georges Desmottes, a top administrator in the Ministry of Public Health and Population, claimed in an exploration of the *minimum vital* all families needed to sustain a decent standard of living: "The problem has to be approached on an objective and scientific basis."[138]

International connections also gave state specialists in family policy greater prestige and more exposure to new ideas. Internationalization after the Liberation took several forms: first, the cross-fertilization of the social sciences, which was especially potent in the field of demography, where American contributions from the Office of Population Research at Princeton and the work sponsored by the Ford, Scaife, and Rockefeller Foundations had a major impact on the French; and second, the development of international organizations, not least UNESCO, that promoted conferences on collaborative projects.[139] French family specialists also took a keen interest in developing the Union internationale des organismes familiaux (UIOF), founded in Paris in 1947 and meeting on a three-year cycle to enable government experts and family association leaders from twenty-four countries to discuss research and policy. Such an endeavor by its very nature reinforced the tendency of participants to play down the politics and play up the science of their common engagement with the family as a "basic," "permanent," and "universal" social unit that had become a "subject for the sciences."[140]

Colonial connections could similarly strengthen an expert's claim to authority. Here, Alfred Sauvy and Robert Debré were the most visible trendsetters. Sauvy, who weighed in frequently on population issues in UN-affiliated venues, spoke out forcibly in print and in policy deliberations on population policy in the French empire, especially in North Africa, where in the late 1940s he had warned of the dire political and social consequences of high birth rates among Muslims. By the 1950s he was using his prestige at INED and on the Haut Comité consultatif de la population et de la famille (HCCPF) to advocate methods of voluntary family limitation for Muslims in Algeria, despite the French anticontraception law of 1920 prohibiting it. As for Robert Debré, his main colonial involvements came through his new Centre international de l'enfance (CIE), which he created in 1950 to educate doctors, nurses, social workers, and teachers about pediatrics and infant hygiene and nurturing—first in Europe, then starting in 1951 in sub-Saharan Africa. Debré's international standing, not only in Africa through the CIE but also through his influence in UNESCO and UNICEF, bolstered his stature in the councils of Paris.[141] International and colonial networks of expertise had long amplified the voices of prominent policy elites.[142] That dynamic intensified after 1945.

Although these trends tended to concentrate power and know-how in the ministries, INED, and the HCCPF, deep knowledge about the state's many forms of family subsidies, family services, and their effects on actual families also came from other sources—from below, as it were, in associations, unions, the family and social security caisses, and an expanding social service infrastructure where lawyers, doctors, psychologists, and social workers labored at the intersection of policy and family life. Certainly Robert Prigent's rise to prominence via union militancy, local knowledge, and the Catholic family movement was a case in point. So too was the emergence of Alfred Lebel and Henri Raynaud as social policy point men, respectively, for FO and the CGT. Raynaud understood as well as anyone that knowledge was a prerequisite of power. As a CGT circular in 1946 put it when instructing local trade union leaders to seek out and train the most capable union members to serve on the newly created caisses, "some basic technical knowledge is indispensable," and because such knowledge was often hard to come by, unions ought to "plan to create a school for [caisse] administrators in every *département*."[143] France's vast new network of self-governing caisses, in short, created opportunities for both seasoned advocates and newcomers to family politics across the political spectrum to cultivate their own forms of expertise at the local level. The distinction between "militants" and "experts" became less clear.

As in the past, Parliament and political parties also served as hothouses for cultivating policy expertise, especially for longtime officeholders and stalwarts on committees. During the Fourth Republic women finally could take advantage of this opportunity. As Priscilla Prestwich has argued, female deputies and senators, especially in the MRP, made a deliberate effort to become self-described *techniciennes,* policy specialists who claimed authority through their mastery of the technicalities of a policy area rather than through the old-boy networks that were commonly denied them. Germaine Poinso-Chapuis certainly took this route by taking a sustained interest in marriage law, alcoholism, and economic planning. Her MRP colleague Francine Lefebvre worked the vineyard of labor legislation. Marie-Madeleine Dienesch did so through the issue of educational reform.[144] The party and trade union press also tended to rely on in-house specialists, such as the CGT's Andrée Cazaudon at *Antoinette,* who wrote regular features on social security and family policy issues. The state's post-Liberation expansion and restructuring of family subsidies, then, had two countervailing effects on the shape and distribution of expertise: it reinforced a concentration of specialized knowledge and cross-policy planning at the (mostly male) summit of the administrative state, and it evoked responses in caisses, parties, unions, and civil associations that expanded the number of voices (often female) who spoke about family policies with considerable knowledge of their own.

Nor were state officials alone in exploiting "scientific" claims to authority over matters of family and natality. The Communist Party and its CGT magazine *Antoinette* claimed for themselves a medical folk hero in Dr. Fernand Lamaze, a French gynecologist at the CGT's clinic for Parisian metalworkers, who after visiting natural childbirth clinics in the Soviet Union in 1951 launched a campaign for the use of the relaxational birthing techniques that came to be associated with his name. Proselytizing for the Lamaze method gave the PCF a chance to stress its pronatalist commitment and to tout "Soviet science"— Lamaze's techniques derived from work on stimulus-response by Ivan Pavlov in the 1920s—all the while employing the seemingly nonpolitical language of scientific expertise in making its case that "painless childbirth" ought to be an option for all women in France, whatever their circumstance.[145] "I decided," Lamaze said in *Antoinette,* "to educate expectant mothers, starting in the seventh month, as in the USSR." But because of the high rate of premature births, "due to the deplorable social conditions in which the wives of French workers lived, I moved the beginning of training up to the sixth month."[146] The Lamaze campaign, then, was rooted in medical and sociological expertise (not in a resistance to the hegemony of the medical establishment, as the natural childbirth movement would later become in the United States), and it was not that far removed from the politics of social class that was the bread and butter of the Communist Party. Sylvie Chaperon has even suggested that the party's promotion of "painless childbirth," a promotion that intensified in 1956, was motivated in part to convey a commitment to women's well-being at a time when *militantes* had been thrown on the defensive by the party's stunning, recalcitrant opposition to birth control.[147]

Likewise, the very birth control movement that the PCF opposed made its own appeal to scientific authority. To a degree this tactic was a necessity. The 1920 law prohibited public advocacy of birth control, including advertising. One way around this was to create a private, nonprofit association focused on research with the legal right to disseminate its findings to its members—which is precisely what birth control crusaders Marie-Andrée Lagroua Weill-Hallé and Évelyne Sullerot did when they created Maternité heureuse (Happy Motherhood), the principal birth control advocacy group of 1950s France. With the goal of protecting women's health and making every child a wanted child, Maternité heureuse published a quarterly bulletin of the same name and distributed it to its 2,000 to 3,000 member-subscribers. The bulletin made its case for contraception and family planning on medical and psychological grounds, not on the basis of women's rights and autonomy as we are accustomed to today, and it drew heavily on the expertise of birth control advocates abroad who had had the benefit of conducting studies under more favorable legal conditions. Maternité heureuse leaders understood they were cultivating expertise on this subject in a French setting that was not only legally rigged against them but also deeply hostile to them on a number of cultural grounds. As founder Weill-Hallé put it, "At first only we women were willing to take on the law, demographers, fearful doctors, cautious jurists, indignant nuns, and mocking men."[148] International connections, moreover, proved as crucial for these women as they did for state elites. In 1958 Maternité heureuse joined the International Federation of Family Planning, and then in 1960 became the more robust and consequential French Family Planning Movement, which would eventually see contraception legalized through the Neuwirth law of 1967.[149]

Although expertise on family matters and maternity expanded during the Fourth Republic through advocacy movements, political parties, and the activities of the caisses, as well as through the ministries and institutes of the state, it also expanded by way of another avenue: the propagation of domestic science. As in other countries, so too in France, efforts to teach young women skills in homemaking and child rearing became common in the late nineteenth century, even before Paulette Bernège in the 1920s became France's most prominent authority on how to adapt the rationalizing ideas of William Winslow Taylor to the everyday activities of household management. Bernège burnished the image of domestic science as *science*, as did the success of the immensely popular Salon des arts ménagers, the annual exposition at the Grand Palais in Paris featuring the latest technological advances in home appliances.[150] The Vichy government made domestic science courses mandatory for girls in the school curriculum. As Claire Duchen has pointed out, by making homemaking more a matter of technical expertise, proponents of domestic science claimed to be elevating the status of the housewife, even as it made her dependent on the experts in this field (and the husband who paid for the appliances).[151]

After the Liberation, domestic science got a big boost from the expanding use of *travailleuses familiales* (home service aides), young women hired for short-term stints in families where mothers were absent or waylaid by childbirth or infirmity. The MPF had popularized the "TF" as a salve to families suffering the burdens of absent fathers. Robert Debré and Alfred Sauvy had even proposed in their Liberation treatise, *Français pour la France,* that all young women perform obligatory national service as family aides. This notion proved a dead letter for lack of public support and state resources. But what did take off in the late 1940s was the use of discretionary funds under the control of the family caisses to fund *travailleuses familiales* to serve families in need.[152] The Ministry of Public Health and Population also put money behind this effort by paying for the training of TFs in the hope of bringing the latest ideas in domestic science to tens of thousands of families across the country. In 1949 the Ministry also established a Certificat des travailleuses familiales to standardize year-long technical training and examinations in fourteen national centers so that TFs would teach by example in the families they served. By the 1950s, then, family workers entered families with a knowledge ranging from Bernège's ideas for maximizing the efficient use of domestic equipment to notions of best practice in cooking, hygiene, family budgeting, and reading to children.[153] As Ministry communiqués summed it up, "The educative role of the family worker is essential, not only in poorly adjusted families but in every family in which they intervene."[154] Cross-class and cross-age encounters were not uncommon, to good or ill effect. One working-class mother described "the exchange of views" with her 20-year-old "bourgeoise" as "très chic," talking as they did about "all the problems of family life, . . . educating children, school problems, coming of age, marriage, even very sensitive conjugal matters, social questions, etc."[155]

Ambitions to use TFs as missionaries of household and parental expertise only rose during the 1950s. The ministry, by raising the minimum age of training to 21 in 1955, sought to make the position a *profession sociale* (social service profession).[156] By the end of the decade it had indeed become more of an adult profession than an apprenticeship for late teens. Professionalization did not, however, quickly translate into expansion. Funding still depended mainly on the caisses, which with their many priorities devoted only 14 percent of their discretionary monies to this purpose, so the number of TFs in the country in the late 1950s still hovered at around 4,500, much where it had been a decade before. Still, *travailleuses familiales* helped make family policy a domain of governance where claims to expertise were widely diffused in civil society. So too did another cadre of specialists, *conseillères ménagères* (household advisers), who as state-trained "experts en Arts ménagers" were hired by caisses, family associations, low-income housing projects, and department stores to disseminate housekeeping know-how at the grassroots, with the likely consequence of making mothers more aware of their rights in the postwar, family-centered welfare state.[157]

Did the proliferation of these many agents of family-related expertise change the political dynamics in the family policy domain? In principle, widely recognized forms of expertise, often formally certified, empowered the "experts" and gave the caisses and the agencies they worked for greater institutional heft. Even a casual reading of the periodical press on such topics as marriage counseling, child-rearing practices, and the importance professionals assigned to mother-child attachments makes it clear than many more types of voices were becoming part of the public conversation about the family.[158] Strictly speaking, policymakers were under little obligation to heed the views of the burgeoning legions of social workers, family aides, household advisers, family association leaders, and feminist advocates, who could all make legitimate claims to informed opinion. Still, there were signs in the 1950s and early 1960s that new voices were getting themselves heard.

Take, for example, the kerfuffle in the Paris region in 1954 over whether social workers in the infant and maternal protection services (PMI) should administer research surveys to the North African families in their purview. The many professional women who did this work—and virtually all social workers in these family-related services were women—carried large caseloads of young families with infants whom they tried to monitor through home visits. To win a parent's confidence in this inherently intrusive business, social workers sought to show they were there to advise, not police, the family—never an easy task but one made more difficult in working with North African families, who had good reason to think services and surveillance were deliberately linked.[159] So when the authorities asked social workers in 1954 to administer surveys to their North African clients, social workers pushed back. CGT members of the local caisses wrote the head of the social services coordinating committee for the Seine region that "we find very regrettable the use of social workers in conducting surveys that do not fall within the normal activity of providing social services," and that in running a survey of North African workers in France "we wonder whether its purpose is essentially social servicing or policing."[160] The administration backed down; an informal coalition of social workers, union representatives, and advocates with influence in the caisses prevailed. The country's expanding social service apparatus and the government's populationist ambitions were giving social service professions greater voice.

Another sign that new voices in family matters were breaking through came in the nascent field of consumer advocacy. Historian Rebecca Pulju has shown that as officials in the economic ministries and the Planning Commission began to give more attention in the 1950s to consumer demand as an engine of growth, they explored ways to use consumer advocates as advisers to state planners and consumers alike. A new state-sponsored Centre de recherche et documentation sur la consommation (Consumer Research and Documentation Center) sent domestic science educators and representatives from the Union française civique et sociale (UFCS) and the Union française de consommation to the United States on a Marshall Plan mission to study consumption. Not long after, representatives from the conservative Catholic UFCS and other women's and family organizations won appointments to the new National Committee of Consumption (Comité national de la consommation), created by the minister of national economy in 1960 to provide expert advice on consumer demand.[161]

Though only a modest foreshadowing of the larger consumer advocacy revolution that was to come in France a decade later, this co-optation of family advocates and domestic science experts into state planning satisfied the mutual ambitions of family-centered activists pushing their cause and state administrators seeking to fathom the mysteries of household consumption in a rapidly changing national economy.

Communication between top state officials and new experts in the family domain took another form in the creation of the much publicized "apartment referendum" of 1959, as historians Nicole Rudolph and Brian Newsome have both examined. De Gaulle's first housing minister for the Fifth Republic, Pierre Sudreau, sought out Catholic activist Jeanne Aubert-Picard to help him find a way to make public housing—the vast archipelago of *grands ensembles* being constructed in the periphery of France's cities—more appealing to the working-class families they were being built for. Aubert-Picard epitomized the new "expert" who found opportunities open up to her in the family policy domain of the 1950s. A veteran of the Catholic trade unions (CFTC), the Catholic youth movement (JOCF), and the MPF, Aubert-Picard had won election as a family association representative to the UNAF, which in turn picked her to represent the family movement in the government's prestigious Conseil économique et social (Social and Economic Council). She became a national figure—though still someone rooted in the everyday realities and associational world of her past, and hence an ideal collaborator for Sudreau, who, though a progressive Gaullist, former resister, and survivor of Buchenwald, was still a Sciences Po graduate and son of the Paris bourgeoisie. By drawing on their respective outlooks and expertise, Aubert-Picard and Sudreau joined forces to create an interview and survey project at the 1959 Salon des arts ménagères whereby thousands of respondents, mostly housewives, weighed in on how they would like to see the domestic spaces in public housing apartments configured. Aubert-Picard also interviewed 300 families residing in the *grands ensembles* about how they would like to refashion their abodes, and she consulted a large number of family associations and several domestic sciences organizations about the subject. Most architects ridiculed this ambitious engagement with residents as an affront to their professional wisdom about how people should dwell. But Sudreau and Aubert-Picard saw to it that their survey findings had an impact on design in the years that followed. Though hardly a bold leap into participatory design planning, the apartment referendum and the teamwork behind it signaled a growing respect for the advice that new kinds of experts, and in this instance even housewives themselves, could provide officials like Sudreau who were willing to listen.[162]

The ubiquity of family life, its centrality to the Catholic and Communist agendas during the Fourth Republic, a small but reviving feminist movement, and the state's investment in demographic growth as a cornerstone of the reconstruction all made it easier in the family policy domain, than say in taxation or industrial policy, for new voices to emerge with claims to expertise. The demographers and economists at INED and the Planning Commission certainly retained their influence, but they could hardly monopolize the policy conversation in a realm so vast and so subject to multiple forms of expert commentary as "the family" had become in the 1950s. Likewise, the sheer expansion since 1945 of the state's role in the regulation and provision of social services having a bearing on families, notably in education, health, and housing, diluted the control any single ministry or institute could exert over policy.[163] No government of the Fourth Republic could dare to imagine concentrating and orchestrating the principal experts and advocates of the family as state officials had tried to do under Vichy and even initially after the Liberation. Top officials were finding it harder to keep strategy in this policy domain simple and coherent. In the capstone speech summing up the deliberations at the 1958 world congress of the Union internationale des organisme familiaux (UIOF), Georges Desmottes, whose career as a family expert in the ministries of public health and population spanned from Vichy to the Fifth Republic, expressed deep disquiet about the mounting difficulty of "inserting" family interests within a state that had grown so complex in functions and that touched families in so many ways. "Under such conditions will the dialogue between family organizations and public authorities be likely to succeed?" The key, he felt, lay in creating some focal point—a ministry, a council, a powerful unit within a ministry, anything—to serve as the animating and coordinating organ of governance and the "familial conscience" of the state.[164] This suggestion, coming from an administrative insider just weeks after the

collapse of the Fourth Republic, could not have been more timely, what
with Charles de Gaulle setting out that summer to design a new republic. It remained to be seen, however, whether Desmottes's notions
of coherent dialogue, coordination, and "family conscience" could be
realized now that the variety of players and perspectives on family
policy had expanded so much under the Fourth Republic.

Family Policy from the Fourth to the Fifth Republic

By the mid-1950s, debates about family policy had sharpened, especially
over the single-wage allowance *(salaire unique)* and the state's influence over the caisses. The *salaire unique,* designed principally to
enable mothers to stay home with children, had critics from the start
in 1939, but its pronatalist and Catholic champions easily prevailed. By
the mid-1950s its defenders were also invoking research about the psychological importance of the mother-child relationship. Proponents of
the *salaire unique* also managed in 1955 to make it available to farm
families and in 1956 to all qualifying families of the self-employed.[165]
Yet the impact of the *salaire unique* on fertility was hard to measure,
and state officials disagreed about how big that impact might be. An
INED survey conducted in 1957 offered evidence that boosting the level
of the *salaire unique* would have little effect on women's employment
or childbearing decisions.[166] Proponents of the policy, of course, believed fervently in its efficacy. They could, after all, point to the fact
that participation in the workforce by mothers with two children
dropped to 17 percent in 1954 from 23 percent in 1947, though a shift
of this sort no doubt had multiple causes.[167]

Claims that the *salaire unique* actually worked as an incentive to
keep mothers at home made critics of the policy all the more determined to oppose it. Business lobbyists complained that many families
with two wage earners managed to get the *salaire unique* fraudu-
lently.[168] The CGT, the FO, and the Communist and Socialist parties
saw it as penalizing working mothers and rewarding the wives of well-
paid *cadres* who could afford to stay home. They called instead for
converting the *salaire unique* into a supplement to the family allowance for all mothers, regardless of employment.[169] In *Antoinette* the

CGT's Madeleine Colin made a point of citing evidence of the *benefits* to children and mothers alike when mothers worked.[170]

The Left's line of criticism of the *salaire unique w*as hardly new. What sharpened the debate more was the growing opposition of self-styled "economic modernizers"—business leaders, planners, and economists associated with the Planning Commission, the *mendé-sistes* at *L'Express* and the civil service, Pierre Mendès France himself, and a number of state-deficit-obsessed Radical Party politicians such as Edgar Faure—all of whom spotlighted productivity, not fertility, as the key to national renewal. They viewed women as crucial to the workforce in an expanding economy still hostage to the nation's chronic labor shortage. The Planning Commission's Second Plan (1951) had called for lowering the *salaire unique* for precisely the purpose of moving more women into employment.[171] By the draft of the Third Plan (1957), planners targeted women as especially important for the more highly trained technical and management positions opening up in industry, a "modernizer's" aim that dovetailed with the growing aspirations of young women, especially in the middle and upper-middle classes.[172]

Although the full force of second-wave feminism in France was still more than a decade away, a shift in expectations about careers for women was under way. As early as 1951 INED's scholarly journal, *Population,* published a study arguing that working wives had more say in the family and "a better situation with respect to their husbands" than nonworking wives—a sign, the researcher claimed, that the evolving condition of women was making the family itself a site of positive, dynamic change.[173] Another sign of shifting outlooks: *Réalités,* the glossy monthly magazine of the "modernizing" bourgeoisie, ran a noteworthy feature in 1955 on careers young women should consider, ranging from the more pioneering terrain of engineering, the high civil service (ENA having been open to women from its founding in 1945), and cinema and radio to the more traditional female careers such as teaching, "colonial nursing," and social work.[174]

To aspire to wider professional horizons, of course, was not necessarily to criticize the *salaire unique*. But this sacred cow of Catholic family policy in the 1940s saw its sanctity diminishing in the 1950s,

and most notably in the professional and business strata. As Remi
Lenoir has pointed out, even the policy's familialist defenders began
justifying it not simply on moral and patriotic principle, as in 1945, but
on the economistic grounds that homemaking contributed to national
income and hence that nonworking mothers deserved the equivalent
of a salary.[175] The Catholic Union féminine civique et sociale, for decades a leading stalwart of full-time motherhood, spoke of the subsidy
as "economically and socially beneficial for the country," not least
because of the purchasing power housewives were exerting in the
economy.[176] The "reconstruction" wing of the CFTC, the most "modernizing" faction in the Catholic trade union movement and hence
often allied with Mendès France on economic matters, sought to defend the *salaire unique* within the very terms of debate the *mendé-
sistes* had framed. The daily absence of mothers from the home, they
argued, "risks having the most regrettable impact on the birth rate and
on the life, health, and mental balance of children," producing in the
long term "a reduction in the size and quality of the future workforce
and a concomitant rise in the burden of unproductive people." A truly
progressive economy, in their view—"a civilization of real work"—
would make homemaking and mothering waged work: "The countries of northern Europe include in their national accounting the
contribution of domestic workers and the Beveridge Plan treats the
married woman, by the very fact of staying at home, as an employee."[177]
If the *salaire unique* still had plenty of advocates, the terms of debates
had moved to the turf of planners, progressives, and business leaders
who talked the talk of economic growth, a loose constellation of what
could be called the "productivists," who were gaining on the lead that
familialists still clung to in the debate.

Alongside the *salaire unique,* issues of governance created a second
major source of tension over family policy in the 1950s. Catholics had
in 1946 secured the independence of the family caisses from the social
security caisses. Parliament wrote that victory definitively into law in
1949. But fears for the autonomy of the family caisses intensified in
the 1950s—for good reason. The ministries and the state's auditing
authority, the Cour des comptes, tightened their oversight of the social
security and family caisses from the late 1940s on; the Cour had its
audit powers boosted in 1949, the ministries acquired more approval

power over caisses budgets in 1950, and then three years later over salary levels and contracts established by the caisses.[178] In the case of the social security caisses, some of the motivation for greater state oversight stemmed from the intensity of the Cold War political rivalries that rattled the caisses themselves, where Communists enjoyed a good deal of influence and clashed with their non-Communist opponents. In family caisses, Communists were weaker and board relations calmer.[179] The extension of state control there stemmed more from conventional political pressures to contain costs and enforce national guidelines for funding services. As Labor and Social Security Minister Daniel Mayer, a Socialist, put it 1949: "The character and size of the funds urgently demand state oversight of their management and use in the best interest of the country."[180] And indeed, state officials could extend their reach into caisses affairs all the way down to locality. The Ministry of Labor and Social Security insisted, for example, despite protest by the CNAF (the national council for the family caisses), that caisses subsidize families sending children to *colonies des vacances* (summer camps) but not family holidays.[181] When a local caisse in Annecy used funds to subsidize winter sports classes for children in 1957, orders came down from the ministry in Paris, via the regional director of social security in Lyon, to stop the subsidy.[182]

State intrusions on such a petty scale hardly constituted a full-scale assault on caisse autonomy. Not so something else far more serious: starting in 1952 the government began to enable local authorities to funnel contributions collected by the family caisses to cover deficits in social security caisses close by. Over the course of the Fourth Republic the government gradually increased the rate of employer contributions to the family caisses (to over 16 percent by the end of the decade), even as rates of population growth, once the baby boom was well under way, held fairly steady. Meanwhile, as early as 1949 the costs of medical care and old-age assistance began to exceed the contributions the social security caisses were taking in. Longer life spans and the baby boom were increasing the proportion of older and younger people in relation to the adult contributors to social security. By 1953 more than 41 billion francs raised for family benefits were shifted over to cover the swelling social security deficit.[183] This kind of thing was precisely what the victorious opponents of the *caisse unique* (a single fund for all welfare state provisioning) had always feared, and now it was the state administration, not the left-wing proponents of the *caisse unique,* that was violating the autonomy of the family caisses. Family advocates cried foul, as did employers, not only on account of the diversion of resources but also because of the *étatisation* this displayed.

Trade union activists castigated the expansion of the state's *tutelle* (oversight) authority just as vociferously, and each confederation had its own critique. CGT leaders, Jacobin in outlook as its Communist leadership was, urged the government to crack down harder on employers who avoided contributions to the caisses, and yet they also excoriated the administration for its "disastrous" *(néfaste)* bureaucratic penetration of the system with its "3,000 circulars, decrees, and laws in three years," as a CGT leaflet put it in 1950.[184] FO (non-Communist) campaign appeals in the 1955 caisses elections, drawing more explicitly on the idioms of the syndicalist and mutualist traditions, condemned the social security system as "centralized, inhumane, and state-controlled," and called for "caisse autonomy" and "eliminating the state's oversight."[185] CFTC (Catholic) leaders, as one might expect, were the most unremitting in highlighting the threat that state oversight posed for the family caisses. René Mathevet and Fernand Besse, key CFTC specialists on family policy in the 1950s, denounced the very notion that family caisses could have a surplus, and hence the diversion of family funds to such things as farmers' pensions.[186] Repeatedly in the pages of the CFTC's newspaper, *Syndicalisme,* they warned of the "ever growing trend toward *étatisation*" and "ministerial supervision of the caisses that is becoming ever more rigid and arbitrary."[187] The specter of *étatisation* had long been a staple in the rhetorical diet of Catholic activists and the CFTC, but the strengthening of the state's *tutelle* authority in family policy and social security now had enough foundation in the facts of the 1950s to make it a focal point of complaint across the spectrum of the trade union movement.

When in 1958 Charles de Gaulle and Michel Debré assumed leadership of the new Fifth Republic as president and prime minister, they encountered a family policy domain where the fundamental tenets of policy—child allowances, tax deductions for dependents, housing subsidies for families with children—still commanded consensus, but where controversy had deepened over the *salaire unique,* the state's *tu-telle,* and the financial autonomy of the family caisses. At first de Gaulle and Debré seemed to signal continuity for family policy: they kept on longtime MRP stalwart Paul Bacon as minister of labor and social security, later named the MRP's rising star Joseph Fontanet to run the Ministry of Public Health and Population, and appointed the venerable Robert Prigent to the Social and Economic Council and to head up a prestigious commission to examine the family benefit system. But in fact, de Gaulle and Debré had come to wager the grandeur of France not so much on family supports as on economic productivity and the capacity of French industry to adapt to competition within the new Common Market. Armed with the recommendations of the Rueff-Armand report on removing obstacles to economic expansion, including its call for job flexibility and day care to support working women, as well as an end to the *salaire unique,* Debré challenged the views of his own Prigent commission when it issued its more conservative report in 1961.[188]

The clash between Debré and the Prigent commission revealed how much had changed in the family policy domain since the Liberation. For one thing, the cleavage had widened between familialists and natalists. Most members of the commission, which included several of the old hands of family policymaking such as Prigent, Georges Mauco, and the UNCAF's Roland Lebel and Roger Monnin, reaffirmed the familialist agenda by making recommendations designed to buttress the autonomy of the family caisses from social security, to index family allowances to hikes in the minimum wage (the better to boost the benefit), and to strengthen support for larger families with stay-at-home mothers. They called for preserving the *salaire unique,* restricting it to families with two or more children, and keeping it going for families until children reached age 21 as long as they were still in school or apprenticeship.[189] Natalist benefits, in their view, such as maternity and prenatal supports or Michel Debré's proposal to provide financial incentives for couples to have children in the first five years of marriage, ought to come from the state budget and not from funds raised through the family allowance contribution. These proposals would expand the pie of the family benefit system.

Two voices on the Prigent commission dissented. One, most likely Michel Debré's father, Dr. Robert Debré, who was regarded as the commission's "most natalist" (rather than familialist) member, opposed the *salaire unique* altogether as an injustice to working mothers. The other, likely agricultural specialist Louis Leroy, objected to provisions that seemed unfair to rural families.[190] But the stance of the commission's majority was clear. They sought to use family benefits to reinforce the conventional family at a moment when many familialists feared that de Gaulle and Debré had forsaken them for their productivist economic agenda. The head of the CNAF put it in 1959, "I feel it like a very deep pain, as do millions of fathers and mothers likewise, this total absence of any allusion to the family in the speeches of General de Gaulle and Prime Minister Debré."[191] Prigent's commission apparently felt it too: "In reality," their commission report claimed, "the public has the right to wonder if France has a family policy or if there are only specific family-related measures taken in a social and economic policy conceived outside of a family perspective per se. This would doubtless explain, for example, the delay over these past years in compensating families for their financial burdens."[192] To press its case further, the commission called on the government to enlarge the authority of the Ministry of Public Health and Population so that it could serve as guarantor of a real family policy.

Prime Minister Michel Debré, who as a key Gaullist policy expert in 1945 would scarcely have dreamed of challenging the familialist establishment (nor needed to when familialism and natalism went hand in hand), now struck back hard—behind closed doors. In July 1961 he wrote directly to his ministers that "family policy has to maintain and consolidate the demographic recovery the country has made since the Family Code [of 1939]." No call, this, for unbridled population growth.[193] He would prefer, he said, to craft a policy that eliminated the *salaire unique* (a position the Labor Ministry apparently supported), raised the ceiling on wages taxed for family allowances and social security, and allowed funds to be moved across social programs (a capacity the Finance Ministry especially wanted the state to preserve). Debré also objected to the class bias he saw in expanding benefits to families with older children in school—something rural and working-class families were less likely to receive. Whereas familialists still insisted on the solidaristic principle that all families, whatever their income, be eligible for the same benefits, Debré spoke for a growing number of business elites and planners who thought it was time to consider means-testing social benefits.[194] Such an approach would enhance the state's ability to encourage women to work and shift resources to families most in need.

Could Debré realistically pursue all these goals over the fierce objections of the family movement and his own blue-ribbon Prigent commission? His own advisors were divided on this question. Some urged him on, others thought the *salaire unique* was untouchable. "Experience proves that a position restricting acquired benefits cannot be maintained for long in the social domain."[195] Sobriety prevailed. Debré relented on the *salaire unique*'s survival—but not on its financing. His Finance Ministry battled successfully with the Ministry of Public Health and Population to keep a lid on the benefit. And indeed, its share in the larger family benefit system, a share that had begun to decline in 1956, continued to slide through the 1960s. In 1967 the benefit finally became subject to rate variations depending on income and the age of the children.[196]

Though the Debré government of 1959–1962 did not bring a sea change to family policy, it did accelerate shifts that had been gathering strength in the 1950s. In this policy domain, as in a number of others, de Gaulle and Debré brought the long reconstruction era to a close and took initiatives that pointed to future developments. Continuities across the divide of the Fourth and Fifth Republics were clear to see, and they troubled staunch familialists. Debré's efforts to shift the balance from familialism to productivism built on momentum, as we have seen, from the 1950s. Likewise, by reasserting the Finance Ministry's control over distributing funds between the family caisses and social security, and by maintaining strong administrative oversight over the caisses themselves, the Debré government sustained what many critics regarded as a process of *étatisation* that had been under way for over a decade. Not for nothing in 1962 (as in 1955) did virtually every organization running candidates for the local caisse elections include a strong anti-*étatiste* statement in its campaign platform, as in, for example, the CFTC's election leaflet castigating the "intolerable stranglehold of the state."[197]

Pivotal though the Debré government was in shifting family policy priorities, change was hardly just an elite-centered, state-driven affair. Nor was it a simple by-product of the Gaullist party's eclipsing of the MRP after 1958, as much as this political transformation wounded the Catholic family movement. No, change in the domain of family policymaking came at least as much from civil society as from the state and party politics. And here the contrast with the tax reform story could hardly be starker. In the tax domain, top-down initiatives, concentrated expertise, weak interest-group mediation, and popular protest combined to make for a volatile trajectory toward reform, whereas the conditions in the family policy domain were nearly the reverse. Here, once the institutional revolution of the Liberation era had altered the policy landscape, ideas for reform came as much from below as above. Expertise became more widely situated, and change came slowly because of a surfeit of interest-group mediation. Conflicts over core issues in this domain—about women and work, means-testing benefits, and governance over the family benefit regime—became more intense in the 1950s simultaneously within the state and in society at large. Familialist, productivist, and natalist factions within the ministries, the Social and Economic Council, the Haut Comité consultatif de la population et de la famille, and other high councils of government all could point to associations, unions, and academic experts who supported their side in debate. Just at the moment when, as we have seen, Georges Desmottes was calling for the elevation of a ministry or agency to give unity and coherence to this realm of state action, state actors drifted farther apart, even in the supposed moment of technocratic supremacy in the early Fifth Republic. At the same time, societal actors—that legion of activists, associational leaders, caisse officials, experts, and quasi-experts who had a claim to knowledge and hence some modicum of authority in this realm—were also gravitating toward a greater variety of competing priorities. Communists and Catholics quarreled within their respective camps about the primacy of child-centered, natalist goals, one the one hand, over women-centered and productivist goals, on the other. The erosion of the 1945 natalist consensus both reflected and facilitated the rising strength of a still-nascent second-wave feminist movement that would put marriage-law reform and contraceptive rights squarely into the center of national political debate by the mid-1960s. When de Gaulle and François Mitterrand squared off in the presidential contest of 1965, they fought over women's rights, not family policy.

Family policy in the early Fifth Republic, then, became both stable and fluid as a domain of state-society relations. The basic policy instruments—family allocations, prenatal and maternity benefits, tax breaks, housing subsidies—remained in place. France kept its rank as Europe's frontrunner in devoting national income to family supports (and its laggard in funding old-age pensions).[198] True, experts continued to disagree on whether family benefits boosted fertility. Pierre Laroque displayed his doubts in the late 1960s when he wrote that the effect on the birth rate came "less perhaps by the material contribution [benefits] make to families than by the climate that they help create around childbirth and the idea of the family."[199] Still, family supports remained popular and were thought to be efficacious: despite commonplace quips that parents cynically had children for the things they could buy with the benefits (famously captured by novelist Christiane Rochefort's *Les petits enfants du siècle:* "the washing machine arrived with the twins"), family allocations still enjoyed overwhelming support in opinion surveys.[200] But the number of authoritative players in this policy domain had grown, as had discordance in their views. Neither the state nor the interest groups enjoyed the coherence and hierarchical discipline they had had in 1945. The family policy domain, in short, became more open to debate, ideas, and new voices. Paths opened up that made possible another wave of innovation in the 1970s and 1980s. A new generation of activists, experts, and politicians negotiated a distinctive blend of natalism, productivism, and feminism to make some of the most robust commitments in Europe to child care, preschool, part-time work, and parental leave. These breakthroughs had their origins in the debates that began to crystallize in the last years of the long reconstruction.[201]

5

Enterprise Politics

The Postwar Nationalizations

BUSINESS ENTERPRISES had long been zones of political combat in France, but at no time more so than in the final months of the German occupation and on through the reconstruction era. Contests of power between workers and management, and between public and private authority, lay in the balance. Not for nothing do most textbooks associate the first postwar years in France with big innovations in commercial enterprise—nationalizations in finance and industry, Monnet-style economic planning, and the establishment in large and medium-sized firms of *comités d'entreprise,* or works committees, giving employees greater voice in the workplace. A worker's right to strike, to join a union, even to participate "through the intermediary of his delegates in the collective determination of working conditions and the management of enterprises," found its way into the 1946 Constitution.[1] So, too, did women's "equal rights to men in all domains," and not least, it was to be assumed, in the workplace.[2] The inner workings of business enterprise—its social relations, decision making, financing, and linkages to the state—became a strategic site of experimentation, and contestation, in the postwar reconstruction. Indeed, France was the one country in Western Europe after World War II that adopted all three major innovations—nationalization, works committees, and planning—in its recovery effort. As historian Claire Andrieu has shown, Britain, West Germany, Austria, and Italy all tried one or two of these innovations, but not all three and not with the transformational ambitions of the French. Only in France did the Left, including the Communists, unite behind these initiatives, and only in France was the Right weakened and divided enough (thanks to collaboration and the Vichy debacle) to allow for such experimentation.[3]

Nationalized enterprises took center stage because it quickly became obvious that reconstruction depended heavily on their success, as did the effort to "modernize" the postwar economy. When the Monnet Plan of 1946–1952 opted to concentrate the vast majority of public investment—and Marshall Plan money—on electricity, gas, and coal, as well as rail transport, cement, and tractors, the spotlight on nationalized companies that were dominant in most of these sectors became brighter still.[4] Nationalized firms, moreover, brought into confrontation and partnership the heaviest hitters in the industrial economy—most of the CGT's biggest and most powerful unions and their Communist allies, many of the most experienced engineers, managers, and government experts in the country, and a number of leading politicians with business backgrounds and their own technical expertise. The state's authority over public enterprises also yoked the everyday life and governance of these enterprises to politics, to the shifting fortunes of political parties and the big interest groups. Nationalized enterprises carried the symbolic freight of their semantic association with the nation in an era where virtually every political party regarded reconstruction as an effort to restore France to a position of preeminence in the European economy, to define "France" for a new era.

Given their strategic and symbolic importance, nationalized enterprises became key sites of contestation throughout the long reconstruction era over the role of the state and the effort to reconcile a top-down recovery drive with democratic renewal. Just how government leaders, state experts, company managers, and trade unions negotiated these issues differed markedly from firm to firm. This chapter explores both the fate of nationalization as a major policy commitment over the long arc of the reconstruction era and the more particular fates of several nationalized firms as they forged different paths to the early

Fifth Republic. Those paths differed because market conditions, technology, company cultures, and the distribution of expertise did much to shape the character of governance and contestation in nationalized enterprise by the early 1960s. So too did the efforts of political elites to harness the nationalized sector to the "modernizing" agenda of the Planning Commission and the postwar reconstruction.

Nationalization as Continuity and Rupture

The French government carried out its postwar takeover of financial and industrial companies in three waves of nationalization. During the initial, "insurrectionary" wave, from September 1944 to the spring of 1945, de Gaulle's Provisional Government used its decree power to nationalize the Renault company, the aircraft engine firm Gnôme et Rhône, and the coalfields of the Nord and Pas-de-Calais. The Renault takeover was a powerful symbolic acknowledgment of the moral authority of the Resistance and a boon to the Communist-oriented CGT, which even by the late 1930s had made Renault's giant Boulogne-Billancourt plant its most prominent industrial bastion. Company owner Louis Renault conveniently died in the autumn of 1944 while awaiting trial for collaboration with the Nazis, making the firm's confiscation easier.[5] Gnôme et Rhône, sharing similar collaborationist notoriety, was combined with Renault's aircraft engine division to become the Société nationale d'études et de construction de moteurs d'avions (SNECMA). As for the northern coalfields, de Gaulle's government nationalized them more out of practical necessity. Miners there, who had forged an extraordinary degree of political solidarity under the oppressive conditions of direct Nazi occupation, insisted on a state takeover and a removal of their collaborationist employers as a condition for mining the coal that was now desperately needed for the renewed war effort against Germany.

The second wave of nationalizations, more than a year later, from December 1945 to May 1946, required more planning and deliberation because it involved so many firms and because the final decisions were made through the wrangling of parliamentary legislation, not decree. In December 1945, the Constituent Assembly nationalized the four largest deposit banks (Crédit Lyonnais, the Société Générale, the Comptoir national d'escompte, and the Banque nationale pour le commerce et l'industrie), which possessed roughly half of all bank accounts.[6] In the words of the MRP (Christian Democratic) deputy François de Menthon, though no radical he, the hope was to "liberate democracy from the power of money."[7] The following spring the Assembly passed bills nationalizing gas and electricity (eventually becoming Gaz de France [GDF] and Électricité de France [EDF]), coal mining nation-wide (creating nine regional state corporations capped by a central authority, the Charbonnages de France), and thirty-four of the largest insurance companies (roughly half that sector).[8] After nearly a two-year hiatus a third wave followed, which was but a faint echo of the previous two. In 1948, under the moderate, MRP-led government of Robert Schuman, Air France became a mixed company (with a minority position for private shareholders), as did two large firms in maritime transport.

Unlike in Britain, where Clement Attlee's Labor government car-ried out nationalizations at a comparatively orderly and deliberate pace from 1945 to 1950, in France decisions came in a punctuated series of more politicized initiatives. Each nationalization differed from the others in the circumstances of its creation and the leadership involved. The French process lacked a clear overall design. What emerged was a diversified collection of public enterprises, each unique in structure, governance, company culture, and relationship to the market.[9]

However disorderly, France's postwar nationalizations had some precedents, so that historians making the case for long-term continu-ities have a lot to go on. Since 1919 the CGT had made nationaliza-tions a centerpiece of its program, and the basic notion that industries like mining, railroads, and insurance ought to be taken out of the hands of the "trusts" (the wealthiest business elite) and put to the service of the nation had become popular in left-wing circles as early as the late nineteenth century.[10] Léon Jouhaux, the CGT's longtime moderate leader, embraced this tradition and would remain a key voice in debates over nationalization on into the 1950s. He viewed public enterprises as vehicles for democratizing economic life and for bringing dyna-mism to crucial sectors of the economy that capitalists alone could not be trusted to run efficiently with an eye to the nation's future. At the same time, Jouhaux shared the CGT's syndicalist heritage of distrusting the state. Public ownership of a company carried the inherent danger of *étatisation*—of the firm becoming a deadened, rigidly controlled creature of the state bureaucracy—and nobody wanted that. To avoid it, Jouhaux insisted, a tripartite board (representing employees, consumers, and the state) would have to govern each public enterprise and oversee its top management.

That idea, plus the notion that nationalizations should go hand in hand with economic planning, became central to the political agenda of the non-Communist Left in the 1930s. "Planiste" Socialists, such as André Philip and Jules Moch, along with Jouhaux's moderate wing of the labor movement, saw the 1936 victory of the Popular Front—the electoral alliance of Communist, Socialist, and Radical Parties—as their chance to make extensive nationalizations a reality. The more moderate Radical Party objected. Communists balked, too, for the sake of keeping the Radicals in the Popular Front and out of a belief that nationalizations, if done before a revolutionary seizure of state power, would only shore up capitalism. As a result, Léon Blum's Popular Front government nationalized only armaments and aircraft construction, and it amalgamated the railways into a single mixed company, the Société nationale des chemins de fer (SNCF), with 51 percent state ownership. This Popular Front experiment with nationalizations, limited though it was, had an enduring political impact. The SNCF experience reassured the Right: private owners of railway firms got plush indemnities from government buyouts and a continuing influence in the firm; workers got no seats on the new company board.[11] By contrast, the aircraft experience inspired the Left: there, workers won some say on the factory floor and representation on company boards and national coordinating committees in Paris. Long-skeptical Communists began to consider whether nationalization might possibly hold some revolutionary potential after all.[12]

Although the Left owned the birthrights to nationalization, Vichy officials did nothing to reverse what the Popular Front had begun. State controls, after all, offered advantages to a right-wing government as well. Pétain's Vichy regime took over the private news service, Agence Havas, which would become Agence France-Presse after the war.[13] Jean Bichelonne, Vichy's technocratically inclined minister of industrial production, welcomed the added leverage public enterprises gave him to regulate the economy, inaugurate state planning, and negotiate with the German occupying authorities over business arrangements. Although Pétain's government refrained from further nationalizations, it did let stand the Popular Front takeovers in railroads and aviation. Meanwhile, the banking law of 1941 arguably did more to curb the autonomy of private bank lending and expand government oversight of credit than did the later nationalizations of commercial banks in 1945.

Still, for all Vichy's dirigisme, it was in the Resistance that postwar planners harbored the grand ambitions for nationalization that were to bear fruit in the Liberation era. Nearly every important planning group in the Resistance made a priority of some version of nationalization. André Philip and the Socialists proffered the most radical vision. They hoped to give government the capacity to plan the economic future by nationalizing transport, banks, insurance, mines, and electricity.[14] At the more sober and conservative end of the spectrum, the de Gaulle–backed Comité général d'études viewed nationalization in more limited terms as a way to take monopolistic firms out of the hands of "trusts."[15] It fell to the National Council of the Resistance (Conseil national de la Résistance, or CNR) to work out a compromise, but the Left's influence was obvious. The CNR's 1944 charter avoided the word "nationalization" but issued a call "to return to the nation the major means of production, the fruit of our common labor, the sources of energy, the riches underground, the insurance companies and big banks."[16]

Given how popular the idea of nationalizations appeared to be in the Resistance and how fervently men like Mendès France, André Philip, and Jules Moch pushed it, it is easy to see the nationalizations of the Liberation era growing right out of the 1930s. In this realm of public policy, as in a number of others, the Fourth Republic began, in a sense, with the Popular Front in 1936. But if we make too much of these continuities, we can underestimate how serious a rupture occurred in 1944 and how much the work of creating nationalized firms in 1944–1946 reflected the impact of events and the volatility of political circumstance. The postwar nationalizations, especially those of the second wave in 1945–1946, were by no means inevitable, despite the momentum for them that seemed to emerge from the National Council of the Resistance.

For one thing, the CNR charter papered over important differences of opinion and ambivalent convictions. Some Communists had not completely jettisoned their doubts about nationalizations. The Christian-Democratic MRP was nothing if not internally divided about many matters of policy. Although the party's leader, Georges Bidault, and the head of the Catholic labor movement (the CFTC), Gaston Tessier, had signed the CNR charter, many members at the grassroots had a more conservative economic outlook. Just how far de Gaulle was willing to go with nationalizations remained unclear. His interest in the idea had little to do with challenging capitalism or enhancing workers' rights and everything to do with buttressing the state's capacity to restore national grandeur. His wartime pronouncements on the subject had a studied vagueness. "No monopoly," he said in 1942 in his speech on the "new democracy" to come with liberation, "will be able to abuse men nor erect barriers to the general interest." A few months later he described a new "economic and social regime where no monopoly or coalition can impinge on the state, nor determine the fate of individuals, and where, as a consequence, the principal sources of our common wealth will be either explicitly administered or at least overseen by the nation."[17] Such statements fell far short a nationalization plan.

Indeed, what made the idea of nationalizations so useful politically in the postwar planning of the Resistance was its very ambiguity. It seemed to offer a method for making fundamental structural changes in an economy that the Resistance, much of the public, and even many Vichy officials believed had let the country down before the war. It satisfied a yearning after the defeat of 1940 for strong medicine against "economic Malthusianism" (habits of risk aversion, protectionism, market cartelization, and other ways of behaving defensively that were thought to shackle entrepreneurial drive). But how much of a change nationalizations would actually bring about was hard to say. Would postwar public enterprises assume the anodyne qualities of the prewar SNCF or something more radical—a genuine sharing of power with employees at the workplace and a powerful coordination of investment at the national level? The uncertainty of the prospect made possible the near unanimity of support for the nationalization clause in the CNR charter, and hence helped hold the fractious coalition of the

Resistance together. So, too, did the nationalism inherent in the very word itself. As early as 1919, advocates for nationalization had made their case on republican grounds as well as socialist ones, highlighting for the general public the national interest at stake in nationalization. During the Occupation the rhetoric of patriotism and anticapitalism became even easier to weave together, given the prevalence of business collaboration with the Germans, so that nationalization could be construed as the logical consequence of purging traitors and "liquidating the trusts."[18] But the patriotic resonance in the call for nationalization made it difficult to gauge how much of a challenge to big business its advocates were prepared to make. On the eve of the Liberation, then, almost everything about a postwar nationalization drive—its reach, its timing, its implications for French capitalism and workers' power—remained unknown. And it would take quite a while for the character of nationalization in France to become clear. As late as November 1945 a mainstream business newspaper would still be asking whether nationalizations would take more a "Western" (Occidental) British form (measured, rational) or an "Eastern" (Oriental) Czech form (vast, political).[19]

Two initiatives, one from societal groups locally, the other from de Gaulle's leadership group at the apex of power, would come to have an enormous impact on the first two waves of nationalization. The societal initiative began late in the summer of 1944. As territory became liberated, especially in cities and towns in southern France and in the coalfields and industrial areas of the northeast, workers and ardent activists in the Resistance began taking control of mines, factories, and offices building. They established management committees to assume authority over the workplace, and in many companies they seized collaborationist employers or sent them fleeing. Resistance work had given many CGT activists the moral authority to carry out this shift in political power in local enterprises. By autumn 1944 de Gaulle's Provisional Government had to acknowledge a wave of "wildcat nationalizations" in the mines of the North. In many southern cities and towns, factory seizures had a similar spectacular aspect, not least in Marseille, where workers pressured de Gaulle's republican commissar to requisition fifteen companies, and Toulouse, where aircraft workers negotiated an "accord de Toulouse" that gave them a prominence on management committees in their companies. As we have seen, workers and activists took command of their place of employment not to rebel against de Gaulle's state-in-the-making but to invite the state to expand its stewardship over the economy on their behalf. These actions reinforced the call for widespread nationalizations and raised workers' hopes that they could win greater voice through public enterprise. Communist leaders dropped any lingering inhibitions about pushing the CNR's nationalization agenda.

The leftward drift of public sentiment at the Liberation gave the grassroots campaign for nationalization additional momentum. According to national polls in October 1944, 65 percent of all respondents, and 79 percent of workers, favored greater employee voice in the management of their firms. In November 60 percent of respondents supported nationalizing the mines, and in December 68 percent of Parisians wanted the city's gas services publicly owned.[20] These figures did not reveal people's underlying views. Did they wish to socialize the economy, or simply bring down the biggest collaborators and the "trusts"? Did they recognize the unions and the government as fresh, patriotic agents better equipped than private entrepreneurs to jumpstart the postwar economy? Or were they simply angry at companies that acquired rare supplies or coal and electricity while ordinary citizens suffered blackouts?[21] Communist ministers Charles Tillon and François Billoux (of Air and Public Works, respectively) privately urged Minister of National Economy Pierre Mendès France to promote nationalizations, "not as socialist measures, which they aren't, but as a national necessity, an effort to put an end to the control of the French economy by those men of the trusts who are guilty of high treason."[22] Patriotic cards were trumps in 1945, and Communist leaders knew how to play them as well as anyone. Still, the mood of the country at the Liberation had clearly moved left on industrial policy. Pierre Lefaucheux, engineer, establishment figure, and company director in the private sector before the war, now spoke of "the bankruptcy of capitalism" that had become apparent when "a whole fraction of the *patronat* rushed into collaboration" in 1940.[23] This broad shift in public sentiment found expression where it mattered most—at the ballot box. There, in October 1945, Communists and Socialists together won a majority in the Constituent Assembly. This victory gave left-wing politicians the power to push forward the second wave of nationalizations.

Alongside these popular pressures to create public enterprises and democratize their management, de Gaulle set about trying to lower the political temperature. He sought delay by announcing that any further nationalizations would have to await the Allied victory over Germany and new elections. At the same time, the big business lobby, though weakened politically by wartime collaboration, urged moderation and probably saved the steel industry from a government takeover.[24] Within de Gaulle's cabinet the battle lines hardened between finance minister and businessman René Pleven, who doubted the wisdom of nationalizations, and the minister of national economy, Pierre Mendès France, who favored tight money to curb inflation, a powerful economic planning agency housed in his own ministry, and extensive nationalizations—in banking, insurance, energy, machine tools, air transport, merchant shipping, and steel. In Mendès France's view all three elements— austerity, nationalizations, and planning—were essential for national recovery and of a piece, because only with extensive nationalizations, he thought, would workers accept austerity and a reconstruction effort that favored investment over consumption.[25] "I believe the country will accept these harsh necessities," he told de Gaulle's cabinet, "if it believes it is for the collective interest and not, as before, for the profit of special interests."[26] This political gamble de Gaulle was unwilling to make. As head of state he opted for the more politically palatable path of easy money, a weaker planning authority (which he gave to Jean Monnet to establish as the Planning Commission), and fewer nationalizations. Mendès France had played out his hand and resigned from the government in March 1945.

With de Gaulle on the brakes and the Left on the accelerator, the second wave of nationalizations finally lurched forward after the Communist-Socialist electoral breakthrough in October 1945. De Gaulle and Pleven had stalled a bank nationalization bill. Now the left-wing parties pushed it through. The spotlight then shifted to Marcel Paul (Figure 5.1), the minister of industrial production and a Communist. Paul had risen to political prominence as a luminary in the Communist trade union movement—first in the 1930s as a leader in the electrical workers union, then as a key figure in the Communist Resistance and a survivor of Nazi torture in France and deportation to Auschwitz and Buchenwald. As minister, he now took the lead in shepherding the nationalization bills for electricity and gas, the coal

FIGURE 5.1 Cabinet ministers Amboise Croizat (center) and Marcel Paul (with the light suit, just behind), 1946. Both men became leaders of their Communist trade unions in the 1930s, Croizat in metalworking, Paul in electricity, and then had harrowing experiences during the war. As labor minister in de Gaulle's Provisional Government, Croizat worked with Pierre Laroque to put social security and family allocations on their postwar footing. As minister of industrial production, Paul orchestrated the big nationalizations of 1946, leaving his mark especially on EDF-GDF (electricity and gas). Mémoires d'Humanité/Archives départementales de la Seine-Saint-Denis. All rights reserved.

industry, and insurance. By May 1946 the Left had moved all these measures through Parliament, where much of the debate focused on how amply to indemnify the former private owners of the companies that would now compose these huge new public enterprises. Although the conservative PRL (Parti républicaine de la liberté) and the Christian Democratic Party (the MRP) championed the cause of owners, in the end most Socialists also went along with generous terms for them, as did even the Communists, who feared the electoral costs of alienating the many small shareholders in the electrical business.[27]

This second great wave of nationalization then suddenly came to a close. Christian Democrats (MRP) made important gains in the June 1946 elections for the Second Constituent Assembly. Though the

MRP had many left-wingers—men and women of a dynamic Catholic Left that had made its mark in the Resistance—the party straddled left and right. Much like de Gaulle, the MRP sought to rein in the Communists and Socialists, who now in the new Assembly could no longer claim a commanding majority. What's more, Socialists began to have their own reservations about pushing the nationalization drive much further. They worried about the rapid ascendency of Communist trade unionists in the burgeoning new public sector. The essential political coalition propelling the second wave of nationalization—a parliamentary alliance of Communists, Socialists, and enough left-leaning members of the MRP to go along—began to disintegrate nearly a year before Prime Minister Paul Ramadier was to throw the Communists out of his government in May 1947. The tepidness of the third wave of nationalizations in 1948 followed as a result.

Meanwhile, within the nationalized enterprises themselves a quiet revolution had gotten under way. Labor activists in the aircraft industry built on the initiatives they had taken during the Popular Front in the 1930s to reassert a significant role for employees in the management of their nationalized firms. And they found an ally in de Gaulle's air minister, Charles Tillon. A longtime Communist himself (though with a streak of independence for which the party would later punish him), Tillon had led the Communists' armed resistance in France during the Occupation. Now as minister, he named to head the aircraft companies men who had their own stellar Resistance credentials and a commitment to work cooperatively with the CGT in their firms. Fellow Communist Marcel Paul, as minister of industrial production, similarly appointed men who could work with the CGT. He named Auguste Lecoeur to run the new coal authority, the Charbonnages de France. Lecoeur, a miner himself and Communist leader of the miners' CGT union, had famously led a coal strike of 1941 that was the first such labor movement challenge to Nazi authorities in France. For the EDF-GDF Marcel Paul named Pierre Simon, a top administrator in the electrical industry as well as in the state's energy bureaucracy who had been fired by the Vichy government, had subsequently been imprisoned (only to escape through help from the Resistance), and was well regarded by the CGT.[28] Pierre Lefaucheux, no Communist either but an engineer and businessman who had risen to the top echelons of the

Parisian Resistance and had acquired strong credibility with the CGT, took up the reins at Renault. For leadership of the SNCF (rail) and its vast rebuilding efforts, the government replaced collaborationist management first with the team of Marcel Flouret and Maurice Lemaire, who were then replaced in 1949 with Pierre Tissier and Louis Armand, the latter a brilliant engineer and a legendary Resistance figure passionately committed to the modernization of the rail system.[29]

Company leadership of this type made it easier for CGT activists to acquire stature and influence within these public enterprises. They won positions on the tripartite governing boards of these firms, not only as employee representatives but often as consumer delegates as well. Liberation-era legislation had also mandated *comités d'entreprise*, or works committees, in all large public and private firms, and in these venues too the CGT solidified power, because it fell to these committees to oversee the many social services—cafeterias, summer camps, medical clinics, benefit programs—that major employers had provided paternalistically in the past. Works committees did not have jurisdiction over a company's core activity, production itself. But in a few nationalized firms—the aircraft companies, Renault, and the EDF-GDF—the government called for mixed production committees, composed equally of employee and management representatives, to advise on methods and conditions on the factory floor. This innovation took these firms one step further beyond the customary exclusion of labor from decision making in the industrial workplace.[30]

As another sign of the labor movement's advance, a good many white-collar employees—engineers, technicians, midlevel managerial staff—threw their support behind the CGT and shared left-wing hopes for making public enterprises the dynamic vanguard of postwar industrial renovation. They hoped, too, that with new high-quality managerial leadership and the expectations for the postwar reconstruction at stake, firms like Renault, the EDF-GDF, and the SNCF would offer new opportunities for meritocratic career advancement.[31] The major union of engineers and technicians in the electrical and gas sectors, for example, argued strenuously for the full nationalization of the production, transport, and distribution of electricity and gas, whereas business moderates had been hoping to keep distribution private.[32]

Labor's crowning achievement in these early days of the postwar nationalizations was the statute Marcel Paul created for employees at the EDF and the GDF in 1946. He got Socialist Prime Minister Félix Gouin to sign the *ordonnance* "on a table corner" shortly before the latter fell from power.[33] The statute established pension and vacation rights, equal treatment for female employees, paid leave for family emergencies, protection from arbitrary dismissal, and advancement on the basis of merit and seniority. In its sharpest departure from conventional company culture, the statute also created codetermination committees giving labor and management representatives oversight of hiring, promotion, discipline, and job descriptions. The Charbonnages de France and the SNCF soon got similar statutes.

The architects of nationalization after the Liberation certainly drew on continuities from the interwar past. Léon Jouhaux's CGT program of 1919 gave them their ideas about tripartite boards. They learned from the first big experiments in railroads and aviation from the Popular Front. But the Liberation marked a rupture as well. Factory seizures and sequestrations in many cities and towns, the leftward shift in public sentiment at the Liberation, the thirst for retribution against the most egregious business collaborators, the CGT's emergence from the Resistance as a powerful instrument of political mobilization both locally and in Paris, and not least, the newfound electoral prowess of the Communist and Socialist parties and the allies they also found in the Catholic Left—all these developments converged to make 1944–1946 a singular moment for advocates of nationalization. By vastly expanding the reach of public ownership and radically altering the internal political life of public enterprises, they used their moment. Whether in the Constituent Assembly, the staff meetings of Marcel Paul's Ministry of Industrial Production, or the new works committees and mixed production committees, champions of nationalization thrived on continuity and rupture in equal measure.

Purging, Taming, and Consolidation

Had labor and the Left managed to stabilize a new status quo as it had emerged in most public enterprises at the end of 1946, the postwar settlement of the Liberation era would have looked very different from what it turned out to be. It would have been based on a new system of shared power in the workplace and the ministries.[34] Inclusion of the Communists in the cabinet and at the head of most of the economic ministries, nationalizations and the voice they initially gave workers in the management of public enterprise, Monnet's first efforts at planning that included representation for labor as well as business—these major institutional achievements for the Left brought social peace to industrial France for almost three years after the summer of 1944. It was a period of low strike rates and high productivity. Communists and CGT militants hammered home relentlessly the productivist slogans of their "battle for production," first to win the war against Hitler and then to jump-start a national recovery—and to burnish their reputations as responsible partners in governance.

The achievements of 1945–1946, however, were anything but stable in the face of France's internal tensions and the advent of the Cold War. The tripartite coalition of Communists, Socialists, and Christian Democrats governing since the Liberation—first with de Gaulle, then without him—came under greater strain. Since November 1946 outright war in Indochina against Ho Chi Minh's Soviet-supported nationalist movement had made Communist participation in the government more difficult, as did the announcement of the Truman Doctrine the following March, whereby American officials openly committed their country to countering the Soviet threat. France's Socialist prime minister, Paul Ramadier, felt growing American pressure to drop Communist ministers from his government, especially given signs that Americans might then invest more in Western Europe's recovery. What brought things to a head were wildcat strikes against wage restraints at Renault and the SNCF. Outflanked by Trotskyists and other radicals to the left, Communists and the CGT felt they had to repudiate Ramadier's wage policy if they were to retain command of their constituents. On May 4, 1947, the Communist Party voted no confidence against Ramadier's economic policy, and the following day the prime minister sacked the Communist ministers in his government. The Cold War division within French domestic political life began to harden, and it congealed all the more the following September when Stalin summoned Communist Party leaders from across Europe to the Polish mountain village of Szklarska Poreba. There the Soviets baptized the new Cominform (Communist Information Bureau), replacing the old Third International of the interwar years. They committed the Communist parties of Western Europe to oppose their "bourgeois" governments by all possible means and to reject the Americans' Marshall Plan, which had been announced three months before. French Communists, abandoning the "battle for production," now threw themselves behind the fierce strikes that followed.

These seismic international and domestic developments set the stage for a protracted struggle for power in France's public enterprises that would make the late 1940s feel like a period of Thermidorean reaction—reminiscent of that phase in the French Revolution when moderates sought to reverse gains of radicals before them. Communist visibility in most public enterprises made these companies obvious sites of combat in the early days of the Cold War. Many business leaders and politicians were eager to see, in the words of an internal memorandum at the CNPF (the business peak organization, the Conseil national du patronat français), a "depolitization" of public enterprises and a "counterpurge."[35] Less than a fortnight after Ramadier fired his Communist ministers in early May 1947, René Mayer, a leading Radical and a centrist, published a remarkable article in *France-Libre* entitled "Democracy and Nationalizations." There he acknowledged the need for some nationalizations in the wake of the Liberation but thought the process had been too feverish and ambitious. He admired Britain's more modest approach, especially in the banking sector (only the Bank of England had been nationalized), and he regarded the sobriety of the SNCF's nationalization in the 1930s as the model that should have been followed. Most of all, he warned of "the danger of trade union influences." "The state," he wrote, "cannot run the political risk of failing in its task of organizing the economy's public sector by seeming to hand that task over to some technocrats who come from the unions. . . . Democracy would have a new danger to dread, which all republicans have a duty to think about." By raising the specter of a technocracy rooted in the very success of the unions to anchor their influence in state enterprise, Mayer was putting to ironic use a rhetoric most commonly deployed after the Liberation by the Left. He concluded by doubling down on this tactic: "If nationalizations are to be in line with the development of democracy, they have to be conceived and realized in such a way as not to crush, under the grip of totalitarian state socialism, democracy itself."[36] The PCF and the CGT, Mayer was all but saying, had come to embody the technocratic threat to democracy by overplaying their hand in nationalized enterprise. He had thrown down the gauntlet for the anti-Communist combat to come in the public sector.

Even though center-rightist René Mayer proved especially clever in invoking democratic principles to promote an attack on Communist power in public enterprise, it was in the widening rift between Socialists and Communists that the bitterest battle lines formed. Socialists were still fully committed to nationalized firms, on whose success, they believed, depended "the possibility of organizing a healthy economy in the service of the collective good, and of liberating the workers and enabling them to fully attain humane conditions."[37] But they worried about the power the PCF had acquired in many public enterprises, or as one party leader put it, "the harm to be done by Stalinists, more anxious to transform nationalized companies into political fortresses in the service of their propaganda than to endow France with an essential means of improving its economy."[38] Hence, Socialists replaced company directors who were too close to the CGT, and new directors in turn shook up their managerial ranks and trimmed back CGT representation on tripartite boards. Keen to limit Communist and CGT influence, officials tended to pull decision making back into the director's office or the ministries. Nowhere was this struggle over industrial authority tougher than in coal mining, where the government and the new leadership at the Charbonnages de France sought to rationalize work methods, cut wage rates, and diminish the power of production committees—actions that CGT leaders condemned in patriotic terms as "the betrayal of the nation's interest and independence."[39] In the great coal strike of 1948 over these issues, the government eventually prevailed after sending troops and armored cars into the mining towns of northern France (see Figure 5.2). Big strikes in nearly all the other nationalized sectors in 1947 and 1948 brought the CGT similar setbacks and crystallized its own internal schism with the non-Communist trade union faction, Force ouvrière (FO), which Léon Jouhaux and Robert Bothereau went on to establish as an independent trade union confederation. After a decisive strike in 1947 in the aircraft

FIGURE 5.2 Soldiers entering a miners' town during the coal strike of 1948. When Communist trade union leaders led miners into an industry-wide strike in October 1948, Interior Minister Jules Moch sent in the army to secure the mines and break up the protest. Eight miners died. After fifty-six days, the government prevailed. The CGT's defeat signaled a reversal for miners in securing a voice within their industry, and it deepened the Communist Party's political isolation in Cold War France. © Pigiste/Agence France Presse.

industry, management carried out draconian cuts in a workforce that everyone recognized was too large for the conditions of the postwar airplane market, reductions that by 1950 had diminished the industry's workforce by half. And aircraft was hardly alone in trimming payrolls. In 1948 Minister of Industry and Commerce Robert Lacoste announced 20 percent cuts in the workforces of the EDF and GDF.[40]

Huge layoffs gave employers opportunities to rid their companies of labor radicals, as did the split between the CGT and FO. Labor's newly won authority at the workplace diminished commensurately. Company directors either reduced the importance of production committees or liquidated them altogether, as did Pierre Lefaucheux at Renault in 1948, at considerable cost to his relationship with the CGT. A decree in 1950 transformed the personnel boards at the EDF from decision-making to consultative bodies.[41] When the dust finally settled in the early 1950s after several years of purging and reorganization, many public enterprises had changed a great deal in management structure, political character, and public image from what they had been before 1947.[42] In the eyes of the Communist press, high civil servants, who like everyone else had condemned in principle *l'étatisation* of public enterprises, had promoted a shift in managerial authority that accomplished just that.[43] Even the more moderate trade union stalwart Léon Jouhaux decried the trend in no uncertain terms. "The progressive slippage of nationalized firms toward state monopoly," as he called the concentration of authority in the ministries and high civil service, "would bring about not workers' emancipation but a totalitarian civilization that destroys the individual."[44]

Taking the measure of the postwar settlement in public enterprise, then, requires assessing the outcome of both the Liberation era and the Thermidorean years that followed. The initial achievements of shared power in 1946 gave way to a more complicated arrangement by the early 1950s that consolidated the place of nationalized enterprises in the French economy and institutionalized a high level of combativeness in labor relations. Surprisingly, unlike in Britain where conservatives in the 1950s campaigned hard for denationalization and managed to achieve it in the steel industry, in France the cause of privatization became marginalized. As Raymond Aron told his conservative readership, the nationalizations were "irreversible," both politically and financially. Private investors, apart from in the insurance sector, in his view, could now scarcely summon enough capital to repurchase these immense firms from the state.[45] To be sure, diehard critics of nationalization in the Senate, André Armengaud and Marcel Pellenc in particular, still had a scattered following. In late 1940s and early 1950s outright opponents of nationalization *tout court*—many of them associated with a laissez-faire wing of the Radical Party—grabbed the opportunity Thermidor offered them to attack the very idea of public enterprise. Some journalists on the business Right went so far as to claim that nationalizations had set France on a course for "dictatorship": "The employer having disappeared, the policeman takes his place. With competition removed, despotism takes hold."[46] Left-wing activists responded just as vehemently, calling their opponents "the gravediggers of industry" and condemning attacks on nationalization as "contrary to the national interest and dangerous for democratic institutions."[47]

But for all the rhetorical intensity of this pro- and anti-nationalization talk in the late 1940s, the notion of reprivatizing the nationalized firms of the Liberation era remained little more than the pipe dream of the doctrinaire laissez-faire Right for the rest of the long reconstruction. Indeed, the big business lobby (the CNPF), along with early skeptics about nationalization in the high civil service, made their peace with the postwar nationalizations, and they did so for several reasons. Most obvious was the comfort they took in the diminished power of the CGT and the Communists in the public sector and the certainty that no new nationalizations would occur. It helped, too, that no single party could claim patrimony to the nationalizations of 1944–1946, which were, in fact, the product of compromise.[48] That political consensus did not, of course, automatically translate into strong business support for public enterprise. In 1949 the Monnet Plan's chief economist, Pierre Uri, had complained about the religious fervor with which some people in the business community seemed to oppose the nationalized sector.[49] That same year the CNPF did register their concerns to Treasury Director François Bloch-Lainé that such a large portion of Marshall Plan aid found its way into nationalized firms.[50] In fact, a good deal of that aid supported a renovation of the private steel industry.[51] And by 1951 the leaders of the CNPF applauded a plea by the SNCF's Louis Armand to call a truce between the defenders and detractors of nationalization. Public enterprises had become increasingly identified with a modernization drive in the French economy that depended on a symbiosis of the public and private sectors. The Charbonnages, EDF-GDF, and SNCF delivered energy and transport at lower than average prices (and more cheaply than in many other European countries), making it obvious that public enterprises were providing a subsidy for the revival and expansion of the private sector.[52] Private businessmen, moreover, became more familiar with the nationalized companies as more of them became appointed to those companies' boards. As a sign of the business Right's adaptation to the new postwar mixed economy, nationalization scarcely appeared as an issue in the parliamentary elections of 1951.[53]

Indeed, by the early 1950s business leaders at the CNPF praised the efficiency of the way nationalized firms were being managed. Robert Fabre, a top staff official at the CNPF, paid public tribute to the importance of the nationalized sector to "the national economy."[54]

What also emerged from the Thermidor of the late 1940s, despite all the strike defeats and political setbacks of 1947–1948, was the CGT's continuing preeminence as labor's voice in the public sector. True, the schism with FO weakened the CGT, as did the migration of many engineers and technicians to the Confédération générale des cadres (CGC), a more moderate white-collar union. Still, nationalized industry remained a strategic bastion for the CGT. The French Communist Party, so ambivalent about nationalization a decade before, now saw public enterprises as prize political turf where it could help shape the country's economic life.[55] Everyone knew the government had a big stake in the success of these firms, which remained central to reconstruction and to maintaining social peace in the country. The unions' exceptional capacity in the public sector to defend pension rights, works committees, social services, and a strong voice with management endured accordingly. CGT activists likely benefited too, ironically, from critiques of nationalization by the laissez-faire Right (and some Americans) that had the effect, as historian Patrick Fridenson has suggested, of bring people closer together within firms.[56]

Differing Paths in Public Enterprise to the Early Fifth Republic

Just how much business practices and employee power within the workplace changed through nationalization varied by industry. The circumstances of their initial nationalizations mattered a lot, but so did the politics of their particular sectors as they evolved in the modernization drive of the Fourth and early Fifth Republics. Likewise, although plans for innovating in these industries—for building additional hydroelectric plants, upgrading equipment in coal mining, and electrifying the railroads—had been around since the late 1930s, only after the nationalizations and in the course of the 1950s did state planners and public enterprises put these ideas fully to work.[57]

Banking

In banking, the fruits of nationalization were hardly worth picking off the vine. The Finance Ministry, which had overseen the nationalization of the four big deposit banks, named well-established company executives to run the nationalized firms. They did little to alter banking practices from what they had been in the 1930s. Indeed, the nationalized deposit banks initially resisted providing medium-term credit to other nationalized industries, preferring to stick to their traditional short-term lending business and thereby forcing the government to rely all the more on the para-public banks like Crédit national and the Caisse des dépôts et consignations, and above all, the Marshall Plan, to finance the postwar modernization drive, starting with the Monnet Plan.[58]

Nor did labor relations change much in the banks. At the nationalized Société Générale a long-established paternalistic culture that rewarded loyalty, excellence, and respect for authority had little room for the new consultative ethos promoted by the CGT.[59] Union representatives did get a small number of seats on company boards at the nationalized banks, but as tradition had it in these firms, top management, not their boards, made the important decisions. Even on the boards, union representatives found themselves sidelined by the banking experts, "outflanked by the technical issues," as one sympathetic left-wing magazine put it.[60] They henceforth chose to restrict their advocacy to matters of salaries and working conditions.[61] Nationalization, then, brought no shift in company culture, and the split in the CGT in 1947 weakened labor's influence further.

The nationalized banks' conservative course derived not simply from labor's limited influence and company leaders who, after mid-1946, felt the Liberation climate had cooled down enough for them to assert themselves.[62] Political and administrative leaders of the Fourth Republic, too, readily accepted a limited role for the big nationalized commercial banks, and they did little to subject these banks to state surveillance and control. The Vichy bank regulation law of 1941 stipulated short-term lending as the principal function of the big deposit banks. De Gaulle's Provisional Government had done nothing to change it. René Pleven, as de Gaulle's finance minister and key life-line to the business elite, had successfully prevented banking nation-alizations from altering the structure of the financial sector. And he ensured continuity for banking leadership.[63] Jean Monnet at the Plan-ning Commission and Treasury Director François Bloch-Lainé, the former a venerated businessman, the latter the son of a banker, were both pragmatists who enjoyed the confidence of the leaders of the na-tionalized banks. They found ways to generate the funds for the mod-ernization drive and reconstruction (a huge sum, really, equal to about a quarter of French national income) without depending overmuch on the nationalized commercial banks.[64] They came up with a clever, un-conventional way for the four nationalized commercial banks to issue medium-term loans to nationalized industry that the big four could then get rediscounted by Crédit national and the Bank of France. The big four, in other words, picked up the profits for what were in effect now short-term loans, and the Bank of France and the Treasury cov-ered the risk. This arrangement, combined with the reliance on Crédit national and the other para-publics, created a mechanism whereby short-term savings transformed into longer-term investment—a key to the modernizing drive.[65] After the Marshall Plan ended in 1952, the logic of this "Treasury circuit"—whereby the Treasury provided credit to industry on the basis of advances from the Bank of France and re-serves deposited from the para-publics—became the principal vehicle for subsiding industry.

Nationalizing the big deposit banks, in short, proved to be an important symbolic political gesture in the Liberation era with small economic consequences for the modernization drive. As François Bloch-Lainé said years later, the postwar British government had done more than the French to control credit by keeping the banks private and exerting closer informal and regulatory control over them through the Treasury and the nationalized Bank of England.[66] Meanwhile, for French labor and the Left the nationalized banks came to epitomize a "failed" nationalization. The moderate-left magazine *Observateur* reported in 1954, "The criteria governing the distribution of credit—solvency, liquidity, profitability—remain the same as those of private banks, without any reference whatsoever to the general interest." Or, in the strident idiom of the Communist Party, in this sector "complicity" between "high civil servants" and "the trusts" prevailed.[67] De Gaulle, Pleven, and the more conservative, Gaullist wing of the Provisional Government of 1944–1946 had no desire to dethrone the country's banking elite. The availability of alternative institutions and funds to steer investment into industry gave them the option not to.

Electricity

At the opposite end of the spectrum from banking was the EDF (and its associated firm the GDF), where the company worked closely with the Planning Commission and preserved a strong web of communication linking workers, management, and the CGT. The witch hunt against Communists, and the workforce cutbacks, had been milder in 1947–1948 at the EDF than in coal mining and aviation, and Marcel Paul's labor statute for the EDF-GDF remained enough intact after Thermidor to keep the firm at the forefront of progressive labor relations in France. Not that the political rupture of 1947–1948 and the onset of the Cold War went unnoticed at the EDF. On the contrary: when the Socialist (and anti-Communist) Robert Lacoste took Marcel Paul's place as minister of industrial production, the happy Liberation-era marriage between Paul's CGT Fédération de l'éclairage within the firm and the top staff of the ministry came to an end. With Paul now restored to his long-established role as head of the CGT's electrical workers federation and the ministry no longer Communist-led, tensions between the state and the firm's workforce over wages became a permanent feature of life at the EDF, as it was at other nationalized companies.

But within the EDF, relations between labor and management remained comparatively positive through the whole era of the long reconstruction, and for a number of reasons. First of all, in the late 1940s and the 1950s the top managers, such as *polytechniciens* Roger Gaspard and Pierre Massé, along with key labor leaders, Marcel Paul and Pierre Le Brun, an engineer and CGT official who had done most to plot the details of nationalizing electricity, shared a great deal in common: a history going back to the 1930s of working in the electrical sector and striving for its centralization and improvement. More important still, they shared a background in the Resistance. Massé, who had been a protégé in the 1930s of electrical industrialist Ernest Mercier, had used his business ties to the Germans to rescue Gaspard from prison. (Gaspard had sought to keep copper out of German hands.) And then Gaspard, in turn, had tried to prevent Marcel Paul's internment by the Nazis, though in the end Paul had to endure Auschwitz and Buchenwald.[68] What's more, these men all identified strongly as founders of the EDF. They had much to be proud of: they had forged a centralized enterprise out of a huge electrical energy sector that at the Liberation included 54 companies running 86 coal-fired power plants, 100 companies running 300 hydroelectric plants, 86 companies transporting that power, and 1,150 firms distributing it to customers.[69] Nationalization brought new coherence to this vast amalgam. And given the importance of the CGT and Marcel Paul's labor statute as key vehicles of integration across such a huge enterprise, it is not surprising that these founders worked hard to prevent the Cold War cleavage from destroying the strong ethos of company loyalty that the EDF's overwhelmingly CGT-oriented workforce felt toward the firm. This effort meant buffering the company both from government attempts to isolate the CGT and from the PCF's inclination to disrupt the CGT's attachment to the firm. As a Communist, Marcel Paul paid a price for the priority he had placed on the firm's success and the autonomy he tried, fairly successfully, to provide his CGT federation from the party. At the Twelfth Congress of the PCF, in 1950, Paul was forced to engage in an exercise of public self-criticism for failing to see that public enterprises could exploit workers as surely as private ones.[70] That the firm Paul had founded owed so much of its early success to the Marshall Plan no doubt did little to help his standing in the party. But the PCF stopped short of purging him, and he continued through the 1950s to serve as a crucial bridge between the CGT and the firm.

The CGT's continuing predominance at the EDF preserved channels of communication between employees and management created in the first years of the firm. In 1946 the CGT enjoyed the support of 80 percent of the workforce. It only dropped to 60 percent during the rupture of 1947–1948. This durability made it difficult for management and the ministries to cut separate deals with minority unions—the CFTC and FO—and with the white-collar employees who joined the Union nationale des cadres, techniciens et agents de maîtrise (UNCM, affiliated with the Confédération générale des cadres) as an alternative to the CGT's rather strong cadre branch in the industry. FO remained weak at the EDF. The more robust electrical branch of the CFTC had a history of cooperating with the CGT going back to the 1930s, and after the Liberation its leading activists identified with the left-leaning and intellectually oriented "Reconstruction" faction of the CFTC.[71] The sharp polarization between the CGT, on the one hand, and the CFTC and FO, on the other, that became so common in industry in the 1950s, never locked into place at the EDF.

What held all these trade union factions together, besides common bread-and-butter issues, was pride in the EDF's status as a nationalized firm, something CFTC leaders called "the mystique of public service," enthusiasm for technological progress, and a conviction that expanding electrical supply was the life force of the nation's recovery.[72] Not every employee, of course, felt the magnetic pull of the EDF's technology-driven, patriotic mission. But most did, and all four labor unions—CGT, CFTC, FO, and UNCM—embraced it unreservedly. Though each union had its special accents—as historian Gabrielle Hecht has argued, the CGT stressed the importance of nationalization and technical advances as key to national independence, FO kept especially vigilant about worker safety in the new nuclear plants emerging in the late 1950s, and the CFTC urged a humanistic approach to technological change—all spoke the language of technical progress, growth, and the virtues of bigness and centralization in ways that harmonized beautifully with what EDF managers and state planners were trying to say and do.[73]

As a sign of how well trade union outlooks harmonized with the firm's leadership, all of the EDF's pivotal strategic decisions about technology won labor's ready support. In its earliest years the EDF expanded electrical production by building dams and tapping the hydroelectric potential of the Alps, Pyrenees, Massif Central, and the Rhine and Rhône rivers. That strategy had begun in the 1930s, and it held special appeal to the Left because "white coal" (water) was such a clean, cheap fuel. Marshall Plan funds proved essential for the expansion of hydroelectric power in the late 1940s.[74] But dam building came with big startup costs—financially always, but socially sometimes too, in cases where dammed-up rivers flooded out villages—and optimal locations for dams were becoming rarer.[75] By the early 1950s the EDF began to shift, not without controversy inside and outside the firm, to a mix of hydroelectricity and a new generation of "thermal" power plants, fueled by coal and increasingly oil. The unions followed all these strategic changes closely and wrote about them in detail in the labor press. Communist deputies and CGT activists weighed in periodically to defend local dam possibilities against arguments for thermal, or local thermal projects (and the coal demand they could create) against arguments for nuclear.[76] But overall, the unions at EDF supported the company's decisions to embrace the new technologies. FO's reporting on the subject, to take but one example, fell easily into step: although dams and their waterfalls were the "cover girls of the history of electricity, . . . hydroelectric and coal power must go hand in hand." They "have to coexist and ensure that energy consumption doubles every ten years."[77] The unions made the same kind of adjustment to nuclear power plants. And here again, labor leaders, like managers, attached nationalistic ambitious to the new technology: FO journalists, for example, expressed the hope that France could quickly catch up with the British, who had gotten a faster start in this domain.[78]

A firm so keen to innovate might have seen more Luddite resistance in a workforce fearful of losing jobs. But the CGT argued successfully for a standing policy of retraining, skill grading, and pay advancements, and EDF management complied, knowing that the labor statute and company culture effectively gave employees permanent tenure. Payroll accounted for only a quarter of production costs, so the benefits of deskilling and layoffs were all the scanter.[79] The commitment to retraining tied workers and the CGT more tightly to the firm.

So too did employee representation in company governance. As in other nationalized companies, labor activists had seats on the company board, as both employee delegates and consumer representatives. Labor also sat on an industry-wide Conseil supérieur de l'électricité et du gaz. And in 1957 advisory committees took shape, with representatives of the employees and of local government, at each of the firm's eighteen regional headquarters.[80] The EDF also had one of the stronger, better-funded social service operations in the nationalized sector, providing for medical services, holiday retreats, summer camps, consumer cooperatives, company cafeterias, and social services for employees and their families. Labor union members ran these operations at the local level—a further source of prestige for the CGT. The national-level oversight body for all this, the Conseil central des oeuvres sociales (CCOS), had union representatives from all the labor factions, but the CGT mostly called the shots and Marcel Paul presided.[81] To be sure, the CGT's hegemony over labor's role in company governance and social service management did not go unchallenged in the Cold War 1950s, especially by the government. Conservative prime ministers in the 1951 to 1954 period in particular, and their minister of industry, Jean-Marie Louvel, removed CGT members from the top company board and put the CCOS under the direct command of government appointees.[82] But the CGT's informal influence in the workforce did not really suffer, nor did its control over local social service operations.

Again in contrast to the nationalized banks, at EDF employees and their trade union leaders acquired forms of expertise that enhanced their influence in the firm and in the national conversation about industrial policy. Labor's role in the founding and ongoing governance of the company, combined with the high skill level of much of the workforce and the advanced technology with which they were associated, gave EDF employees a prominent public profile in the nationalized sector. The unions kept abreast of the technological, financial, and marketing decisions that shaped the company's evolution. Employee leadership, not least in the white-collar, engineering ranks of the CGT, gained knowledge about energy production and the business of the firm that found expression in the labor press and in labor's intervention on boards and committees. It showed, too, in the way the EDF learned by the late 1950s to create widespread, complex power outages as a form of labor protest that still provided electricity to hospitals and other emergency services that needed it.[83] EDF employees mastered the art of the strategic short protest. The continuity of the CGT's leadership elite, with experience going back to the 1930s, only strengthened its claims to expertise.[84]

When Charles de Gaulle came to power as president of the new Fifth Republic, along with his prime minister, Michel Debré, the EDF commanded prestige as the country's most efficient and innovative nationalized firm. It continued to provide the country relatively cheap electricity, and it had become profitable enough to begin to rely partially on self-financing and the bond market for investment capital, even if the lion's share still came from the Treasury.[85] Its efforts to bring France's first nuclear power plants on line and to export hydroelectric technology to the Third World dovetailed with de Gaulle's pursuit of national grandeur and Debré's economic nationalism. Eager to bolster economic planning in the new Republic, Debré choose EDF executive Pierre Massé to head the Planning Commission. The transition from Fourth to Fifth Republic, in short, went smoothly for the firm.

But it did little to take the edge off the combative relationship the unions, and especially the CGT, continued to have with the government over wages in the industry. The unions still directed their claims-making efforts toward the state—because the EDF was a state-owned monopoly enterprise, its salaries, pricing policy, and long-term plans still all required ministerial approval, as they had in the Fourth Republic. Indeed, through the period of the long reconstruction, it was the prime minister himself who made final decisions about EDF wage rates.[86] Michel Debré, along with Minister of Industry Jean-Marcel Jeanneney, adopted an especially hands-on approach to EDF labor issues because energy policy loomed large in their ambitions for economic expansion. Despite Debré's visceral disdain for Communist influence in the nationalized sector, he and Jeanneney, in hopes of cultivating labor's investment in the new regime, reinstated CGT representatives to the EDF's company board and opened a pathway for bringing the CCOS back under the control of an employee-elected board.[87] But on wages, Debré stalled, to workers' frustration. Workers' dismay over wage rates had only deepened in the course of the 1950s: they lagged behind private sector averages, and all the more so because the effort to provide the country cheap energy and rail transport had made salary hikes at the EDF (and the GDF and SNCF) especially stingy.[88] Hence, the Debré government found itself under continual pressure, including from rail and electrical work stoppages in 1961, to redress these grievances. As one of Debré's staff experts pointed out to the prime minister in a private communication, the government had a clear stake in finding a "solution to these [wage-gap] problems" because they "risked, by increasingly aggravating social tensions, compromising the climate of cooperation that the High Council of the Plan has deemed so necessary for 1962."[89] Debré and de Gaulle had indeed pinned big hopes on a post-Algerian-war expansion of France's industrial capacity, which they envisioned would also be buttressed by an "économie concertée" (orchestrated economy) in which employers, unions, state experts, and firms like the EDF would bring a new level of coordination, planning, innovation, and social peace to the French economy.[90] These ambitions implicitly gave the EDF's employees, and their trade union leaders, leverage in the Fifth Republic, especially insofar as their firm remained at the forefront of technological innovation and the keystone to any energy strategy for the country. Although keen to stanch public sector wage hikes in his fight against inflation, Debré relented. EDF workers got wage gains of 11 to 18 percent over two years, a notable win, though not enough to keep the wage issue from festering onward.[91]

Although EDF workers and their CGT union leaders made some progress on the wage front in the early years of the Fifth Republic, the new regime did not usher in a fresh era of labor strength as had the Liberation. The CGT's efforts to challenge the EDF's pricing system that gave favorable rates to big business customers and not to households and small business came to naught.[92] No revival of co-management along the lines of the Liberation-era comité mixte à la production appeared on the horizon. Indeed, as historian Robert Frost documented, a new trend began to take shape in the early 1960s that by the end of the decade would alter the culture of the firm: the ascendency to the top managerial ranks of economists who increasingly came to challenge the grip on leadership that Liberation-era engineers had held in the company. In 1962 Michel Debré and his minister of industry, Jean-Marcel Jeanneney, removed long-term EDF head Roger Gaspard, signaling the end of the reconstruction era at the firm.[93]

Coal

That said, through the long reconstruction at least, the EDF stood out among public enterprise firms as an enterprise where the blend of top-down administrative initiative and bottom-up trade union participation and employee voice preserved something of the left-wing leaders' vision for nationalization right after the war. This, as we have seen, stood in sharp contrast to banking. The case of coal, the Charbonnages de France, represented a middle path between these two

poles. There the promise of nationalized enterprise as a site of productive investment, efficient management, and employee voice started
out hopefully enough during the "battle for coal" in 1945–1946. The
CGT and the Communist Party commanded authority in the coalfields, not least via local and regional boards and the tripartite board at
the top of the Charbonnages.[94] Pit committees, which CGT militants
had creating in the first months of the Liberation period in many mines,
gave miners themselves a voice in how daily operations proceeded.
The CGT quickly built on this foundation to establish more formalized
production committees at the pits of the Charbonnages during the
"battle for coal." Mining engineers, too, many of whom flocked to
the CGT, participated in these committees, lending a more collaborative ethos to what in the mining world had traditionally been a rigid
chain of command.[95]

The scope and violence of the 1948 coal strike and Jules Moch's repression of it eviscerated much of this achievement. In a fifty-six-day
test of strength between the CGT and the state, triggered initially by
Socialist Robert Lacoste's effort to trim back some of the gains of the
miners' statute—but fueled fundamentally by the early Cold War power
struggle between the Communists and their former tripartite government partners—the CGT withdrew mine security personnel from the
mines. Moch sent in the army, 8 miners died, and 3,000 miners were
fired. The labor statute survived, much as its counterpart had after 1948
at the EDF, but the government ejected the CGT from the Charbonnages board.[96] Instead of enjoying a form of dual power within enterprises and in the Ministry of Industry, CGT activists now found
themselves ostracized by the government and top managers of the firm,
even though they still enjoyed a good deal of authority and respect in
local mining communities. Nowhere in France did the industrial conflicts of 1947 and 1948 create a greater fissure between labor and top
management than they did in the coal industry. Bitterness hung in the
air like coal dust for the rest of the reconstruction era.

Three major developments in the 1950s—the creation the European
Coal and Steel Community (ECSC) in 1950, huge investments in new
mining equipment via the Monnet Plan (with Marshall Plan money)
and the Second (Hirsch) Plan, and the growth of oil and gas as alternative sources of energy—did nothing to improve relations between

miners and top managers at the Charbonnages, or with their ministerial overseers. For one thing, each of these changes had the effect of
concentrating authority at the top levels of the Charbonnages and in the
government. When it was initially created out of eighteen private mining
firms in 1946, the Charbonnages had a decentralized structure—a set of
nine regional mining clusters, each with a director and tripartite
board, and a central coordinating authority in Paris with a staff.[97] But
gradually over the 1950s the size, function, and power of the central
staff grew as it was called upon to negotiate on behalf of the Charbonnages with the ECSC's High Authority in Luxembourg and with the
Planning Commission in Paris.[98] The same mediating role enhanced
the authority of the Ministry of Industry, as did the latter's contacts
with American officials, such as David Bruce at the Economic Cooperation Authority, who were promoting the creation of the ECSC and
channeling Marshall Aid into the Monnet Plan.[99]

The ECSC, investment, and new sources of energy also had the
effect of pressuring the Charbonnages to trim its coal-mining workforce.
The Coal and Steel Community gave French businesses and household
consumers of coal greater access to Germany's abundant supply, especially its superior coking coal, and while French negotiators were able
to extract the promise that the French coal industry would not have to
reduce its output by more than a million tons a year to accommodate
German coal imports (French production was 60 million tons in 1952–
1953), the effect of the ECSC was to constrain the future of French
coal.[100] More important still was the impact of the rising productivity
in the mines, especially in the leading coal regions of the Nord, Pas-
de-Calais, and Lorraine. New equipment, much of it purchased from
American suppliers via Marshall Plan aid, along with improved transport systems and surface operations, boosted average output per underground worker a remarkable 62 percent between 1946 and 1954, and
productivity only continued to rise.[101] Miners' work routines changed
as well. No longer organized into crews, miners worked as individuals
with new coal-cutting machines and were supervised closely and paid
for output. With the production committees of 1945–1946 long since
abandoned by the firm, miners no longer had a vehicle for channeling
their everyday mining expertise into management's planning of the
work. Morale suffered accordingly. As sociological studies in the 1950s

revealed, miners expressed deep ambivalence about a modernizing of the mines that had the effect of degrading the work and producing a finer, more silicosis-inducing, form of coal dust.[102]

And indeed, rising productivity empowered managers to shrink the workforce of an industry whose market was in steady decline. From a peak of 356,000 miners in 1947 the workforce dropped by 31 percent to 244,000 in 1958.[103] The greatest threat to workforce levels, long-term, was beginning to arrive in the form of cheap Middle East oil and natural gas from Lacq (near Pau at the base of the Pyrenees), with potentially more coming from Algeria down the line. In 1959 coal supplied 59 percent of France's energy, down from 83 percent in 1938.[104] By the end of the Fourth Republic the government's energy policy had lost whatever coherence it was thought to have a few years earlier, pulled in several directions at once by the choices between hydroelectricity, coal-fired and oil-fired thermal, the unknowable potential of nuclear on the horizon, the geopolitical uncertainties of France's North African future, and not least a deepening crisis of overproduction of coal in the ECSC.

With the new Fifth Republic, Jean-Marcel Jeanneney, de Gaulle and Debré's minister of industry, made his first priority bringing order to the energy tangle by establishing a multiyear plan for the Charbonnages. To begin with, he formally redefined the relationship between the central office of the Charbonnages and the regional coal districts so as to better acknowledge the former's accretion of power and to strengthen the hand of the center over the periphery in the industry. The center now took explicit control over production programs and investment.[105] Jeanneney also diminished what little remained of the Charbonnages' autonomy from the ministry. As he said years later in an interview, "The Ministry of Industry, through the Charbonnages de France, had nearly total mastery of the coal industry, subject to trade union reactions, and through a series of regulations it also controlled the commercial side of coal (profit margins, import licenses, etc.)."[106] Then in 1960 Jeanneney announced his "Plan d'adaptation des houillères," or what became known as the Jeanneney Plan. It called for cutting French coal production during 1960–1965 to 53 million tons (from 58.7 million tons), scaling back employment, and transferring miners from the Center and Midi (the southwest of the country) to the more productive mines of Nord, Pas-de-Calais, and Lorraine.[107] (Some miners who were transferred to German-speaking towns in Lorraine would come to describe their fate as "deportation.")[108] Jeanneney targeted un-profitable coal pits, including those in the town of Decazeville, for closing by 1965. Although the Jeanneney Plan had provisions designed to ease the pain—indemnities to laid-off workers and early retirees, and a fund to support job development in the most effective mining com-munities—it struck the trade unions as a catastrophe and a sign of their isolation from the halls of power in the Charbonnages. It also signaled the diminished influence in the Fifth Republic of local deputies such as Paul Ramadier, who for his whole career had defended the mines of the Albi region, including Decazeville.[109]

A sector that had been strike-free since 1948 now became the early Fifth Republic's most spectacular arena of labor combat. It began in late 1961 when the Charbonnages began to implement the scaling down of Decazeville. There an entire town and its surrounding communities, including the bishop in Rodez, rallied behind miners and their supervi-sors, who together occupied the mines in a sit-down strike that captured the attention of the whole country. All three major trade unions (CGT, CFTC, and FO) united in defiance of Jeanneney, the Charbonnages' top brass, and what a joint union committee called "the world without soul and without ideals that is called technocracy."[110] This anti-technocratic rhetoric pitting everyday miners and a local economic ecology dependent on their well-being against a distant, soulless Paris, played in a left-wing key a melody we have already seen in its right-wing version on the Poujadist right. And it harmonized with the left-leaning Social Catholicism of local clergy and CFTC militants in the mining towns, especially in Lorraine.[111] After 250 miners began a hunger strike and then a wave of sympathy work stoppages and other protests spread across the southwest, Jeanneney finally negotiated an end to strife by granting better severance and retirement pay for the miners of Decazeville without reneging on his plan to trim back the industry. The unions accepted that was the best they could get.

As it turned out the Decazeville drama was but a dress rehearsal for a massive strike one year later that shut down the entire Charbon-nages for thirty-five days. The Jeanneney Plan had set the table for con-flict, and so too did pay grievances. Wages had lagged in the public sector, especially for miners. When in March 1963 miners threatened a walkout for an 11 percent wage hike, de Gaulle and his new prime minister, Georges Pompidou, took the extraordinary step of requisitioning the mines. They overplayed their hand, for when miners struck anyway, the weight of public opinion supported them. As in the Decazeville struggle, the Church hierarchy sympathized with the miners, as did much of the national press. De Gaulle and Pompidou conceded the wage hike, as had Jeanneney the year before. They also offered a fourth week of paid vacation, and made vague (empty, as it turned out) promises to reconsider the future of the industry. The strike, recognized as a blow to de Gaulle's prestige, announced the arrival of more combative labor relations to the Fifth Republic.[112]

Still, the 1962 and 1963 coal strikes did little to reorder the power dynamics within the Charbonnages. The miners' unions had won wage hikes and layoff provisions and a measure of political pride, but neither a future for their industry nor a stronger voice in managing its decline. Unlike in the EDF, where employees and their unions retained influence within the enterprise, in the Charbonnages miners retained much less within the firm; their negotiating leverage in 1962 and 1963 came from their success in winning allies and popular support outside the company. And that supporting public cared less about the future of coal per se than about the miners and their circumstances.

Nationalization, then, which first promised empowerment for miners, became a boon principally for the state and coal consumers, especially businesses that benefited most from a Charbonnages charged with producing cheap coal, not a profit. As analysts concluded by the end of the 1950s, nationalization enabled the government to improve the industry—its organization, investment financing, and production methods—in ways private owners would not have done, or done so quickly.[113] So tight was the government's grip on the industry that even the leader of the more moderate CFTC union in mining spoke in the 1950s of the irony of having abolished private capitalism in the coalfields only to have "the government institute state capitalism."[114] The Fifth Republic, by strengthening executive authority and giving ministries more autonomy from local parliamentary deputies in mining districts, only enhanced the state's control further. With de Gaulle's government firmly committed to opening up French industry to the wider international economy—and Jeanneney was an especially fervent supporter of adapting to the competitive pressures of Europe—the Communist Party's anti-ECSC diatribes in the early 1960s had no consequence.[115] By the mid-1960s the industry's continuing decline became ineluctable. Its workforce would shrink to 41,000 by 1975.[116]

Railroads

What, then, about that other huge state monopoly enterprise, the national railroad (the SNCF): Did it evolve from the Liberation to the early Fifth Republic more in the manner of the EDF or the Charbonnages? In one respect it resembled the latter: what with two bruising strikes, it had an especially tumultuous Thermidorean passage in 1947–1948. The first strike, in June 1947, originated in the rank-and-file grassroots over government-imposed bread quota reductions and wage rates. All the railway unions had to sprint to get out in front of the protest, once it started, and it was remarkable how much solidarity was achieved in this effort, not only between the rival trade union confederations but also between the white-collar employees and blue-.[117] The CGT made the most of the moment—trumpeting "the total unity of all railway workers of every leaning, religion, and rank."[118] The second strike, for two searing weeks in November and December 1947, was altogether different. This was a Communist-instigated, solely CGT affair, a political strike designed to disrupt the regime in early days of the Cold War. It divided the confederations, damaged the blue-collar/white-collar alliance, and confirmed many non-Communist CGT militants in their determination to launch Force ouvrière (FO) as a separate, anti-Communist confederation. Both the June and December strikes also did the SNCF some damage of another sort: they provoked commuters dependent on the rails to use emergency bus services and other road transportation, to the delight of a road transport lobby in fierce competition with the rails.[119]

But unlike in the Charbonnages, in the SNCF the state's strike repression, though violent, did not lead to mass layoffs and widespread firings of CGT militants. CGT representatives lost their seats on the national board of the SNCF (and would not get them back until 1972, much later than at EDF), and about sixty-five employees were dismissed.[120] But as in the EDF, a history of labor-management consultation at the SNCF going back to the interwar years and then galvanized in the secret networks of the Resistance—the much celebrated "bataille du rail" (battle of the rails)—helped to buffer the blows of Thermidor. CGT members continued to serve on local and regional labor-management committees. The railway workers' employment statute—which like the EDF's included favorable health and pension benefits, and some extras, such as free rail travel for employees and their families and early retirement ages—also survived the repressive backlash of 1947–1948. The SNCF's board of directors made a point of hailing "railway workers' strong professional ethos and the sense of devotion."[121] Pride in the railway endured. As in the EDF, then, the company went into the 1950s with decent channels of communication between employee unions and management, and workers continued to identify strongly with the firm, its public service mission, and the link between the strength of the railroad and an image of France as a modernizing country.[122]

And modernize, the SNCF certainly did. Right after the Liberation the SNCF concentrated on repairing the devastating rail network and purchasing huge numbers of rail cars and locomotives from the Americans, and by the 1950s the firm bet its future on electrifying the network. Marshall Plan money launched the effort. Even larger amounts of state funding followed. Powerful new electric locomotives replaced steam engines at an impressive pace. The SNCF's technical feats in the 1950s—a speed world record in 1955 and a reputation as Europe's most efficient train system by the end of the decade—made a hero of company director Louis Armand. He was celebrated in the pages of *Réalités* as the very embodiment of France's new postwar elite, "the orchestra leader of progress," who described himself as having to "take into account thought and action at the same time."[123] Productivity figures told the company's story: passengers and freight per kilometer grew 60 percent between 1938 and 1955, the average daily distance traveled by locomotives nearly tripled between 1938 and 1963, and the number of employees at the SNCF dropped to 364,000 in 1958, down from 490,000 in 1947.[124]

Railway productivity did not, however, trigger the same level of fear in the workforce as it did in coal. Low retirement ages, generous pensions, confidence in the SNCF's future, and pride in technical improvements made workforce declines more palatable to the railway unions than to their counterparts in the Charbonnages.[125] To be sure, some workers paid heavily for the productivity drive. The CGT cried foul if jobs disappeared when the company closed lesser-used secondary lines in remote rural districts, although, notably, militants tended to blame "the Americans" rather than the firm for these decisions.[126] But everyone knew railroads mattered—70 percent of the country's domestic transport still went by rail in the early 1950s—so the company's achievements tended more to buttress than sap company loyalty.[127]

Management and labor also shared a common stake in defending the rails against the rising competition of the roads. Since its founding in 1937 the SNCF had benefited from a republican tradition of viewing railroads as the centerpiece of a national transport system designed to knit the country together and promote its economic development. This outlook undergirded a dirigiste approach to price setting and taxation in the private road transport business so as to keep roads from undercutting the rails. But by the late 1940s the road transport lobby, the Fédération nationale des transporteurs routiers, had become a powerful force in arguing for deregulating rates.[128] In 1949 Transport Minister Christian Pineau, less wedded to dirigisme than his predecessor Jules Moch, used decree powers granted by Parliament to give private trucking companies more room to grow and put the SNCF under more competitive pressure.[129] Although a much more thoroughgoing liberalization of transport pricing and taxing would not come until the 1970s, top civil servants in the Transport Ministry through the 1950s and into the early Fifth Republic became increasingly sympathetic to the road lobby. They found rail strikes disruptive and economists persuasive in using the logic of marginal cost pricing to argue for price deregulation.[130] Controversy over road-rail competition throughout the period of the long reconstruction brought employees and management at the SNCF into common cause against ministerial officials, who more often than not saw issues of transport coordination differently.

With the new Fifth Republic, de Gaulle and Debré put their executive muscle behind the twin goals of continuing to electrify the rail system and making the transport sector more commercially competitive. The government's major compass-setting for economic policy generally, the Rueff-Armand Report of 1960 on obstacles to economic expansion, highlighted the need for marginal cost pricing, not least in the transport sector—a position more favorable to roads than rails, despite Armand's now-former association with the SNCF.[131] But what most preoccupied the Debré government, and Debré himself, about the SNCF was wages. Just as at the EDF, at the SNCF wages had fallen behind those in the private sector, enough so that in 1959 the railway unions united behind a decision to challenge the new regime with a major nationwide rail strike. It was a risky move for the unions: a significant, though unknowable, number of workers had approved of de Gaulle's return to power and new republic, which the Left had opposed.[132] Debré and de Gaulle, in the meantime, had come to see counterinflationary policy and currency stabilization as their preeminent economic policy objective, and wage constraint in public enterprise as their most powerful instrument to achieve it. On June 12, 1959, a week before the anticipated strike, Prime Minister Debré went on radio and television to dramatize what was at stake for the government's first real test of political will on the labor front. "At the end of last year," he told his national audience, "after having put an end to our first evil—governmental instability—by having the nation approve new institutions, General de Gaulle completed his work by putting an end to a second evil—inflation." But, he warned, "this rectification has its adversaries," who, he almost said, in a phrase he had crossed out on his text before delivering the speech, "don't want France to become France again." Instead of so blatantly impugning their patriotism, he sought to drive a wedge between the CGT and the railway workers by appealing to the latter's ethic of public service. "I can't believe," he said, "that railroad workers would agree to put themselves at odds with this rectification [especially] in a public enterprise where the sense of national interest has always been high"[133] Debré then met directly with union leaders to convey how intimately he knew the railway workers' world. Debré's staff reminded him to emphasize, as he most likely did, how much advisory power the unions already had at all levels of the SNCF hierarchy and how advantageous retirement and welfare benefits were in the enterprise.[134] When, just days before the strike deadline, Debré played his strongest card—the threat of requisitioning the railroads, with all the penalties that might entail for strikers—the unions backed down.[135] De Gaulle's government had won its biggest labor confrontation until the battles in the coalfields in 1963.

The SNCF, then, followed a trajectory of evolution as a nationalized enterprise closer to that of the EDF than of the Charbonnages. As in the electrical industry, in railways the workers, engineers, and white-collar managers embraced the state's modernization strategy for their sector, and a great many of them had a level of skill and expertise that gave them a voice in the internal functioning of the firm. Both companies, of course, had plenty of political friction—trade union rivalries, built-in employee-management conflicts that nationalization did little to transcend, and above all deep antagonism between employees and the ministries that supervised wage restrictions in the public sector. Compared to the EDF, labor relations were rougher at the SNCF, where brief, usually localized, work stoppages became almost commonplace in the 1950s. And SNCF chief Louis Armand held a particular animus for Communists and the CGT—a case where the Resistance experience sowed resentment over competing claims to the heroic legacy instead of creating bonds between top management and labor leaders, as at the EDF. Still, these forms of endemic conflict at the SNCF were a far cry from the bitterness and distrust that beset the Charbonnages, much less the unreformed, paternalistic condition of social relations in the nationalized banking sector.

Pundits and politicians during the long reconstruction tended to speak of the virtues and vices of nationalization as if it were a single industrial policy, but in reality it was a bundle of distinct trajectories. Banking, the EDF, the Charbonnages, and the SNCF: each evolved over the long reconstruction in accord with how their employees, managers, attending ministries, and state experts clashed and negotiated and in so doing created unique public enterprises. And their circumstances varied. In banking, employees and their unions never had a serious opportunity to challenge the established order in their firms, and much the same could be said of the nationalized insurance sector. In coal, the brutal reversals of 1948 and the ensuing changes in market conditions, work organization, and technology destroyed most miners' hopes for nationalization as a means for their empowerment. The CGT's mining leader, Auguste Lecoeur, captured that disillusion succinctly in 1950: "The state is more rapacious than the private employers. With the state, the only arbitration is that of combat." His FO counterpart echoed: "We have a boss today as yesterday: he has changed his name, that's all."[136] But in industries where public enterprises had brighter economic prospects, where labor and management could agree on technological strategies to match those opportunities, and where they could salvage from the battles of 1947–1948 enough of the participatory apparatus for governance that had been built in 1945–1946, there employees, company brass, and their state sponsors and regulators would remain invested in their firms' success as nationalized enterprises. These conditions prevailed, in differing degrees, in the EDF, the SNCF, Renault, and the aircraft firms. In those companies, too, in contrast to banking and coal, the unions could more reliably use the weapon of work stoppages—usually localized and sporadic in the EDF and the SNCF, more concentrated and spectacular at Renault—to negotiate with the state. In nationalization, then, variation came with the territory, and all the more so as firms evolved.

Variation also made it more challenging for state officials to coordinate the often contradictory relationships between public enterprises. The SNCF and Renault, for example, had competing stakes in the protracted, vexed effort to find a transportation policy that satisfied the interests of the rail and road lobbies.[137] Finding an energy policy, as Jean-Marcel Jeanneney struggled to do, that might optimize the EDF's strategic flexibility while giving the Charbonnages a future proved to be a technical and political challenge of the highest order. And wage policy in the public sector was hardly a thing of rationalistic beauty. The Finance Ministry created a wage coordination commission, but it could do little more than keep track of how wage conflicts varied across public enterprises and how the several *ministères tutelles* (oversight ministries) were dealing with them.[138] To compound the challenges of coordination, the state itself was a congeries of separate authorities, sometimes working in harmony in overseeing a policy choice in given enterprise, but often not. The Ministry of Finance might clash with the relevant oversight ministry (Defense, Industry, Public Works), or the Ministry of National Economy, or the Planning Commission. And even within the Finance Ministry, the Treasury Department, which oversaw investment in public enterprises, often looked at things differently than did the Budget Department, which oversaw budgets and salaries.[139] When Michel Debré began as prime minister, he hoped to reduce this friction between ministries and agencies, the better to strengthen the state's control over the nationalized sector. "There is an excess of independence in public enterprises and nationalized firms and an absence of [state] oversight," he complained.[140] But even though he did manage to assert direct control over the appointment of the heads of public enterprises, he could do little to diminish ministerial competition and streamline the state's oversight authority. Variation among firms, then, endured on into the Fifth Republic, as did the unique relations each firm had with its state allies and supervisors.

Administrative Power and Industrial Democracy

Ambiguity had made the idea of nationalization a convenient vehicle of unity for the Resistance. In the 1950s and early 1960s the variation in the forms and political character of public enterprises also made it easy for groups to draw their own conclusions about this legacy of the Liberation. Overall, nationalized firms became an accepted part of the landscape, little feared by most business leaders and increasingly appreciated by planners, engineers, and economists for providing cheap energy and transport and for developing new technologies, production methods, and pricing strategies. Much of the state's financial investment in public enterprise found its way to the private suppliers of equipment and materiel for the EDF, SNCF, and Charbonnages.[141] The state took on financial risks for innovations that private firms would likely have evaded or taken longer to get to.[142] As Jean-Marcel Jeanneney wrote in 1954, while still a Sorbonne professor and not yet minister of industry, "although the nationalized sector has come about in a somewhat irregular fashion, no party in France proposes, at least openly, the return of nationalized undertakings [enterprises] to private industry."[143] On the left, labor activists no longer romanticized nationalization as inherently revolutionary. Indeed, from the late 1940s on, a number of left-wing theorists questioned whether a public enterprise could be anything but a creature of *l'état-patron*, the state as just another boss.[144] Still, labor and the Left had played a huge role in shaping the public sector. In the EDF, the GDF, the SNCF, Renault, and the aircraft companies they retained enough influence, and empowering expertise, to sustain these firms as laboratories of industrial democracy on into the Fifth Republic.

To be sure, after 1948 top officials did shift more authority to company heads and the ministries at the expense of the production committees and tripartite boards of the firms. When ministers sought to restructure aviation, electrify the rails, rationalize coal production, or plan the shift from hydroelectric power to coal plants and then to nuclear power, they turned to top civil servants and the expertise of engineers and economists, not to the deliberative, representative bodies of the Liberation era, to determine these new directions. By the 1950s, moreover, company directors became mainly responsible for technical operations and industrial relations, whereas the main work of planning investment and project development moved into the ministries. Ministers further enhanced their authority by using a talented cadre of state auditors to oversee company operations and by clutching the purse strings of public enterprise—their grip made all the tighter by the Finance Ministry's restrictions on self-financing and its insistence on financing via loans rather than capital.[145]

Even so, the democratic values that founders had invoked in creating nationalized enterprises—the importance of public service and the national interest, the transparency of these enterprises to public scrutiny, their accountability to Parliament, and the role that representative bodies were supposed to play in their management—endured. When Prime Minister René Mayer, a tough-minded neoliberal, decreed in 1953 that all the tripartite boards would be reduced in size and that a fourth kind of representative—"persons known for their industrial or financial competence" (that is, for their technical expertise and their ties to the supervising ministry)—would be added to them by ministerial appointment, outcries came from many quarters, and not just the Communist Party. And critics were just as withering in repudiating Mayer's claim that the ministries retained a right to veto board decisions deemed contrary to the "general interest."[146] In the pages of *Le Monde* the now-aging labor moderate Léon Jouhaux lamented that "the nationalized industries have been transformed into statized organisms."[147] Many parliamentarians, too, felt Mayer's technocratic Jacobinism would subvert their own supervisory authority over the nationalized sector. In 1955, in a stunning reversal, Parliament abrogated Mayer's decree and reinforced parliamentary oversight authority.[148]

Parliamentary oversight, of course, provided one form of democratic participation in the nationalized sector—democracy from a distance, if you will. But it also diminished the independence of firms in the same way ministerial controls did. Back in 1946, under the political circumstances of the Liberation when left-wing parties had a majority in Parliament and had a big say over the activities of oversight committees in the National Assembly, Parliament's role could complement a CGT strategy of expanding employee authority within the workplace. But in the mid-1950s, with the Cold War raging and Communist deputies more isolated in the National Assembly, parliamentary oversight and workplace democracy were more at odds. When Pierre Mendès France became prime minister in 1954, he called in his investiture speech for building closer ties between the Planning Commission and nationalized enterprises, something that in theory might make the latter more democratically accountable. Yet here too the withdrawal of the CGT from the Planning Commission and the evolution of the Commission during the 1950s into a bigger, more expert-laden institution and less of a gathering place for dialogue between civil servants and interest group spokespersons, made this avenue for democratizing public enterprise narrower than the Left had initially hoped.

The shift from the Fourth to the Fifth Republic only furthered these trends. By strengthening the executive branch over Parliament, de Gaulle's new Constitution fortified the role of the ministries and enhanced their supervisory authority in the public sector. As economic nationalists, de Gaulle and Debré remained deeply invested in the success of the major public enterprises, but they also regarded wage restraint as essential to the monetary stabilization they viewed as a pillar of the new regime. A focus on cost containment also reflected the government's emerging preoccupation with making France more competitive in the new Common Market and in a European economy fueled increasingly by mass consumption, and not just by investment and production as had been case right after the war.[149] The government's economic agenda, in short, kept labor in public enterprise on the defensive in the early years of the Fifth Republic, which in turn made it tough to advance the cause of participatory democracy in the nationalized sector.

The question, then, of how to combine a concentration of authority in the hands of top experts in the companies and the ministries with a cultivation of democratically structured consultative bodies within enterprises and in broader sector-wide and national planning areas remained very much alive. What got settled by the mid-1950s was the economic legitimacy of nationalized enterprise. What remained unsettled were issues of social democracy in industrial enterprise, and these matters would emerge again as central concerns in the late 1960s when the possibilities of industrial reform would once again animate debate in the unions and the student movement. This time, however, the movement to democratize the workplace would come not from the PCF, which grew satisfied merely to protect the nationalized sector as a bastion of CGT influence, but from a new generation of leftists who had come to see Gaullist technocracy and Communist "bureaucratic centralism" as equally complicit in a new industrial status quo.[150]

6

Reformer Dilemmas

Pierre Mendès France and Michel Debré as Renovators of the Republic

AFTER WITNESSING European fascism and the Vichy regime, no politician or high-level civil servant could remain oblivious to the danger that the rule of experts posed for French democracy. Key architects of postwar policy, such as Jean Monnet at the Planning Commission or Pierre Laroque in the social policy arena, championed democratic principles even as they pushed their policy agendas as experts behind the scenes. They knew that the success of the dirigiste state required agencies of public participation—planning committees, local social security boards, and family fund boards with ample union and business representation—to bring daylight, advice, and legitimacy to an increasingly powerful administrative state. They understood, too, the opposite principle: that any serious democratic revival depended on experts who could master the technical challenges of making economic planning work and a welfare state solvent. But how to render compatible, rather than contradictory, state-led renovation and democratic participation was hardly self-evident under the best of circumstances—and it was all the less so amid government instability (cabinets lasted an average of six months in the Fourth Republic), Cold War divisions on the left, and after 1953 the insurgency of a Poujadist movement that made the attack on "technocratic" Paris one of its clarion calls.

Two men who served as both experts and politicians played a big role in shaping the postwar conversation in France over how to rejuvenate the country through the use of centralized administrative authority and to nurture democratic participation at the same time. Prolific writers both, Pierre Mendès France (1907–1982) and Michel Debré (1912–1996) left visible, decades-long records of how they thought about these matters. Their careers in public office left evidence of how they managed them in practice.

Just five years apart in age, both men were born in Paris into Jewish, or in Debré's case partly Jewish, families. After training in law, they worked their way precociously into high government posts by the late 1930s. Both men made their marks as major policy thinkers in the Resistance and then served in de Gaulle's Provisional Government of 1944–1945. Both were in Parliament in the Fourth Republic, Mendès France most famously as prime minister in 1954–1955 when he negotiated France's exit from the Indochina war after the army's defeat at Dien Bien Phu, opened a pathway to Tunisian independence, and for a brief period—later ritualistically referred to by his admirers as his woefully short "seven months and seventeen days" in office—raised hopes, especially among urban professionals and the young, that a heretofore unstable Fourth Republic could be made to work with charismatic leadership. *Mendésisme,* a term its namesake disliked, would thereafter stand for a modern and efficient France, technical progress, rigor, social justice, youth, and an escape from political gridlock and economic Malthusianism.

Michel Debré, though nominally in Mendès France's Radical Party, became a Gaullist insider after 1944 and devoted himself in the 1950s to the General's return to power. He wrote policy tracts for the Gaullist cause and penned a number of mass-circulation middle-brow books that sought to expose the Fourth Republic in all its pathology. When de Gaulle took power in 1958, Debré drafted the Constitution of the Fifth Republic, which Mendès France opposed, and went on to serve as de Gaulle's first prime minister from 1958 to 1962. Together, Debré and de Gaulle put into everyday practice the executive-centered system of governance that had eluded them in 1945.

Despite their common political origins and parallel careers in the republican mainstream, Mendès France and Debré by the early 1960s came to represent opposing perspectives on the Fifth Republic. Each served as a standard-bearer for his respective camp, Debré as a right-leaning Gaullist, Mendès France as a left-leaning republican allied more openly than he had been before with Socialists and an emerging decentralist, associationalist Left (which came to be called the "Second Left" in the 1970s). Both men had styled themselves as "democratic reformers" seeking to adapt the French state to the requisites of a postwar national recovery. They saw the future of democracy itself as being at stake in their disagreements about reform. At the heart of their differences lay their answers to the question of how to transcend the conflict between top-down, expert-led rule and democratic participation. Their struggles with this question tell us a lot about how key political elites regarded this problem, and why it would remain so unresolved, indeed so politically charged, at the end of the reconstruction era.

Politics and State Service in the Interwar Years

Pierre Mendès France made his first serious effort to think about the relationship between policy expertise and democratic values in his doctoral thesis in law, which he defended in 1928. He wrote it on the Poincaré government's fiscal policy of 1926, that combination of budget cuts, tax hikes, debt consolidation, and currency stabilization that eventually tamed France's postwar inflation. Raymond Poincaré, conservative nemesis of the Cartel des Gauches government of 1924–1926, hardly seemed the obvious topic for a young Mendès France on the left of the Radical Party. He had joined the party at age 16 after hearing party head Édouard Herriot speak in Paris. As a law student, he became a leading militant in the Ligue d'action universitaire républicaine et socialiste (LAURS), a student group associated with the party.[1] He also became passionately interested in economics, which was then mainly a law school subject (and a marginal one at that), and he admired Poincaré for his technical command of financial questions, his "devotion to the public good," and his "sense of the state."[2] Indeed, Poincaré, despite his politics, still embodied the republican virtues of patriotism, rationalism, and probity that the young Mendès France had already come to embrace from his own Third Republic education and his upbringing in a nonobservant but militantly Dreyfusard Jewish family. To the end of his life Mendès France would include Poincaré in his personal pantheon of heroes (along with Jules Ferry, Jean Jaurès, and eventually Léon Blum and Charles de Gaulle).[3]

Mendès France nonetheless managed in his thesis to blend an appreciation for Poincaré's technical mastery, his "intelligence," "authority," and "sang-froid," with a stinging indictment of what he regarded as the two deep flaws in Poincaré's approach. The first was Poincaré's willingness to privilege the state's own financial solvency over the health of the larger economy. "We will encounter technical steps," he told his readers, "taken because they bring the state one, two, or three millions [francs] while they make the country lose ten, fifteen, or twenty million."[4] This Mendésean conviction—put public finance to the service of economic growth, not vice versa—would make him an early and prominent French proponent of Keynesianism a decade later.[5] Second, and worse still in Mendès France's view, was Poincaré's blindness to the "social repercussions" of his policy. "While he lined up his columns of figures and his experts looked for what taxes they could still raise," Mendès France wrote, "M. Poincaré could have felt the shuddering of the country he was crushing . . . the shopkeepers without clients, the wage-earners without work, the poverty, the unemployment, the bankruptcy."[6] Mendès France concluded his thesis with a warning: "Once again, alas, our politically democratic Republic has not been economically just. The technical soundness, the success even, of M. Poincaré should not make us forget the injustices committed or accrued."[7] Binding together the intelligent use of economics and a commitment to justice and equity—that challenge would come to define his own sense of mission when in the 1930s he positioned himself as the leading young economic expert in the Radical Party.

Meanwhile, Mendès France made his worries about the improper use of expertise even more explicit in a short book he published in 1930 on the new Bank for International Settlements (BIS), a brainchild of the Young Commission to facilitate the payment of inter-allied war debts and German reparations.[8] He welcomed the BIS as an antidote to narrow economic nationalism, applauded its proficiency, and wondered wistfully if, had it been founded in 1920, "we would have known, perhaps, neither the Ruhr adventure nor the revival of chauvinism that followed it, nor the German bankruptcy, nor the bankruptcy of France! . . . We would have fortified and modernized democracy!"[9] But by empowering experts accountable to bankers, not governments, the bank, in his view, embodied the threat of a new "business Bonapartism."[10] Unaccountable to governments or any pan-European authority yet to be invented, the technical wizards of the BIS were, in his view, paving the way for a new internationalism of private interests, rather than a much-longed-for postwar internationalism of peoples. The unchecked power of BIS technicians signaled a wider trend of ceding too much power to autonomous experts. What was needed instead, Mendès argued, was a reassertion of political authority, the invention of new European political institutions to match innovations like the BIS, and the recruitment of experts from "the major administrations of the state," who by tradition and training would have "a broad, impartial, and objective conception of the general interest."[11] Here was Mendès France as the Jacobin republican, elevating the common good and the duty to serve it.

Given his admiration for Poincaré and for Radical Party leaders who were also strong in economics, such as Joseph Caillaux, the architect of the income tax, and Georges Bonnet, the civil servant turned politician who wrote a preface to Mendès France's published thesis, it was not surprising that he chose to pursue a political career.[12] Indeed, electoral politics gave Mendès France a way to bridge economic expertise and left-wing republicanism. In 1929, uninspired by the prospect of a legal career in Paris, he took up a law position in Louviers, a market town in the department of the Eure in Normandy, where he then established himself in the local Radical Party. The gamble paid off handsomely: in a tight election in 1932 he beat the conservative incumbent to become, at age 25, the youngest deputy in Parliament. (He also became mayor of Louvier three years later.) His star rose swiftly within the party. Well known to Herriot, Bonnet, and Caillaux from his student days, he was tapped to give the principal economic speech at the Radical Party congress at Toulouse in 1932. There, tacking more sharply to the left than the party fathers might have wished, he spoke in the accent of his fellow Young Turks, like Jacques Kayser, Pierre Cot, and Jean Zay, who saw in the Great War and now the Great Depression ample reason to scuttle the laissez-faire traditions of the party and opt for a more dirigiste approach. Repudiating fiscal orthodoxy, Mendès France called for government borrowing, greater reliance on the income tax, and policies that would shift resources from nonproductive to productive sectors of the economy. And with echoes of wartime republicanism, he urged a more equitable sharing of sacrifice in a time of crisis.[13] Productivity, renovation, equity, sacrifice: Mendès France had already captured the themes that would shape his approach to state-led, growth-centered economic policy for the rest of his career.

But could the state administration and the Third Republic command the authority that dirigisme required? A long-simmering debate on state reform came to a boil once the Depression hit France, and Mendès France joined the argument. He did so in 1933 in an article on fellow Radical Joseph Caillaux and conservative André Tardieu, two political heavyweights who clashed over how to strengthen state authority. Caillaux thought it a matter of leadership and political will. Tardieu, by contrast, called for "constitutional measures" that, according to Mendès France, would give the prime minister power to dissolve the chamber of deputies, trim back parliamentary initiative, carry out a political purge of the administration, and exploit the use of referenda. Siding with Caillaux, Mendès France regarded the constitutional route as illusory, a "pitiful program in the face of our immense current difficulties." What the French people wanted, he argued, was "a reform in political customs, in leaders' mentality, . . . and the audacity of their decisions, . . . [so as to further] the primacy of the general interest over special interests . . . and the speed of implementation." To accomplish all this, he concluded, "it is not necessary to change something in our laws: we have to have men, with all that that implies in the most powerful sense of the word."[14] Echoing his conclusions about Poincaré's fiscal policy and the Bank for International Settlements, Mendès France offered enlightened political leadership as a remedy—assertive political elites who used their authority to take action, harness the experts, and subordinate private interests to the public good. His confidence in the potentiality of enlightened leadership (and, later in his career, enlightened citizenship as well), and his distrust of constitutional change, would remain a hallmarks of his approach to reform—in sharp contrast to Michel Debré, who would eventually take André Tardieu's path and bet heavily on constitutional reform.

Although just a bit younger than Mendès France, Debré came of age politically amid the full blast of political, economic, and international crisis in the mid-1930s rather than in the late 1920s when Mendès France could still regard the Cartel des Gauches as a hopeful referent. Born in 1912 in Paris of physician parents, Michel Debré grew up in a wealthy and cultivated bourgeois household that valued art, intellect, and the professions of law, medicine, civil service, and the academy, in contrast to the brasher world of business and politics that Mendès France's more middle-class family was accustomed to. Debré's mother, an accomplished doctor, died when Michel was 17. His father, Robert Debré, world-renowned as a pioneer in pediatrics, became a policy luminary in his own right, working with Alfred Sauvy to shape pronatalist policy and medical reform during the Fourth and early Fifth Republics.[15] Father Robert descended from a long line of Ashkenazi Jews from Alsace who had resided in the same town as Léon Blum's Alsatian family. Michel's paternal grandfather had been a rabbi. But by the time Michel came along, the Robert Debré household was assimilated, secular, and if fairly apolitical, certainly avowedly republican and vaguely center-Left.

Michel strongly identified with his father, and even as adults they remained close companions.[16] He briefly considered going into medicine himself, but knew his father's career would always overshadow his. Still, the concreteness and precision of the healer's profession appealed to him. In his writing and lecturing about government, Michel Debré often fell upon the use of medical analogies to describe the state. Speaking with students at the new École nationale d'administration in 1947, he likened civil servants to doctors who drew on an empirical science of observation to carry on their real work as practitioners.[17] And he loved to think about the state as a stricken organism. Criticizing the ill effects of excessive centralization, he wrote shortly after the war: "Our state by dint of its centralization has become a veritable skeleton: the living cells that make for the life of the body are always inert; its atrophied muscles can no longer move without an exhausting effort."[18] Organicist metaphors were commonplace, of course, in discussions of state and society. But it is easy to sense in Michel's emulation of his father an inclination to see the work of the civil servant and reformer as a matter of science and professionalism, not politics. He wrote late in life in his memoirs, "Throughout my life I have made the comparison between these men of science and the political men I spent my time with. The comparison rarely favors my colleagues, however more often they may be cited by journalists and even historians."[19]

Michel Debré's most important initiation into policymaking occurred in November 1938 when, at the age of 26, he joined Finance Minister Paul Reynaud's policy staff. Reynaud became a model for him of political rectitude. The road to this post had taken Debré from the Lycée Louis-le-Grand, to studies at the Paris Law Faculty and at Science Po (like Mendès France), where he wrote a thesis on state regulation of the artisanal trades, and then to the prestigious corps of the Conseil d'État, which he joined in 1934 being first on the list of candidates. His father's connection to the banker André Istel, a close confident of Reynaud, brought Debré to the finance minister's attention. What Debré brought to this post was legal talent, a gift for writing, a strong sense of himself as a *serviteur de l'État* (a servant of the state), and a patriotic conviction that previous governments, including the Popular Front that he had initially welcomed, had failed to meet Hitler's challenge. He was intellectually predisposed for ministerial activism, having just published an article in *Sciences Politiques* advocating a more dirigiste role for the state in the French economy:

> The state must be alive to its new mission and conceive its activity scientifically rather than acting purely according to politics. . . . The problem is no longer to decide whether or not the French economy will be managed; the only choice is between shilly-shallying, letting numerous pilots each follow their own course, and firm direction provided by one, good pilot.[20]

As a dirigiste Debré sang in harmony with Mendès France and many other Young Turks. But unlike Mendès France, who had entered into Parliament full of idealism about leadership and worries about the role of experts in a democracy, Debré had opted for the *grands corps de l'État* and the role of the high-level civil servant. From his vantage point it was not uncommon in the 1930s to think that in some policy domains administration ought indeed to supersede politics.

Such convictions about the use of state authority and expertise—the need for "one good pilot"—served Debré well in Reynaud's staff. The young legal civil servant was immediately put to work drafting the famous decree laws that within days would abolish the 40-hour week (enabling employers to require longer hours), triggering the general strike of November 30, 1938, that devastated the CGT. He did not hesitate to take the assignment; he had regarded the forty -hour week as a colossal mistake from the beginning.[21] Sharing an office with the young Alfred Sauvy, Debré also played an important role drafting the 1939 Code de la famille (Family Code). This project, too, spoke to his convictions: Adolph Landry, a parliamentary champion of pronatalist policy and a family friend, had convinced him of the gravity of France's demographic crisis.[22] Debré served as well on the Comité de réorganisation administrative, dubbed in the press the Comité de la hache (the hatchet committee), which embarked on one of the most extensive surveys of the state apparatus that has ever been undertaken in France, with an eye toward administrative efficiency.[23]

What's striking about Debré's staff experience is how much he prized it as formative of his own political personality. He wrote extensively in his memoirs about his ten-month stint with Reynaud as a brief, if all too tardy, triumph of reason after years of governmental ineptitude and political self-serving. Among the country's leading politicians, in his view, only the maverick Reynaud had the courage to see what needed to be done, "by opposing academic conformism in monetary policy, military conformism in armaments, national conformism in demography."[24] Of self-doubt Debré showed barely a trace. He saw in the 40-hour week only an obstacle to production, which by 1938 in some plants it surely was, but scarcely recognized it as a symbolic achievement for workers that could have a bearing on morale, productivity, and the industrial climate in the rearmament drive. The wider political ramifications of policy initiatives little interested him. He took enormous pride in having been one of a "very small number of civil servants" who drafted the family code, which, as he later said, "gave new authority to the health ministry, . . . affirmed the state's responsibility [in this domain], . . . [and] opened a thirty-year period when, despite changes in regime, demographic preoccupations would remain dominant in the minds of political authorities."[25] Working, as

he put it, at the "hinge" *(charnière)* between administration and politics, this experience of writing decrees and legislation that changed the
social fabric of his country gave him a sense of vocation as a *serviteur
de l'État* that he would retain for the rest of his life.[26]

Serving on Reynaud's staff also put him on opposite sides of the
policy barricades from Mendès France. The latter regarded the Reynaud
decree laws of November 1938 as "unjust" and "ineffective."[27] As a
Popular Front loyalist, Mendès France objected to Reynaud's wholesale
attack on the 40-hour week and the CGT, and even more to regres-
sive tax measures that Reynaud imposed to help finance rearmament.
Reynaud's approach—restoring business confidence and reversing
capital flight by implementing the anti–Popular Front agenda of the
big-business Right—flew in the face of what Mendès France had tried
to achieve just eight months earlier when Léon Blum, given the opportunity to form a new, though short-lived, government, appointed
him undersecretary of finance. Aided immensely by the brilliant economic journalist Georges Boris, Mendès France drafted a bold economic
plan to boost rearmament. It called for capital controls, progressively
structured tax hikes, price controls, a capital levy of up to 17 percent,
government loans from the Bank of France, and longer working hours
in defense plants. The plan won approval in the Chamber of Deputies, only to die in the Senate, where a recalcitrant Caillaux, troubled
especially by the capital levy, led the counterattack. Though stillborn,
this effort to launch economic planning on the eve of a new world war
was an important moment in the history of French planning and a
baptism for Mendès France in ministerial policymaking. Under Boris's
tutelage, he now came to embrace Keynesian strategies of fiscal management and pump-priming, and he shed whatever reticence about
planning he harbored from his classical economics training.[28] The Reynaud strategy of November 1938, then, was a double blow to Mendès
France—against both the vision of social justice associated with the
Popular Front and the *planiste* style of dirigisme he had come to be
identified with.[29]

By the time war broke out in the autumn of 1939, Debré and Mendès
France had acquired different perches within and outlooks upon gov-
ernment service in the French Republic. Though both had welcomed
Blum's Popular Front government in 1936, they found themselves on

opposite sides in 1938 when centrist republicans had to choose between trying to resuscitate the Popular Front or bury it, as Daladier and Reynaud succeeded in doing. Mendès France's brief planning effort in 1938, his association with Boris and Blum, his admiration for the Roosevelt New Deal, which he long regarded as a policy model for the Popular Front, all kept him leaning left. He remained, moreover, unwilling to castigate the constitutional structure of the Third Republic or the principle of parliamentary government that undergirded it. In his work as a deputy he seemed to find the balance he was looking for between policy expertise and the salutary, democratic habits of serving a local constituency—trying, as it were, to practice the virtues and avoid the sins of a Poincaré.

Debré, by contrast, had taken the royal road to becoming a high-level civil servant through the Conseil d'État and a minister's policy staff, and this path gave him a different outlook—little angst about the tyranny of the experts or their marriage to private interests and plenty of appreciation for the beauty of decree laws as a way around Parliament. From where Debré sat, it was the power of the deputy, not the expert, that threatened to compromise the national interest. Even so, despite his drift to the center-Right since 1936 and his role in reversing the legislative gains of the Popular Front, Debré showed little interest in the more right-wing corporatist ideas that made Salazar's Portugal a fashionable compass point on the radical Right. Nor was he drawn to the technocratic authoritarianism of Jean Bichelonne that was to find such purchase in the Vichy regime. Debré remained a Jacobin republican and a centrist, and from the perspective of the divisive French 1930s, not in the end all that distant from the dirigiste Radicalism of a Mendès France.

Their apprenticeships in government service had had, after all, much in common. Each man had found models in republican mavericks, be they Poincaré, Blum, or Reynaud. Each had inserted himself within influential, and partially intersecting, policymaking networks—Mendès France through Georges Boris and Georges Bonnet with their connections to the Radical and Socialist Parties, Debré through Reynaud and mentors at the Conseil d'État such as Alexandre Parodi and Pierre Laroque. They would later rely on these connections to rise in the Resistance. Like many young governmental elites of the

REFORMER DILEMMAS

Depression-torn 1930s, Mendès France and Debré both placed a high value on technical competence and the bold use of state authority. Their common legal training at the Paris Law Faculty and Sciences Po had given them both a foundation in administrative law and constitutional theory that further solidified their "sense of the state" and their confidence that it was legitimate to expand government authority.[30] Though unambiguously committed as democrats (unlike a number of Young Turks of the period), both men had a technocratic side—Mendès France with his newfound fascination with planning and his ambition to become the Radical Party's leading economist-politician, Debré with his talent for drafting complex social and economic legislation. The trauma of defeat and the long years of Occupation and Resistance that followed would give them an even deeper reservoir of common experience, as would the disappointments they encountered in the Liberation period.

Bruised Architects of a Liberated France

Service in the Resistance earned both men prominence in the Liberation government of Charles de Gaulle; their subsequent dismay over political setbacks in 1945 colored their vision of democratic reform for the rest of their lives. Neither man had an easy time finding his way into the engine room of the Resistance movement. Mendès France first had to endure arrest, imprisonment, and a humiliating trial by the Vichy government on trumped-up charges of desertion. Only after escaping through the window of his prison cell in Clermont-Ferrand and living on the run for months did he find safe passage from Geneva to Lisbon to London, where his friend Georges Boris had established himself as an advisor to de Gaulle. Mendès France insisted on serving in the RAF, but after months of flying bombing missions over France he finally heeded de Gaulle's call in late 1943 to become commissioner of finance in the Comité français de libération nationale (CFLN), de Gaulle's Liberation government in the making. This post reconfirmed Mendès France's stature, which he had already achieved by 1938, as the center-Left's leading young economic policy parliamentarian. The war years may have subjected Mendès France to a harrowing personal odyssey and painful separation from his family, but Free France rather easily enabled him to resume his journey on the political and professional path he forged in the Popular Front.

For the younger Michel Debré, by contrast, work in the internal Resistance of metropolitan France catapulted him to a level of influence he could not have anticipated before the war. Taken prisoner as a soldier in the fighting of June 1940 and imprisoned near Orléans, he managed to elude German guards during a work detail and slipped into the unoccupied southern zone. He soon resumed his duties at the Conseil d'État, which had relocated to a suburb of Clermont-Ferrand. France's defeat shook him deeply and may have had something to do with his conversion to Catholicism during the grim early phase of the Occupation. He nonetheless remained republican to the core (though scornful of the Third Republic) and ached to continue the fight clandestinely. Debré said later of this period that he drew inspiration from Fichte's *Discours à la nation allemande* and from the Prussian reform of 1806 when Stein, Scharnhorst, and Gneisenau used defeat at the hands of Napoleon as an opportunity to recast the nation and army root and branch. Incongruous as a Prussian precedent may have seemed in 1940, to Debré it symbolized the kind of state-focused, elite-led reform he now hankered for, though under something other than a collaborationist Vichy regime.

Debré found that something in de Gaulle's France Libre (Free France). While on temporary diplomatic assignment in Morocco in the spring of 1941, he met with Emmanuel Monick and René Courtin, who urged him to help build the internal resistance and its links to London while still working in the unoccupied zone as a civil servant. This he did until he came under suspicion of the Vichy police in late 1942.[31] He then moved to Paris, went fully into the underground, and assumed such complicated duties as raising funds for the Resistance from the Parisian bourgeoisie and recruiting new prefects and Commissaires de la République to take over the administration after the Allied invasion. Through Alexandre Parodi, his former mentor at the Conseil d'État, he also became one of nine members of the Comité général des experts, renamed the less overtly elitist Comité général des études (CGE), one of the key groups de Gaulle looked to for charting policy directions for a liberated France.[32] This assignment secured Debré's ascendancy, at age 31, into what has been called the governmental resistance—a network of elites planning the restoration of a republican state, in contrast to the political resistance of party militants, and especially Communists, who built the Resistance as a social movement.[33]

The CGE also enabled Debré to establish himself as a leading advocate of constitutional reform. Much of his thinking found its way into the influential post-Liberation booklet that he wrote with Emmanuel Monick, *Refaire la France: L'effort d'une génération*.[34] There they sketched out most of the major social and economic policy prescriptions of de Gaulle's Provisional Government—nationalizations, social security, pronatalism, and an encouragement of immigration by Europeans (but not others). An unapologetic nationalism gave the book its rhetorical force: "[France], like it or not, will have to choose its fate: that of a great power or a small power, of a state that plays a global role or one that restricts itself to its own existence."[35] Debré's long-standing worry about population decline also found ample expression in the text: unless things changed, he said, "in a few generations France will be a country without wealth, without an empire, without culture . . . without Frenchmen."[36] But undergirding the whole program was Debré's preoccupation with institutional change, especially the need for a strong executive. Debré and Monick called for a more rationalized Parliament (an advisory upper house, and a weightier lower house with a six-year term), a reformed civil service, a single-district majoritarian electoral system, suffrage for women, an extra vote for heads of household (the family vote), and most startling of all a "republican monarch," a strong president elected by a large electoral college to a twelve-year term with the power to name the prime minister and dissolve the assembly.

Since the late 1930s Debré had regarded weak government as the biggest source of the nation's troubles. His thinking owed a good deal not only to André Tardieu but also to René Capitant, a law professor at Sciences Po (and an important future Gaullist in his own right), who in 1936 lectured on the unorthodox constitutional theories of his own teacher, Raymond Carré de Malberg. The latter, who drew on German political thought, had argued before World War I that French parliamentary government had failed to maintain a true separation of legislative and executive powers, and as a result the dominance of the Chamber of Deputies over the whole of government had effectively replaced popular sovereignty with parliamentary sovereignty. Carré de Malberg's critique of the Third Republic gave Debré a way to free himself, as Nicholas Wahl has argued, "from the grip of traditional theories that he now considered unrelated to French realities."[37] With his strategic location in the CGE and his co-authorship of *Refaire la France,* Debré now seized the opportunity to offer a remedy he understood might be hard for the public to swallow. But given the divisions inherent in the country and the discredit that defeat had heaped on the Third Republic, Debré and Monick regarded robust executive authority as the sine qua non of national renewal, writing that if the French did not achieve such a reform, "our political institutions will lack their keystone and France will have neither the stability nor the permanence of power."[38] Debré emerged from the Resistance elite as the country's most determined champion of the strong executive, even more sure of himself on this point than de Gaulle himself. Indeed, he said later that among Resistance leaders he seemed like "the white crow," because he "said the state had to be legitimate, independent and authoritarian, that is to say, having authority."[39]

Once the liberation began in the summer of 1944, Debré got the opportunity to practice the kind of administrative leadership he idealized in his Resistance texts. As Commissaire de la République (Republican Commissar) in Angers, he presided over the restoration of republican authority in the Loire region he knew from his childhood. When he replaced the Vichy prefect "in the name of General de Gaulle and the republic" and sat down at his desk, he thought, as he described it later, "Je suis devenu l'État [I became the state]."[40] Like other commissars he rushed to impose his authority before the American army or politically ambitious liberation committees tried to fill the power vacuum of Vichy's collapse, and he went on to establish judicial procedures for liberation trials and to tackle the challenges of acute shortages, infrastructure repair, labor recruitment and wages, and support for the families of POWs and deportees. He also assumed a pedagogical role by speaking to groups across the region about the urgency of setting aside the old struggles over social class and religion in order to create a "Fourth Republic that would be the opposite of the Third" and to make France a major industrial force and the leading military power in Europe. His speeches, he wrote later, seemed to surprise a peasant world that "had been deluded for four years with the theme of 'return to the land.' "[41] More troubling still, by early 1945, as some semblance of normalcy returned to the Loire, he sensed a passivity in his audiences, despite their applause. He wondered how "the new democracy would be able to produce and sustain leaders capable of getting the French to rise above themselves."[42] Luckily for him, just as he began to see the job of commissar becoming routine and action shifting to the capital, de Gaulle summoned him to his staff for higher duties in Paris in the spring of 1945, most notably to establish the new École nationale d'administration (ENA; National School of Administration) that he had advocated in the CGE and that he now convinced de Gaulle was a national priority.

The ENA gave Debré the perfect place to apply his ideas about state service: remaking France, he had said in his wartime writings, required "remaking the state," and what better way to start than a new grande école to staff the high civil service.[43] State administrators, he told de Gaulle, had long been too easily absorbed by the petty affairs of provincial and local governance. The ENA, as he put it, would give its students "a sense of the state, . . . make them understand the responsibilities of the Administration, make them taste the grandeur and accept the demands of the métier."[44] It would also create policy generalists who could compete for a single grands corps examination and hence begin to break up the self-perpetuating insularity of the separate grands corps de l'État. A curriculum emphasizing economics and social policy would better equip graduates to staff the postwar dirigiste state. Debré also hoped the school would draw students from beyond the usual recruiting grounds of the Parisian bourgeoisie, and he scandalized his colleagues by insisting on giving access to women, a commitment deriving in part, perhaps, from the example set by his mother.[45] The ENA soon proved disappointing as a vehicle for democratizing entry into the high civil service. But in altering the training of young fonctionnaires and in centralizing their recruitment into the state, the ENA became a landmark innovation of the Liberation period. It confirmed Debré's reputation as a state reformer. Moreover, the way de Gaulle pushed through the ENA reform—by ordinance rather than law because he believed he could not pass it in the Assembly—gave

Debré one more experience in which the nation seemed best served by administrative action rather than politics.[46]

Then came crushing disappointment. In January 1946 de Gaulle resigned, having failed to seize control of the constitution-writing process. Debré had wanted de Gaulle to adopt his own wartime ideas for a new constitution and push them through by means of a popular referendum. He likewise had wanted de Gaulle to have municipal elections promptly after the Liberation (rather than after the POWs returned, as de Gaulle decided to do) so as to undercut the power of the local liberation committees, where Communists in many districts predominated. With quick municipal elections behind him, Debré thought, de Gaulle could move swiftly to promulgate a constitution and secure its popular approval.[47] Something like this approach de Gaulle followed—in 1958, when he asked Debré to draft the constitution of the Fifth Republic to take it directly to the people in a referendum. But in 1945 de Gaulle felt compelled to respect the political muscle of the Communists, Socialists, and MRP, who called for the election of a Constituent Assembly to draft a constitution. Debré never got over it. He felt de Gaulle had squandered an opportunity to force through the key institutional reforms a robust state required—a constitution with a strong executive and an electoral law mandating majoritarian electoral districts with single-round elections to foster the development of a British-style two-party system. At the thirtieth anniversary of the Liberation in 1975, Debré still claimed that de Gaulle could have spared the country a weak Fourth Republic had he acted accordingly.[48]

In this respect the militant Debré of 1945 had something in common with Pierre Mendès France, who also collided with de Gaulle's political pragmatism. In June 1944 de Gaulle appointed Mendès France to his Provisional Government as head of a new Ministry of National Economy. Hoping to capitalize on the nation's patriotic ardor at the Liberation before it dissipated, Mendès France argued for a tough anti-inflationary monetary policy, prompt nationalizations, and a strong economic planning authority housed in his own ministry. Mendès France believed each initiative reinforced the others. Nationalizations and planning would empower the state to channel investment toward national priorities to maximize growth, which in turn would make a salutary but initially painful monetary rigor more politically palatable. Together these initiatives would realize the ambitions of the Resistance for state-led economic renovation.

But Mendès France suffered setbacks on all three fronts.[49] Other economic ministries, especially the Ministry of Production that Vichy had invented and that de Gaulle now put in the hands of (the rather conservative) Socialist Robert Lacoste, resisted the notion of subordination to Mendès France's planning authority. De Gaulle, moreover, preferred to postpone nationalizations until the war ended and national elections gave his government genuine legitimacy. That left monetary policy, on which Mendès France staked every card remaining in his hand. The ingredients for potentially ruinous inflation were clear to see: a surfeit of currency (money in circulation had tripled between 1939 and 1944), acute shortages of nearly every kind, an entrenched black market, and wage earners yearning for higher salaries. To avert calamity, Mendès France called for tough measures: controlling wages and prices, taxing capital, freezing accounts, confiscating illicit wartime profits, and most controversial of all, imposing a mandatory exchange of old currency for new, at reduced rates, so as to sharply diminish liquidity. Mendès France's supporters saw this as a choice between rigor and laxity. His chief opponent, Finance Minister René Pleven, regarded it as a choice between "dogmatism" and "the spirit of practicality."[50] Pleven and most of the rest of de Gaulle's cabinet knew how bitterly bankers opposed these measures, and they feared the social unrest that might ensue in the countryside. They recommended instead a much more limited currency exchange and a more innocuous policy of issuing government bonds to soak up some liquidity. Mendès France found little support for his approach in the Constituent Assembly, least of all from Communists trying to court peasants and rally workers to the "battle for production." De Gaulle might still have salvaged the Mendés France strategy, but he too opted for practicality. "The country is sick and wounded," he later wrote. "Why throw it into dangerous convulsions when in any event it is going to recover its health?"[51] Mendès France resigned from his ministry in April 1945.

This pivotal policy defeat did a great deal to shape the way Mendès France would continue to combine the roles of expert and politician after the war. For one thing, he had gathered into his confidence a dynamic group of other young experts, mostly high-level civil servants like François Bloch-Lainé, Gabriel Ardant, Roger Goetze, and others whom one might call the state's emerging in-house economics intelligentsia. He worked closely with them as an equal, and they recognized the mutual benefits of collaboration.[52] They saw him as one of them, as a fellow colleague in the rational pursuit of national renewal. Maintaining this fraternal connection with a growing technical cadre of state economists and managers in the high civil service would remain as important to Mendès France, personally and politically, as his agricultural electoral base in the Louvier and the Eure. He would further cultivate this connection to young economic experts, such as Valéry Giscard d'Éstaing and Simon Nora, by teaching economics at the ENA in 1947 and 1948 and agreeing in 1952 to serve as the first president of the new Commission des comptes et des budgets économiques de la nation, a body Nora created to nurture the state's role in national income accounting and economic forecasting.[53]

The 1944–1945 episode in de Gaulle's government also proved formative for Mendès France in another respect: as minister he experimented with using radio broadcasts to reach out rather intimately to the public and defend his policies. On twenty consecutive Saturdays between November 1944 and the end of March 1945 he exhorted his listeners to work more, consume less, and shun the black market for the sake of the "reconstruction, rectification, and renovation of France."[54] He adopted the posture of pedagogue, prophet, and cheerleader as he reported on scarcities and the country's efforts to overcome them. Saving his strongest rhetoric for his final broadcast, shortly before his resignation, he told his listening audience: "Inflation is the triumph of immorality and social inequity. . . . When price hikes are certain, you get rich most surely by holding back merchandise, hoarding it, and crossing your arms, while useful investment with long-term profits in a depreciated currency remains unattractive."[55] This effort to establish a direct connection to the public marked a radical departure in ministerial leadership in France. Mendès France had found obvious inspiration for it in FDR's fireside chats and in Churchill's wartime speeches. "I think a great people such as us," he told them, "want to be spoken to frankly, and I saw with my own eyes, when my unit was stationed in England, that another great people accomplished great things because they were spoken to frankly."[56] This use of the radio also gave Mendès France a means, insufficient though it was, to raise his visibility and hence his influence in the absence of having the backing of a powerful political party or parliamentary alliance. He would make even bigger use of the radio chat when he returned to power as prime minister in 1954.

His stint as minister of national economy also confirmed Mendès France in his commitment to operate as crusader, at once both rationalist and moralizing, for economic renovation, even at the cost of political isolation. As a politician he was perfectly capable of striking bargains and making compromises; he would never otherwise have survived for decades as a deputy in an agricultural district. But in matters of broad national economic policy he functioned more as the expert-in-power than the politician. He and Georges Boris had complete confidence in their approach to nationalization, planning, and monetary discipline; it was merely a matter of getting others to see the light. Just as de Gaulle brooked no compromise when it came to restoring France's place at the table of the Allied powers, so too Mendès France regarded economic renovation, along rationalist and dirigiste lines, as policy terrain subject to scientific rationality that ought to transcend ordinary politics. After witnessing the miracles of American and British economic mobilization in the war, the logic of state-led economic expansion and a Keynesian revolution for France, he believed, ought to speak for itself. He knew the conventional wisdom about the political impracticality of his monetary plan. But as he told Jean Lacouture years later, "Must [a politician] be content to adapt to the possibilities of the political situation and renounce what he believes to be true?"[57]

The lesson he learned from his policy defeat in 1944–1945, then, was not to be more bending, but quite the opposite—to negotiate in advance the conditions he required to preside over a ministry. After de Gaulle resigned and the Socialist Félix Gouin invited him to join a new government in January 1946 as minister of the economy, Mendès France agreed only on the condition that the parliamentary majority of Communists, Socialists, and MRP would consent in advance to roughly the same austerity policy he failed to get the year before and grant him plenary powers to put his plan into action. He was looking for a way to be a Colbert (Louis XIV's famed financial strongman) within a parliamentary republic. But the parties refused, and he declined the post. He would spend the rest of the 1940s playing a more marginal role in Parliament and devoting most of his energy to representing France in a number of highly technical assignments in international finance at the International Monetary Fund, the United Nations, and the Banque internationale pour la reconstruction et le développement (BIRD).

Mendès France and Debré met similar setbacks in 1945. To be sure, they had sharply differing strategies. Mendès France directed his attention at economic discipline and renovation—a society-centered approach entailing only modest change in the structure of the state. Nationalization had ample precedent in the interwar years. And he was willing to build on, rather than radically revamp, the new planning agency that Vichy had created with the Délégation générale à l'équipement national. In this respect Mendès France still operated within the paradigm Joseph Caillaux had sketched out in 1932, which viewed policy and leadership rather than constitutional change as the path to reform. Debré now took the opposite tack, seeking to reshape the state itself. He viewed the "republican monarch" as paramount and sought constitutional change to establish it. His was a state-centered approach to reform not unlike Tardieu's rejoinder to Caillaux.

Even so, Mendès France and Debré shared more in common in 1946 than at any time in their careers. They both had bet heavily on de Gaulle's support and lost. As much as Mendès France would later object to the very idea of a "republican monarch," he wished as much as Debré did in 1945 that de Gaulle would embrace his own strategy of reform, circumvent parliamentary opposition, and make the case for austerity directly to the people. Likewise his futile effort to secure plenary powers in early 1946 further illustrated the need he felt to work around parliamentary recalcitrance for the sake of economic rigor, if only on a temporary basis. The two men, then, shared the expert's impatience with parties and political notables, left and right, who in 1945 had stood in the way of what they each believed with a certainty the country needed.

Divergent Engagements with the Fourth Republic

During the Fourth Republic, Debré fashioned a political career that mirrored how Mendès France had already managed to blend the worlds of policy expertise and parliamentary politics. Professionally, they came to resemble each other as politician-experts, a leadership type that would become more common in the postwar era, and especially the Fifth Republic, as more and more graduates of the ENA and the École polytechnique took up political careers. Mendès France, in fact, has been credited with inspiring, by force of his example, many young *énarques* (ENA graduates) in the 1960s to enter politics.[58] Politically, however, the two men grew farther apart, and dramatically so after 1956, when they took diametrically opposed positions in response to the regime crisis that beset the Fourth Republic during the Algerian war.

Debré's political career grew directly out of his Resistance activity and his engagement with Gaullism as a policy expert. In 1946, after taking part alongside Mendès France and Jean Monnet in Léon Blum's mission to Washington to negotiate loans and debt forgiveness from the United States, resulting in the famous Blum-Bynes Accords, he decided to take the plunge into electoral politics. At de Gaulle's suggestion, he ran on the Radical Party list for a parliamentary seat in the Loire in 1946, and lost. Two years later he tried again, this time winning a Senate seat representing Indre-et-Loire, in the same region he had presided over in 1944 as a republican commissar. He would keep the seat for the rest of the Fourth Republic. Though nominally in the Radical Party, he worked assiduously as a Gaullist pamphleteer and policy expert, publishing books, articles, and policy briefs. Like Mendès France, he taught courses at the ENA on government. In the Senate he became something of a specialist on Germany, drawing on his own deep-seated convictions about the continuing German menace as well as on the knowledge he acquired in 1947, when he served ten months as general secretary of German and Austrian affairs for the Ministry of Foreign Affairs. He became a leading senatorial adversary of the (eventually unsuccessful) campaign for a European Defense Community, which would rearm West Germany, and he criticized too the European Coal and Steel Community, which he regarded as a fig leaf for the reassertion of German industrial power.[59] Above all, he established himself in the 1950s as the most acerbic and outspoken republican critic of the Fourth Republic as a regime. In a series of pungent, polemical books, *La mort de l'État républicain* (1947), *La République et son pouvoir* (1950), and *Ces princes qui nous gouvernent* (1957) he made his case that governments in the Republic had an intrinsic and fatal absence of power and that only a radical constitutional reform could prevent the nation's imminent, catastrophic decline.

Debré had developed most of these constitutional ideas by the Liberation. A deep-felt and quite conventional form of republican nationalism formed the foundation of his thinking. He set his compass by Ernest Renan, who defined the nation as "a grand solidarity, created by the feeling of sacrifice that one makes or is prepared to make still. . . . A plebiscite every day."[60] This willful attachment to a historically constructed community, rather than geography, ethnicity, or language, had made France *the* model nation, in Debré eyes, but it also made it all the more essential that the nation have the strong state it required. Debré emerged from his Provisional Government experience as the most stridently Jacobin voice in the republican center-Right— committed to the state as the guarantor of popular sovereignty and national unity and hostile to organizations, policies, and loyalties that might undermine that unity. Like de Gaulle, he viewed a strong state with a rejuvenated civil service and a powerful executive as a means to insulate government from popular pressures.[61] Of course, the postwar strength of the Communist Party posed a special threat. But Debré's Jacobinism drew on something even deeper than anti-Communism: a sense that, despite the voluntarist ethos at the heart of French national belonging, ordinary citizens could never be fully trusted to put national interests ahead of their own. He wrote in *La mort de l'État républicain:*

> Citizens don't have children, but the nation needs arms and brains: so the state encourages natality and organizes immigration. Citizens work with outmoded methods and produce little of value, whereas the nation needs fresh, productive capital: so the state imposes economic reform. Citizens forget their dependence on lands abroad and despise their colonies, but the nation needs raw materials, commerce and expansion: so the state preserves the empire.[62]

His litany went on. Only the state, in short, could rescue the nation from decline.

De Gaulle could have hardly said it more bluntly, and by the time Debré published this in 1947 he had become part of a small circle of de Gaulle loyalists building the Rassemblement populaire français (RPF) with the aim of bringing de Gaulle back to power. Just as he did in the days of the Resistance CGE, Debré wrote well-informed policy papers on an astonishing range of subjects—nationalized enterprise, education, housing, social security, radio, food supplies, the electoral system, taxes, the use of Marshall Plan funds, and of course constitutional reform—all in preparation for what some Gaullists still hoped might be a sudden return of the General followed by a period of emergency rule and national renovation.[63] It was an odd mix of policy pragmatism and a political fantasy for a kind of replay of the Liberation that in the late 1940s, at least, was quite out of touch with reality. Debré was one of the few members of the Gaullist inner circle who expressed skepticism that the RPF offered a realistic vehicle for bringing de Gaulle back into power.[64]

One might infer from Debré's Jacobin rhetoric and his zeal for playing draftsman for a new France that he yearned for an expert's paradise, freed from the reins of politics. But in virtually everything he wrote on the state during the Fourth Republic, Debré insisted on the centrality of democratic principles. "Democracy," he wrote in *La mort de l'État républicain*, "is perfectly suited to this conception of the [strong] state," for only a state that was fortified against the fragmenting, corrupting influence of parties and pressure groups could guarantee justice and individual liberty, which he saw as the essential attributes of democracy.[65]

Yet Debré was too serious a thinker to believe it was enough to simply proclaim that a strong state was essential for democracy. What makes his writing about the state interesting was his continuing search for ways to reconcile his primary commitment to restoring authority to the state with the need to preserve its democratic character, without which France would no longer be France or worthy of its standing as a great nation. He worried about the dangers of administrative tyranny, and he admired much in the political culture of Britain and the United States. In his postwar university lectures, for example, he spoke of the need for state administrators to acquire the degree of professionalism and independence from political authorities that he felt the British had established with Macaulay's reforms in the nineteenth century and that the French still needed to emulate.[66] He also understood that administration ultimately had to be accountable to elected officials. "To leave politics to the administration, that is, to *fonctionnaires*," he told students, "is to break the unity of national action and undermine society's morale."[67] He even went so far as to endorse Tocqueville's celebration of New England town government, where locally elected officials were accountable to neighbors and thereby empowered to supervise the local bureaucracy.[68] Such an arrangement offered the perfect antidote to administrative authoritarianism. From Tocqueville, too, and from his own frustrations with the entrenched bureaucratic traditionalism he found in Paris, Debré took much more seriously than one might have expected the ill effects of an excessive centralization, which he saw could sap the very state he sought to strengthen.[69]

Yet if Debré's turn to electoral politics and his insistence on democratic accountability tempered his administrative Jacobinism, he remained fervently statist in his strategic vision, seeing national renewal as depending first on buttressing state authority, and not the reverse, as Mendès France was inclined to do. He remained, too, an *haut fonctionnaire* (high-level civil servant) in his manner of operating, writing feverishly about the illness of the Fourth Republic and the remedies he would prescribe. Like Mendès France, he derived a good deal of satisfaction from talking with constituents and the local officeholders who gave him his mandate. But he never became a party man, and indeed when stumping in his district he made his independence a point of pride: "I am not indoctrinated into a party," he would say.[70] He lived elective office much as he envisioned it in his democratic theory—as a distant form of public accountability that linked the political leader to the nation without nurturing the parties and intermediary bodies he found so destructive of the state.

Likewise, his commitment to decentralization hardly qualified as Tocquevillean, despite the kind gestures toward New England municipal government. What he really worked for, in his writing and later as a minister in the 1960s, was not so much decentralization as "deconcentration"—not an effort to transfer authority to local political

officials but to make the central state's agents more effective at the
local level. By reducing the number of departments by half, to forty-
seven (a plan he pushed several times in his career to no avail), he hoped
to strengthen the autonomy of prefects from local pressure groups, who
had made them, as he put it contemptuously, just another "deputy" for
the department.[71] He also fought hard against any reform that promised to give meaningful political authority to the regions. To be sure,
Debré's conception of the state depended completely on democratic
institutions—free elections that made leaders accountable and gave legitimacy to a state whose raison d'être was to serve the nation. But he
associated democracy principally with the defense of liberty and
freedom from tyranny, not with public participation in policymaking;
anything resembling direct democracy (apart from referenda) he regarded
as anathema. In his diagnosis, Fourth Republic democracy suffered from
too much interest group involvement, not too little.

The Pierre Mendès France of the early and mid-1950s in many ways
agreed with Debré on the nature of the illness, though he continued to
differ on what to do about it. Like Debré, he lamented the stranglehold
that entrenched pressure groups and self-serving political parties had
on policy. Even the much-heralded Planning Commission of Jean
Monnet, in Mendès France's view, was too timid a form of dirigisme:
it had done too little to challenge the traditional business practices of
private industry or harness the considerable resources of the new
nationalized sector.[72] By the early 1950s, Mendès believed, France's
postwar drive for economic renovation had dangerously stalled.

But Mendès France also continued to believe that the solutions lay
in leadership, not in Debré's presidentialist recasting of state authority.
"The restoration of the state," he said at the Radical Party congress in
1953, "is not a matter of policing or violence; it will be achieved, irre-
sistibly, on the day the country recovers the feeling, lost a long time
ago, of having a supportive and decisive government that knows what
it wants and says it faithfully to the country, and that governs with no
goal but the public good, justice, and the nation's progress."[73] He also
believed leaders had the institutional tools they needed to shepherd the
country's "reconstruction" and "modernization," especially if they
could inspire in citizens the sense of transcendent national purpose
that the Liberation and the final push against Germany in 1945 had

given them.[74] The state had sufficient formal authority; it was a matter of shifting, as Mendès France's protégé Simon Nora phrased it, from a *dirigisme de protection,* those time-honored practices of sheltering the traditional sectors, to a *dirigisme d'expansion.*[75]

Ironically, only ending a war—in Indochina—would enable the country to recover the sense of common national purpose, the collective psychological war footing, that Mendès France yearned for. Only peace would make it possible to "restore to France its prosperity, its rank, and its capacity to achieve its mission."[76] Or so Mendès France argued before Parliament in 1953 in making the case for transferring resources from their "unproductive" use in a doomed colonial war to their "productive" investment in economic modernization at home. A deeply indebted, cash-poor government could not do everything at once. "To govern," as he so famously summed up the point, "is to choose."[77] When after Dien Bien Phu in 1954 the National Assembly, rather begrudgingly, voted for his investiture as prime minister with a mandate to negotiate an end to the war, he put into practice the style of leadership he thought country required. Mendès France came to the prime ministry with personal authority none of his parliamentary peers could claim. Years of service as an economic expert representing France internationally had given him credibility: by the 1950s economics was beginning to eclipse law as the reigning paradigm for legitimizing policy choices.[78] His standing with young economists in the administration had only risen as a result, and he rewarded them in turn. An unprecedented number of young graduates from the ENA, as many as twenty, took up cabinet staff positions in his government. He gave them, especially Simon Nora and Claude Gruson from the national accounting and forecasting staff (SEEF), sweeping responsibility to draft an economic program.[79] As parliamentarians, only Edgar Faure and Félix Gaillard matched Mendès France in economic expertise, but they lacked his maverick standing in Parliament and his willingness to defy its customs. Mendès France named ministers directly to his cabinet without negotiating beforehand with party barons. He refused to count the Communist Party as part of his voting majority on the Indochina question, so as to strengthen his negotiating hand with the Vietnamese. Most of all he made the signature feature of his leadership its public visibility, in contrast to the image of Parliament as a closed club of insulated powerbrokers.

Visibility came through three channels: the practice of what he liked to call a "contractual" relationship to Parliament in which he spelled out in advance his policy proposals and secured a working majority for them in advance; a skillful courting of the printed press—*Le Monde, France Observateur*, and especially *L'Express*, which Jean-Jacques Servan-Schreiber and Françoise Giroud had founded in 1953 to bring Mendès France to power; and the use of the Saturday radio chats he had first experimented with in 1944–1945 to establish a direct, emotive connection to the public. His plain-spoken clarity, his charm in making his listeners complicit in his own causes ("I ask you, don't let Sunday go by without thinking at least a few moments about the help you can lend me [in Geneva]"), and his lavish use of the first-person singular to personalize his authority made these broadcasts a milestone in the cultivation of public opinion.[80] His fellow lawmakers much resented his efforts to circumvent Parliament. And rightly so: his visibility, his reliance on technical staff in the high civil service who regarded him as a champion of their modernizing agenda, and his public approval ratings (reaching 60 percent)[81] had the effect, if only momentarily, of strengthening the executive in relationship to Parliament. It seemed as if he might achieve much of what Debré was calling for but within the framework of assembly-centered government. Parliament soon disabused him and the country of this illusion. Despite breaking the leadership mold, he still depended on a fragile parliamentary coalition, which in February 1955 fractured over Algerian policy. In the end, he served in office too briefly, and with too narrow a focus on urgent foreign policy problems—Indochina, Tunisia, German rearmament—to achieve much of what his career as a politician-expert had prepared him to do for the economy. To be sure, his government did take important initiatives in regional planning and industrial decentralization, in the public sponsoring of scientific research, and in nuclear power and nuclear weaponry. He, Simon Nora, Alfred Sauvy, and other experts in his entourage succeeded, too, in changing the national conversation about the economy by bringing into the airwaves, the press, and the halls of Parliament the steady invocation of "productivity," "expansion," and "reconversion," and the denigration of the "Malthusian" practices of France's producers.[82] If nothing else, this proliferation of productivity talk made it harder for Poujadists on the right and Communists on the Left to define the debate.[83] Mendès France's government also helped prepare France for what in 1957 would become the Common Market. Simon Nora, Claude Gruson, and François Bloch-Lainé convinced Mendès France that the country had recovered enough since 1945 to face the salutary competitive pressures of the international market. Hence, his government argued for liberalizing exchange controls and lowering tariffs, and it went ahead to create funds for retraining workers and converting outmoded companies to adapt accordingly.[84] But this was policy incrementalism, hardly the heroic shift from war fighting to productivity building Mendès France had hoped for.[85] When Gruson pleaded for a renewed commitment to ambitious planning to match the shift to trade liberalization, or when Nora urged Mendès France to take over the Finance Ministry directly (and push out Minister Edgar Faure), he refused on the grounds of economic and political pragmatism.[86] Nora, Gruson, and others in the young experts' entourage ended the seven months and seventeen days aggrieved and disappointed.[87]

The collapse of the Mendès France government also intensified frustrations on the center-Left with government instability under the Fourth Republic, because by raising expectations Mendès France had suddenly become the system's most spectacular casualty. For some *mendésistes* a journey eventually leading them into the Gaullist camp of a new Fifth Republic began here.[88] But for Mendés France himself, brevity in power inspired him to try to wrest control of his own Radical Party from its more conservative leaders and to crusade for the reform—not the Gaullist replacement—of the Fourth Republic.

What kind of reform? In a celebrated speech on the "crisis of democracy" in 1955 he called for nothing short of a transformation of French political life.[89] He had a few practical proposals: give the prime minister greater authority to dissolve Parliament and to use decree powers to flesh out the details of broad legislation; and replace the electoral system of proportional representation with a return to single-member district elections that under the Third Republic had tied deputies more closely to their voters. But his targets for change went far beyond the machinery of state, and he warned against making the constitution a "scapegoat" for the country's ills. The crisis ran much deeper than that: France had become a nation of citizens "estranged" from an "imposter state" (a term he borrowed from André Malraux) that appeared "disinterested in their fate." The parties had been captured by "oligarchies and clans." Leaders in government, the press, and the pressure groups had lost an understanding of the "general interest." As a result, too many voters had become abstentionists or something worse, Communist Party voters with no serious communist convictions, which to Mendès France was abstentionism by another name. "True democracy," which Mendès France defined as "an intimate association" or "fusion" of "the state and citizen," required, on the one hand, intellectually honest leaders who spoke the truth and proposed "clear, distinct, and limited solutions to problems," and citizens, on the other, who had a powerful sense of civic duty. He called for making voting mandatory and abstention subject to a fine. He exhorted citizens to democratize their parties by becoming active militants, to talk about national issues "at work, in the factory, on the street, and in the café," to ignore small factions and marginal movements, and to devote themselves instead to the big parties that alone "will be able to shape the national destiny." To do otherwise meant "resigning yourselves to dictatorship and all its consequences." Here, then, was Mendès France in full pedagogical form. Just as he had in his own governing style, so too in this prescription for reform, he had sought to revitalize the Republic by cultivating greater dialogue between the executive and the people. Pressure from above and below, he hoped, would empower the modernizers in all the major parties to push aside traditionalists who stood in the way of national progress.[90] Radio, the mass press, and public opinion polling gave this vision a mid-twentieth-century feel. But it was also easy to hear the late nineteenth-century echoes of Léon Gambetta and Jules Ferry, republican state-builders who also had been preoccupied with creating republican citizens.

Mendès France never got the chance to implement even the more practical aspects of this agenda. Much admired in "modernizing" circles of the non-Communist Catholic and secular Left, he nonetheless lacked a broad political base. True, he retained his ties to *L'Express*, and he created his own journal, *Les Cahiers de la République*, which kept his ardent supporters enlisted in the *mendésiste* agenda of economic progress, democratic reform, and, increasingly, Third World development. But he succeeded neither in returning to power in the 1956 elections nor even in prevailing over his rivals in the Radical Party. His position on Algeria further weakened his capacity to be a coalition builder: though staunchly committed to keeping Algeria French, he urged negotiating with the rebels as the way to do so, a view (like Camus's) that earned him disdain from supporters of both independence and Algerie française (keeping Algeria French).[91] The Communist Party distrusted him, and the Poujadists scorned him paradoxically as both un-French (that is, Jewish) and the quintessence of Parisian technocracy. Even the more moderate labor Left expressed a bit of the latter. "The Mendès France government," wrote R. Le Bourre critically in *Force Ouvrière*, "marks an important step in the forward march of technocracy."[92] As the Republic descended into even deeper crisis over the Algerian war, Mendès France's niche in the political landscape narrowed to the point where he no longer had power to define the debate on the future of the regime. That power was shifting to the combatants in Algeria and to men like Michel Debré who were trying to engineer de Gaulle's return to power.

Indeed, Debré, who had admired "le style Mendès France" (if not all the Mendès France choices) in 1954, had taken the collapse of the government in 1955 as further evidence that de Gaulle's return was only a matter of time. By 1957 Debré's verbal attacks on the Fourth Republic had acquired a radical, even insurrectionary tone.[93] In *Ces princes qui nous gouvernent* he focused his ire on the entire governing elite—its top 1,000 or so politicians, civil servants, academics, journalists, and leaders of industry, labor, and the Church—who tolerated the "deplorable institutions" of the Fourth Republic for the sake of their own power. He likened their blindness and fatalism to that of the Vichy elite. "In truth," he argued, "the regime little by little ceases to be legitimate."[94] To Debré's mind the rot was obvious. After all, Mendès France's government, which momentarily appeared to resuscitate the Republic, collapsed in failure like all the others. More voters in the 1950s seemed to support anti-system parties—Communists, Gaullists, Poujadists—than otherwise. And the bankruptcy of policy, in Debré's view, was clear—in the sluggishness of economic change in industry and the countryside, in the woeful state of the nation's housing, in the self-delusion of turning to a supranational Europe to contain German and American power. What outraged him most was imperial decline.

He had always viewed the Empire as fundamental to France's place in the world and an essential economic and demographic asset. Imperial strength figured prominently in his postwar vision in *Refaire la France*. Dien Bien Phu had dismayed him, and even more so the loss of dominion over Tunisia and Morocco and the humiliation in Suez. As a result, Algeria became his Verdun, a location of imperial defense beyond compromising. Once the war there deepened in 1956, he dropped his inhibitions and declared the Fourth Republic in full-scale crisis. In *Ces princes* he called openly for a "government of public safety"—an interim government of "reconstruction" with General de Gaulle as its head.[95]

What Debré imagined in *Ces princes* resembled his 1940 fantasies of a Prussian Reform, though this time conceived within the formal framework of France's democratic republic. He ended the book with an appeal to the *princes*: "[If] half of you demand of your political leaders that they put an end to outmoded institutions and bygone morays, so that room can be given to a government of public safety, which can resist, then who would dare oppose this pressure from above?"[96] This revolt from above by the nation's elite could, if it had the will, bring back de Gaulle, who represented "honor, the national interest, popular support, the law."[97] Once installed, a new government of public safety could, over what Debré estimated would be a period of eighteen months to four years, carry out urgent reforms—innovations in industry, agriculture, taxation, housing, education, and most of all, government itself, by creating the strong presidency and majoritarian electoral system he had advocated since 1944. Debré had no qualms about a top-down revolution: he believed this entire scenario—return of the savior, a government of public safety, a new regime—would have the support of a French public as disillusioned with their leaders as he was. They would usher the General to power much as they had in 1944. To promote such a climate and to keep the pressure on the "princes" in power, Debré created *Le Courrier de la Colère*, a biweekly newspaper that between November 1957 and the collapse of the Republic in May 1958 featured his regular drumbeat for de Gaulle's return and a government of public safety.[98] This politician-expert now entered into the ambiguous business of inciting rebellion from above in the cause of a renewal of French democracy.

In March 1958 he tried to enlist Pierre Mendès France into a now rapidly radicalizing Gaullist movement by asking for his help to install de Gaulle in power for six months with exceptional powers to (supposedly) restore peace in Algeria.[99] The gesture did not seem as quixotic then as it may to us now. Many Gaullists in Parliament, after all, had supported Mendès France's investiture in 1954 and his peace agreement with the Vietnamese, and Mendès France had a good deal in common with Debré and de Gaulle: ambition for executive power, a distrust of parties, confidence in experts, planning, and dirigisme, and a desire to restore France's rank in the world. Although calling Mendès France the General's John the Baptist, as some observers did later, makes too much of these similarities, it remains the case that *mendésisme* and *Gaullisme* drew on a common reservoir of people, ideas, and aims.[100] But Mendès France would have nothing of Debré designs, which offended his sense of legality and his loyalty to the Republic. For all their similarities in diagnosing the ills of the regime, the two men differed starkly in their view about what the country needed most. For Debré (and de Gaulle) it was state authority, from which all else would follow—grandeur, economic progress, and civic engagement. For Mendès France, it was economic progress and a revival of citizenship—which he believed the French state of the Fourth Republic, if in proper hands like his own, was still in a position to inspire.

The Draftsman and the Critic
of the Fifth Republic

When de Gaulle returned to power in June 1958 under threat of a military coup emanating out of Algiers and amid a parliamentary crisis that Debré had helped to engineer, the General and his draftsman at last had the chance to replay the Liberation with the script Debré had wanted all along. Algeria made all the difference. "It was the war in Algeria," Debré wrote later, "that revealed there was no longer a state. I had known it for ten years."[101] Political fears in May had been palpable, especially among political elites. "The Republic had only one defense between itself and fascism," Jacques Fauvet wrote in *Le Monde*, "and that was the person of General de Gaulle."[102] Even Georges Boris and Pierre Mendès France, who rarely indulged in hyperbole,

FIGURE 6.1 Protesting de Gaulle, 1958. Pierre Mendès-France (front row, third from left) and other left-wing leaders head up the march of May 28, 1958, in Paris along the traditional protest route from the place de la Nation to the place de la République. Somewhere between 150,000 (the police estimate) to more than twice that (the left-wing press estimate) demonstrated their opposition to de Gaulle's bid to replace the Fourth Republic with a new regime. Also in the front row are Socialist André Philip, second from the left, Edouard Daladier, fifth from the left, and François Mitterrand, sixth from the left. Keystone France / Gamma Keystone / Getty Images.

had expressed worries about a "fascist danger" many months before the end of the Fourth Republic.[103] Still, Mendès France would not countenance de Gaulle's liquidation of that republic, especially under the threat of a coup. Would that block fascism or pave its way?[104] He would go on to lead a large demonstration in the Fourth Republic's defense, four days before de Gaulle's investiture into office (see Figure 6.1). The oppositional gesture was futile, as everyone knew: with broad public approval, Parliament gave de Gaulle six months of exceptional powers, which he used to issue an extraordinary series of ordinances on a wide variety of policy matters—prompting Raymond Aron to call the episode "six months of Roman dictatorship."[105] Above all, he set Debré to work as minister of justice to draft a constitution.

Debré's text delivered much of what he had called for during the Occupation in *Refaire la France:* a presidency insulated from parliamentary pressure, elected by a large electoral college of about 80,000 public officials, and empowered to name a government, dissolve Parliament, issue referenda, and claim exceptional powers in moments of national emergency (the famous Article 16). The text also created a Constitutional Council to rule on the constitutionality of legislation, and it required parliamentarians to forfeit their seats if they were named ministers. Both these provisions reinforced a separation of powers. Debré's drafting process entailed compromise. He and de Gaulle had wanted, for example, a stronger Senate to further dilute the authority of the National Assembly. But bargaining on secondary matters paid off as Debré shepherded the text through a large constitutional consultative committee that gave jurists and parliamentarians enough of a say to enable most of the major political parties to claim some authorship of the document. After a vigorous public relations campaign to sell the new constitution to the public, four out of five French voters approved it in a national referendum. Only the Communist Party and a small coalition of other left-wing opponents to de Gaulle, including Pierre Mendès France, tried to mount a countercampaign, which was poorly funded and doomed before it was started.

It took the exercise of power, however, and not just a text, to fashion new modes of authority. The strong presidentialism we now take for granted in the Fifth Republic was not fully apparent at the beginning.[106] As Debré explained to the Conseil d'État in August 1958, it was still formally a parliamentary regime, and indeed he had hoped in vain to do more to replicate the British parliamentary system that he admired. Neither he nor de Gaulle had tried to establish a full-scale presidential system along the lines of the United States. Hence, to concentrate power in the executive they made full use of the tools the new constitution gave them. Once elected president, de Gaulle named Debré as his prime minister and together they created a government unprecedented in its reliance on "technicians," elite civil servants drawn heavily from the *grands corps*. A number of these experts became ministers: eight served in de Gaulle's emergency government of 1958 (most notably in Foreign Affairs, Interior, Armed Forces, and Overseas

Territories), and even more were added in the Debré government of 1959.[107] The technocratic profile of Debré's government became even sharper when, in a cabinet shake-up in 1960, they made civil servant Wilfred Baumgartner of the Bank of France the new minister of finance, replacing Antoine Pinay, the most distinguished parliamentarian in the government and a symbol of conservative probity in the Fourth Republic.[108] Expert-ministers, in contrast to the usual parliamentarians and party leaders who ran ministries, were thought to stick closer to their specialties and assigned territory, leaving Debré and de Gaulle more in control of general policy.[109] And the two men insisted on discipline. When Antoine Pinay wandered beyond his territory in a cabinet meeting, de Gaulle replied: "So the Finance Minister is now interested in foreign affairs?"[110] General De Gaulle and Debré also quickly established large, talented staffs in both the Elysée (presidential) and Matignon (prime ministerial) Palaces to plan policy, and they appointed special, sometimes secretive, commissions to chart direction and make budgetary decisions even over the heads of ministers.[111] Never before in the history of republican France had parliamentary politicians been so overshadowed in policymaking by top government leaders and the elite civil service. As the venerable political scientist André Siegfried put it, "Hence the regime takes on the character of a technocracy in which the chief of state absorbs into his person the political leadership of the country, properly speaking. . . . It will be . . . the republic of administrative talents, the 'capable ones,' as Gambetta called them, and all the prestige of political direction will reside at the summit in one person."[112]

Although De Gaulle and Debré made much of fact that they had broken with the Fourth Republic past, this technocratic turn in French governance had been a long time coming. Amid rupture there was plenty of continuity. For one thing, nearly all the elite civil servants on whom De Gaulle and Debré most depended, men like Robert Blot (tax administration), François Bloch-Lainé (financial administration), Roger Goetze (former budget director), and Maurice Pérouse (at the Treasury), had been top-level administrators in the Fourth Republic. Although Debré's government drew more heavily on elite civil servants in the prefectural and diplomatic corps, the Conseil d'État, and the military than from the economic planning experts in the *mendésiste*

crowd, a number of the latter, such as Michel Jobert, became important in the de Gaulle regime.[113] What's more, many of the policies de
Gaulle and Debré rammed through by ordinance, especially in such
matters as health and hospital reform, state-sponsored research, industrial decentralization, and regional planning, had their origins in the
early 1950s and especially in modernizing efforts of the Mendès France
government of 1954–1955, when policy experts and the more forward-
looking factions of key interest groups in business, the unions, and the
academy had worked together to chart the next stages in the country's
economic and social transformation.[114] As much as de Gaulle and Debré
scorned the former republic, they recycled its policies and personnel,
especially those associated with their sharpest critic in 1958, Mendès
France.

If a greater reliance on expert ministers and staff teams empowered
Debré and de Gaulle at the expense of their ministries, to say nothing
of Parliament, it also enabled the Elysée to poach prerogative from
Matignon. Where the constitution had left ambiguous the division of
authority between the prime minister and the president, de Gaulle set
precedents in behalf of the latter. He asserted his authority in ap-
pointing ministers, resolving policy disputes, and initiating referenda.
He even encroached on Debré's authority to manage the government's
relationship to Parliament. In 1960 when a majority of deputies called
for a special session of Parliament to respond to complaints from
farmers about the state's rural modernization policy, de Gaulle stunned
them (and Debré) by refusing their request to convene.[115] But it was
Algeria that gave the General his main opportunities to consolidate
his power. Once he opted for a referendum on self-determination for
Algeria in September 1959 and began working his way toward negotiations with the FLN, he put Debré, still a diehard on keeping the
territory French, in the position of having to implement a policy he
would otherwise have disavowed. Many of de Gaulle's opponents in
Parliament applauded the General's move toward a negotiated settlement in Algeria, and hence they supported a broad interpretation of
presidential powers in this area. When the "week of the barricades" in
Algiers in 1960 and the army putsch of 1961 created national emergencies, Socialists in Parliament were among the first to endorse de
Gaulle's request for emergency powers.[116] Referenda, decree power,

the symbolic wearing of his uniform, and other public displays of his authority on radio and television: de Gaulle's use of all these instruments of authority won over many a deputy, professor, and journalist who in a time of peace would otherwise have excoriated him as a latter-day Bonaparte. The war, then, enabled de Gaulle to enlarge his symbolic authority and acquire unambiguous control of what became known as his "reserve domain" of policy in foreign and military affairs.[117]

Debré responded to these encroachments on the prime ministry with less equanimity than observers at the time assumed. *La Gazette de Lausanne* conveyed the commonplace skepticism about his autonomy: "There are no longer ministers in the Debré cabinet. There are high civil servants. . . . The holders of ministerial portfolios are the executors of a policy that isn't theirs, nor even the prime minister's. The real head of government is the president."[118] But what Debré's archives now reveal is a man more ambivalent about de Gaulle's aggressive presidentialization of power than the public realized. To awake one morning to discover that de Gaulle had changed the price of milk infuriated him.[119] "You can't imagine," he wrote to Pompidou in 1961, "how alone I am and how much the ministers complicate my task by dealing directly with the staff of the Elysée."[120] He resented his dwindling role in foreign affairs, his having been sidelined on Algeria, and de Gaulle's meddling over shake-ups of the cabinet.[121] Because Debré understood that even in the Fifth Republic the legislative branch had to be managed and courted, he found de Gaulle's intrusions in parliamentary affairs especially troubling and even compromising of presidential authority: "Let's not diminish the president of the republic by obliging him to be in permanent contact with Parliament."[122] He likewise realized that because "a government composed largely of civil servants will find itself in a different position vis à vis Parliament," it would be wise, he wrote de Gaulle, to have "one or two ministers especially charged with parliamentary relations."[123] Although strategically Debré remained committed to a strong presidency, tactically he thought it required a more respectful sharing of power between the two executives and a better orchestrated consultation with Parliament than de Gaulle wanted. Once the Algerian war ended and de Gaulle began to contemplate a more radical way to consolidate presidential power (via direct election), de Gaulle replaced Debré, to the chagrin of much of Parliament, with a more compliant staff insider, Georges Pompidou.

The elevation of experts and the relegation of professional politicians to the margins in the Debré government provoked strong reactions. As Brigitte Gaïti has argued, the beginning of Gaullist rule in 1958–1959 became the moment when journalists, academics, and politicians in considerable numbers suddenly discovered "technocracy" as a worthy subject of controversy, inaugurating a decade of intense commentary in France over the vices and virtues of expert rule.[124] The Communist Party, as the only big party to oppose de Gaulle from the outset of the regime, was quick to equate "Bonapartism," "monopoly capitalism," and Gaullist "technocracy." Jacques Duclos accused de Gaulle of using the referendum to create "like Napoléon III a plebiscitary system."[125] From Communists such barbs carried less political sting for de Gaulle and Debré than when they came from potential allies of the center and the Right, and especially from politicians in the new Gaullist party, the UNR (Union pour la nouvelle République), who found their own subordination in policymaking galling. In 1960, after Debré's government presented to the National Assembly its plans for agricultural modernization—plans designed by elite civil servants and the "modernizing" activists in the Young Farmers movement (the CNJA)—a number of UNR deputies balked at what they regarded as too radical an assault on the rural order, criticizing "views that are sometimes too technocratic," as one of them put it, "and hence more dangerous than useful." Another warned the government "never to yield to a technocratic dream." "To me family farming is quite different from a simple economic formula."[126] If de Gaulle and Debré sought to rescue policymaking from the clientism and logjam of the Fourth Republic by circumventing Parliament, it was not surprising that legislators, even supporters of de Gaulle, would fling "technocrat" as an epithet—with its connotations of elitism, cold abstraction, and detachment from "human" experience—to defend the potential losers in the stepped-up modernization drive of the early 1960s.

Though obviously a "modernizer" with his own history of collaboration with some of the experts in Debré and de Gaulle's orbit, Pierre Mendès France nonetheless established himself quickly as the regime's most distinguished and intransigent critic. He never reconciled

himself to what de Gaulle achieved in establishing a stable new republic, a republic born illegitimately under the "threat of a military
coup."[127] For years he predicted its imminent collapse.[128] He opposed
de Gaulle's investiture, the Constitution of 1958, and the direct election
of the presidency in 1962, which he viewed as an instrument to further
consolidate de Gaulle's power and render the citizenry, ironically, more
passive. No longer tethered to his conservative rural constituency
after losing the election of November 1958, Mendès France migrated
to the breakaway Left-minority of the Socialist Party, the PSU (Parti
socialiste unifié). Then in 1962 he published his most important statement on democratic reform, *La République moderne (A Modern Republic)*, which found a large audience and confirmed his stature as
the leading critic of the regime.

The book served as Mendès France's extended rebuttal to the institutional and political revolution de Gaulle and Debré carried out
during the first three years of the new republic. He castigated them for
arousing the public's fear of the Communist Party (whose influence
he regarded as limited) and for personalizing power so radically in
the presidency: "Without realizing it, they are moving backward to the
Bonapartist orbit that has dogged the country persistently for the last
century and a half and has led to catastrophic setbacks each time it
has come to the fore."[129] Latter-day Bonapartism of this kind, in his
view, only exacerbated the trend toward citizen passivity he had diag-
nosed a year before. "Under the Fourth Republic the people felt cheated,"
he now admitted, "[but] under the Fifth they feel they are being treated
like children."[130] Like other critics of the de Gaulle–Debré government, Mendès France also targeted its technocratic overreliance on
experts. Not since the early 1930s had he concentrated his fire so
squarely on the problem of the expert in power. Now in the opposition
and no longer on the defensive for similar charges against his own
government, he placed "the dangers of bureaucracy and technocracy"
at the center of his final chapter in the book on "the place of the citizen" in a modern republic.[131]

His answer to technocracy was threefold. The first was his usual
republican pedagogy, though this time with a twist: he argued for the
importance of teaching all citizens economics, the better to stand
up for themselves in the face of experts. "Of all the great industrial

nations," he said, "France is, perhaps, the one where public opinion is least well informed about economic problems" and hence most inclined to leave them to the experts.[132] Economic literacy had become imperative for moving beyond representative democracy to the kind of participatory democracy he now felt the country needed. Second, he embraced with newfound enthusiasm the essential role that trade unions and other associational groups needed to play as counterweights to the technocratic state. Before he published *A Modern Republic*, Mendès France had positioned himself principally as a reform-minded statist within the Radical tradition, with its Jacobin confidence in the capacities of the state and its citizenry to work toward a rational and just social order. Now he embraced the associationalist side of Radical republicanism, reflecting his connection to the PSU, small *mendésiste* enclaves within the labor movement, and the Club Jean Moulin, where left-leaning policy thinkers talked of an *économie concertée* that better integrated interest groups into the work of state economic management.[133] But what role should unions and associations play? Mendès France rediscovered the virtues of planning, the third element of his anti-technocratic approach and the keystone of his "modern republic."

Mendès France had long been associated with planning, but it had faded in his thinking in the 1950s. Now he returned to it as a way to promote participatory democracy and give coherence to the state and direction to national life: "In times of war, everyone knows that defense needs take precedence over all others; every man at his post knows that his attitude must conform to the demands of the battle. The Plan should have the same precedence in time of peace."[134] He called for converting the Social and Economic Council into the Senate. Under the Fourth and Fifth Republics the Council was an advisory body of interest groups. Mendès France hoped that if it became the second legislative chamber, it would give a democratic imprimatur to the Plan. He also advocated creating a supremely powerful planning ministry with authority over the other economic ministries. The planning cycle, moreover, would be brought into line with the electoral calendar so as to focus Parliament's attention more squarely on the Plan. And he looked to planning as a way to enhance the role of the trade unions in national life. "Without this," he wrote, "the Plan . . . would remain bureaucratic and technocratic and subject to other

influences with no democratic checks and balances."[135] He envisaged
the Plan, then, to be as much a political as an economic institution, a
way as much to harness the participation of the citizenry as to render
coherent the state's role in the economy.

A Modern French Republic served Mendès France as his principal
frame of conceptual reference for the rest of his political life. Gaullism
in power had freed him to become a full-fledged oppositional politician,
which in turn enabled him to articulate more directly than he had
before what price French democracy was paying for the rule of experts. By naming the problem of technocracy, like so many others had
done in the early 1960s, and by responding to it with the associational
turn and the Plan, he offered something new, what Pierre Rosanvallon
has described as an original synthesis of classical republicanism (with
its focus on the state-citizen relationship), an organic or social conception of democracy (built around associations), and a rationalist approach that appealed to experts.[136] His associationalist turn in the
early 1960s, moreover, was, in theory at least, good politics. It brought
him into closer harmony with the PSU, and it played on an important
potential weakness in the Gaullist regime—its image as presiding ar-
rogantly at too high a remove from the rest of the country. In fact, as
we have seen in our explorations of industry, the retail trade, family
policy, and immigration, the regime remained more responsive to
interest-group politics than most observers at the time perceived or
Debré and de Gaulle wanted to project. Their government did reach
out to some groups, most famously to the Young Farmers movement
to help modernize agriculture and to Catholics in the making of the
Debré law of 1959 authorizing public subsidies to religious schools.
Still, the main thrust of de Gaulle and Debré's strategy was to insulate the executive from pressure groups and Parliament, and they usually
took care to include members of key intermediary groups on commissions and boards only as individuals, not as representatives.[137] Mendès
France's newfound enthusiasm for organized groups in civil society,
and especially the unions, made perfect sense as a way to define himself in opposition to a regime Debré and de Gaulle regarded as a mo-
narchical republic.

But if Mendès France's text went farther than anything he had said
before about how to democratize a technocratic state, it failed to serve

as a practical program for the Left. For one thing, Mendès France had turned to planning when it was losing favor with many of his own allies, such as Gabriel Ardant and François Bloch-Lainé.[138] Although Mendès France argued that the same hierarchical structure of planning from periphery to center could be carried right on up to Brussels and the Common Market, European integration was beginning to make the Plan harder to realize in practice. His vision of planning, moreover, still reflected a rationalist perspective that underestimated the difficulty of getting disparate groups to find common ground. He retained the optic of a central planner, seeking to overcome the state's incoherence: "Time and again in the last fifteen years, a particular service or department, a minister, or Parliament itself, has taken decisions that, although individually justifiable within a given field, upset, and sometimes very seriously upset, the essential emphasis and priorities of the Plan. Planning, in fact, can only be really fruitful . . . if all individual decisions bow to it."[139] The Plan remained a force for centralization, a way to organize a vast national conversation in which the center prevails over the local, and the general over the particular, though in theory everyone will have had a say.[140] The twin goals of expanding the community of voices contributing to the Plan, not least labor's, while at the same time making the Plan more effective and coherent than it had ever been before in France, made sense logically. But it was as likely to intensify the conflict between the technocratic and the democratic as to diminish it.

A further obstacle to building Mendès France's "modern republic" was his own political isolation. Despite the powerful role he imagined for the trade unions in his planning republic and in his profession-based Senate, and despite, too, his call for revitalizing the *comités d'entreprise* (company committees) to become genuine organs of employee power in management, he himself still had only the loosest links to the labor movement. *A Modern French Republic* had its patronizing passages about labor: "The acquisition of more rights and greater outlets for action [for unions] involves facing up to wider and more difficult tasks. This is what maturity means, and it is a natural development in social life, just as it is in the life of the individual."[141] He kept in contact with Pierre Le Brun in the CGT, but Le Brun was a relatively marginalized figure fascinated with planning. Mendès France knew a few more militants in FO. But FO and the CFTC never warmed to his ideas for Senate reform, or even to his ambitions for labor in the planning apparatus, which they took as a threat to their autonomy from the state.[142] Only the small "Reconstruction" faction of the CFTC, people like Paul Vignaux and Edmond Maire who were disillusioned with the MRP, maintained close connections to Mendès France, whom they saw as kindred modernizing spirit and an ally in the political elite. Most labor militants viewed him as far too removed from working-class realities to understand them. "To be brutally frank," FO militant Georges Rino said years later, "he knew nothing about it."[143] The CGT's Jean Magniadas associated him with the "technocratic illusions that *mendésisme* peddled."[144] Even as sympathetic a colleague as Edmond Maire found that in his "relationship to the worker's world, he hit all the republican keys," that is so say, legalistic, abstract, motivated by a drive to see "a greater social cohesion come through an equality before the law that remained to be achieved."[145] Mendès France's vision for democratizing the country, in short, depended heavily on mobilizing a complex, divided labor movement with which he had little credibility.

More crippling still in turning his ideas into action was his own categorical refusal to run for the presidency in the Fifth Republic, despite the feeling of many people that he should. As early as 1963 he made this choice clear. As an opponent of the direct election of the president, he refused as a matter of principle—and perhaps pride—to seek the office.[146] François Mitterrand later said Mendès France also worried that his candidacy would occasion a revival of anti-Semitism akin to what happened in 1936 when Léon Blum came to power.[147] His anxiety was not so far-fetched. Rabid Poujadist pamphleteers were not the only danger here. A UNR leaflet in the 1958 election campaign had dared to say: "To vote Mendès France is to vote against de Gaulle, to vote against France, to vote Jewish. So vote French, vote UNR."[148] Whatever his motives, he settled into a role of statesman and doctrinal leader of the non-Communist opposition, which left the way open to Mitterrand to run against de Gaulle.

In the late autumn of 1965, during the run-up to the presidential elections, Pierre Mendès France and Michel Debré squared off in a series of radio debates on the station Europe No. 1 (see Figure 6.2).

FIGURE 6.2 Radio duel. Pierre Mendès-France (far left) and Michel Debré (far right) at their microphones in their radio debate of 1965. In three two-hour broadcasts these eminent politician-experts of the non-Communist Left and the Right debated over the domestic and foreign policy issues at play in the presidential race between François Mitterrand and incumbent president Charles de Gaulle. They also argued over executive authority and democracy in the French Republic. Keystone Pictures USA/Alamy Stock Photo.

Listeners found the first two debates so enthralling that the station sponsored a third encounter—for a total of six hours of what Debré later called his "duel" with Mendès France.[149] Many people regarded it as the highlight of the campaign season, and for good reason: French radio listeners had never heard anything like it. An extended, freewheeling debate between major political antagonists was unprecedented in a country where radio and television were government controlled, though not entirely government owned.[150] Europe No. 1 was private, but it was still restricted in what it could broadcast in public affairs. Hence, the 1965 "duel" expanded the airwaves as a political space. It also crystallized the terms of debate between what had become the ruling Gaullist establishment and the non-Communist Left opposition. A towering presence, of course, was the man not in the studio, Charles de Gaulle. He went on to win a second presidential term, his first by popular election, in an unexpectedly close second-ballot contest with François Mitterrand. But the two radio protagonists who spoke on behalf of their candidates were titans in their own right, and they used the opportunity to promote views about policy and democratic reform that they had held since the first years of the Fifth Republic.

Behind their disagreements over such matters as inflation, Germany's resurgence, and the Common Market, it was easy to hear in the broadcasts a deeper war of words between a Debré eager to defend de Gaulle's consolidation of executive authority and a Mendès France keen to convey that the General was putting democracy itself in danger. Each man new the other's game well. Debré reiterated his conviction that liberty and suffrage were the essence of democracy, which only strong leadership could protect: "Democracy exists only where the elected authorities are capable of governing."[151] He ridiculed Mendès France's notion of contractual governance. A government that binds itself to Parliament or the electorate with a plan for four or five years— that "notion of contract," he said "is one of those theoretical ideas that is conducive to sapping authority."[152] Mendès France was hardly less blunt in response: "At the present time we no longer have democracy; all the power and all the fundamental decisions are made by one man."[153] And he mocked Debré for his inconsistencies: "In 1958 you declared the election of the president by universal suffrage to be a bad procedure that harbored the risk of dictatorship; in 1962 you suddenly found it to be an excellent idea."[154] Drawing from *A Modern Republic*, Mendès France called for "a system in which everyone in the country who wants to participate in national life—the local governments, the *groupes de pensée*, the parties, the unions—will be able to intervene, a system where all the decisions will not devolve purely and simply to one man."[155] The debate dramatized more explicitly than listeners had heretofore heard a duel of many years running over how best to restore state authority and transcend the tension so acutely expressed in the long reconstruction era between democracy and elite, expert rule.

Nothing quite like the Debré–Mendès France debate happened again— such a high-profile, open-ended, and lengthy exchange by politician-experts who represented contesting sides in a campaign in which they were not candidates. Thereafter, candidates themselves would take the stage in the more formalized and formulaic genre of the televised debate. In 1965 these two men stood in as eminent policy thinkers for the Right and the Left. Neither of them ran parties, much less a political or social movement. But few doubted their status as leading spokesmen for their respective camps. As men of state and politician-experts they embodied in their ideas and their careers two sides of a two-decade-long argument in the republican center over how to reform the state.

Their differences in outlook in the 1960s had roots in their political comings-of-age in the 1930s. In his first important published writing, Mendès France had expressed his anxieties about unfettered technocratic power and the marriage of experts and private interests, just as Debré had come to his convictions by 1940 that France needed top-down, Prussian-style reform. But we ought not read too much into their early years. After all, they had much in common in the Liberation, not least a similar dismay at paths not taken in 1944 when de Gaulle opted against the reforms each cherished most. Resistance work made Debré much more the politician than he had been in the 1930s, just as government service in the late 1940s made Mendès France more the expert and the expert's politician than he had been before. Furthermore, the experience of opposition had as much impact on each man's thinking as did the experience of state power, perhaps more. Years as a Gaullist conspirator out of power in the 1950s radicalized Debré in his view that France needed a sharp rupture to consolidate the power of the executive. Likewise, only in full-fledged opposition in 1958 and after did Mendès France return to his critique of technocracy and embrace associational democracy as an antidote to Gaullism.

For all of their growth as strategists of reform, however, neither Debré nor Mendès France came fully to terms with the dilemma that haunted all republican reformers in the postwar years—the inherent tension, that is, between reviving democracy by giving greater voice to the many, while pursuing a state-led modernization drive with winners and losers and under the direction of the expert few. Debré, who helped to make the early Fifth Republic so expert-dominated, thought it was sufficient to check technocratic authority with a powerful president and prime minister accountable to the people. If he ever complained of the power of "technocrats," it was in relationship to Brussels and the Common Market, which he disparaged foremost because it was supranational but also because its officials were insufficiently unaccountable to political authority.[156] Mendès France, by contrast, was much more willing than Debré to acknowledge the technocratic drift of postwar French society, though he stopped short of developing a radical critique of technocracy per se. What troubled him most was the systematic collusion of experts with either private power, as in his critique of the Bank for International Settlements in the 1930s, or with the Gaullist state, as in his widely cited article on the problem in 1965. There he criticized how closely tied the young graduates from the ENA, the École polytechnique, and other *grandes écoles* had become to the upper reaches of Gaullist administration, in effect undermining the professional independence of the high civil service and concentrating expert power all the more.[157]

Yet if by the 1960s Mendès France had come to envisage how democratic planning, a reformed Senate, a more informed and engaged citizenry, and a bigger role for unions and other associations might serve as countervailing forces to the concentration of administrative power in France, he did little to create a roadmap to get there. He remained too much the expert, and not enough the politician, to create what he envisioned. True, as mayor of Louvier and deputy for the Eure, he proved himself a formidable local politician. The work with local constituents and dialogue with local voters that he had made much of in his writings on democracy appealed to him, and he was good at it. But like Debré, he never established himself as an effective party builder or party leader. His reform effort in the Radical Party of 1955–1956 came to naught. Nor was there much incentive in the Fourth Republic to build a political machine or national organization beyond the local base. He cultivated two vineyards: one in the Eure, the other in the highest reaches of the civil service, the young economics intelligentsia, and an international policymaking elite. The middle strata of political life—the world of political parties and unions and business groups and chambers of commerce—he knew less well.

Likewise, some of his closest associates criticized him for his insufficient ambition and his lack of appetite for the political game.

François Bloch-Lainé believed that, in reaction to parliamentary in-competence in the Third Republic, Mendès France made a mistake of blending too readily in his own life the roles of expert and politician. He would have been wiser, Bloch-Lainé thought, to focus more on get-ting power and using it rather on than being the expert committed to being right.[158] Mitterrand criticized his indifference to parliamentary coalition building and his reluctance to rub shoulders with the movers and shakers of the Fourth Republic. At two points in the reconstruc-tion era Mendès France might have done more to build the infrastruc-ture of party and associational democracy he advocated in *A Modern Republic:* first, in 1944–1946 when the left-wing world of parties and unions had greater fluidity than it would have after the Cold War began to freeze the organizational ground in 1947; and second, in the 1958–1962 period when a reconfiguration of the Left opposition offered a similar, if less propitious, opportunity. In 1944, however, he was still a long way from coming to his associationalist republicanism, and party building was the last thing on his mind as he sought to sell his policy rigor and discipline to a skeptical de Gaulle and an even more skeptical left-wing coalition of Communists, Socialists, and Christian Democrats. When the chance came again to rethink his relationship to party building and the unions in early days of the Fifth Republic, it was probably too late for the man to change his political personality. Michel Rocard would later complain of Mendès France's failure to use the PSU to build a national political base for himself in the 1960s. He remained too independent and aloof.[159] Unlike colleagues in the more traditional Left, he harbored, despite his associationalism, a dis-comfort with the "social"—with the open-ended and potentially un-controlled mobilization of classes, factions, and interests that, if undisciplined by the Plan, might derail the sound economic manage-ment on which the future of his France depended.[160] The one social group Mendès France celebrated most, youth, was too diffuse to pose that danger.

If Debré had similar difficulties cultivating parties, interest groups, and the "social," it was more from conviction than temperament. Like Mendès France he worked best at the local and ministerial levels, the bottom and the top of the political food chain.[161] Throughout his career he remained suspicious of parties and lobbies as a threat to state autonomy. In practice, of course, the Gaullist state of the early Fifth Republic worked closely with family associations, the Young Farmers, some business factions, and other groups. But Debré had little interest in legitimizing social bargaining as such, much less in revitalizing this organizational landscape as a site for participatory democracy. He did work to build the UNR, which at its Strasbourg Conference in 1961 he called a "secular instrument of Gaullism," by which he meant a centralized transmission-belt party built for the purpose of explaining to militants and hence to the country what he and de Gaulle wanted to do.[162] Neither of them had any intention of making the party the kernel of a social movement.

De Gaulle, after all, drew inspiration from an enduring French myth of the heroic figure, standing outside ordinary politics and parties, who in moments of crisis charts a course for national renewal. Debré, too, embraced the myth, and not simply out of admiration for the General. From his service in Paul Reynaud's staff, through the Resistance CGE, his work as a republican commissar and founder of the ENA, and on to his role in destroying and replacing the Fourth Republic, Debré repeatedly practiced a style of governance that relied, not on forging a new consensus of parties and social partners, nor even on mobilizing a citizenry. Instead, he remained the Olympian drafter of texts, a philosopher-prince who, when moments of crisis created an extraordinary concentration of authority at the center, sought to implement a few key ideas that preoccupied him throughout his life. He left an enduring stamp on the institutions of his country. But he also helped institutionalize a style of governance that concentrated power in the executive and the ministries, while keeping civil society at a distance (formally and publicly at least, if not always in practice, as we have seen in several policy domains). As Mendès France had warned, such an approach to government, born of crisis, has a way of encouraging crisis as well, as it did in May 1968 and in lesser waves of strikes and street demonstrations ever since. Debré's legacy was thus more complex than he may have wished—a stronger state, yes, but also a crisis-prone dynamic of elite rule and popular protest that he never intended.

Mendès France's legacy had its ironic complexity as well. May 1968 gave him the pleasure of seeing his prophecy of regime crisis at least momentarily fulfilled. For several days he even enjoyed the prospect, though fleeting it proved to be, of returning to power in partnership with François Mitterrand. But May 1968 also exposed the limitations of his style of opposition as a politician-expert. When the Gaullist regime stumbled into its crisis, the political work to create a coherent leftist opposition had barely begun, and Mendès France himself had done too little to advance it. May 1968 also brought into the foreground of French politics a host of new visionaries and utopians on the Left who took notions of participatory democracy, self-management, and decentralization into far more radical territory than Mendès France had intended. If in 1962 *A Modern Republic* stood out as a biting critique of Gaullist power, it looked anodyne, establishmentarian, even statist and technocratic in its own right, in comparison to the radical critiques of authority that became more commonplace a few years later. Mendès France could rightly claim a prominent place in the genealogy of the Second Left that would emerge in the 1970s. But May 1968 also confirmed him as a transitional figure of the Resistance generation who, even as a democratic reformer, could not break with all the habits of an expert in the dirigiste state.

7

Algerian Anvil

War and the Expansion of State Authority

FRANCE'S POSTWAR RECOVERY differed from that of other countries in Western Europe in a crucial respect: the French pursued the long reconstruction while fighting two more major wars—in Indochina until 1954, followed immediately by the Algerian war of 1954–1962. The British, Dutch, and Belgians had important, episodic military engagements in the late 1940s and 1950s in response to nationalist rebellions against their colonial rule, but even the British combat against the Mau-Mau in Kenya paled in comparison to the full-scale wars the French fought, and lost, trying to hold on to their most valued overseas territories. The Indochina war cost the French dearly, even though the Marshall Plan and direct American military aid gave the French government the wherewithal to pursue domestic recovery and colonial war at the same time. Yet, for all the sacrifice, wastage, and diverted attention the Indochina war entailed, the Algerian war dwarfed it in its impact on the metropole. French authorities never declared the Algerian conflict a war as such, preferring to call the Algerian nationalists simply "outlaws" so as to deprive them of any potential political standing, but this war mattered hugely: the scale, brutality, and proximity of the combat, plus the stakes in an imperial territory uniquely integrated—administratively, legal, politically—into France itself, made it impossible to keep that war from having its own profound effects on relations between the state and its citizens in the final years of the long reconstruction. How, then, did the Algerian war change the role and authority of the state in metropolitan France and the ways people contended with that authority?

One answer to this question is obvious, even banal. The Algerian war, or rather deep conflicts over how forcefully to fight it, triggered a popular revolt in 1958 by European settler-citizens in Algiers and, in their support, an army near-coup that led to the collapse of the Fourth Republic. A frightened Parliament in Paris, bereft of easy alternatives, brought Charles de Gaulle back into power after years in the political wilderness to create the Fifth Republic as the presidential regime he had long advocated. War as an occasion for state-making rarely gets more direct than that. But well before the May 1958 crisis, the war had inspired government officials to expand the state's role in French society along three key dimensions: what might be called population management, with its subsequent effects on the state's handing of immigration; economic and social planning; and the intensification of executive authority. In all three dimensions top civil servants and ministerial officials enhanced their authority and further deepened the tension between administrative power and democratic governance.

Population Management

Consider first the state's expanding role in managing North African populations within the metropole. Algerian migration into metropolitan France got its real start in the First World War, grew only modestly in the interwar years, and finally began to surge in 1947 when Algerians acquired the right to travel and work in the metropole. Algeria, after all, was deemed to be not a colony in the usual sense but a veritable part of France itself. The 1947 reform, of a piece with a broader French strategy to liberalize the wider empire the better to hold on to it, granted Muslim Algerians full citizenship, though not political equality, much less meaningful political power.[1] Still, basic citizenship status made it easier to get jobs in France, especially in entry-level industrial jobs in factories like Renault, which as a nationalized, trend-setting firm in labor relations was in the vanguard in hiring

Algerians. The Algerian population in the metropole—and the figures here are notoriously uncertain—shot up from about 50,000 in
1945 to about 260,000 in 1954 when the war began, mostly single
men living in barrack-style dormitories, rundown residential hotels,
or the shantytowns that were expanding rapidly in the outskirts of
Paris, Lyon, and Marseille. By war's end in 1962 that number grew to
roughly 410,000, including many families, making the war years a
period of heavy migration for Algerians, relative to most other foreign
populations coming to France.[2]

In the early years after World War II, French authorities had moved
heaven and earth to encourage white Europeans, even former German
POWs, to come to France to redress a serious labor shortage. Algerian
migration, by contrast, they sought to avoid, or strictly contain. In 1946
the top civil servant administering population policy at the Ministry
of Public Health and Population, Emmanuel Rain, declared North African manpower "undesirable."[3] Rain's ministry did respond positively
to a desperate plea by the Ministry of Industrial Production for North
African labor recruitment into mines in the metropole, but only on the
condition that the workers be sent back when they were no longer
needed. Manpower Director Jacques Maillet at the Labor Ministry
made a similar plea for North African labor to build hydroelectric
dams.[4] The energy needs of the immediate post-Liberation moment,
then, trumped the prejudice against recruiting non-Europeans, but only
if the laborers were temporary. When, after 1946, state authorities lost
much of their power to send Algerians home and the flow of migrants
swelled, Rain and other populationists advocated ways to discourage
migration and slow the rate of population growth in Algeria, which they
saw as a threat to metropolitan France. Ideas abounded in ministerial
discussions: mounting an information campaign in Algeria to convey
how tough life could be for migrants in the metropole and to falsify
the rumors about the good wages to found there; tightening medical
screening at migrants' points of departure or arrival; and stimulating
Algeria migration away from the metropole toward other French overseas territories.[5] Fernand Boverat, the old warhorse of interwar popu-
lationism and a postwar member of the Haut Comité consultatif de
la population et de la famille, took the extreme position of denying
that the legal reforms of 1946 and 1947 actually granted Algerians any-

thing approaching the rights and duties of citizenship. He called for the state to reassert its authority to repatriate migrants and to enforce a clear numerical quota on migrants as was done in the United States.[6]

But Boverat was wrong about the law and wrong, too, about the sheer feasibility of choking the flow of tens of thousands of Arab- and Berber-speaking migrants seeking work in the metropole. Boverat's fellow Haut Comité member, the more savvy and academic Alfred Sauvy at the Institut national des études démographiques (INED), had a better grip on this reality. Though he had not abandoned the ethnocentrism that had colored his immigration policy prescriptions in 1945, he had a keen sense of what you might call Realdémographique. As he reported to the Ministry of Public Health and Population, rural poverty and declining rates of infant mortality in Algeria, due largely to improvements in pediatric public health, were fueling a growing demand for jobs that the Algerian economy alone could not provide. The pressure for migration, once the legal barriers had been removed, was ineluctable. Moreover, any campaign for "birth control," Sauvy said, employing the English term, "risked provoking a nationalist and religious counter-reaction . . . and casting French authorities in a bad light in international opinion." Better, he thought, to use the migration flow to advantage, to encourage Algerian Muslim families, and not just single men, to settle in mainland France, especially in "the villages of the Midi." In the long run, the mixing of peoples in the metropole held greater potential for integration and assimilation than in Algeria itself, which he saw condemned to a long future of segregation.[7]

Sauvy's begrudging realism and cautious optimism about Algerian migration signaled a wider, gradual opening up to the possibilities on the part of government and business leaders in the late 1940s and early 1950s. To be sure, in many quarters in France there remained outright racist hostility to Algerian migration, and plenty of conflict over whether the government ought to strive to integrate or isolate the newcomers. All the same, many employers in manufacturing and mining, still in need of labor and finding European immigration insufficient, expressed a desire to hire North African laborers. And indeed, the expanding opportunities for Algerian migrants in the 1950s would be urban and industrial, not "in the villages of the Midi," as Sauvy hoped. After 1954 the government did make something of an effort to resettle a small number of Algerians on available farmland in hill villages of southern France, but not much came of it. Transplanted Algerian families fleeing rural poverty in Algeria were unlikely to overcome conditions in France that were fueling a rural exodus there as well. A skeptical planning report had pointed out in 1947, "There's little or no land or available property in France except in those few zones where the soil is poor, the climate harsh, the crop unpredictable, the output risky, and the life hard."[8] No, the immediate future of migration labor market was in the car plants, chemical factories, and coal mines of France's bigger cities and semi-rural industrial districts.

Above all, though, what radically altered the government's approach to migration was the growing threat of anticolonial rebellion and then the outbreak of the Algerian war itself in late 1954 and its escalation into a full-blown conflict in 1955. The war raised the stakes of migration exponentially: French officials and employers became much more invested in making Algerian migration work. For one thing, immigration served as a safety valve for an Algerian labor market whose weakness only fed the ranks of the nationalist movement. For another, Algerian migrants provided a labor force in the metropole to fill jobs vacated by increasing numbers of young Frenchmen conscripted to fight in the war. By 1956 the French had 450,000 troops in Algeria. Over the course of eight years, 2.7 million Frenchmen would see duty in the war.[9]

Algerian migration had a catch, however: it brought into the metropole, especially Paris, potential supporters for the Algerian insurgency. Even before 1954, supporters of Messali Hadj's nationalist movement, organized via the Mouvement pour le triomphe des libertés démocratiques (MTLD), had staged a number of significant street demonstrations in Paris (Figure 7.1), some of which involved violent clashes with the police and mass arrests. Once the rival FLN (Front de libération nationale; National Liberation Front) took the initiative to lead the insurgency against French authorities, a bloody, brutal struggle also ensued—both in Algeria and in the metropole—between these leading factions of the nationalist movement, in which the FLN eventually prevailed. By 1958 the FLN succeeded in securing from Algerian migrants in France active and passive forms of attachment to the movement, especially through an extraordinary system of collecting monthly payments from employed migrants.[10] Involvement

FIGURE 7.1 Algerians demonstrating in Paris on Bastille Day, July 14, 1953. Since 1951, Algerian migrants in Paris who were associated with Messali Hadj's Mouvement pour le tromphe des libertés démocratiques (MTLD; Movement for the Victory of Democratic Freedoms) had joined in the Left's traditional march on Bastille Day. In 1953, 5,000 to 6,000 MTLD demonstrators used the event to call for Algerian independence. Police efforts to break up the protest led to clashes in which seven people died and hundreds were wounded. Hadj is featured here on the poster. Vergne/Mémoires d'Humanité/Archives départementales de la Seine-Saint-Denis.

in an insurgent state in the making, coerced though it was, was unprecedented in the history of French immigration. Before then, immigrants in the metropole, whatever their nationality, had always had a difficult time establishing political leverage for themselves in France, and this was especially the case for North Africans. But the Algerian war gave Algerian migrants an unusual kind of leverage, the power that derived from their real or imagined connection to the liberation movement, as well as from the rights Algerians acquired as citizens in 1947. The war reframed in government eyes the meaning, and hence the stakes, of migrants' success or failure in settling into orderly, stable lives the metropole.[11] French officials thus sought to manage, support, control, and repress this implicitly empowered population, and in doing so they transformed the state's role in the country's migration regime.

Managing Algerian migrants took two forms—social services and policing—and a complex blending of the two. As a number of scholars have shown, this form of intervention was both new and not so new.[12] Between the world wars, the state offered comparatively little in the way of social services to the Italians, Belgians, Poles, Spaniards, and eastern European Jews who made up the bulk of the immigrant populations in that period. But North Africans were different, or so French officials assumed because of their race, religion, colonial status, potential interest in anticolonial politics, and hence the danger they were believed to pose to social order. In 1925 the Paris Prefecture of Police established the Services de surveillance, protection et assistance des indigènes Nord-Africains (SAINA; North African Surveillance, Protection, and Assistance Service), or the North African Brigade, to provide hostels, infirmaries, and a job placement center—but also to collect information on individuals and to keep this population under surveillance and under a continuous threat of harassment, arrest, and deportation. In 1935 the prefecture went one step further by building in the suburb of Bobigny the so-called Franco-Muslim hospital, a segregated facility much criticized by Communists and Algerian nationalists and much resented by many migrants escorted there by public health officials and the police.[13] Some public officials at the time understood there was a price to be paid for all this surveillance. In a study of "the problem of North African labor migration to France," Pierre Laroque, the future architect of the social security system, wrote that "the link between police services and social services was excessive" and that "the social is sacrificed to information."[14]

Given this criticism even before the war, and then the abuses of police power during Vichy, the practice of linking services and policing was bound to come under scrutiny after the Liberation. In 1944 de Gaulle's minister of interior, Adrien Tixier, who had played an important role in scuttling efforts to establish overt ethnic criteria in screening immigrants, abolished the North African Brigade. He sought to establish clearer lines of separation between social services, supervised principally by the Ministry of Public Health and Population or the Ministry of Labor, and policing. Tixier also reasoned that if Algerians now were citizens in any meaningful sense, they ought not be targets of special police units. Police disagreed, claiming the Tixier reform sacrificed an effective way to penetrate the hidden world of North African life in the urban fabric. In fact, the reform proved to be less radical than it seemed. Though dispersed into regular police units, a number of former members of the North African Brigade, including some of North African origin themselves, still worked in their old migrant beats, rounded up nationalist activists, and kept up connections with their informants. They won back much of their lost authority in 1953 when, after deadly clashes with Messali Hadj's MTLD demonstrators in a Bastille Day march, the government established the Brigade against Aggression and Violence (BAV). Half of the Brigade's officers spoke a North Africa language, so its purposes were clear despite the obscurity of its name: to discern and handle the growing presence of Algerian nationalists in the Paris region.[15] But it was the war itself that fully freed the Prefecture of Police and indeed the leadership of the Ministry of the Interior itself to reverse the Tixier reform. After 1954, efforts to blend services and policing returned anew. And it was in this domain, in the elaboration of new forms of social service provision and police activity, that the war changed the scope and character of the state.

To begin with, government authorities significantly enlarged the range of services and social subsidies offered to Algerian migrants. By the mid-1950s more women and children were leaving Algeria to join their husbands and fathers in the metropole—not in huge numbers yet, that would come in the 1970s, but noticeably enough all the same. Between 1954 and 1962 the number of Algerian families in French grew from 7,000 to 30,000.[16] Many of them came to escape the war, and French authorities sought to support this new development more fervently than they had in the late 1940s because they now regarded women as the key to assimilation and as a politically moderating influence on men.[17] Government officials developed public services, and subsidized a great many local private services as well, targeted especially for Algerian women. Activities ranging from French cooking classes to lessons in family budgeting, everyday *politesse,* shopping, cleaning, infant care, child rearing, hospital-based childbirth, and enrolling children in school all supported a vision of the family as a vehicle of integration. The approach promoted a conventional, patriarchal model of the European family that resonated, at least partially, with Algerian patriarchal norms.[18] Meanwhile, the Ministry of Labor stepped up its efforts to prepare men for the labor force, subsidizing language instruction, job placement, medical services, and occupational training.[19] Public officials' ambition for shaping migrants' lives, in short, grew apace.

But what that ambition implied for a larger vision of population management was far from clear, at least initially. Three ministries, in fact, competed for primacy in promoting services—the ministries of Labor, Public Health and Population, and the Interior—each with its own policy logic and bureaucratic ambitions. In keeping with priorities since the Liberation, Public Health and Population put its emphasis on family services, whereas Labor focused on the mostly male migrant workforce, with an eye toward keeping paths open for workers to return to Algeria when metropolitan labor markets tightened. As the war intensified, however, it was Interior, with its focus on public order and police surveillance, that got the upper hand. The Interior Ministry already had a head start when as early as 1948 it had assigned several high-level administrators, called IGAMEs—inspecteurs généraux de l'administration en mission extraordinaire (special inspectors)—to each of the large military districts covering metropolitan France to oversee the government's many forms of institutional contact with Algerians migrants. This innovation gave the ministry an administrative infrastructure, and a new level of in-house expertise, to build on in the 1950s.[20] Then in 1955 the government instituted mandatory identity cards for all citizens wishing to travel between Algeria and France. This initiative provided a pretext for arbitrary identity checks of Algerian migrants, group roundups, and eventually quite violent police entries into domiciles.[21] It gave police greater license to bust down doors—and much else.

The Interior Ministry also took a bold step to enhance its influence in the social service realm: it appointed Algerian civil servants in the Algerian colonial administration to become conseillers techniques pour les affaires musulmanes (CTAMs; technical advisors in Muslim affairs). They now served as intermediaries between migrants and the state by working with prefects, and IGAMEs in the metropole coordinated the full range of services—medical, housing, social work, and public assistance—that touched Algerian migrants in France. In a real sense the CTAMs, who formerly had been lifelong residents of Algeria, were migrants themselves. But with the power of the prefects backing them up and with their intimate knowledge of the world migrants came from, they commanded attention from the many ministerial branches they engaged with, as well as from the network of around 200 service organizations around the country concerned with Algerian migrants.[22] The number of CTAMs grew from a mere four in 1952 to thirty-four by 1962. Their expertise and their strategic importance to the administration underscored a key assumption: that to make the migration system succeed in places like Paris and Lyon and Roubaix, the Interior Ministry had to import colonial knowledge into local service networks.[23] And no problem seemed too trivial for CTAM attention. Their reports could be microsurgical in scope: a missive on the grades, schoolwork, sports activities, and family troubles of individual Algerian students in school; an effort to get another school to provide its three Algerian charges with meals that respected Muslim dietary restrictions; and so on.[24] The government took CTAM surveillance seriously, for as an Interior Ministry circular prescribing their activities put it, there was "a tight connection between social problems and problems of public order."[25]

The Interior Ministry took yet another step in blending services and policing when in 1956 it won jurisdiction over the government's initiative in housing for migrants—the SONACOTRAL (the Société nationale de construction de logements pour les travailleurs algériens), a government-funded public-private agency to build hostels and *cités de transit* (temporary housing). The latter resembled large mobile home parks with fixed rectangular units designated especially for families. The authorities hoped that moving Algerians from shantytowns, especially the big one in Nanterre, into *cités de transit* and eventually into HLMs (low-cost permanent public housing projects) would integrate them into more ethnically diverse communities and break what ties they might well have had to FLN cadres in the *bidonvilles*. But the Interior Ministry had a more explicit policing agenda as well for the SONACOTRAL. To the dismay of officials in the Ministry of the Labor, who objected to the new agency becoming merely "a pacification

enterprise,"[26] SONACOTRAL hostels were managed by former policemen, army officers, and colonial administrators who placed a
priority on political surveillance.[27]

Tensions grew between Labor Ministry officials, public health
authorities, and social workers, on the one hand, who were often
deeply troubled by the blurring of lines between services and policing,
and Interior Ministry officials and policeman, on the other, who were
committed to it. Social workers in family services in the Paris region,
for example, pushed back in 1954 against government requests to administer a survey questionnaire in home visits to gather information
on their North African clients. CGT-affiliated social workers in particular wrote officials to repudiate the request and to question whether
the survey was "essentially for service provision or policing." As a
city council member pointed out at a discussion of this dispute, "the
role of social workers is particularly delicate with these families,
and if the latter knew about the questionnaires they would shut them
out."[28] The survey was stopped, but not the continuing pressure to
combine service with surveillance. At a meeting bringing together
social service administrators and social work representatives in late
1955, the assistant director of the Caisse régionale de sécurité sociale
named the problem squarely. "The infant and maternal protection
service," he said, "is charged with two missions: a familial mission
of counseling and a surveillance mission of a repressive kind. This
second mission is incompatible with the first, and it puts the social
worker at risk of losing the family's confidence." Amid an escalating
war in Algeria, the problem was easier to describe than resolve. The
group referred it to further study.[29] As historian Amelia Lyons has argued, even though a good many social workers did their best to keep
police out of their business, the police nonetheless maintained strong
lines of communication with the country's vast service network, and
Algerians themselves had no illusions to the contrary.[30]

Algerians also had a festering grievance about a key feature of
family services: inequity in the provision of family allowances. *Allocations familiales*, which had already become an important part of the
wage package for many salaried employees in industry in the 1930s,
became virtually universalized as a big piece of the postwar social
security system in France and the central pillar of pronatalist policy.

But architects of the system, such as Pierre Laroque and Robert Prigent, deliberately designed family allowances to support natality in the metropole, rather than in the colonies or even in the four overseas departments (DOM) of Martinique, Guadeloupe, French Guyana, and Réunion. Outside the metropole, the family allowance system became a complex patchwork. DOM residents got them, but at much lower rates (and also erratically enforced) so as to discourage high fertility, and they fought for decades to achieve equity with recipients in the metropole.[31] In French West and Equatorial Africa, where officials worried about low fertility rates in an urban working class whom they viewed as key to developing the region, the trade unions eventually succeeded in 1956 to get family allowances for waged workers.[32] Meanwhile, in the protectorates of Morocco and Tunisia, employees of European origin had won access to the system, but their indigenous counterparts had not.[33] Algeria, as always, had its own exceptional arrangement. As early as 1942, Algerian migrant employees in the metropole (whether North African or European in family origin) became eligible for standard family allowances if their families resided with them in the metropole. But if they were "Français musulman d'Algérie" (FMA, or Algerian Muslim French, a term that emerged after 1944 when citizenship was extended to everyone in Algeria) and if their family still resided in Algeria, they got the benefit at much lower rates—from about one-third to two-thirds the Paris rates, and the larger the family, the greater the inequity. This approach remained intact in the Fourth Republic. As in the DOM, the authorities' fear of high fertility drove policy for an Algeria where non-Europeans outnumbered Europeans nine to one. FMA families in Algeria were also deprived of a hefty set of benefits available in the metropole: prenatal and maternity subsidies, a special supplement for families with a single wage earner, a childbirth leave allowance, and after 1949, housing benefits. To add to Algerians' sense of injustice, employers of migrants with families still in Algeria contributed the full freight to the national family welfare fund, in effect creating a surplus without the employee getting the full benefit.[34]

This glaring discrimination fueled migrants' resentment and gave Algerian nationalists a powerful propaganda point. It also provided the French trade unions a way to connect to Algerian migrants.

Left-leaning social Catholics and the CFTC (the Catholic trade union federation), committed as they were to a strong family policy on both confessional and egalitarian grounds, put the issue at the center of their advocacy for migrants. As one CFTC leader stressed, it was particularly galling to Algerian migrants to see Italians have the unique right as migrants to send family allowances back to their families in Italy at the full French metropolitan rates (a special feature of the Franco-Italian immigration accord of 1946) even after many an Algerian soldier had served in the Allied campaign in 1943 to liberate the Italian peninsula. The CFTC was observant enough to emphasize, too, that Algeria migrants who had managed to become self-employed in France (as butchers, grocers, or mechanics, or as owners of boutiques, cafés, or restaurants) had to contribute to the national family fund without receiving allowances themselves. Until 1955 the benefit extended only to salaried workers.[35] Government authorities, aware that all these inequities risked fueling the nationalist movement, remained loath to raise allowance rates in Algeria for fear the money would find its way into the nationalists' hands. Instead, to quiet critics, Pierre Laroque created the Social and Sanitary Aid Fund in 1952 to begin using the family allowance fund surplus to boost social services targeting Algerians in the metropole—a move that scarcely disguised the continuing inequity in Algerians' social citizenship.[36]

If Algerian migrants had plenty to alienate them from state authorities in the metropole—the blurring of policing and services, the sheer force of policing in their neighborhoods, the inequities built into the welfare state—tensions became greater still when, in March 1958, the interior minister of what turned out to be nearly the last government of the Fourth Republic named Maurice Papon prefect of police for the Paris region. Papon arrived at a pivotal moment. Rebellion in the ranks of the Paris police over delays in being paid a "danger bonus," which climaxed with a couple thousand policemen marching on the National Assembly, gave Papon his chance.[37] Best known to us now for his role in deporting Jews in Bordeaux during the German Occupation, Papon had risen to prominence as the IGAME (or superprefect) of the much-embattled Constantine and Bône region in eastern Algeria in 1956. Before that he had served directly under the notoriously tough Paris police prefect Jean Bayot, going after Algerian nationalists in the city, and he also earned stripes overseeing brutal antinationalist actions in Morocco. He brought now to the French capital a commitment to use the most violent police methods his experience had taught him to root out FLN militants and intimidate the Algerian population into passivity—in a Paris region that by 1961 would have had 180,000 Algerians, making it second only to Algiers as an Algerian urban center.[38] He also brought hardened army officers with experience in rural Algeria to establish a new Service d'assistance technique aux français musulmans d'Algérie (SAT), which, like the old North Africa Brigade, was to provide migrants help with employment matters, housing, updating papers, and welfare, all the while creating an immense card file on 70,000 Algerian residents in Paris.[39] At a new "identification center" in the Bois de Vincennes, police registered more than 67,000 Algerian migrants by 1960 and subjected nearly 4,000 to interrogation.[40] Papon also brought in sociologists with deep knowledge of North Africa for advice on disrupting the FLN in Paris. He harnessed, too, experienced Algeria hands of another sort: Harkis, Algerian Muslims serving in the French army in Algeria, to work their way into FLN strongholds in the Paris region and dismantle FLN networks. Algerians who were subsequently swept into police custody routinely suffered savage beatings. Torture became more commonly used for interrogations, as was the importation of another instrument of the war in Algeria, internment. In 1959 police started sending what by the end of 1961 would be 15,000 suspected militants into camps at Larzac (Aveyron), Thol (Haute-Marne), Saint-Maurice-l'Aroise (Gard), and Vadnay (Marne).[41] As Emmanuel Blanchard has argued, Papon's steps had the effect of militarizing the police, and hence of breaking with a long tradition in France of distinguishing clearly between the police and the army.[42]

Meanwhile, in October 1958, in accord with the strategic vision inherited from the Fourth Republic, Charles de Gaulle's new Fifth Republic government opted to spend a great deal more money on services in the hope of encouraging a steady flow of migration to relieve pressure in Algeria. To energize and coordinate this ramping up of the service effort, the government tapped Michel Massenet, a graduate of the new École nationale d'administration and former IGAME for the Lyon region, to oversee a big new social service initiative, the Fonds d'action sociale (FAS; Social Action Fund). He reported directly to Prime Minister

Michel Debré. Much of the FAS money came from the family allowance fund surplus, and Massenet embraced the service mission with the enthusiasm of a crusader: "No migration in the world," he said, "is supported by such a tight set of public and private initiatives, welcome centers, transit centers, housing centers, specialized administrative offices, projects devoted to adult literacy, and so on."[43] Massenet also signaled that there ought to still be some boundary between social work and police work. He refused to attend cabinet meetings when high-level police officials were present.[44]

Massenet was hardly alone in trying to protect an expanding social service apparatus designed to integrate migrants while serving an administration increasingly waging a war against many of them. At a private conference in early 1959, CTAMs and other service professionals worried openly that "the mass of migrants," as a summary memo put it, "caught between the demands and violence of the 'separatist agents' [FLN activists], on the one hand, and the actions of the police, on the other, seems exhausted and disoriented." And the problems were only worsening. "After the terrorist wave of the past summer," the memo continued, "many Muslims feel the widespread suspicions of the metropolitan public, and even of their comrades at work." CTAMs worried, too, that employers might be becoming more hesitant to hire Algerians, and migrants more reluctant to use the support services available to them—if they were laid off, for example, they might choose to avoid employment bureaus and unemployment benefits by relying instead on family and friends or simply returning to Algeria.[45] Implied here was the CTAMs' concern that distrust of a policing state thickened the barriers between migrants and the state's services.

Massenet's ambitious new thrust with the Social Action Fund certainly gave CTAMs and service providers more tools to address these concerns, but Papon's logic of repression and brutalization relentlessly held sway. The war seemed to ensure it. In the fall and summer of 1961 the metropolitan-based leaders of FLN stepped up their attacks on the police, and Papon's use of police terror escalated as well. Papon, indeed, hankered for tougher action, received the green light to do so from de Gaulle and Debré, and imposed a nighttime curfew on Algerians in the Paris region to ramp up the tension. When, on October 17, in the evening, 30,000 Algerians in Paris staged a massive, deliberately peaceful march into the center of the city to protest the curfew and display the strength of the FLN, Papon unleashed the full force of police violence. Many dozens of Algerians were killed (some credible estimates put the number as high as 200), and 11,500 were rounded up into the Vélodrome d'Hiver stadium (site of the "Vél d'Hiv" roundup of Jews in 1942). It was the deadliest episode of police repression of a street demonstration in the modern history of Western Europe, an episode continuous with a tradition of colonial massacre that many of the perpetrators, not least Papon among them, had brought to the capital. Michel Massenet immediately recognized the political costs. As he wrote to his superiors, "in several days the work of several years has been destroyed."[46]

When only five months later de Gaulle's government and the FLN negotiated a peace settlement through the Evian Accords, Papon's hot war against the neighborhoods came to an end as well. But much of the state's newly acquired capacity for managing migrant populations endured. Indeed, it was put to an extraordinary test in the months immediately following the Evian Accords when nearly a million European Algerians, *pieds noirs,* fled to France to claim their right to be French and escape the violence of a newly independent Algeria. A new Ministry of Repatriation put the social service network of the country to work for them and won many of these newcomers priority access to public housing. SONACOTRAL set aside 30 percent of its housing for them.[47] De Gaulle's government made no such effort for the approximately 100,000 Harkis who, upon escaping FLN reprisals and then getting to France on their own, found themselves deemed refugees, not repatriated citizens, and were shunted into camps and then into isolated settlements where many were to languish for years.[48] The expanded social service capacity of the state, then, proved its utility during the paroxysms of 1962 much more for some new arrivals than for others.

More important still were the consequences of service expansion—its institutions and the expectations it created—for the state's immigration management after 1962. SONACOTRAL continued as a key component of the government's effort to relocate people out of the shantytowns. It was rebranded SONACOTRA (Société nationale de construction de logements pour les travailleurs) in 1963 to signal its new effort to house not only Algerians but also workers from France's other current or former possessions.[49] Social services became more of a centerpiece of the government's immigration policy as agencies and funding programs expanded the hostels, job training, and large array of family and hygienic activities for all immigrant populations, not just Algerians (who, despite the war, were still regarded as "important assets" to a French economy with a continuing labor shortage).[50] This shift represented a major recasting of the state's function in the domain of immigration. Before the Algerian war the state focused principally on greasing the wheels of the labor market for immigrants and their employers—aiding in recruitment, policing illegal immigration, managing repatriations when jobs became scarce. After the Algerian war the state made welfare servicing a focus of its immigration strategy. A key Interior Ministry memorandum in 1963 made the case to the prime minister for precisely this adaptation of the state's approach to Algerian migration to the entire immigration regime. Recognizing that France now faced stiff competition from Germany for immigrants, where wages were higher, Interior Ministry officials called for using Massenet's Social Action Fund to help the full spectrum of immigrant populations adapt to France. Housing was crucial, of course, but so were other things: "material aid, advice on administrative matters, family assistance, especially for spouses, French courses, professional training, courses to help children get a leg up in French schools."[51] To that end Michel Massenet continued to run the robust Social Action Fund out of the prime minister's office, now on behalf of the Spaniards, Portuguese, Algerians, and West Africans who became the main new sources of labor for the boom years of the 1960s and early 1970s.[52] In the realm of immigration the state's role enlarged and became more focused on managing, settling, and in principle at least, adapting immigrants to the labor market. Oversight for this work remained centralized in the office of the prime minister.

The state's policing role in the management of immigrant populations also continued to bear the imprint of the Algerian war experience. Outright police terror ended with the war, but Papon remained at the helm of the Paris Prefecture until 1967. Perpetrators of police violence remained at their posts. His Service d'assistance technique

(SAT), with its meticulous methods of monitoring the Paris region, neighborhood by neighborhood (*quadrillage* in the language of the army's Algerian war strategy), remained intact. But the scope of this activity actually expanded after the war. Now the target population for all this police attention diversified beyond Algerians (who continued to come to France as laborers under the terms of the Evian Accords and subsequent agreements) to include the growing number of migrants from Mali, Senegal, Madagascar, and other former colonial countries where police surveillance of colonial subjects had had a long history.[53] Moreover, the wartime ethos within the police—fierce loyalty to their organization, engrained habits of racial stereotyping—lived on in the force. Though in principle immigrants in the 1960s enjoyed greater legal protections from police abuse than Algerians had had during the war, police found ways to ignore them. "There were actions," a former prefectural official later admitted, "that we carried out together [in the force] and that certainly didn't appear in the inquiry reports because they violated the law. The context was different than now; there weren't journalists ready to publish no matter what."[54]

The state, then, expanded along two dimensions in the immigration domain from what it had been before the Algerian war—as a service provider and as a policing instrument for governments striving to manage or intimidate non-European populations whose integration into French society was seen as a problem, a challenge, and by those on the far right, an impossibility. This expansion, moreover, went hand in hand with a concentration of authority over these activities at the highest levels of government, most notably into the prime minister's staff and the Ministry of the Interior. Finally, whereas the end of the Algerian war made it easier once again to separate service provision from policing, the legacy of that blending experience remained. Service providers found it difficult to dispel immigrants' continuing, and often justified, suspicions that assistance came at the price of potential exposure to police harassment. True, experience engendered savvy. Many Algerian migrants and their spouses had learned to navigate this landscape by avoiding the service providers that were most tied to the police, by cultivating relationships with social workers, and by demanding the benefits to which they were legally entitled.[55] And that knowledge spread. Portuguese and black African immigrants who came to France in the 1960s and 1970s acquired similar skills and agency. Still, for Algerian migrants the wounds of the war years cut deep and were too often kept fresh by patterns of continuing police harassment long after the war. When, in the dozen years or so after 1962, Algerians living in France had opportunities to opt for naturalization, they did so at lower rates than other immigrants.[56]

Planning's Reach

If the pressures of the Algerian insurgency inspired state officials to enhance their social service and policing tools of population management, the Algerian war had similar effects on the state's role in economic and social planning. On October 3, 1958, five days after winning public approval of his Fifth Republic Constitution, de Gaulle traveled to Constantine, Algeria's most predominantly Muslim-populated big city, to announce an ambitious plan for economic and social development. The Constantine Plan had its origins four years earlier when Pierre Mendès France's government charted a ten-year plan for Algeria designed to addressed what experts such as anthropologist Germaine Tillion and many others regarded as the social and economic roots of the rebellion—chronic underemployment and depressed standards of living made worse by rapid population growth and a lack of investment. The Constantine Plan was nothing if not ambitious: a five-year design to create 100,000 new jobs in the metropole for Algerians and a staggering 400,000 new jobs in Algeria itself, more than a quarter of which in what was hoped would be a new booming industrial sector based on oil and gas production in the Sahara, a new steel complex near the coastal city of Bône, and an array of light industries such as textiles, food products, and other consumer goods. Planners hoped to spur industrial growth in cities and towns other than Algiers and Oran, an idea much in keeping with the metropolitan craze of the 1950s to decentralize French manufacturing away from Paris. Agrarian plans were no less ambitious: the redistribution of 250,000 hectares of land and a revolution in agricultural methods nurtured by an army of experts, one for every 200 farmers, combined with big irrigation and electrification projects, marsh drainage, and road building. The plan also included new housing for a million people and schooling for two-thirds of

Algeria's boys and girls. Another goal stood out: something resembling what today we would call "affirmative action," the setting aside of 10 percent of the posts in the civil service in metropolitan France and Algeria for Muslim Algerians. This public commitment to civil service hiring put real numbers on an objective that the Guy Mollet government in 1956 had already decreed in general terms and that paralleled a wider effort to "indigenize" state employment throughout sub-Saharan French Africa. Finally, the Constantine Plan also served as the vehicle to launch Michel Massenet's Social Action Fund for the metropole (financed in part, as we have seen, by the discriminatory family allowance surplus). All this wasn't cheap. The five-year plan came with a price tag of $4 billion, and $1 billion was in fact spent during the first two years of the plan's implementation.[57]

French leaders did little to hide their political motives for the plan. De Gaulle described it as a way "to preserve and develop ties that exist between the Algerian and French communities."[58] Speaking to the French National Assembly shortly after his Constantine announcement, de Gaulle explained that "insofar as the economy develops, political solutions [will] take shape."[59] When in late 1958 he appointed Paul Delouvrier (Figure 7.2) to be his highest-ranking civilian official in Algeria (his *délégué général*) and to make the Constantine Plan a reality, he told Delouvrier, "You are France in Algeria. . . . In that role you have to pacify and administer [Algeria], but at the same time transform it."[60] Yves Le Portz, head of the main funding conduit for the plan (the Caisse d'équipement pour le développement de l'Algérie) declared openly in Algeria that "the necessity of industrialization is essentially social. The idea is to create a new elite of workers and supervisors who increasingly serve as a real foundation for development and democracy."[61] New extractive industry and manufacturing in Algeria, planners thought, would also tighten the economic bonds to a metropole (and a new European Common Market) that would provide an outlet for products and a larger labor market for Algerian workers.[62] Government planners also regarded the agrarian reform as a way for private property to nurture "the development of an elite differentiated from the masses"—social engineering in the hope of building a third force, a new Muslim elite keen to keep Algeria, if not formally French, at least tightly associated with France.[63] Indeed, as

FIGURE 7.2 Launching the Constantine Plan in Algiers, 1959. Prime Minister Michel Debré (standing, far right) describes details of the plan to promote the economic and social development of Algeria. Accompanying him were Paul Delouvrier (seated, center), charged with overseeing the plan, and Nafissa Sid Cara (seated, left), a secretary of state within the office of the prime minister, the first woman in the Debré cabinet and the first Muslim to hold cabinet rank in France. The plan did little to change the course of the war, but it had a large impact on Algeria's economy and institutions and on the place of planning in French politics. Photoreportage Trampus–Paris/ICharta.

historian Philip Naylor has argued, de Gaulle cared less that the plan reach all its economic goals than that it help maintain France's strategic position in Algeria, even after independence, were that to happen. As Delouvrier admitted later, they had to pursue the Constantine Plan without breathing a word about that possibility.[64] French authorities, in fact, continued to fund some industry even after the plan as an institution ended after 1961.[65]

How much confidence French leaders had in the plan's premise—that social and economic development would lead to a political settlement of the French-Algerian conflict—is hard to say. Some experts thought the reverse: that only with a political resolution, be it independence or some revamped Algerian association with France, could development be made to work. In advising Pierre Mendès France in

1956, for example, economist George Boris reminded his boss that "it would be illusory to give priority to action in the economic and social domain; on the contrary, immediate political reform seems indispensable to insure the efficacy of any economic development plan."[66] The politics, in his view, preceded the economics. By the time the Constantine Plan was under way in 1959, that logic had become all the more compelling, as even the plan's overseer, Paul Delouvrier, acknowledged. "The solution to the Algerian problem," he said, "can only be political."[67] In the end, de Gaulle pursued the military, political, and economic fronts simultaneously, with General Challe's offensive in the Algerian countryside, de Gaulle's own September 1959 speech holding out the prospect to the Algerian people of a referendum on self-determination, and his full and continued support for the Constantine Plan.

The plan's implementation nonetheless fell far short of its goals. The war both facilitated and compromised the plan. The presence of 450,000 French soldiers in Algeria enlarged the market for goods and construction: monumental quantities of locally produced beer, for example, became an astonishing portion of the caloric intake fueling the French army.[68] But as the war dragged on, it became more difficult to attract the private capital needed to finance about half the plan. Once industrialists realized that de Gaulle saw independence as inevitable, they refrained from investing, despite the lure of tax breaks and loan guarantees. They worried, too, that an independent Algeria might nationalize French firms, especially after the FLN's Ferhat Abbas said as much to the Scandinavian press in early 1960, mentioning the banks, railroads, mines, and Saharan oil as likely targets for state takeovers.[69] To calm business nerves, the Constantine Plan's top industry committee pondered beefing up the state's subsidies to firms for the risks they were running, but in the end decided against it, except in special cases, for fear of fueling the anxiety further.[70] Investors' belief that capital flight had followed independence in neighboring Morocco and Tunisia dampened confidence too.[71] As did old-fashioned business conservatism: some firms, especially in textiles, were content to regard Algeria as a lucrative colonial commercial outlet for products and not as a place to set up plants that might undercut metropolitan production.[72] Whatever the cause, the lack of private investment took its toll. From 1960 on, 61 percent of the funds for the Caisse d'équipement came from the state.[73] New industry produced only 20,000 jobs in Algeria from the end of 1958 through 1961.[74]

More serious still, the army's brutal campaign of rural displacement crippled the agrarian program. Over the course of the war the army forced three million inhabitants into resettlement camps or one of the "one thousand new villages" that were little more than internment camps by another name, isolated from the terrain and transport nodes of potential rural reform.[75] The FLN, moreover, made it dangerous for rural families to take possession of redistributed land. In late 1960 the original goal of distributing land to 15,000 households was revised to a mere 1,800 households.[76]

Nor did the plan have as much propaganda value as de Gaulle had hoped for. As to be expected, the FLN condemned it as part of France's war against Algerian independence, and many left-wing critics in Paris dismissed it as "neocolonial" and paternalistic.[77] Delouvrier's staff prepared lengthy texts with talking points to answer just this kind of attack.[78] But it was harder to dismiss the sting when the more mainstream leadership in Algiers of the trade union confederation Force ouvrière disowned the plan in June 1960 because "it lacked the approval of the Muslim majority . . . and could not be fruitful as long as the Algerian conflict endures."[79]

The plan's agenda for initiatives within the metropole brought mixed results. Michel Massenet put the resources of the new Social Action Fund amply to work in expanding services to migrants, but he and Prime Minister Debré had a tougher time getting businesses to create the annual increase of 20,000 new jobs for Algerian migrants in the metropole that the plan called for. Trends in 1959, the first year of the plan, alarmed them. A survey of firms in Lyon revealed that in the mild economic slump of that winter, Algerian migrants were laid off in much higher proportions than were workers of metropolitan origin.[80] Troubling, too, was the fact that CTAMs, with their close connections to the street, reported that "since the Constantine speech, a large number of Algerian migrants consider work as a right, and in the face of difficulties getting hired easily call out the injustice of it, especially if they find themselves in competition with foreigners."[81] Massenet knew the many reasons for the "hostile discrimination" against Algerians: employers' prejudices about their abilities, worry about their association with FLN violence, and fears about worksite sabotage and fights with fellow workers.[82]

With the political stakes for successful migration only getting higher, Massenet and Debré finally went on the offensive with employers in 1960. They directed prefects around the country to pressure firms "with a mixture of authority and persuasion" to hire, train, and when possible house Algerian migrants in preference to foreign workers.[83] Massenet also convened two meetings in Paris, one with top executives of nationalized firms, the other with private sector leaders, to impress upon them the patriotic imperative of hiring Algerians and to call them to account for their record so far. Among nationalized firms, Renault stood out as exemplary, as government officials were accustomed to pointing out, with nearly 2,700 Algerians employed, including some in skilled jobs.[84] But other nationalized firms highlighted the obstacles they faced in doing better by Algeria migrants. The EDF, SNCF, and Charbonnages pointed to their obligations to boost labor productivity and cut payroll. Air France and defense-related industries claimed security concerns. By contrast, Massenet got a less defensive reception from private sector business leaders, especially in chemicals, building construction, sugar refining, and public works, where many Algerians worked. But none of the private executives uttered a word about targets for future Algerian employment as Renault had done (at 10 percent), and none of the business leaders, public or private, embraced a commitment to expand in-house training to the degree Massenet wanted.[85] In the end this exercise in what Americans at the time would have called "jawboning"—persuading by force of authority rather than outright incentives or punishments—revealed how important Algerian migration had become to the de Gaulle–Debré government as a part of the Constantine strategy and how limited their weapons were to make it expand.

For all these many shortcomings in fulfilling the Constantine Plan, French leaders did come closer to reaching goals on a few fronts: 142,000 housing units were built or renovated in Algeria's larger cities by 1962, the number of Muslim children attending primary school rose 70 percent from 1958 through 1960, and 10 percent of the jobs in public administration in Algeria did indeed go to Muslims, though a smaller percentage got them in the metropole.[86] As historian Martin Evans has argued, the plan may have had some positive impact for Algerian women—a key target for hearts and minds—with its clauses for improving women's education and access to public sector jobs. Opportunities in social work and nursing expanded after 1959.[87] All told, the Constantine Plan in three years created 80,000 to 100,000 jobs in Algeria, albeit only a quarter of its five-year goal. And for many years after the war, much of the new Algeria's industrial growth—pipelines from recently discovered Saharan oil and gas reserves, petrochemicals in Arzew, steelmaking in el-Hadjar, hydroelectric power—owed a lot to investments made under the plan.

In mainland France the plan's aftereffects took two forms. The plan had created a context for imagining what the future of French-Algerian relations might be after independence, and in that respect figured in the minds of both French and Algerian negotiators of the Evian Accords. France's commercial and financial engagements with a new Algerian republic and its continuing importance as a destination for Algerian migrants owed not a little to investments, precedents, and habits formed under the aegis of the plan. In addition, the plan had an impact on the stature and scope of planning in the Fifth Republic.

To discern this effect, consider first what mixture of continuity and change the Constantine Plan represented in the history of state planning in France. Continuities are easy to see. To begin with, the plan had been years in the making, the product not of overnight scrambling once de Gaulle came to power in May 1958 but of considerable prior thinking. In 1954, Interior Minister François Mitterrand in the Mendès France government, sensing that Algeria might soon explode, appointed the Maspétiol Commission to draft a plan for economic and social development. Then in 1956 the governor general of Algeria, Robert Lacoste, harnessed planners and high-level civil servants to the task of turning the Maspétiol report into a detailed ten-year plan, which soon thereafter became the basis of the Constantine Plan. On each of these plans the work was done by many of the same civil servants—for example, Michel Piquard and Salah Bouakouir, who were to become top deputies on Delouvrier's staff.[88] And continuities went still farther back. In its economic assumptions and organizational methods, the plan drew heavily on the French experience in the metropole after

World War II—the Monnet Plan of 1946 that set investment targets for important portions of France's reconstruction and served as a vehicle for directing Marshall Plan funds into basic industry and infrastructure. Several of the Constantine Plan's designers and administrators had cut their teeth working with Jean Monnet on the rue de Martignac, most notably Paul Delouvrier himself, who served as the first financial director of the Monnet planning group in 1946–1947.[89] Jean Vibert, whom in 1959 Delouvrier picked to be the administrative director of the Constantine Plan, had previously overseen the overseas work of the Planning Commission in the mid-1950s. Delouvrier even brought the head of the Commission himself, Pierre Massé, to serve on the Constantine Plan's top council. Not surprisingly, then, the organizational structure Delouvrier and Vibert put into place resembled the Monnet Plan's vast hierarchical network of committees that co-opted large numbers of people into the planning process. The Constantine Plan set up five broad overarching committees—agriculture, industry, social and cultural action, regional development, and overall coordination—as well as a dozen departmental committees for each of the three departments of Algeria. All told, 1,800 people took part in this activity, including 300 in the metropole, 80 of whom were civil servants, and 1,500 in Algeria, of whom 300 were civil servants, 900 European colonists *(pieds noirs),* and 600 non-European Algerians, of whom 50 were civil servants. This vast enterprise, much like the Monnet Plan, was designed to give planners a sense of reality and economic actors a sense of political and psychological investment in the Plan. It also served as a running seminar on development and "modernization."

Alongside these continuities, however, there was novelty as well. Most obviously, the Constantine Plan pursued social objectives as seriously as economic ones, and its economic goals were intrinsically linked to the effort to transform the social and political landscape. Job creation, education, support for cultural programs and welfare, agrarian training, home construction, changing the social composition of the civil service—all these efforts were in principle supposed to complement, intimately, the bread-and-butter projects of creating new businesses, luring French firms into new territory, and building infrastructure. Monnet Plan planners had measured success in terms of productivity, output, and growth; Constantine Plan planners measured success in terms of job creation, living standards, and property owner-ship. The ambition of the planners, in short, expanded to tackle eco-nomic underdevelopment, and in so doing sought to combine the economic coordination of the postwar Monnet Plan with both the co-lonial tradition of social uplift—the "civilizing mission," rebranded as "development" by the 1940s—and an old metropolitan repertoire of social initiatives associated with Catholic charities, municipal socialism, agricultural education, and public school proliferation of the late nineteenth century.[90] The economic challenges of poverty and underemployment and the political challenges of "pacification" forced Delouvrier and his colleagues to be far more ambitious than the Monnet Plan team in using state planning to transform a society.

The Algerian war, then, became a crucible through which state planners in France gained confidence in what planning might do. Al-geria, of course, was hardly the sole arena where the planning imagi-nation enlarged: over the course of the Algerian war the Planning Commission in the metropole had steered the French economy through the post–Monnet Plan era of Plan II (1952–1957) and Plan III (1958–1961), with each plan being wider in scope; and ideas about the relationship between economic innovation and social engineering traveled through international circuits of intellectual exchange—academic conferences, the UN, and foundation-sponsored research—with growing velocity in the 1950s.[91] But in the French case the Algerian war was a significant arena because the Constantine Plan was given such publicity—indeed, publicity was part of the point—and because in Algeria planners would see ideas sprout quickly as schools, roads, apartment complexes, and industrial plants across the territory. The experience reverberated back into the metropole. Shortly after Paul Delouvrier left his post in Algeria at the end of 1960, he was tapped to run what would soon be-come an immense new planning authority for the Paris region, to himself become, as it were, a latter-day Haussmann. (He would soon become associated with France's vast experiment in new towns.) If Delouvrier had not had this track record of navigating the scale, poli-tics, and public relations of the Constantine Plan in an Algeria turned upside down, de Gaulle and Debré would likely not have named him to tackle the planning challenges of the Paris region. And he assem-bled around him a tight team—Michel Picard, Robert Buron, Jean

Mascard, Jean Vaujour—all of whom had Algerian experience to draw from. Bernard Hirsch, who had directed public works in Mauritania and Mali before becoming Delouvrier's man to head the new town development of Pontoise-Clergy, would later suggest that Parisian regional development could be construed as "colonialism in reverse."[92] Not that the Constantine Plan made Algeria a "laboratory of modernity" for mainland France, as scholars have regarded some consequences of colonial architecture and planning. But it confirmed politicians, planners, and civil servants in their conviction that the state had the capacity and vocation to reshape the economic and social landscape in France itself, and that they were the men to do it.[93]

This enlarged ambition for social as well as economic planning soon found expression in Plan IV for France. When the Planning Commission announced the broad outlines of this Plan in the summer of 1962, hundreds of thousands of *pieds noirs* residents of Algeria were migrating to the Hexagon with little prospect of return. Plan IV addressed the challenge head-on, calling for job creation and housing expansion to enable these emergency newcomers to settle quickly throughout the country, especially in regions targeted for new growth. The hope was to integrate them through a policy of dispersal, rather than concentration—the kind of sociologically inflected aim that carried echoes of the Constantine Plan experience.[94]

Constantine rebounded in another way as well. De Gaulle and Debré ramped up a grand national policy of industrial decentralization—an effort, launched during the Mendès France government in 1954–1955 on the basis of ideas going back to the 1940s, to tackle the problems of economic underdevelopment in the backwaters of the metropole. Delouvrier had understood the Constantine Plan to be in part a campaign of industrial decentralization, a struggle to entice French industry to set up branches and factories in Algeria, to shift resources from the center to the periphery, and to keep the two big cities of Algiers and Oran from growing so large that their European majorities would become minorities.[95] Back in the Hexagon, planners made industrial decentralization the core strategy for transforming what Jean Gravier had famously dubbed the "French desert" of the country's marginalized regions.[96] Like Delouvrier and his team, many planners and administrators assigned to regional development had experience in the colonies, often Algeria. (By the mid-1960s, 30 percent of France's prefects, who were given considerable responsibility for making the regional development effort work, had served as civil servants in Algeria, and another 12 percent in the colonies.[97]) The Constantine Plan, for all its desultory results and dubious purposes, was a valuable initiation for many of these officials, who in the 1960s and 1970s would seek to synthesize job training, technical education, housing construction, and industrial investment to integrate Brittany, Languedoc, the outer rim of the Paris region, and a number of other parts of the "desert" into a rapidly expanding French economy. And the Constantine Plan effect was not limited to top state officials. It made visible to a broader public a more job-oriented conception of planning and the government's willingness to throw enormous resources into territorial development in response to political crisis. It invited comparisons, and many were made, between underdevelopment in the colonies and underdevelopment at home. And it exposed the magnitude of the sums the state was prepared to spend for these purposes. In 1960 the head of the Social and Economic Council cited the Constantine Plan explicitly as the kind of regional development project the government ought to provide for France. Rural activists and regional elites made the same point more sharply—most notably in Brittany, where they used the Algerian precedent to support their own demands for a "Constantine Plan for Brittany."[98] The Constantine Plan alerted regional advocates to what they felt they deserved.

Ironically, then, even though the Constantine Plan failed to capture the Algerian imagination as de Gaulle had hoped, it seems to have reinforced within the Hexagon the mystique of planning as an instrument of state power and as a focal point for making claims on the state. Just when the Constantine Plan was revealing its limitations, de Gaulle himself embraced planning as never before. In his memoirs Michel Debré recounts the General showing him a preliminary draft of his May 8, 1961 (VE Day) speech, in which he sought to rally the country to a future of growth, prosperity, and national greatness beyond the Algerian morass. "What task, what ambition?" de Gaulle asks rhetorically. "The development of France." He goes on to declare the "obligatory character" of the Plan's objectives—a gesture toward a command economy that stunned even the Jacobin-inclined Debré. At the latter's urging, as Debré tells it, de Gaulle dialed his text back, though in the revised speech he still attempted to give the Plan new authority to harness the energies of the country. "The Plan must become an essential institution," he proclaimed, "more powerful in its actions, more open to collaboration with the certified bodies of science, technology, the economy, and labor. . . . For all Frenchmen it must be an ardent obligation."[99]

Dubbing it an "ardent obligation" indeed caught attention, and it fed discontent, long-festering but heating up with the new Fifth Republic, over what critics on the Left felt was undemocratic about the planning process. For all the many Monnet-style committees that engaged business, labor, outside experts, the ministries, and the government's statistical and forecasting bureaus in sharing the information that went into making the Plan, the process still had a technocratic aura. The Communists and the CGT had been excluded from the process of making Plans II and III. De Gaulle and Debré, moreover, had pushed through a revised Plan III in 1959 without giving Parliament a chance to discuss and approve it, as it had the previous two Plans. Goal setting for the Constantine Plan had been heavily top-down, a product of expert calculation and the political objectives of de Gaulle and Debré. For critics already disturbed by a government awash with high-level civil servants as cabinet ministers and a Parliament weakened by the Fifth Republic Constitution, de Gaulle's enthusiasm for a Plan with greater heft seemed to confirm the technocratic direction in which he was taking the country. Fresh calls for democratic planning came accordingly—from Pierre Mendès France, who, as we have seen, made it central to his 1962 treatise on the "Modern Republic"; from the CFTC and especially its intellectuals associated with the "Reconstruction" monthly; from Gaullist academics such as Leo Hamon and René Capitant; and from "modernizing" elites in the Club Moulin who advocated giving Parliament and interest groups, writ large, a meaningful say over the "big options" that would then shape the details of the Plan.[100] Even Pierre Massé, the head of the Planning Commission, felt compelled to speak up for more of a deliberative role for Parliament and the Social and Economic Council. The goal of democratic planning would remain important to much of the Left throughout the 1960s, even though the power of the Planning

Commission would gradually decline vis-à-vis the ministries and the impact of the Common Market.[101]

Boosting and Resisting Authority

The war had not only reinforced the visibility of planning. It also provided a context for leaders to concentrate executive authority and consolidate the Fifth Republic as a presidential regime. The Constitution that Charles de Gaulle and his key lieutenant, Michel Debré, created in 1958 established the strong executive these leaders, and many others since the 1930s, had advocated as a remedy to unstable government. But it did not establish the presidentialism we now take for granted as synonymous with de Gaulle's republic. Only through navigating toward a conclusion to the war and facing down an army minority willing to defy him to keep Algeria French, and most notably the OAS (the secret army organization of military diehards who resorted to terrorism and assassination in 1962), did de Gaulle get the powerful presidency he wanted. To be sure, the Constitution trimmed back parliamentary power by giving the Council of Ministers, under the leadership of the prime minister and the president, more authority to initiate bills, control the legislative agenda, and decide whether to take action by rule making (the American equivalent of executive orders) or lawmaking (passing bills through Parliament). It also permitted the appointment of nonparliamentarians to cabinet ministries. What was not at all clear in 1958 was how the president and the prime minister would share power, or how they would use the emergency powers that the Constitution allowed for.[102] By picking Michel Debré as his prime minister, moreover, de Gaulle only deepened the initial mystery of how authority would be distributed, given that the two men had a long history of collaborating together.

The Algerian war gave de Gaulle a protracted series of crises through which he managed to enlarge and clarify his authority. Historians disagree on whether and for how long de Gaulle tried to win the war.[103] In any event, by the autumn of 1959 suspicions grew in the officer corps and in the European settler community that he had come to regard independence as acceptable, and in January 1960 army dissidents and European settlers in Algiers staged a revolt—the so-called week of the barricades—in the hope of scuttling his presidency in virtually the same manner by which they had propelled him to office nineteen months earlier. De Gaulle donned his uniform, took to the airwaves of radio and television, and appealed to the public and the army rank and file to stand by him. The method worked, as it did fifteen months later, in April 1961, when army dissidents attempted a coup in Algiers and de Gaulle took to the airwaves again, this time invoking the emergency powers granted by Article 16 of the Constitution. De Gaulle made the stakes remarkably clear. "In the name of France," he said to the nation and especially to the young soldiers listening on their transistor radios at their posts in the Algerian countryside, "I order that all means, I repeat all means, be used to bar the route to these men until such time as they are overcome. I forbid every Frenchmen, and in the first place every soldier, to carry out any of their orders."[104] Both these radio and television performances, reminiscent of his radio speech from London in June 1940, consecrated de Gaulle as the embodiment of the republic in the eyes of a French public, the majority of whom by now were eager to have done with the war.

This drift in the public mood also enabled de Gaulle to make extravagant use of a political weapon provided for in the Constitution: the referendum. On three occasions de Gaulle asked the voters to endorse his initiatives: in January 1961 to approve of the principle of self-determination in Algeria (winning by 75 percent), in April 1962 to approve the Evian Accords ending the war (winning by 90 percent), and in October 1962 to approve the direct election of France's president by universal suffrage (often referred to as the second founding of the Fifth Republic, winning by 62 percent, although, given abstentions, by just 46 percent of the electorate).[105] This latter victory, by no means a foregone conclusion because so much of the political and intellectual establishment opposed the direct presidential election, got a fillip from the harrowing attempt on de Gaulle's life by OAS assassins (one of four failed attempts) in August 1962, which buttressed his stature and reminded the public a president might one day need to be replaced through a process with popular legitimacy. De Gaulle would go on to use referenda several more times in the 1960s, consolidating a form of plebiscitary rule that his opponents on the Left likened, with some justification, to the nineteenth-century Bonapartist precedents of the First and Second Empires. This tool, after all, had the ill-disguised effect of not just approving the proposition at issue but renewing the president's mandate and reaffirming his claim to authority. The direct appeal to the people, both over the airwaves and via the referenda, elevated the president and diminished the power of Parliament.

Algeria also made the president's preeminence over the prime minister unmistakably clear. By seizing command of the government's Algeria policy, de Gaulle gradually made foreign policy, military affairs, and national security the *domaine reservé* (privileged domain) of the president, which, again, is something we take for granted now, but it wasn't then. De Gaulle was all the more eager to establish this privileged domain of policy control because Prime Minister Debré, though loyal to him personally, was a strong proponent of a French Algeria. Every major shift in Algerian policy came at de Gaulle's initiative and through his broadcast speeches. The General, moreover, solidified his control by expanding the presidential staff to include a large number of technical advisors with expertise and authority much exceeding what the prime minister, and more specialized ministries, could muster on their staffs. De Gaulle also used the Algerian crises to set precedents for naming and dismissing high-ranking government officials, which in 1958 might have been thought to be the prerogative of prime minister. The most notable instance impinged on Debré's maneuverability directly. When by late 1960 the divergence between the two men's approach to Algeria became too great, de Gaulle named a close confident, Louis Joxe, to head a newly created Ministry of Algerian Affairs, in effect marginalizing Debré in the peace talks that followed. And when Michel Debré resigned in the spring of 1962 soon after the signing of the Evian Accords, it was widely understood that de Gaulle had dismissed him, establishing the precedent that the prime minister served at the pleasure of the president. Until then it was more commonly assumed that the constitutional clause about prime ministerial resignation was designed to enable the prime minister to leave office when he chose. Like all the other aspects of presidential rule— marginalizing Parliament, exploiting constitutional provisions for emergency powers and referenda, the building of an expert-laden presidential staff, direct appeals to the public through the broadcast media—the subordination of the prime minister came a great deal more easily than it would have without the Algerian war.[106]

De Gaulle's four-year effort to strengthen the presidency, from 1958 to 1962, restores the shift from the Fourth to the Fifth Republic as an important moment of rupture in the history of the French state. But if we broaden the scope to executive authority, and not just presidential power, then 1958 also appears as a moment of continuity. In 1955 and 1956 the French government took two steps, with far-reaching consequences, that expanded administrative authority. The first was the State of Emergency Law of April 1955, and the second was the Special Powers Law of March 1956—both adopted to address the crisis in Algeria. The State of Emergency Law, developed under the governments of Pierre Mendès France and Edgar Faure in winter of 1954–1955, gave prefects everywhere, as well as the governor general of Algeria, the power to impose curfews, to close public places, cafés, movie houses, and meeting halls, and to confiscate arms, seize newspapers and books, censor the press and the radio, even move people from their place of residence (soon enough, crucially, into internment camps). True, Mendès France and the Left thought this use of ramped-up executive authority would be brief, after which the government could then tackle the entrenched problems of underdevelopment. But in fact these new powers gave the state the means to fight a protracted war both in Algeria and in the metropole. The following spring the Special Powers Law, approved by all political parties except the Poujadists and some mainstream conservatives such as Paul Reynaud, went even further to enhance executive authority for fighting the war. It gave greater powers to the Ministry of the Interior, to the Ministry of Defense and the Army, and to a new Ministry of Algeria (under the tough-minded Socialist Robert Lacoste, who was battle-hardened from the strike repression of 1948), and it gave the government the authority to use "any exceptional measure required by circumstances with a view to the reestablishment of order, the protection of persons and property and the safeguard of the territory."[107] The scope of executive authority expanded exponentially. These two laws together proved pivotal in diminishing parliamentary oversight of the war, and they set precedents for the exceptional powers provision of Article 16 in the Constitution of the

Fifth Republic and other uses of executive authority after May 1958. The State of Emergency and Special Powers Laws, originally inspired by the desire of Fourth Republic politicians, civil servants, and military officials to fight the FLN, also gave de Gaulle legal tools to fight the ultras of the other side in 1960 and 1961.[108]

The war, then, enabled, inspired, or provoked politicians and high-level civil servants of the Fourth and Fifth Republics to transform the state in at least three ways: expanding its role in managing populations, enlarging the ambitions of state planners to combine social and economic goals for the country's own escape from underdevelopment, and consolidating executive authority. All these changes had the effect of enhancing the role of policy experts, top civil servants, and the president himself in the early years of the Fifth Republic—the Massenets, Papons, Delouvriers, Debrés, and de Gaulles, who though divergent in their politics shared a common conviction that national reconstruction and grandeur derived first and foremost from the use of centralized executive authority.

At the same time this expansion and concentration of state authority engendered its own opposition. State expansion and societal resistance had often gone hand in hand in the past, and this dialectic applied in the Algerian war years as well. In this respect, too, the continuities prevailed from the Fourth to the Fifth Republic, because the political contours of opposition shifted more in 1955–1956 than they did in 1958. In the early 1950s, opposition to the state's policing and repressive authority engaged both the Communists and the Algerian nationalist movement within the metropole, working in an awkward informal alliance: awkward, not only because most Algerian nationalists had no desire to subordinate their cause to anyone else's political agenda, but also because the French Communist Party, although uncompromising in its support of Ho Chi Minh's Communist-oriented war of independence in Indochina, still regarded Algeria as exceptional and a part of France. Even so, many Algerian migrant workers participated in the Communist-led street protests against the visit of American general Ridgway to Paris in 1952. Indeed, the sole fatality in bloody clashes with police that day was an Algerian Communist activist, Belaïd Hocine.[109] In July 1953 the party and the CGT staged large demonstrations and citywide work stoppages in Paris to protest the deadly police attack on the Bastille Day marchers from Messali Hadj's MTLD.[110] Above all, links between Communists and Algerians had emerged in the opposition culture of the everyday workplace. Many Algerian migrants became involved in the CGT, and their union activism, especially at Renault, served them well in learning organizing methods and building networks when they became active in the FLN's Paris underground.[111] Indeed, union activists suspected some employers of systematically firing the more highly educated Algerian migrants for fear of the leadership role they might play among their compatriots.[112]

After 1954, however, tensions deepened between an Algerian nationalist movement fully committed to a war of independence and a PCF whose leaders clung to the goal of creating a socialist Algeria still linked to France. The PCF argued, too, that an independent Algeria would fall into the American orbit.[113] When in 1955 the government adopted its State of Emergency Law, Algerian workers carried out street demonstrations and clashed with police largely on their own. And when the PCF deputies in Parliament voted for Mollet's Special Powers Law of 1956 for fear that to do otherwise would jeopardize the PCF's strategic priority of building a new popular front with the Socialists, Algerians in France felt deeply betrayed. The burden of protest in Paris against the Special Powers Law, then, fell heaviest on the shoulders of Algerian migrants themselves. The MTLD and the FLN orchestrated a march in Paris of 10,000 people, following the call to prayers, an initially peaceful affair that led to hours of battling with the police and to a great deal of destruction of commercial property.[114]

After 1956, resistance to the state's expanded authority in the metropole took number of different forms, each shaped by how oppositional groups positioned themselves in relationship to the war. Algerian nationalists challenged the state's police power by far the most directly by defying government restrictions against demonstrations and then in 1960 and 1961 carrying out armed attacks against Papon's police and Harki personnel in Paris. It was in defiance of Papon's October curfew, designed in part to stem these attacks, that the FLN mounted its most spectacular display of resistance to state authority—the nonviolent demonstrations of October 17, 1961, which the police were to immortalize in blood with deadly force. Meanwhile the Communist Party shored up its position at the moderate end of the oppositional spectrum by advocating peace and a negotiated settlement. Party leaders never lost sight of the fact that its working-class constituency made up a major part of France's conscript army. The PCF did allow the CGT to play a more militant role in organizing demonstrations and work stoppages on behalf of the peace movement, which in turn served to keep Algerian migrants connected to trade unions. In the final three years of the war the CGT played a role in hundreds of marches and work actions across the country. Still, the yawning gulf between the FLN's revolutionary defiance, on the one hand, and the PCF's cautious ambivalence, on the other, created space for a New Left to emerge as the galvanizing force behind a more avowedly anticolonial and antigovernmental opposition. Dissidents within the Communist Party, not least a number of women in the Union des femmes françaises, lent support to a wave of protests in 1955 and 1956 by reservists who, when called to serve in Algeria, demonstrated at railway stations and disrupted the movement of troop trains to the south.[115] By 1959 university students, faced with narrowing avenues to avoid conscription, emerged as a principal force behind the antiwar movement. The Union nationale des étudiants de France (UNEF) became a leader in organizing the biggest demonstrations in final years of the war. By 1960 celebrated intellectuals, filmmakers, and publishers, left-wing Catholic activists in the CFTC and elsewhere, and not least, Socialist dissidents who in 1960 broke with the SFIO to form the Parti socialiste unifiée (PSU) coalesced behind the cause of ending the war quickly and negotiating the terms of independence with the FLN. Shared outrage over government's use of torture, mass-scale internment, and press censorship, and its abuse of special powers, held this disparate coalition together, even if only a tiny minority of the opposition, such as Francis Jeanson's money-and-arms-running network, went so far as to give material and ideological support to the FLN.[116] Antiwar politics, in short, provided opportunities for new actors, Algerian and French, inside and outside the long-established parties and unions of the Left, to call into question the expansion of state authority during the war and to bring new energy into the rituals of protest—petitions, marches, symbolic work stoppages, and clashes with police—that proliferated exponentially in the final years of the war. These rituals gave New Left activists an arena in which to shape a new political relationship to the Fifth Republic.[117]

De Gaulle's own crablike walk to peace—guiding the country step-wise to accept self-determination by the Algerian people while continuing to battle the FLN mercilessly to strengthen his government's negotiating position in the Evian talks—had paradoxical effects on the antiwar opposition. De Gaulle's position and theirs increasingly converged even as war continued through 1961. Antiwar voices had a way of bolstering de Gaulle's authority within a government and an army still divided over conceding independence, even as de Gaulle's recalcitrance in negotiations spurred the antiwar movement to battle more. The emergence of the diehard OAS, and above all the extraordinary violence it carried out, including several attempts on de Gaulle's life, in its efforts to keep Algeria French, in the short run helped de Gaulle close some distance between the General and his antiwar opposition. But OAS violence, especially in the metropole, also brought together the PCF, CGT, New Left, and Algerians living in mainland France in a shared feeling of common vulnerability and a unity behind the demand that de Gaulle's government should do more to end OAS violence and the war. This momentary unity found expression in an immense demonstration on February 8, 1962, its violent repression by the police, and the subsequent deaths of eight demonstrators crushed at the Charonne Métro station as they were trying to escape police batons. A million people turned out for the funeral procession five days later, accompanied by a general strike in Paris and tens of thousands of demonstrators in other cities.[118] It was to be the largest political possession of the streets in Paris between the Liberation moment of August 25, 1944, when de Gaulle presided over the ritual, and May 1968, when demonstrators tried to bring him down.

The Algerian war, then, may have served as the occasion for the governments of the Fourth and Fifth Republic to expand state authority along the several dimensions discussed here—population management, planning, and executive power—but in doing so it also provided plenty of opportunity and inspiration for the growth of counter-movements and counter-sensibilities. Most colonial wars leave scars of all sorts but rarely serve as transformative moments for the metropolitan states that wage them. By contrast, the Algerian war, so exceptional in its magnitude and in its intimate involvement of the metropole—it was the largest colonial war fought by a European colonial power—left an

important and lasting legacy, not least the consolidation of a Gaullist
state endowed with newfound authority and an accompanying contes-
tatory political culture.

How much the war changed the French state and the relations between the state and society was underappreciated at the time. After
1962 de Gaulle's government and much of French society were eager
to put the war experience to rest, move forward, and suppress the mem-
ories of the brutality, torture, insurrection, and assassination that had
occurred. De Gaulle much preferred to situate his regime in a different
collective memory—that of June 18, 1940, and the Liberation of 1944.
He made spectacular theater of the pantheonization of Gaullist Resistance hero Jean Moulin in 1964.[119] But the Algerian legacy was there
all the same. True, the Gaullist state of the 1960s and 1970s owed a
great deal to the innovations of the Second World War and the Liberation era—nationalizations, planning, a national social security system.
But it also owed something important to another war, the one people
in France for a long time tried to forget and are now more willing to
recall. The Algerian war helped to make the Gaullist state the epitome
in Western Europe of not just economic dirigisme, but social dirigisme
as well, and it concentrated authority even more than the most ambitious of all the state Jacobins, Michel Debré himself, had imagined possible in 1944. It would be incorrect to say that the Algerian conflict
gave de Gaulle, Debré, and their predecessors in the latter years of the
Fourth Republic, who were state-builders in their own right, a war they
wanted. But it gave them circumstances they exploited: the emergency
conditions that wars often provide leaders to expand state functions
and centralize authority. Yet, because it was the war that wasn't declared as such, and because emergency powers could only go so far in
silencing opposition in the metropole, the war also gave pressure groups
and citizens room to maneuver and to hone their repertoires of
contention—most especially in the uses of public demonstrations and
ritualized combat with police. These repertoires, too, became part of
the Algerian war's inheritance for the Fifth Republic.

Conclusion

In 1960 Alexander Werth, the *Manchester Guardian's* legendary observer of France, wondered whether a "daddy-knows-best" mood had overtaken the country. "If, in spite of everything, de Gaulle at last succeeded in making peace in Algeria," he noted, it was not clear whether "the French democratic tradition [would] become revitalized."[1] These were not idle musings. De Gaulle proved masterful in using the Algerian war to strengthen executive authority, to which the still towering General lent a marshal and paternalistic aspect. This approach to leadership in the Fifth Republic also made for an easy marriage with "technocratic" authority, a reliance on seasoned high-level civil servants, scientific and academic experts, and a few policy-savvy politicians who shared de Gaulle's impatience with party and pressure-group politics. Nothing signified this marriage more clearly than de Gaulle's appointment of a large number of nonparliamentarians to his cabinet, the dramatic expansion of technical expertise in the presidential staff, and the downgrading of Parliament in policymaking, even to an extent that made his loyal prime minister, Michel Debré, uncomfortable.

The ascendency of policy experts had deep roots in France, but it had accelerated rapidly, as we have seen, after the Liberation and through the long reconstruction. In some key perches of the state during the Fourth Republic, at the Planning Commission and the Treasury, for example, top civil servants like Étienne Hirsch and François Bloch-Lainé could operate with extraordinary autonomy as governments rose and fell around them.[2] De Gaulle's consolidation of presidential power in 1958 (and further in 1962) gave even greater influence in the new Fifth Republic to experts and administrative elites, men like Jean-Marcel Jeanneney and Paul Delouvrier and the first graduates of the École nationale d'administration *(énarques)*, like Michel Massenet. As British political scientist F. F. Ridley observed in the 1960s, the British civil servant tended "to see the functions of government rather negatively as the adjustment of conflicting interests," whereas in France "the technocratic-administrator does have a sense of responsibility for modernization."[3] And a sense of entitlement to authority. As Simon Nora reflected later, "We were a small number who knew better than others what was good for the country.... And this sentiment, which I express here a bit ironically, nourished the technocratic strata."[4]

It took the full span of the long reconstruction era—to 1962 with the end of the Algerian war and the shift to the direct election of the presidency—for government officials to consolidate "technocratic-administrative" authority to the degree Nora's remark implies. Remarkably, the paradigm of "reconstruction" continued to serve de Gaulle and Debré in the early Fifth Republic as a way to justify their constitutional and policymaking agenda. They saw it as completing the work of the Liberation even as they also claimed to be ushering France into a new era. And indeed, it took until the 1960s for the French to complete the most challenging projects of physical reconstruction after the war, such as the rebuilding of the port city of Le Havre, as well as to restore stability to public finance, overcome a sense of demographic panic, and see the industrial initiatives of the late 1940s take deep root in the economy. Above all, it was only in the early years of the Fifth Republic that the key political consequence of the reconstruction era became visible—namely, that remaking France after World War II intensified, rather than diminished, the clash between administrative authority and democratic participation. That reality, while discernible in the Fourth Republic, became obvious by the early 1960s with the full flowering of debate about the vices and virtues of de Gaulle's "technocratic" state.

The visibility of France's economic achievements by the end of the long reconstruction only reinforced the self-confidence of policy experts and top civil servants. For achievements there were. By 1962 France had reached a level of gross domestic production 250 percent higher than what it had been in 1946, and it was poised to have the highest average annual growth rate in Western Europe during the 1960s.[5] State investment in public and private enterprise, industrial restructuring, most notably through the nationalized sector, and rising labor productivity all contributed to this accomplishment, as did the capacity of firms to respond to the competitive pressures of the new Common Market.[6] Furthermore, despite leaders' fears of losing an empire, decolonizing the export economy midway through the reconstruction era helped to expand it within Europe. In 1953, 37 percent of French exports went to the nonmetropolitan territories in the franc zone, and only 19 percent to Belgium, the Netherlands, Luxembourg, West Germany, and Italy; by 1962 it was the reverse.[7] The success of the reconstruction reconfirmed the confidence most French elites had placed in an aggressively dirigiste approach to the country's economic development. And this comfort with state guidance would last. Even after the neoliberal turn of the 1980s and 1990s, France would continue to have a more state-centered economy in comparison to Britain, Germany, or the United States, as measured by tax revenue, public employment, and public spending as a proportion of GDP.[8] The effects of this reconstruction experience, moreover, spilled beyond the borders of France. As many scholars and journalists have observed, the French emphasis on elite guidance, strong administrative governance, and weak parliamentary power had a big impact on the evolution of the European Union, starting with Jean Monnet and Robert Schuman's conception of the European Coal and Steel Community run by a technocratic "High Commission."[9] Analysts in search of the origins of today's "democratic deficit" in the European Union would do well to look there and at Monnet's notion of building Europe gradually through elite-led institutions.

Yet, tracing the rise of "technocracy" and its contribution to France's postwar economic success tells only half the story. The long reconstruction also left an equally consequential legacy for parties, pressure groups, and social movements seeking to master their own methods of contention, advocacy, and negotiation in France's modernizing, state-directed postwar economy. Although welcomed by the majority in Parliament and a public that would soon thereafter ratify by a wide margin the Constitution of a new Fifth Republic, de Gaulle's return to power in May 1958 galvanized an opposition, mobilizing more than 150,000 demonstrators into the place de la République. Despite tough restrictions on marches and protest as the Algerian war ground on, the "politics of the street" returned with a vengeance over the course of the de Gaulle–Debré government, most notably with postwar France's bloodiest night of police violence on October 17, 1961, and with the immense demonstrations in February 1962 for peace and against police repression. From disparate quarters, critics of the regime spoke out against the concentration of authority in the new "Gaullist state." Although not everyone regarded "technocrat" as an epithet after so much government instability in the Fourth Republic, "technocracy" did become a negative watchword of the early 1960s, as social scientists made it an object of study and as writers, from conservative Catholics to Trotskyists, anarchists, and others in an emerging New Left, made it a target of their anti-Gaullist critique.[10] The Communist Party issued pamphlets and newspaper diatribes haranguing "Bonapartist Gaullist technocracy." Some Christian Democrats in the MRP, seeing their party's voting ranks diminished by the ascendency of the Gaullist party and the relegation of Parliament to the margins, castigated "technocracy" and spoke of democracy "going on vacation, or to sleep, or even buried."[11] The remarkably wide, if ultimately ineffective, political coalition that rallied against de Gaulle's referendum for presidential direct election in October 1962 (Figure C.1) came together to form the "cartel of the noes," dubbing themselves the "Cartel of Democrats" united to defend the "principles of republicanism."[12] Pierre Mendès France would sustain the critique on into the mid-1960s. He accused de Gaulle of imagining France as an ocean liner: "The pilot at the helm, the crew at their posts, the passengers (49 million Frenchmen!) in their cabins!"[13] In short, the tensions between the Gaullist state and societal groups endured—and grew: farmer rebellions in 1961 and 1963, a politically damaging miners' strike in 1963, a harshly fought presidential election in 1965, and full-blown regime crisis in May 1968, a series of major rent strikes by immigrants in public housing in the 1970s—all exposed the fissures that lay just beneath the stable surface of the Fifth Republic.

The Gaullist state thus was hardly the smooth-sailing ocean liner Mendès France claimed de Gaulle wanted. On the contrary, it emerged in 1962 from the long reconstruction era still very much intertwined or in combat with societal groups and subject to lobbies and social move-

FIGURE C.1 Parisian voters contemplate their choices for the referendum of October 1962. De Gaulle asked voters to support his proposed constitutional change to elect the president directly, rather than by an electoral college. Left-wing parties and some leaders on the right, urging "non," feared that this further strengthening of the executive would weaken Parliament and damage democracy. Voters approved the change by 62 percent, a Gaullist victory that is sometimes called the second founding of the Fifth Republic. Keystone France/Gamma Keystone/Getty Images.

ments beyond the state's control. Ironically enough, as political scientist Ezra Suleiman has shown, administrative centralization and the decline of Parliament could sometimes make a state especially susceptible to the influence of private interest groups if they could focus their leverage on a key bureau or minister in Paris. Private groups could also exploit the state's internal rivalries, which were as common in the Fifth Republic as they had been in the Third and Fourth.[14] Sociologist Pierre Grémion has argued, moreover, that the expansion of the state into realms of regulation, local housing, and town planning, for example, spawned new intermediaries between state and society, center and periphery, who in turn could negotiate new limits to state authority.[15]

The French state that emerged from the long reconstruction, then, had a dualistic relationship to French society: in many arenas it was imperious and autocratic, prone to trigger protest in response; whereas in other arenas it was flexible and responsive, adept at negotiating with pressure groups to get things done. The policy domains we have explored in depth here displayed this duality, as well as the concomitant variation in the way societal groups learned to engage with the government's direction of the postwar reconstruction. In the domain of taxation, top-down state initiatives sparked the largest tax rebellion in French history, which in turn forced the government to modify its policies to salvage the basic thrust of its reforms. At the opposite end of the spectrum, in the family policy domain, ideas for reform came equally from civil society and the state, and much of the implementation of policy took place through a vast, decentralized network of local funding bureaus (caisses) subject to elected bodies. Ministries and their experts, often at odds with one another over new policy directions, learned they needed to build alliances with family associations of various stripes. The immigration domain took yet another course. There, Communists and trade unionists wielded exceptional influence over the recruitment of foreign workers until 1948, when Cold War politics marginalized these players. Ministerial officials and big business leaders shared command in this domain until the Algerian war shifted the ground once again. This war gave Algerian migrants an implicit leverage that made the government deeply invested in making a trans-Mediterranean migration system work, which in turn led de Gaulle and Debré to further concentrate authority in this domain into the hands the prime minister and the Interior Ministry. Finally, in the domain of nationalized enterprise, the tension between administrative governance and democratic participation varied by sector or enterprise. The nationalized banks barely changed their practices from what they had been before the war, nor did they alter their tough, paternalistic labor relations. Électricité de France (EDF), by sharp contrast, radically reorganized a whole industry and embraced technological change, with its unions weathering the anti-Communist turmoil of 1947–1948 to claim a comparatively strong role in company affairs thereafter. Though still a company run from the top, EDF built more of a culture of industrial democracy than did other public enterprises. The Charbonnages de France (coal) started out in 1945–1946 as a bastion of left-wing power but descended, after devastating strikes and purges of Communists in

1948, into an unrelenting purgatory of poor labor relations and workforce contraction that pitted workers against the state. Managers, employees, and state officials involved in the nationalized railways (SNCF), the Renault auto firm, and the aircraft industry forged paths between these extremes.

What accounts for this variation among policy domains and business sectors? Comparing them along three dimensions across the full span of the long reconstruction reveals a lot about why they evolved differently as arenas where state officials and societal actors struggled over how to revive democratic participation amid a top-down, state-led modernization drive. The first and most obvious dimension was the *degree of fit* between the government's modernizing plans and the way societal groups perceived their own self-interest. Shopkeepers and coal miners, for example, came to recognize themselves as outsiders to the politics of "modernization and reconstruction." Shopkeepers were outsiders in two respects in the 1950s: they lacked a reliable and powerful pressure group (although Léon Gingembre's Confédération générale des petites et moyennes entreprises would partially rectify that in the 1960s), and they symbolized the traditional economy that the modernizers hoped to change. They consequently feared both the immediate impact of the state's tax reform efforts in the 1950s and the longer-term effects of the state's support for big retailers. Feeling cornered, they opted for Poujadist revolt and Poujadist candidates at the polls. Likewise, coal miners came to see themselves as victims of the state's rationalizing agenda, be it the new work methods and mechanization in the mines, the new market structures via the Coal and Steel Community, or the new competitive fuels (oil and nuclear) edging out coal. The subsequent contraction of the workforce pitted miners against the state in no uncertain terms. Unlike shopkeepers, miners had well-established unions, but these organizations had lost their leverage with the state after the devastating strike defeat of 1948. When miners struck again in 1962 and 1963 to try to salvage their future, they had to look outside the state for allies, to local communities and the Church, because they had little recourse for support within the government. The strength of the Poujadist revolt had won shopkeepers some continuing leverage over tax policies and small business protection in the 1960s and 1970s, but miners learned how little power they had to renegotiate their fate in a rapidly evolving energy economy.

In the family policy domain, by contrast, as well as in such nationalized firms as the EDF, the SNCF, Renault, and the aircraft companies, societal groups found it easier to negotiate their role in the state's project of economic transformation. There the fit was much tighter between the state's modernizing agenda and the perceived self-interest of societal groups, be they in the family caisses, which shared the state's pronatalist priorities, or in the technology-savvy unions of the EDF, the SNCF or Sud-Aviation, which supported the strategic priorities the state established in energy and transportation policy. Not that relations between the state and labor went entirely smoothly in these nationalized firms. De Gaulle and Debré's insistence on tight wage constraint in public enterprises turned workers in these companies into aficionados of the short-term strike. But these antagonisms were nothing in comparison to the battles shopkeepers and miners fought, quite literally with the police, to defend their interests. In short, the content of the state's plans for the new postwar French economy did a lot to shape the nature of relations between the state and society in particular policy domains, as did the capacity of societal groups to position themselves accordingly.

Policy domains also varied along a second dimension—the *distribution of expertise* inside and outside the state. Here the family policy domain stood out for the extraordinary breadth of that distribution. True, doctors, public health officials, and demographers brought a special expertise to this domain. But so did a host of others—economists, social workers, family aid workers, Catholic charity professionals, trade union journalists, and staff specialists—all of whom knew a lot about what kinds of wage subsidies and social services would benefit the families they worked with. The very expansion of those services and decentralization of decision making into the local family caisses during the long reconstruction era further proliferated the number and kinds of people, many of them women, who could assert themselves with claims to knowledge and hence to authority—operating as experts—in this policy domain. No state ministry or agency, moreover, monopolized expertise in this area. A half dozen ministries, each with its own specialists and points of view, weighed in. Such widely distributed knowledge-based authority in this domain made for broad public participation in policy debate, as did the periodic election of representatives to the family caisses. The caisses also gave trade unionists, family associations, Catholic activists, and employers power to set localized priorities on how money should be spent on services, holiday camps, and other family-related programs. This highly decentralized discretionary authority made this policy domain exceptional in the reconstruction era.[16] Correspondingly, policy change would come slowly, incrementally even, in this domain—a gradual sea change from stay-at-home natalism to policies supporting working mothers would take decades—but come it would through complex, multilayered negotiation.

In sharp contrast, expertise remained quite narrowly concentrated in the taxation domain. There, highly trained professionals in the Finance Ministry and its tax administration, along with top civil servants such Maurice Laure and Paul Delouvrier and a few exceptionally knowledgeable politicians such as Edgar Faure and Antoine Pinay, commanded the expertise required to think strategically about public finance. A shopkeeper could figure out what a tax rate meant for his or her business, but not what it meant for the state's ledger, much less for meeting the goals of the national Plan. What conventional negotiation there was in this domain remained where it had long been since the Third Republic—in the specialized committees of Parliament, the financial press, and the experts employed by the big-business Conseil national du patronat français. The experts, in short, resided at the top, not in the localities or unions or the newly organized cadres of the Poujadist movement. Even Poujadist deputies in Parliament proved ineffective as policy advocates. The consequences of this narrow distribution of expertise were enormous. State experts initiated reforms in taxation and its enforcement, and shopkeepers and their allies revolted, radically reducing the flow of revenue to the state. Revolt forced the experts to compromise. In its own violent and politically destabilizing way, the Poujadist revolt was a form of democratic participation in a domain where the Finance Ministry held a near monopoly on expertise.

The distribution of expertise in the immigration domain fell between the polar opposites of family policy and taxation. As in the family domain, a wide variety of societal groups—unions, businesses, and religious and political organizations—cultivated their own specialists in immigration matters. They knew the statistics, legal complexities, and geography of immigration, and a lot about what immigrants went through to find and keep jobs in France. The Office national d'immigration (ONI) gave trade unions a key arena to grow their own experts, and an expanding network of social services also gave social workers influence in this domain. Several ministries, moreover, competed for authority over immigration policy, especially Labor, Interior, and Public Health and Population, each with its own experts, logics, and priorities. But for all this breadth in the distribution of expertise and the concomitant influence it gave to many groups inside and outside the state administration, two large contextual changes empowered government leaders to privilege some experts over others during the long reconstruction. Cold War cleavage after 1947 enabled the government to diminish the ONI and with it the influence of unions and the Communist Party over immigration. The government marginalized immigrant advocacy organizations as well. And then the Algerian war allowed top officials, and after 1958 especially de Gaulle and Debré, to give the Interior Ministry the upper hand in this domain. As for the immigrants, particularly Algerian migrants who became such an important portion of the expanding workforce in the 1950s, they found themselves, like shopkeepers, treated as outsiders to their own policy domain—marginalized within the trade unions and criminalized for their association with the Algerian nationalist movement. Without their own experts at the table on a regular basis, they relied on demonstrations and the politics of the street, even if legally prohibited from doing so. Not until the 1970s and 1980s would immigrants finally acquire the legal and political space they needed to create robust institutions of political representation, acquire respect for their expertise, and play an important role in setting the agenda for policy debate.[17]

The distribution of expertise and the degree of fit between societal groups and the government's modernizing projects had an important bearing on how confrontational the political climate became within policy domains, but so did a third dimension—the *coherence of state efforts* to shape policy in a given domain. "The government's doctrines and actions must be a coherent whole," de Gaulle told the nation in a major radio address in 1945, and such an aspiration seemed essential as the state guided the postwar reconstruction.[18] But coherence in policy priority-setting and action can be difficult for any state to achieve, and in postwar France it varied across domains.[19] It was considerable in the taxation domain. Once Marshall Plan officials and the key experts in the Finance Ministry made the urgency of better public finance unmistakably clear in the late 1940s, the tax administration proceeded with impressive discipline to move forward with the TVA tax and the attack on fraud. This state coherence around tax policy had political consequences: it made it all the more difficult for Poujadists to exploit divisions within the government and hence sharpened the confrontational character of the tax revolt.

Coherence proved more difficult to achieve in the immigration domain, especially early on in the reconstruction era when three ministries competed for preeminence and opinions differed widely within government about the value of non-European migration. Over time, coherence grew as the Interior Ministry took greater control of the Algerian migration system and as the government came to rely increasingly on employers to directly recruit European immigrants (mostly Italians, Spanish, and Portuguese), whose status could then be "regularized" by the state at employers' request. These two developments had the effect of diminishing the role of the trade unions and immigrant advocacy groups in policymaking in this domain.

If state action became more coherent over time in immigration, it became less so in the domain of family policy. Strong consensus over natalist priorities in the first years of the reconstruction era gradually gave way to a split within the government over the importance of encouraging mothers to remain at home versus urging them to enter or return to the workforce. This latter, "productivist" position appealed to many feminists and employers, if for different reasons, and it divided experts in the ministries. By the time of Debré's government in 1959–1962, a leading veteran state administrator in this domain, Georges Desmottes, despaired of how disharmonious the voices had become within the government over priorities in family policy. Growing incoherence within the state had the consequence of giving societal groups new opportunities to push their own priorities and to find allies within the government to support them.

Coherence varied, too, within the domain of nationalized enterprise. There, executives and trade unionists became highly skilled in exploiting divisions and rivalries within the state administration. They knew how to cultivate allies in their oversight ministries (Transport for the SNCF, Industry for the EDF, and so on) and to play on the tension between the Budget Department and the Treasury within the Finance Ministry. Debré's efforts to establish a unified wage policy in public enterprise, as well as his government's attempts to create a fully coordinated set of policies for energy and transport, came to naught. Nationalized industries would continue to pursue their distinctive trajectories in alliance with the agencies and ministries they had worked with during the reconstruction era—and hence the disparate fates of banking, coal, the EDF, and other firms. This pattern of sectoral diversity would continue on into the 1960s and 1970s, as the French state sought more vigorously than anywhere else in Western Europe to steer industrial development in the public and private sectors. Dirigisme worked well in high-technology sectors where the government had savvy private actors to work with, including unions committed to technological change, and where the state's procurement, ownership, or regulation still gave it the upper hand—in nuclear power, for example, or high-speed rail, aerospace, telecommunications, or architectural *grands projets* in Paris. Not so in steel and shipbuilding, where the state had less leverage and less cooperative partners. There, projects flagged.[20] In agriculture, to take a mixed case, success with mechanization and land consolidation in the 1960s came at the cost of rural unrest and required close partnership between state elites and the Young Farmers movement, a postwar association that challenged the older farm lobby and developed a strong corporatist relationship with the Gaullist Ministry of Agriculture.[21] State effectiveness, in short, depended not just on the state's authority to maneuver, which varied by sector, but also on able private partners and public-private collaborations, increasingly facilitated in the Fifth Republic by the growing practice of *pantouflage*, the parachuting of high-level civil servants from government to top managerial posts in the private sector.[22]

When de Gaulle and Debré built the Fifth Republic, they sought to build coherence out of the congeries of politics that made governing a country "with 246 cheeses" so difficult, as de Gaulle like to say. Constitution-writing and Algerian war-making gave them much of what they needed to do this. They harnessed the capacities, experience, and confidence of the policy experts left to them by the Fourth Republic. They were not afraid to use the powers of surveillance, incarceration, and tough, often brutal, policing that governments had intensified during the Algerian war. All the same, they also had to learn to accept a good deal of policy incoherence, even as they sought to make the state appear to be more fully in command. Above all, de Gaulle and Debré had to learn how to govern within the policy domains that the long reconstruction had transformed—each with their distinct logics, interest-group dynamics, and repertoires of contestation that made the Fifth Republic, like the Fourth, a regime of multiple configurations of the state, not just *l'État*. Democratic renewal, after all, had taken many forms during the long reconstruction—from tax rebellion, street demonstrations, and short, highly disruptive electrical and transport strikes to the everyday functioning of a vast network of locally elected family and social security caisses. Fifth Republic governments had to adapt accordingly. In doing so, however, they still remained committed to relying heavily on top civil servants and policy experts to set the course of the state's modernizing projects in nearly all policy domains, and all the more so after the autumn of 1962 when, with a peace settlement and a strong presidency at last based on direct election, de Gaulle finally got the kind of republic he had wanted in 1945. This combination of concentrated executive authority, administrative governance, expert-led policymaking *and* democratic renewal would make the young Fifth Republic at once both stable and volatile—a polity with strong state leadership as well as a confrontational style of politics that could spill into the streets.

In this respect the massive protests and strikes of May 1968 were not so much the last gasp of an insurrectionary tradition harking back to the French Revolution, 1848, and the Paris Commune, as was said at the time. Rather, 1968 was a moment when protesters appropriated that tradition to confront the practical realities of top-down government in the modern-day Gaullist state. They drew, too, on the momentum of protest politics from the era of the long reconstruction and the Algerian war. And they created a specter of regime crisis that has haunted Fifth Republic political life ever since. When, in more recent years, Catholic organizations, unions, or students have mobilized demonstrators by the hundreds of thousands to protest policy initiatives by the state—as happened over private school funding in 1984, pension reform in 1995, and employment rules for young people in 2006— governments have backed down for fear of losing control. In France, more so than elsewhere in Europe, students, workers, public employees, immigrants, and other constituencies have kept street politics central to their repertoire of democratic politics. To be sure, de Gaulle and his successor in the presidency, Georges Pompidou, repeatedly pointed to the state as the source of France's progress, order, and unity. And yes, the rise of a talented political and administrative elite after 1945 lent a dynamism to France's undeniably successful postwar recovery. But the challenge of counterbalancing administrative rule with democratic participation persisted, even deepened. By consigning an important measure of democracy to the streets, the state in the Fifth Republic served as much to sow as to quell disorder—making that, too, a legacy of France's long reconstruction.

Notes

Abbreviations

AEF	Archives économiques et financières (Ministry of Finance archives)
AHR	*American Historical Review*
AN	Archives nationales (French National Archives)
AP	Archives privées (of the French National Archives)
APP	Archives de la préfecture de police (Paris)
AS	Archives des associations (of the French National Archives)
BB	Judicial archives at the French National Archives
CAC	Centre des archives contemporaines (of the French National Archives)
CNRS	Centre national des recherches scientifiques
DE	Archives Michel Debré
DV	Paul Delouvrier Papers
FHS	*French Historical Studies*
FNSP	Fondation nationale des sciences politiques
FPCS	*French Politics, Culture & Society*
IHTP	Institut d'histoire du temps présent
JMH	*Journal of Modern History*
JO	*Journal Officiel de la République Française*
MS	*Le Mouvement social*
PA	Alexandre Parodi Papers
PUF	Presses universitaires de France
PUR	Presses universitaires de Rennes
VS	*Vingtième Siècle: Revue d'Histoire*

Introduction

1. Unless otherwise noted, all translations in this book are my own. On the physical destruction of France during the Second World War, see Jean-Pierre Rioux, *The Fourth Republic* (Cambridge: Cambridge University Press, 1987), 18–21; Richard F. Kuisel, *Capitalism and the State in Modern France: Renovation and Economic Management in the Twentieth Century* (Cambridge: Cambridge University Press, 1981), 187; Maurice Larkin, *France since the Popular Front: Government and People, 1936–1986* (Oxford: Oxford University Press, 1988), 117–119; Dominique Barjot, "La reconstruction des infrastructures (1944–1953)," and Danièle Voldman, "La reconstruction des habitations," both in *La France de 1945: Résistances, retours, renaissances,* ed. Christiane Franck (Caen: Presses universitaires de Caen, 1996), 325–336, and 353–360; and Dominique Veillon, *Vivre et survivre en France, 1939–1947* (Paris: Payot & Rivages, 1995), esp. 289.

2. Quoted in Simone Gros, *Pierre Mendès France au quotidien* (Paris: L'Harmattan, 2004), 122–123.

3. Quoted in "Dans le mouvement ouvrier et familial," in *Femmes, famille et action ouvrière: Pratiques et résponsabilités féminines dans les mouvements familiaux populaire (1935–1958),* ed. Geneviève Dermenjian (Villeneuve d'Ascq: Groupement pour la recherche sur les mouvements familiaux, 1991), 77.

4. René Remond, "Les Français veulaient-ils modernizer la France?," *L'Histoire* 44 (April 1982): 95. See also Jon Cowans, "Vision of the Postwar: The Politics of Memory and Expectation in 1940s France," *Memory and History* 10 (1998): 68–101.

5. Jean Monnet, *Mémoires* (Paris: Fayard, 1976), 306.

6. *Combat* 34 (September 1942), in *Les idées politiques et sociales de la résistance (Documents clandestine—1940–1944),* ed. Henri Michel and Boris Mirkine-Guetzévitch (Paris: PUF, 1954), 145.

7. On dissent from this statism in the postwar years, see Gérard Bossuat, "The Modernization of France: A New Economic and Social Order after the Second World War?," in *The Postwar Challenge: Cultural, Social, and Political Change in Western Europe, 1945–58,* ed. Dominik Geppert (Oxford: Oxford University Press, 2003), 160–162.

8. Speech of 15 November 1941, quoted in Charles de Gaulle, *La France sera la France: Ce que veut Charles de Gaulle* (Paris: Le rassemblement du peuple français, 1946), 12–13.

9. Moch quoted in Henri Michel, *Les courants de pensée de la Résistance* (Paris: PUF, 1962), 513; *Combat* in Jacqueline Lévi-Valensi, ed., *Camus at Combat: Writing, 1944–1947,* trans. Arthur Goldhammer, with a forward by David Carroll (Princeton: Princeton University Press, 2006), 13.

10. As quoted in Michel, *Les courants de pensée,* 692–694.

11. "Programme du Conseil National de la Résistance," 15 March 1944, in Michel and Mirkine-Guetzévitch, *Les idées politiques et sociales,* 215–218.

12. On modernization theory in the early postwar era, see especially Frederick Cooper and Randall Packard, introduction to *International Develop-*

ment and the Social Sciences: Essays on the History and Politics of Knowledge, ed. Cooper and Packard (Berkeley: University of California Press, 1997), 1–41.

13. Marc Bloch, *Strange Defeat: A Statement of Evidence Written in 1940* (New York: Norton, 1968), 175. On Bloch's book as a Resistance text, see Donald Reid, "Narratives of Resistance in Marc Bloch's *L'Étrange Défaite,*" *Modern and Contemporary France* 11, no. 4 (2003): 443–452.

14. As quoted in Andrew Williams, "France and the New World Order, 1940–1947," *Modern and Contemporary France* 8, no. 2 (May 2000): 196.

15. On repertoires of contention, see Doug McAdam, Sidney Tarrow, and Charles Tilly, *Dynamics of Contention* (Cambridge: Cambridge University Press, 2001), 14–18; Tilly, *Contentious Performances* (Cambridge: Cambridge University Press, 2008), 1–30.

16. On the concept of policy domains, see Paul Burstein, "Policy Domains: Organization, Culture, and Policy Outcomes," *Annual Review of Sociology* 17, no. 1 (1991): 327–350. For the related concept of policy networks, see Patrick Kenis and Volker Schneider, "Policy Networks and Policy Analysis: Scrutinizing a New Analytical Toolbox," in *Policy Networks: Empirical Evidence and Theoretical Considerations,* ed. Renate Mayntz (Boulder, CO: Westview Press, 1991). On the analytical utility of comparing policy domains, see Frank R. Baumgartner, "The Many Styles of Policymaking in France," in *Chirac's Challenge: Liberalization, Europeanization, and Malaise in France,* ed. John T. S. Keeler and Martin A. Schain (New York: St. Martin's Press, 1996), 85–101; and Martin J. Smith, *Pressure Power and Policy: State Autonomy and Policy Networks in Britain and the United States* (London: Harvester Wheatsheaf, 1993).

17. Other domains could serve these analytical purposes, too—such as agricultural policy, though there much of the story of "modernization" happened in the 1960s. Housing and urban planning could be another example, though that vast territory readily breaks down into several policy domains that already have inspired major historical studies. On agriculture, see John T. S. Keeler, *The Politics of Neocorporatism in France: Farmer, the State, and Agricultural Policy-Making in the Fifth Republic* (New York: Oxford University Press, 1987); and Venus Bivar, "The Ground beneath Their Feet: Agricultural Modernization and the Remapping of Rural France, 1945–1976" (PhD diss., University of Chicago, 2010). On housing and urban planning, see Nicole C. Rudolph, *At Home in Postwar France: Modern Mass Housing and the Right to Comfort* (New York: Berghahn Books, 2015); Kenny Cupers, *The Social Project: Housing Postwar France* (Minneapolis: University of Minnesota Press, 2014); Rosemary Wakeman, *The Heroic City: Paris, 1945–1958* (Chicago: University of Chicago Press, 2009); Danièle Voldman, *La reconstruction des villes françaises de 1940 à 1954: Histoire d'une politique* (Paris: L'Harmattan, 1997); W. Brian Newsome, *French Urban Planning, 1940–1968: The Construction and Deconstruction of an Authoritarian System* (New York: Peter Lang, 2009); and Sabine Effosse, *L'invention du logement aide en France: L'immobilier au temps des Trente glorieuses* (Paris: Comité pour l'histoire économique

et financière de la France, 2003). Change came to the education domain more in the Fifth Republic than in the Fourth. See Antoine Prost, *Du changement dans l'école: Les réformes de l'éducation de 1936 à nos jours* (Paris: Éditions du Seuil, 2013).

18. As quoted in Ezra N. Suleiman, *Politics, Power, and Bureaucracy in France: The Administrative Elite* (Princeton: Princeton University Press, 1974), 25.

19. As quoted in Marc-Olivier Baruch, "Les élites d'État dans la modernization," in *De Gaulle et les élites*, ed. Serge Berstein, Pierre Birnbaum, and Jean-Pierre Rioux (Paris: La Découverte, 2008), 95.

20. On the tension within French republicanism between rationalism and popular sovereignty, see Sudhir Hazareesingh, *Political Traditions in Modern France* (Oxford: Oxford University Press, 1994), 66.

21. For a fuller treatment of how this tension emerged from the revolutionary period and continued to change over the course of the nineteenth and twentieth centuries, see Herrick Chapman, "The State," in *The French Republic: History, Values, Debates*, ed. Edward Berenson, Vincent Duclert, and Christophe Prochasson (Ithaca, NY: Cornell University Press, 2011), 163–172.

22. Antoine Picon, "French Engineers and Social Thought, 18–20th Centuries: An Archeology of Technocratic Ideals," *History and Technology* 23, no. 3 (September 2007): 197–208.

23. Pierre Rosanvallon, *L'État en France de 1789 à nos jours* (Paris: Éditions du Seuil, 1990), 63.

24. Philip Nord, *France's New Deal: From the Thirties to the Postwar Era* (Princeton: Princeton University Press, 2010).

25. On the early references to technocracy in the 1930s and the more commonplace uses of the term in France after World War II, see Delphine Dulong, "La technocratie (au) miroir des sciences sociales: La réflexion technocratique en France (1945–1960)," in *La question technocratique: De l'invention d'une figure aux transformation de l'action publique*, ed. Vincent Dubois and Delphine Dulong (Strasbourg: Presses universitaires de Strasbourg, 1999), 77–91. See also the discussions of technocratic authority in Gabrielle Hecht, *The Radiance of France: Nuclear Power and National Identity after World War II* (Cambridge, MA: MIT Press, 2009), 28–38; Gérard Brun, *Technocrates et technocratie en France, 1918–1945* (Paris: Éditions Albatros, 1985); Jean Meynaud, *Technocratie: Mythe et réalité* (Paris: Payot, 1964); Philippe Bauchard, *Les technocrates et le pouvoir* (Paris: Arthaud, 1966); F. F. Ridley, "French Technocracy and Comparative Government," *Political Studies* 14, no. 1 (1966): 34–52; Ezra N. Suleiman, "The Myth of Technical Expertise: Selection, Organization, and Leadership," *Comparative Politics* 10, no. 1 (October 1977): 137–158; Jean-Claude Thoenig, *L'ère des technocrates: Le cas des ponts et chaussées* (Paris: L'Harmattan, 1987); and James C. Scott's treatment of "authoritarian high modernism" in *Seeing Like a State: How Certain Schemes to Improve the Human Condition Have Failed* (New Haven, CT: Yale University Press, 1998), 87–102.

26. Jackie Clarke, *France in the Age of Organization: Factory, Home and Nation from the 1920s to Vichy* (New York: Berghahn Books, 2011).

27. Richard F. Kuisel, "Technocrats and Public Economic Policy: From the Third to the Fourth Republic," *Journal of European Economic History* 4 (1973): 53–99; and Nord, *France's New Deal*. See also Stanley Hoffmann, "The Effects of World War II on French Society and Politics," *FHS* 2, no. 1 (Spring 1961): 28–63; Robert O. Paxton, *Vichy France: Old Guard and New Order, 1940–1944* (New York: Norton, 1972); Kuisel, *Capitalism and the State*; Michel Margairaz, *L'État, les finances et l'économie: Histoire d'une conversion, 1932–1952*, 2 vols. (Paris: Comité pour l'histoire économique et financière de la France, 1991); Andrew Shennan, *Rethinking France: Plans for Renewal, 1940–1946* (Oxford: Clarendon Press, 1989); and Herrick Chapman, *State Capitalism and Working-Class Radicalism in the French Aircraft Industry, 1928–1950* (Berkeley: University of California Press, 1991).

28. Isser Woloch, "Left, Right and Centre: The MRP and the Post-War Moment," *French History* 21, no. 1 (March 2007): 85–106.

29. On Socialist membership figures and Blum's postwar hopes, see Philip M. Williams, *Crisis and Compromise: Politics in the Fourth Republic* (Garden City, NY: Anchor Books, 1966), 100, 103.

30. On the challenges of integrating expertise and public voice in a democracy, see Michael Schudson, "The Trouble with Experts—and Why Democracies Need Them," *Theory and Society* 35, nos. 5–6 (December 2006): 491–506.

31. See, for example, Hubert Bonin, Sylvie Guillaume, and Bernard Lachaise, eds., *Bordeaux et la Gironde pendant la Reconstruction, 1945–1954* (Talence: Éditions de la Maison des Sciences de l'Homme d'Aquitaine, 1997); William I. Hitchcock, *France Restored: Cold War Diplomacy and the Quest for Leadership in Europe, 1944–1954* (Chapel Hill: University of North Carolina Press, 1998); and Alan S. Milward, *The Reconstruction of Western Europe, 1945–51* (Berkeley: University of California Press, 1984).

32. For Pierre Mendès France's two investiture speeches, 3 June 1953 and 17 June 1954, see his *Oeuvres complètes* (Paris: Gallimard, 1985, 1986), 2:431–460, 3:50–57.

33. On the linkages between reconstruction and empire, see Frederick Cooper, "Reconstructing Empire in British and French Africa," and Nicholas J. White, "Reconstructing Europe through Rejuvenating Empire: The British, French, and Dutch Experiences Compared," both in *Postwar Reconstruction in Europe*, supplement 6, *Past and Present* (2011): 196–210, 211–256.

34. David Feldman, preface to *Postwar Reconstruction in Europe*, supplement 6, *Past and Present* (2011): 6, 9–11; and, in the same issue, Mark Mazower, "Reconstruction: The Historiographical Issues," 28. See also, in the same issue, the essays by David Edgerton, "War, Reconstruction, and the Nationalization of Britain, 1939–1951," and Adam Tooze, "Reassessing the Moral Economy of Post-War Reconstruction: The Terms of the West German Settlement in 1953."

35. Jean Fourastié, *Les Trente glorieuses, ou, la Révolution invisible de 1946 à 1975* (Paris: Fayard, 1979). For a critical perspective, see Céline Pessis, Sezin Topçu, and Christophe Bonneuil, eds., *Une autre histoire des "Trente glorieuses": Modernisation, contestations et pollutions dans la France d'après-guerre* (Paris: La Découverte, 2013).

1 · Liberation Authorities

1. On material depravation during the Occupation, see Kenneth Mouré, "Food Rationing and the Black Market in France, 1940–1944," *French History* 24, no. 2 (2010): 262–282.

2. Charles de Gaulle, *The Complete War Memoirs*, trans. Jonathan Griffin and Richard Howard (New York: Simon and Shuster, 1959), 7, 646, 689.

3. http://www.charles-de-gaulle.org/pages/espace-pedagogique/le-point-sur /les-textes-a-connaitre/discours-de-lrsquohotel-de-ville-25-aout-1944.php.

4. Gordon Wright, *The Reshaping of French Democracy* (New York: Reynal and Hitchcock, 1948), 52.

5. On French Communist attitudes toward the state, see Herrick Chapman, *State Capitalism and Working-Class Radicalism in the French Aircraft Industry, 1928–1950* (Berkeley: University of California Press, 1991), 10, 59–63, 302–306; Tony Judt, "Une historiographie pas comme les autres: The French Communists and Their History," *European Studies Review* 12, no. 4 (October 1982): 464–465; Philippe Buton, *Les lendemains qui déchantent: Le Parti communiste français à la Libération* (Paris: Presses de la FNSP, 1993), 237–242; and Jean-Marc Berlière, "L'épuration dans la police," in *Le rétablissement de la légalité républicaine (1944)*, Actes du colloque organisé par la Fondation Charles de Gaulle, la Fondation nationale des sciences politiques, l'Association française des constitutionalistes (et la participation de l'Université de Caen), 6–8 October 1994 (Paris: Éditions Complexe, 1996), 499.

6. James D. Wilkinson, *The Intellectual Resistance in Europe* (Cambridge, MA: Harvard University Press, 1981), 45–46, 52–55; André Bendjebbar, *Libérations rêvées, libérations vécues 1940–1945* (Paris: Hachette, 1994), 44–45. On post-Liberation distrust of state policing and surveillance, see Stefanos Geroulanos, "An Army of Shadows: Black Markets, Adaptation, and Social Transparency in Postwar France," *JMH* 88, no. 1 (March 2016): 60–95. On the MRP and the state, see Andrew Shennan, "The Origins of Postwar France," *Historical Journal* 27, no. 4 (December 1984): 1043.

7. Jean-Paul Sartre, "The Republic of Silence," in *The Republic of Silence*, ed. A. J. Liebling (New York: Harcourt, Brace, 1947), 498–500.

8. Olivier Wieviorka, *The French Resistance*, trans. Jane Marie Todd (Cambridge, MA: Harvard University Press, 2016), 317.

9. De Gaulle, *The Complete War Memoirs*, 564.

10. Quoted in Robert Aron, *France Reborn: The History of the Liberation, June 1944–May 1945*, trans. Humphrey Hare (New York: Charles Scribner's Sons, 1964), 50. On de Gaulle's visit to Bayeux, see also René Hostache, "Bayeux, 14 juin 1944: Étape décisive sur la voie d'Alger à Paris," in *Le ré-*

tablissement, 231–242; Charles-Louis Foulon, *Le pouvoir en province à la Libération* (Paris: Armand Colin, 1975), 101–106. Raymond Triboulet recounts his experiences in *Le rétablissement*, 249–250.

11. Herbert R. Lottman, *The Purge* (New York: Morrow, 1986), 66.

12. Kim Munholland, "The United States and the Free French," in *De Gaulle and the United States: A Centennial Reappraisal*, ed. Robert O. Paxton and Nicholas Wahl (Oxford: Berg, 1994), 91.

13. On republican commissars, see Foulon, *Le pouvoir en province*, and Steven Philip Kramer, "The Provisional Republic, the Collapse of the French Resistance Front and the Origins of Post-War Politics: 1944–1946" (PhD diss., Princeton University, 1971).

14. Charles de Gaulle to "Quartus" [Alexandre Parodi], 31 July 1944, Fondation nationale des sciences politiques (FNSP), Archives Alexandre Parodi, PA 11.

15. Wieviorka, *The French Resistance*, 335–336.

16. See Diane de Bellescize, "L'intérim gouvernemental des secrétaires généraux," in *Le rétablissement*, 129–163.

17. Charles de Gaulle, "Discours prononcé devant l'Assemblée consultative provisoire, 25 juillet 1944," in *Oeuvres complètes*, vol. 3: *Discours et messages* (Paris: Plon, 1970), 84.

18. Francois Rouquet, *L'épuration dans l'administration française: Agents de l'État et collaboration ordinaire* (Paris: Éditions du CNRS, 1993), 116–117; Henri Rousso, "L'épuration en France: Une histoire inachevée," *VS* 33 (January–March 1992): 78–105.

19. François Bloch-Lainé and Jean Bouvier, *La France restaurée, 1944—1954: Dialogue sur les choix d'une modernisation* (Paris: Fayard, 1986), 74. On purges in the administration, see also Peter Novick, *The Resistance versus Vichy: The Purge of Collaborators in Liberated France* (London: Chatto and Windus, 1968), 89–90; Robert O. Paxton, *Vichy France: Old Guard and New Order, 1940–1944* (New York: Norton, 1972), 333–343; Marc Olivier Baruch, *Servir l'État français: L'administration de France de 1940 à 1944* (Paris: Fayard, 1997), 570–575.

20. For accounts of August 25, see Serge Berstein, "L'arrivée de de Gaulle à Paris," in *Le rétablissement*, 365–368; de Gaulle, *The Complete War Memoirs*, 643–651; Jean Lacouture, *De Gaulle*, vol. 1: *The Rebel, 1890–1944*, trans. Patrick O'Brian (New York: W. W. Norton & Company, 1993), 571–576; Aron, *France Reborn*, 287–298.

21. On hopes for a new army and a *levée en masse*, see H. R. Kedward, *In Search of the Maquis: Rural Resistance in Southern France, 1942–44* (Oxford: Clarendon Press, 1993), 225–226; Grégoire Madjarian, *Conflits, pouvoirs et société à la Libération* (Paris: Union Générale d'Éditions, 1980), 113–114.

22. On army integration, see Jean Delmas, "La réunification de l'armée," in *Le rétablissement*, 543–552; Col. Pierre Le Goyet, "Quelques aspects du problème militaire français pendant la libération du territoire," and Lt.-Col. Roger Michalon, "L'amalgame F.F.I.—1re armée et 2e D.B.," both in *La libération de la France*, Actes du colloque international tenu à Paris du

28 au 31 octobre 1974 (Paris: Éditions du CNRS, 1976), 559–584 and 593–665; Madjarian, *Conflits*, 103–114; Alexander Werth, *France, 1940–1955* (London: Hale, 1957), 233–235.

23. As quoted in Philippe Buton, "Le PCF à la fin de l'année 1944," in *Le rétablissement*, 745. On dissolving the patriotic militias, see also Buton, *La joie douloureuse: La libération de la France* (Paris: Éditions Complexe, 2004), 153–155; Jean-Pierre Rioux, *The Fourth Republic, 1944–1958* (New York: Cambridge University Press, 1987), 47–48; Madjarian, *Conflits*, 145–164; Kramer, "The Provisional Republic," 103–104; Foulon, *Le pouvoir en province*, 228–229.

24. De Gaulle, *The Complete War Memoirs*, 654.

25. Robert Gildea, *Fighters in the Shadows: A New History of the French Resistance* (Cambridge, MA: Harvard University Press, 2015), 408–409.

26. On de Gaulle's reinvention of the royal entry, see Laurent Douzou and Dominique Veillon, "Les déplacements du Général de Gaulle à travers la France," in *Le rétablissement*, 652–659. On presidential tours in the Third Republic, see Nicolas Mariot, *Bains de foule: Les voyages présidentiels en province, 1888–2002* (Paris: Éditions Belin, 2006).

27. On communication difficulties during the Liberation period, see Henri Frenay, *La nuit finira* (Paris: La Livre de Poche, 1974), 210; Buton, *La joie douloureuse*, 138.

28. Pierre Laborie, "La libération de Toulouse vue par le pouvoir central," in *La Libération dans le midi de la France*, ed. Rolande Trempé, Actes du colloque organisé par les Universités Toulouse-Le Mirail et Paul Valéry de Montpellier les 7 et 8 juin 1985 (Toulouse: Éché, 1986), 166–167; Aron, *France Reborn*, 397.

29. As quoted from the newspaper *La République du Sud-Ouest*, 17 September 1944, in Douzou and Veillon, "Les déplacements," 650.

30. For an analysis of de Gaulle's oratorical strategies, the use of his voice, and how reporters covered his tours, see Evan Laurence Spritzer, "Politicizing French Radio: Crises, Communities, and Competing Voice, 1934–1954" (PhD diss., New York University, 2015), chap. 5.

31. Charles-Louis Foulon, "La Résistance et le pouvoir et l'État dans la France libérée," in *Le rétablissement*, 192.

32. Charles-Louis Foulon, "Prise et exercice du pouvoir en province à la Libération," in *La libération de la France*, 509. On regional variations in the strength of CDLs, see also Jacqueline Sainclivier, "Le pouvoir résistant (été 1944)," in *Les pouvoirs en France à la Libération*, ed. Philippe Buton and Jean-Marie Guillon (Paris: Éditions Belin, 1994), 31–34.

33. Maurice Agulhon and Fernand Barrat, *C. R. S. à Marseille: "La police au service du peuple," 1944–1947* (Paris: Armand Colin, 1971), 45.

34. Fabrice Virgili, *Shorn Women: Gender and Punishment in Liberation France*, trans. John Flower (Oxford: Berg, 2002), 50–53. See also Meghan Koreman, *The Expectation of Justice: France, 1944–1946* (Durham, NC: Duke University Press, 1999), 108–115; Claire Duchen, "Opening Pandora's Box: The Case of *Femmes tondues*," in *Problems in French History*, ed. Martyn Cornick and Ceri Crossley (New York: Palgrave, 2000), 213–232; Corran

Laurens, "'La Femme au Turban': Les femmes tondues," in *The Liberation of France: Image and Event*, ed. H. R. Kedward and Nancy Wood (Oxford: Berg, 1995), 155–179.

35. Koreman, *The Expectation of Justice*, 96. On *indignité nationale*, see Anne Simonin, *Le déshonneur dans la République: Une histoire du l'indignité, 1791–1958* (Paris: Grasset, 2008).

36. Foulon, *Le pouvoir en province*, 153.

37. Raymond Aubrac, *Où la mémoire s'attarde* (Paris: Éditions Odile Jacob, 1996), 134. On Ingrand's experience, see the report of the republican commissar in Clermont-Ferrand, 23 January 1945, archives of the Ministère de l'Intérieur, Administration Générale, AN F1a 4021; Foulon, *Le pouvoir en province*, 153. On the purge in Marseille, see the reports of the republican commissar, 15 November 2 and 15 December 1944, AN F1a 4023; Lottman, *The Purge*, 125–128. On the pressures for purges locally, see also Megan Koreman, "The Collaborator's Penance: The Local Purge, 1944–45," *Journal of Contemporary History* 6, no. 2 (July 1997): 177–192.

38. Report of the republican commissar, Lyon, 13 September 1944, AN F1a 4022.

39. Ibid., Dijon, 16 January 1945, AN F1a 4021.

40. Ibid., Marseille, 15 October, 15 December 1944, AN F1a 4023; Agulhon and Barrat, *C. R. S. à Marseille*, 46–97; Georges Carrot, *Le maintien de l'ordre en France au XXe siècle* (Paris: H. Veyrier, 1990), 216–218; Aubrac, *Où la mémoire s'attarde*, 131–132.

41. Carrot, *Le maintien de l'ordre*, 219–221, 256–258. See also Claude Angeli and Paul Gillet, *La police dans la politique—1944/1954* (Paris: Grasset, 1967); Dimitri-Georges Lavroff, "Les compagnies républicaines de sécurité," *Recueil Sirey*, November 1959, in the archives of the Ministère de l'Intérieur, MI 25590; Philip John Stead, *The Police of France* (New York: Macmillan, 1983), 90–91.

42. On labor's movement for management committees and requisitions, see Antoine Prost, "Un mouvement venu d'en bas," and Post, "Le retour aux temps ordinaires," both in *Les nationalisations de la libération: De l'utopie au compromis*, ed. Claire Andrieu, Lucette Le Van, and Antoine Prost (Paris: Presses de la FNSP, 1987), 65–88; Madjarian, *Conflits*, 165–182; Buton, *Les lendemains qui déchantent*, 148–154; Robert Mencherini, *La Libération et les entreprises sous la gestion ouvrière* (Paris: L'Harmattan, 1994).

43. Chapman, *State Capitalism*, 257–261; see also Rolande Trempé, "Aux origines des comités mixtes à la production: Les comités de libération d'entreprise dans la région toulousaine," *Revue d'Histoire de la Deuxième Guerre Mondiale* 131 (1983): 41–63.

44. Fabrice Grenard, *La France du marché noir (1940–1949)* (Paris: Payot, 2008), 261–263.

45. Note on "Marché libre et suppression de certaines taxations," 5 June 1945, in the dossier on CDLs, AN F1a 4020. See also, Kramer, "The Provisional Republic," 133–151; and the report of the republican commissar, Chalon-sur-Marne, 15 June 1945, AN F1a 4020.

46. Report of the republican commissar, Poitiers, 17 November 1944, AN F1a 4026. On popular attitudes toward the black market during the Occupation, see Lynn Taylor, "The Black Market in Occupied Northern France, 1940–44," *Contemporary European History* 6, no. 2 (July 1997): 153–176.

47. Werth, *France, 1940–1955*, 237; Danielle Tartakowsky, "Manifester pour le pain, novembre 1940–octobre 1947," *Les Cahiers de l'IHTP* 32–33 (May 1996): 475.

48. Foulon, *Le pouvoir en province*, 241; Tartakowsky, "Manifester pour le pain," 475.

49. George H. Gallup, *The Gallup International Public Opinion Polls: France, 1939, 1944–1975*, vol. 1: *1939, 1944–1967* (New York: Random House, 1976), 21.

50. For a general picture of the 221 demonstrations, as well as a description of the role of the UFF and the Mouvement populaire des familles, see Tartakowsky, "Manifester pour le pain, 472–473.

51. Report of the republican commissar in Nancy, 15–31 May 1945, AN F1a 4024.

52. Report from the Commissaire de Police, Chef du Service des Renseignements Généraux de la Haute-Loire au Préfet de la Haute-Loire au Puy, 31 January 1945, AN F1a 4021; report of the republican commissar in Nancy, 15–31 May 1945, AN F1a 4024.

53. Madjarian, *Conflits*, 281; Tartakowsky, "Manifester pour le pain," 471.

54. Rebecca Pulju, *Women and Mass Consumer Society in Postwar France* (New York: Cambridge University Press, 2011), 40–41.

55. On the rejection of Mendès France's plan, see Michel-Pierre Chélini, *L'inflation, état et opinion en France de 1944 à 1952* (Paris: Comité pour l'histoire économique et financière de la France, 1998), 266–281; Kuisel, *Capitalism and the State*, 191–199; Bloch-Lainé and Bouvier, *La France restaurée*, 66–71, 76–84. On support from republican commissars, see Foulon, *Le pouvoir en province*, 185.

56. Michel Margairaz, "L'État et les restrictions en France dans les années 1940," *Les Cahiers de l'IHTP* 32–33 (May 1996): 38–40.

57. Bloch-Lainé and Bouvier, *La France restaurée*, 84. Jean Monnet doubted the feasibility of austerity in such a depleted economy. See Michel Margairaz, "Finances, financement et financiers de la reconstruction en 1945: l'ancien et le neuf," in *La France de 1945: Résistances, retours, renaissances*, ed. Christiane Franck, Actes du colloque de Caen (17–19 mai 1995) (Caen: Presses universitaires de Caen, 1996), 319.

58. Report of the republican commissar in Nancy, 15 October–15 December 1944, AN F1a 4024.

59. Kenneth Mouré and Fabrice Grenard similarly emphasize the post-Liberation state's weakness in confiscating illicit profits from collaboration and the black market, in "Traitors, *Trafiquants*, and the Confiscation of 'Illicit Profits' in France, 1944–1950," *Historical Journal* 51, no. 4 (December 2008): 988–990.

60. Douglas Johnson, "General de Gaulle and the Restoration of the Republic," in *The Jacobin Legacy in Modern France: Essays in Honour of Vincent*

Wright, ed. Sudhir Hazareesingh (Oxford: Oxford University Press, 2002), 156–157.

61. Andrew Shennan, *Rethinking France: Plans for Renewal, 1940–1946* (Oxford: Clarendon Press, 1989), 68.

62. Kramer, "The Provisional Republic," 270–272.

63. William I. Hitchcock, *France Restored: Cold War Diplomacy and the Quest for Leadership in Europe, 1944–1954* (Chapel Hill: University of North Carolina Press, 1998), 33–34.

64. See, for example, Nathalie Carré de Malberg's analysis of the financial conservatism of state administrators, in "Les inspecteurs des finances et la défense du franc (1934–1935)," in *Du franc Poincaré à l'écu*, Colloque tenu à Bercy les 3 et 4 décembre 1992 (Paris: Comité pour l'histoire économique et financière de la France, 1993), 125–169.

2 · Available Hands

1. Jacques Desmarest, *La politique de la main-d'oeuvre en France* (Paris: PUF, 1946), 193–194.

2. On labor during the First World War, see ibid., 31–49; John N. Horne, *Labour at War: France and Britain, 1914–1918* (Oxford: Oxford University Press, 1991); Antoine Prost, "Workers," in *The Cambridge History of the First World War*, vol. 2: *The State*, ed. Jay Winter (Cambridge: Cambridge University Press, 2014). On women workers, Laura Lee Downs, *Manufacturing Inequality: Gender Division in the French and British Metalworking Industries, 1914–1939* (Ithaca, NY: Cornell University Press, 1995).

3. Gary S. Cross, *Immigrant Workers in Industrial France: The Making of a New Working Class* (Philadelphia: Temple University Press, 1983), 35–36. On foreign and colonial workers, see also Tyler Stovall, "Colonial Labor in France during World War I," *Race and Class* (October 1993); Stovall, "The Color Line behind the Lines: Racial Violence in France during the Great War," *AHR* 103, no. 3 (June 1998): 737–769; Laurent Dornel, "Les usages du racisme: Le cas de la main-d'oeuvre coloniale en France pendant la première guerre mondiale," *Genèse* 20 (September 1995): 48–72; John Horne, "Immigrant Workers in France during World War I," *FHS* 14, no. 1 (Spring 1985): 57–88.

4. On comparing American and French immigration, see Catherine Collomp, "Immigrants, Labor Markets, and the State, a Comparative Approach: France and the United States, 1880–1930," *Journal of American History* 86, no. 1 (June 1999): 41–66; Nancy L. Green, *Ready to Wear, Ready to Work: A Century of Industry and Immigrants in Paris and New York* (Durham, NC: Duke University Press, 1997).

5. On policing immigrants, see Mary Dewhurst Lewis, *The Boundaries of the Republic: Migrant Rights and the Limits of Universalism in France, 1918–1940* (Stanford: Stanford University Press, 2007); Clifford Rosenberg, *Policing Paris: The Origins of Modern Immigration Control between the Wars* (Ithaca, NY: Cornell University Press, 2006).

6. On labor regulation during the 1930s, see Desmarest, *La politique*, chaps. 4–6; Joel Colton, *Compulsory Labor Arbitration in France, 1936–1939*

(New York: King's Crown Press, 1951); Val R. Lorwin, *The French Labor Movement* (Cambridge, MA: Harvard University Press, 1954), 76–84; Julie Fette, *Exclusions: Practicing Prejudice in French Law and Medicine, 1920–1945* (Ithaca, NY: Cornell University Press, 2012).

7. Desmarest, *La politique*, 97.

8. Cross, *Immigrant Workers*, 196, 200.

9. See especially Vicky Caron, *Uneasy Asylum: France and the Jewish Refugee Crisis, 1933–1942* (Stanford: Stanford University Press, 1999); Michael R. Marrus and Robert O. Paxton, *Vichy France and the Jews* (New York: Basic Books, 1981), 58–71; Denis Roland, "Extradition ou réémigration? Les vases communicants de la gestion xénophobe des réfugiés espagnols en France," in *Exils et migration: Italiens et espagnols en France, 1938–1946*, ed. Pierre Milza and Denis Peschanski (Paris: L'Harmattan, 1994), 47–69; Louis Stein, *Beyond Death and Exile: The Spanish Republicans in France, 1939–1955* (Cambridge, MA: Harvard University Press, 1979).

10. Lorwin, *The French Labor Movement*, 87.

11. Desmarest, *La politique*, 122. On recruiting women into war production, see ibid., 113–120; and Hanna Diamond, *Women and the Second World War in France, 1939–48: Choices and Constraints* (Harlow, UK: Longman, 1999), 29–31.

12. On women's employment during the Occupation, see Diamond, *Women and the Second World War*, 31–48.

13. Robert O. Paxton, *Vichy France: Old Guard and New Order, 1940–1944* (New York: Columbia University Press, 1972), 170–71. See also Ralph Schor, *Histoire de l'immigration en France de la fin du XIXe siècle à nos jours* (Paris: Armand Colin, 1996), 170–174.

14. Marrus and Paxton, *Vichy France and the Jews*, 5–21.

15. Julian Jackson, *France: The Dark Years, 1940–1944* (Oxford: Oxford University Press, 2001), 331–332.

16. Herrick Chapman, *State Capitalism and Working-Class Radicalism in the French Aircraft Industry* (Berkeley: University of California Press, 1991), 246.

17. Schor, *Histoire de l'immigration*, 166–167.

18. Paxton, *Vichy France*, 292–293, 311. Before launching the STO, Premier Pierre Laval negotiated a "relève" policy to exchange volunteer workers to Germany for repatriated French POWs, at a ratio of three to one. Few volunteered, and even released POWs were still required to work in Germany. Alan S. Milward, *The New Order and the French Economy* (Oxford: Clarendon Press, 1970), 110–124, 165–177; Paxton, *Vichy France*, 292–293, 311, 368–370; Diamond, *Women and the Second World War*, 36–37.

19. Desmarest, *La politique*, 186.

20. Ibid., 205.

21. On the survival of corporatist ideas in the Resistance and early postwar years, see Andrew Shennan, *Rethinking France: Plans for Renewal, 1940–1946* (Oxford: Clarendon Press, 1989), 274–278.

22. *Liberation*, 22 November 1944.

23. A Vichy decree of May 1944 had put many workers on the government dole at three-quarters pay if they were temporarily thrown out of work because of war damage; Parodi took advantage of their dependence to assign many of them to other jobs. *Combat*, 8 February 1945.

24. See the annex to the memorandum, le Ministre du Travail et de la Sécurité Sociale à Messieurs les Directeurs Régionaux du Travail et de la Main-d'oeuvre, 22 March 1945, archives of the Groupement des industries métallurgiques et minières de la région parisienne, AN 39AS 966.

25. See Henri Raynaud, "La mobilisation de la main-d'oeuvre pour activer le redressement économique," *Le Peuple*, 20 October 1944.

26. On giving priority to these workers, see Commission Nationale Provisoire de la Main-d'oeuvre, compte rendu, 18 December 1944, AN 39AS 966.

27. Pieter Lagrou, *The Legacy of Nazi Occupation: Patriotic Memory and National Recovery in Western Europe, 1945–1965* (Cambridge: Cambridge University Press, 2000), 108.

28. Sarah Fishman, "Grand Delusions: The Unintended Consequences of Vichy France's Prisoner of War Propaganda," *Journal of Contemporary History* 26, no. 2 (April 1991): 244–254, esp. n. 57. See also Megan Koreman, *The Expectation of Justice: France, 1944–1946* (Durham, NC: Duke University Press, 1999), 73–91; Lagrou, *Legacy of Nazi Occupation*, 106–128, 163–164, 179–191.

29. Christophe Lewin, *Le retour des prisonniers de guerre français* (Paris: Publications de la Sorbonne, 1986), 77–82. See also Sarah Fishman, *We Will Wait: Wives of French Prisoners of War, 1940–1945* (New Haven, CT: Yale University Press, 1991), chap. 9; and Yves Durand, *La captivité: Histoire des prisonniers de guerre français, 1939–1945* (Paris: Fédération nationale des combattants prisonniers de guerre et combattants d'Algérie, Tunisie, Maroc, 1980).

30. On German POWs in France, see Fabien Theofilakis, *Les prisonniers de guerre allemands: France, 1944–1949* (Paris: Librairie Arthème Fayard, 2014); and Valentin Schneider, *Un million de prisonniers allemands en France, 1944–1948* (Paris: Éditions Vendémiaire, 2011).

31. Desmarest, *La politique*, 47–48.

32. Jean-Pierre Rioux, *The Fourth French Republic, 1944–1958* (Cambridge: Cambridge University Press, 1987), 20. On Tollet's views, see Commission Nationale Provisoire de la Main-d'oeuvre, 28 December 1945, AN 39AS 966.

33. On Tollet and Maillet's views on de-mining operations, see the compte rendu of the meeting of the Commission Nationale Provisoire de la Main-d'oeuvre, 28 December 1945, AN 39AS 966.

34. La Documentation Française, "Les problèmes du travail et de la main-d'oeuvre en France depuis la Libération," *Notes Documentaires et Études*, no. 650 (19 June 1947): 13. Available in the archives of the Ministère du Travail, Direction de la population et des migrations, CAC 770623, art. 68.

35. POWs were paid ten francs a day, half of which went to the prisoners directly, and half to a savings account, the contents of which they could withdraw when they were repatriated to Germany. Ibid.

36. The CGT pressed this issue both locally and on the Commission Nationale Provisoire de la Main-d'oeuvre. See the compte rendu of that body, 2 July 1945, Parodi Papers, PA 16.

37. Commission Nationale Provisoire de la Main-d'oeuvre, compte rendu d'activité pour la période du 7 au 21 mai 1945, Parodi Papers, PA 16.

38. Ministère des Affaires Étrangères, Commissariat général aux affaires allemandes et autrichennes. Memorandum to the Président du Gouvernement Provisoire de la République Française, 26 September 1946, Libération des prisonniers de guerre d'origine sarroise, Georges Bidault Papers, AN 457AP 135.

39. La Documentation Française, "Les problèmes du travail et de la main-d'oeuvre en France depuis la Libération," *Notes Documentaires et Études*, no. 650 (19 June 1947): 12–15. Available in CAC 770623, art. 68.

40. *La Semaine Économiques et Financières*, 1 September 1945.

41. Jackson, *France*, 294–295.

42. Commission Nationale Provisoire de la Main-d'oeuvre, compte rendu, 7 May 1945, Parodi Papers, PA 16.

43. Ibid., 31 August 1945, AN 39AS 966.

44. On the unions and dirigisme, see Robert Goertz-Girez, *La pensée syndicale française: Militants et théoriciens* (Paris: Armand Colin, 1948), 161–163.

45. Desmarest, *La politique*, 5.

46. On ideas for labor representation during the interwar period, see Chapman, *State Capitalism*, 112–115.

47. Alain Bockel, *La participation des syndicats ouvriers aux fonctions économiques et sociales de l'État*, with preface by Pierre Lavigne (Paris: R. Pichon and R. Durand-Auzias, 1965), 59–63.

48. Colin Dyer, *Population and Society in Twentieth-Century France* (New York: Holmes and Meier, 1978), 40, 127.

49. Desmarest, *La politique*, 192, 210, 242–260, 266.

50. See, for example, the minutes to the meetings of the commission de la main-d'oeuvre at the Commissariat général du Plan (1953–1955), AN 80AJ 49.

51. On the productivism of the CGT in 1945–1947, see Chapman, *State Capitalism*, 268–272.

52. Commission Nationale Provisoire de la Main-d'oeuvre, compte rendu, 20 February 1945, Parodi Papers, PA 16.

53. Diamond, *Women and the Second World War*, 168–169.

54. Antoine Prost, "L'évolution de la politique familiale en France de 1938 à 1981," *Le Mouvement Social* 129 (October–December 1984): 7–28.

55. The INED study found that the percentage of women in the population who were working was rising—to 36.7 in 1946, up from 34.2 in 1936. See Jean Daric, *L'activité professionnelle des femmes en France: Étude statistique, évolution, comparaisons internationales* (Paris: PUF, 1947), 84–93. Jean Fourastié later argued that female employment outside agriculture jumped to 220 per thousand in 1946 from a rate of 202 per thousand in 1936. See Jean Fourastié, "La population active française pendant la sec-

onde guerre mondiale," *Revue de l'Histoire de la Deuxième Guerre Mondiale* (January 1965): 8. Both studies are cited in Diamond, *Women and the Second World War*, 170.

56. Ibid., 173–177.

57. Jacques Desmarest, at the Conseil d'État, was a rare voice of optimism in the immediate postwar years about women as an untapped source of labor, though he also endorsed pronatalist goals. See *La politique*, 214–215.

58. For more on pronatalism, see Chapter 4 on family policy.

59. Published under the pseudonym Jacquier-Bruère (Paris: Plon, 1945), 22–24.

60. Charles de Gaulle, *Discours et messages* (Paris: Plon, 1970), 530 (cited in Patrick Weil, "Racisme et discrimination dans la politique française de l'immigration: 1938–1945 / 1974–1995, *VS* 47 [July–September 1995]: 54–55).

61. Desmarest, *La politique*, 266.

62. Pflimlin's view as recorded in the procès-verbal of the meeting of the Sous-Commission du Plan d'Immigration, 12 April 1946, archives of the Haut Comité consultatif de la population et de la famille, CAC 860269, art. 8.

63. Schor, *Histoire de l'immigration*, 194; Georges Tapinos, *L'immigration étrangère en France, 1946–1973*, Institut national d'études démographiques, Travaux et Documents, cahier 71 (Paris: PUF, 1975), 16.

64. Robert Debré and Alfred Sauvy, *Des Français pour la France: Le problème de la population* (Paris: Gallimard, 1946), 226. On Sauvy and the creation of INED, see Paul-André Rosental, *L'intelligence démographique: Sciences et politiques des populations en France (1930–1960)* (Paris: Éditions Odile Jacob, 2003); and Philip Nord, *France's New Deal: From the Thirties to the Postwar Era* (Princeton: Princeton University Press, 2010), 178–189.

65. Xavier Lannes, *L'immigration en France depuis 1945* (Le Haye: Martinus Nijhoff, 1953), 9.

66. On Mauco, see Sandrine Bertaux, "'Processus' et 'population' dans l'analyse démographique de l'immigration en France (1932–1996)," in *L'invention des populations: Biologie, idéologie et politique*, ed. Hervé La Bras (Paris: Éditions Odile Jacob, 2000), 241–254; Patrick Weil, "Racisme et discrimination dans la politique française de l'immigration: 1938–1945 / 1974–1995," *VS* 47 (July–September 1995): 77–102; Greg Burgess, "The Demographers' Moment: Georges Mauco, Immigration and Racial Selection in Liberation France, 1945–46," *French History and Civilization* 4 (2011): 167–177; Karen H. Adler, *Jews and Gender in Liberation France* (Cambridge: Cambridge University Press, 2003), chap. 5; Nord, *France's New Deal*, 176–178; and Georges Mauco, *Les étrangers en France* (Paris: Armand Colin, 1932).

67. Weil, "Racisme," 88.

68. Schor, *Histoire de l'immigration en France*, 195; Weil, "Racisme," 87–93.

69. Debré and Sauvy, *Des Français*, 227–232.

70. Mary Lewis, "Immigration," in *The French Republic: History, Values, Debates*, ed. Edward Berenson, Vincent Duclert, and Christophe Prochasson (Ithaca, NY: Cornell University Press, 2011), 236.

71. Weil, "Racisme," 92–93.

72. On the CADI, see Stéphane Courtois, "Le PCF et la question de l'immigration, 1936–1948," in Milza and Peschanski, *Exils et migration*, 486–489; and Alexis Spire, *Étranger à la carte: L'administration et l'immigration en France (1945–1974)* (Paris: Grasset, 2005), 38–43. Its affiliated associations included such organizations the Comité italien de libération nationale, the Comité polonais de libération nationale, the Union nationale espagnole, the Union des patriotes russes, the Front national arménien, the Comité d'unité et de défense juive, and a dozen others. See the dossier on "main-d'oeuvre immigrée" in the Maurice Thorez and Vermeersch Papers, AN 626AP 165. Alongside CADI, the Mouvement national contre le racisme (MNR) also emerged from the Resistance to battle anti-Semitism and advocate for immigrants and refugees after the war.

73. Spire, *Étrangers à la carte*, 38–45; Gérard Noiriel, *Immigration, antisémitisme et racisme en France (XIXe–XXe siècle): Discours publics, humiliations privées* (Paris: Fayard, 2007), 494–497.

74. Kowalski, as Gérard Noiriel has pointed out, was a pioneer in France in affirming immigrant rights and in "succeeding in inserting the word immigrant into the republican vocabulary." Noiriel, *Immigration, antisémitisme et racisme*, 488.

75. On the need for skilled foreign workers, see the discussion of the Commission Nationale Provisoire de la Main-d'oeuvre, compte rendu, 8 October 1945, AN 39AS 966. On the conflicts among the ministries over immigration policy, see Spire, *Étranger à la carte*, chap. 1; Weil, "Racisme"; Patrick Weil, *La France et ses étrangers: L'aventure d'une politique de l'immigration, 1938–1991* (Paris: Calmann-Lévy, 1991), 53–63; Schor, *Histoire de l'immigration*, 194–198; Noiriel, *Immigration, antisémitisme et racisme*, 486–524; and James F. Hollifield, *Immigrants, Markets, and States: The Political Economy of Postwar Europe* (Cambridge, MA: Harvard University Press, 1992), 51–56.

76. Léon Gani, *Syndicat et travailleurs immigrés* (Paris: Éditions Sociales, 1972), 30–43.

77. Spire, *Etrangers à la carte*, 93–95; Noiriel, *Immigration, antisémitisme et racisme*, 496.

78. Lannes, *L'immigration en France*, 10.

79. On the history of the Société générale d'immigration, see Cross, *Immigrant Workers*, 55–63; and Ralph Schor, *L'opinion française et les étrangers, 1919–1939* (Paris: Publications de la Sorbonne, 1985), 211–220.

80. La Documentation Française, "Les avantages démographiques et économiques de l'immigration," *Notes, Documentaires et Études*, no. 940 (1 July 1948): 10.

81. Weil, "Racisme," 96–97.

82. La Documentation Française, "Les problèmes du travail," 10.

83. Weil, *La France et ses étrangers*, 323n49.

84. See the Aide-Memoire sent to the U.S. Department of State, 7 July 1947, U.S. State Department Central Files, FW 851.504/7-747, in microfilm collection, pt. 2, reel 10.

85. Conseil d'Administration, ONI, procès-verbaux, 25 July 1946, archives of the Conseil national du patronat français, AN 72AS 95.

86. La Documentation Française, "Les avantages," 11; Tapinos, *L'immigration étrangère*, 28–29.

87. Tapinos, *L'immigration étrangère*, 29. The French negotiated also to recruit Germans from the American-occupied zone in Germany. See the exchange of notes in 1946 and 1947 between French and American officials, as well as the Accord technique franco-américain relative au recrutement de main-d'oeuvre volontaire pour la France en zone américaine d'Allemagne, 5 February 1948, U.S. State Department Central Files, 851.504, microfilm collection, pt. 22, reel 10. They also worked out recruitment arrangements in the British-occupied zone. Compte rendu, Commission Interministérielle de l'Immigration, 8 January 1948. Released German POWs seeking French residency were screened by a departmental committee that included government, labor, and employer representatives. Compte rendu, Commission Nationale Provisoire de la Main-d'oeuvre, 16 June 1947, CAC 860269, art. 8.

88. Schneider, *Un million*, 131.

89. "Les Mouvements de population dans le Monde" [Secret], Président du Conseil, 10 May 1947, SDECE, Georges Mauco Papers, AN 577AP 4.

90. Debré and Sauvy, *Des Français*, 228.

91. Rapport Annuel 1950, Service des Mines, Arrondissement minéralogique de Paris, Inspection du Travail, CAC 770623, art. 68.

92. Compte rendu, Commission Interministérielle de l'Immigration, 8 January 1948, CAC 860260, art. 8.

93. Ministère des Affaires Étrangères, Direction Générale des Affaires Administratives et Sociales, Note, Problème de l'immigration, 7 November 1946, Bidault Papers, AN 457AP 135.

94. For "a lost taste for work," see M. Cassan's remarks, and Director General of Population Emmanuel Rain's repudiation of that view in the compte rendu of the Commission Interministérielle de l'Immigration meeting of 6 November 1946, CAC 660269, art. 8. For a good discussion of how French officials, employers, and CGT activists viewed Polish DPs, see Laure Humbert, "From Soup-Kitchen Charity to Humanitarian Expertise? France, the United Nations, and the Displaced Persons Problem in Post-War Germany" (PhD diss., University of Exeter, 2014), chap. 3.

95. On the Banatais episode, see Humbert, "Soup-Kitchen Charity," chap. 3; and Noiriel, *Immigration, antisémitisme et racisme*, 516.

96. La Documentation Française, "Les avantages," 12. Nor did the numbers improve that much after 1947. According to Chevalier, only another 10,914 DPs came to France in 1948, and during the first four months of 1949 another 3,586 arrived. Louis Chevalier, "Bilans d'une immigration," *Population* 5, no. 1 (January–March 1950): 137–138. These numbers fell far short of the 50,000 DPs government authorities had said in early 1947 they were prepared to take (Humbert, "Soup-Kitchen Charity," chap. 3). On DP recruitment, see also Daniel Cohen, *In War's Wake: Europe's Displaced*

Persons in the Postwar Order (Oxford: Oxford University Press, 2011), 106–108; and Tara Zahra, *Lost Children: Reconstructing Europe's Families after World War II* (Cambridge, MA: Harvard University Press, 2011), 154–156.

97. La Documentation Française, "Les avantages," 12.

98. Compte rendu, Commission Interministérielle de l'Immigration, 8 January 1948, CAC 860269, art. 8.

99. To observe these assumptions at work, see, for example, the comptes rendus of the Commission Consultative Nord-Africaine at the Ministry of Labor, 72AS 95. Also, La Documentation Française, "Les avantages," 9–10.

100. Clifford Rosenberg, "Albert Sarraut and Republican Racial Thought," in *Race in France: Interdisciplinary Perspectives on the Politics of Difference*, ed. Herrick Chapman and Laura L. Frader (New York: Berghahn Books, 2004), 36–53.

101. Commission Consultative Nord-Africaine, compte rendu, 20 November 1946, 72AS 95.

102. Ibid., 21 December 1946.

103. *New York Herald Tribune*, 29 January 1949.

104. On purging the CGT, see Sous-Direction de la Main-d'oeuvre Étrangère, Note pour M. le Ministre, 1 June 1949, CAC 770623, art. 142; Note pour M. le Ministre, 4 June 1948, CAC 770623, art. 142; and Spire, *Étrangers à la carte*, 99–104.

105. Spire, *Étrangers à la carte*, 102.

106. Note à l'attention de M. Segalat, 16 April 1948, Mauco Papers, AN 577AP 3.

107. Le Ministre des Affaires Étrangères à M. le Président du Conseil (Secrétariat Général), Réorganisation des service chargés de notre politique d'immigration, 21 June 1948, Bidault Papers, AN 457AP 135.

108. On the reorganization of ONI, see Rapport sur le réforme des organismes chargés de définir et d'exécuter une politique de l'immigration, présenté par M. Delaporte, Conseiller Référendaire à la Cour des comptes, 6 June 1948, CAC 770623, art. 143; Note pour M. le Ministre, Réorganisation des services de l'immigration, CAC 770623, art. 142; Memorandum, Daniel Mayer, Ministre du Travail, à M. le Président du Conseil, 14 June 1948, CAC 770623, art. 142; Robert Schuman, le Président du Conseil, à M. le Ministre du Travail, 8 June 1948, CAC 770623, art. 142; Direction de la Main-d'oeuvre, Note pour M. le Ministre, Modifications immédiates à apporter à l'ONI en attendant réformes de structure, 19 May 1948, CAC 770623, art. 142.

109. ONI, Conseil d'Administration, procès-verbal, 17 February 1950, CAC 770623, art. 141; Spire, *Étrangers à la carte*, 102.

110. R. Maisonneuve, "Contre toute immigration nouvelle," *L'Union des Métaux*, March 1949; and compte rendu, Commission Nationale de Main-d'Oeuvre, 28 March 1950, CAC 860269, art. 8.

111. Spire, *Étrangers à la carte*, 74.

112. On the effects of anticommunist repression on immigrants, see especially Noiriel, *Immigration, antisémitisme et racisme*, 497–509; Courtois, "Le

PCF"; and Spire, *Étrangers à la carte*, 70–81, also 79 on the effort to revive something like the CADI.

113. Robert Fabre, Note for Villiers and Mayolle, Situation de l'Office National d'Immigration, 27 December 1949, AN 72AS 95.

114. Memorandum, Daniel Mayer, Ministre du Travail, à M. le Président du Conseil, 14 June 1948, CAC 770623, art. 142; Secrétariat Général du Gouvernement, Note à l'Attention de M. Segalat, 21 April 1948, Mauco Papers, AN 577AP 3.

115. Vincent Viet, *La France immigrée: construction d'une politique, 1914–1997* (Paris: Fayard, 1998), 239.

116. Spire, *Étrangers à la carte*, 106–107.

117. Noiriel, *Immigration, antisémitisme et racisme*, 524. See also Martin A. Schain, *The Politics of Immigration in France, Britain, and the United States: A Comparative Study* (New York: Palgrave Macmillan, 2008), 47.

118. Noiriel, *Immigration, antisémitisme et racisme*, 518.

119. Chapter 7 pursues this subject.

3 · Shopkeeper Turmoil

1. Texte définitif du Programme d'Action de la Résistance, 15 August 1944, annex 7 in Claire Andrieu, *Le programme commun de la Résistance: Des idées dans la guerre* (Paris: Les Éditions de l'Érudit, 1984), 173.

2. Jean-Pierre Rioux, *The Fourth Republic, 1944–1958* (New York: Cambridge University Press, 1987), 259.

3. On the relationship of Poujadism to Pierre Nicoud's movement and the National Front, see Nonna Mayer, *La boutique contre la gauche* (Paris: Presses de la FNSP, 1986).

4. *Le Petit Robert* now defines Poujadism as an "attitude based on self-interested claims and a rejection of socio-economic evolution."

5. Dominique Veillon and Jean-Marie Flonneau, introduction to *Les temps des restrictions en France (1939–1949)*, ed. Veillon and Flonneau, *Les Cahiers de l'IHTP* 32–33 (May 1996): 8.

6. Lynn Taylor, *Between Resistance and Collaboration: Popular Protest in Northern France, 1940–45* (New York: St. Martin's Press, 2000), 34–37; Maurice Larkin, *France since the Popular Front: Government and People, 1936–1986* (Oxford: Clarendon Press, 1988), 98. On rationing and price controls, see especially Kenneth Mouré, "Food Rationing and the Black Market in France, 1940–1944," *French History* 24, no. 2 (2010): 262–282; Kenneth Mouré and Fabrice Grenard, "Traitors, *Trafiquants*, and the Confiscation of 'Illicit Profits' in France, 1944–1950," *Historical Journal* 51, no. 4 (December 2008): 969–990; Fabrice Grenard, *La France du marché noir (1940–1949)* (Paris: Payot, 2008); and Stefanos Geroulanos, "An Army of Shadows: Black Markets, Adaptation, and Social Transparency in Postwar France," *JMH* 88, no. 1 (March 2016): 68–81. See also Hervé Dumez and Alin Jeunemaitre, *Diriger l'économie: L'Etat et les prix en France, 1936–1986* (Paris: L'Harmattan, 1989), 60–95; Rioux, *The Fourth Republic*, 21–28, 122–123, 126–127; Richard F. Kuisel, *Capitalism and the State in*

Modern France (New York: Cambridge University Press, 1981), 216–217, 269; François Caron, *An Economic History of Modern France* (New York: Columbia University Press, 1979), 267–276; and Hubert Bonin, *Histoire économique de la IVe République* (Paris: Économica, 1987), 103–114.

7. On the black market in cards, see Taylor, *Between Resistance and Collaboration*, 125–134.

8. Ibid., 116. See also the classic fictional account, Jean Dutourd's *The Best Butter*, trans. Robin Chancellor (New York: Simon and Schuster, 1955).

9. Taylor, *Between Resistance and Collaboration*, 134–136.

10. Jean-Pierre Rioux, "La révolte de Pierre Poujade," in *L'histoire: Études sur la France de 1939 à nos jours* (Paris: Éditions du Seuil, 1985), 257.

11. On interest groups relevant to shopkeepers, see Jean Ruhlmann, *Ni bourgeois ni prolétaires: La défense des classes moyennes en France au XXe siècle* (Paris: Éditions du Seuil, 2001); Sylvie Guillaume, *Les classes moyennes au coeur du politique sous la IVe République* (Talence: Éditions de la Maison des Sciences de l'Homme d'Aquitaine, 1997); Cédric Perrin, "Les entreprises artisanales et la politique économique de l'État en France (1938–1970)" (doctoral thesis, Université François Rabelais de Tours, 2001); Steven M. Zdatny, *The Politics of Survival: Artisans in Twentieth-Century France* (New York: Oxford University Press, 1990); and Joseph Jones, "Vichy France and Postwar Economic Modernization: The Case of the Shopkeepers," *FHS* 12, no. 4 (Fall 1982): 541–563.

12. See Jones, "Vichy France"; and Ruhlmann, *Ni bourgeois ni prolétaires*, 55–59.

13. Frank L. Wilson, *Interest-Group Politics in France* (New York: Cambridge University Press, 1987), 101–102. See also Henry W. Ehrmann, *Organized Business in France* (Princeton: Princeton University Press, 1957), 172–184.

14. For details on these protests, see Chapter 1.

15. Archives du Ministère de Justice, Division criminelle, AN BB18 3736, 33 A 47/F 2 (Agen).

16. AN BB18 3736, 33 A 47/F 28 (Millau).

17. Ibid., F 4 (Dijon).

18. Ibid., F 22 (Nantes).

19. AN BB18 3737, 33 A 47/F 87 (Campel).

20. AN BB18 3736, 33 A 47/F 31 (Meaux).

21. AN BB18 3737, 33 A 47/F 91 (St-Aignan-sur-Cher).

22. Ibid., F 95 (Dax).

23. Ibid., F 88 (Rosières).

24. AN BB18 3736, 33 A 47/F 38 (Genouilly).

25. Ibid., F 2 (Agen).

26. AN BB18 3737, 33 A 47/F 67 (St-Étienne); AN BB18 3736, 33 A 47/F 18 (Vorey).

27. AN BB18 3737, 33 A 47/F 101 (Rennes).

28. AN BB18 3736, 33 A 47/F 15 (Clisson et Pornic).

29. Ibid., F 19 (Sille-le-Guillaume).

30. Ibid., F 38 (Genouilly).

31. On the "Mayer Plan," see Caron, *Economic History*, 274–276; Bonin, *Histoire économique*, 140–141; Rioux, *The Fourth Republic*, 184–185; and Kuisel, *Capitalism and the State*, 216.

32. On these reforms, see Stephen Walker Owen Jr., "The Politics of Tax Reform in France, 1906–1926" (PhD diss., University of California at Berkeley, 1982).

33. Carl S. Shoup, "Taxation in France," *National Tax Journal* 8, no. 4 (December 1955): 326.

34. Frédéric Tristram, *Une fiscalité pour la croissance: La direction générale des impôts et la politique fiscale en France de 1948 à la fin des années 1960* (Paris: Comité pour l'histoire économique et financière de la France, 2005), 119.

35. On the French tax system, see Jean-Yves Nizet, *Fiscalité, économie et politique: L'impôt en France, 1945–1990* (Paris: Librairie générale de droit et de jurisprudence, 1991); André Neurisse, *Histoire de l'impôt* (Paris: PUF, 1978); Gabriel Ardant, *Histoire de l'impôt*, 2 vols. (Paris: Fayard, 1972); Warren C. Baum, *The French Economy and the State* (Princeton: Princeton University Press, 1958), 130–165. On the sales tax, see "Evolution historique des taxes sur le chiffre d'affaires," 2 July 1957, AEF Z 814.

36. Alexis Spire, "L'inégalité devant l'impôt: Différences sociales et ordre fiscal dans la France des Trente glorieuses," *Revue d'Histoire Moderne et Contemporaine* 65, no. 2 (April–June 2009): 165.

37. Nicolas Delalande and Alexis Spire, *Histoire sociale de l'impôt* (Paris: La Découverte, 2010), 64.

38. Roger Eatwell, "Poujadism and Neo-Poujadism: From Revolt to Reconciliation," in *Social Movements and Protest in France*, ed. Philip G. Cerny (London: Frances Pinter, 1982), 73.

39. Baum, *The French Economy*, 143.

40. On the Pleven–Mendès-France duel, see Chapter 6.

41. For his account of the war years, see Roselyne Chenu, *Paul Delouvrier ou la passion d'agir: Entretiens* (Paris: Éditions du Seuil, 1994), 55–115.

42. Tristram, *Une fiscalité*, 120–127 and, for the CGT plan, 641–666.

43. Lettre de David Bruce, chef de la mission du plan Marshall en France à Henri Queuille, président du Conseil, le 5 décembre 1948 (F 30 2862), reprinted in François Bloch-Lainé and Jean Bouvier, *La France restaurée,1944—1954: Dialogue sur les choix d'une modernisation* (Paris: Fayard, 1986), 303–305. See also Irwin Wall, *The United States and the Making of Postwar France, 1945–1954* (Cambridge: Cambridge University Press, 1991), 169–170; Frances M. B. Lynch, *France and the International Economy: From Vichy to the Treaty of Rome* (London: Routledge, 1997), 83, 94–95; Frances M. B. Lynch, "A Tax for Europe: The Introduction of Value Added Tax in France," *Journal of European Integration History* 4, no. 2 (1998): 76; Michel Margairaz, *L'État, les finances et l'économie: Histoire d'une conversion, 1932–1952* (Paris: Comité d'histoire économique et financière de la France, 1991), 1114–1115.

44. Lynch, *France and the International Economy*, 97.

45. On the Loriot Commission and its composition, see Tristram, *Une fiscalité*, 296; Baum, *The French Economy*, 161; and Sylvie Guillaume, *Antoine Pinay ou la confiance en politique* (Paris: Presses de la FNSP, 1984), 103.

46. Delalande and Spire, *Histoire sociale de l'impôt*, 62.

47. On this aspect of the French tax system in comparative context, see Arnold J. Heidenheimer, Hugh Heclo, and Carolyn Teich Adams, *Comparative Public Policy: The Politics of Social Choice in Europe and America* (New York: St. Martin's Press, 1983), 185. For some flavor of how tax inspectors regarded the territory under surveillance, see Yvonne Mathé, *La longue marche d'une auxiliaire des impôts* (Paris: Comité pour l'histoire économique et financière de la France, 1988); Marcel Mompezat, *Journal d'un percepteur* (Paris: Comité pour l'histoire économique et financière de la France, 1992); and Catherine Jumeau, ed., *Vies de percepteurs: Fragments autobiographiques, 1918–1993* (Paris: Comité pour l'histoire économique et financière de la France, 2001).

48. On the amnesty and wartime fraud, see Ministère des Finances, "Dix ans de contrôle fiscal en France," February 1955, annex 4, p. 8, archives of the Ministère des Finances, Direction Générale des Impôts, AEF Z 806. On efforts to reorganize the tax services and tighten up auditing methods in 1952 and 1953, see the procès-verbaux of the Conseil d'administration de la Direction Générale des Impôts, esp. 10 January 1952, 17 January 1952, 21 October 1952, and 21 January 1953, AEF Z 826.

49. Quoted in Ministère des Finances, "Dix ans de contrôle fiscal en France," February 1955, annexe, "Les exhortations à la répression de la fraude," p. 8. On the tax administrations qualms about amnesty, Tristram, *Une fiscalité*, 222.

50. Tristram, *Une fiscalité*, 268.

51. On CGT and CFTC interest in TVA, see *Le Peuple* as quoted in *L'Aube*, 20 December 1948; and Henry Ehrmann, *Organized Business in France* (Princeton: Princeton University Press, 1957), 315.

52. Chenu, *Paul Delouvrier*, 143–144; Ehrmann, *Organized Business*, 316. Many large employers would have preferred accelerated capital depreciation, but they settled for TVA. On business opinions, see Tristram, *Une fiscalité*, 331–335.

53. Delalande and Spire, *Histoire sociale de l'impôt*, 71.

54. The principal works on the Poujadist movement include Stanley Hoffmann, *Le mouvement Poujade* (Paris: Armand Colin, 1956); Romain Souillac, *Le mouvement Poujade: De la défense professionnelle au populisme nationaliste (1953–1962)* (Paris: Presses de la FNSP, 2007); Dominique Borne, *Petits bourgeois en révolte? Le mouvement Poujade* (Paris: Flammarion, 1977); Jean-Pierre Rioux, "La révolte de Pierre Poujade," 248–266; Annie Collovald, "Les Poujadistes, ou l'échec en politique," *Revue d'Histoire Moderne et Contemporaine* 37 (January–March 1989): 113–133. See also Pierre Poujade, *J'ai choisi le combat* (Saint-Céré: Société Générale des Éditions et des Publications, 1955); Poujade, *L'histoire sans masques* (Cestas: Elytis Éditions, 2003).

55. Souillac, *Le mouvement Poujade,* 45.

56. Ibid., 41.

57. Tax officials recognized connections between resistance to *contrôle économique* and the Poujadist rebellion. See Direction Générale des Impôts, *La réorganisation des régies financières,* annexe, "Dix ans de contrôle fiscal," February 1955, AEF Z 806.

58. Gérard Vincent, "Groupes et catégories socio-professionels," in *Société et culture de la France contemporaine,* ed. Georges Santori (Albany, NY: SUNY Press, 1981), 167.

59. Borne, *Petits bourgeois en révolt?,* 14–15.

60. Note pour le Ministre, Situation et perspectives du contrôle fiscal à la fin de mai 1956, AEF Z 608. On the geography of the movement, see Souillac, *Le mouvement Poujade,* 43, 52.

61. Note pour le Ministre, Situation et perspectives du contrôle fiscal à la fin de janvier 1956, 9 February 1956, AEF Z 827.

62. Rioux, *The Fourth Republic,* 257; and Rioux, "La révolte de Pierre Poujade," in *La France de 1939 à nos jours* (Paris: Éditions du Seuil, 1985), 255.

63. Poujade, *J'ai choisi le combat,* 114.

64. Philip M. Williams, *Crisis and Compromise: Politics in the Fourth Republic* (Garden City, NY: Anchor Books, 1966), 176.

65. Ibid., 179.

66. Pierre Allix, Rapport au Ministre, Plan concernant les mesures propres à permettre l'exercice normal du contrôle fiscal, 1 June 1954, AEF Z 806.

67. Souillac, *Le mouvement Poujade,* 154–155.

68. Ibid., 153.

69. Note pour le Ministre, Plan de détente fiscale et de reprise du contrôle fiscal, 17 September 1954, AEF Z 806. On efforts to appease the rebellion, see also Nizet, *Fiscalité,* 139–141.

70. Letter from the Directeur des Contributions Indirectes à M. le Chef du Service d'Étude et de Contrôle Fiscal, 24 November 1954. AN BB18 4193, dossier 5 A 54 F 37.

71. Pierre Allix, Rapport au Ministre, 1 June 1954, AEF Z 806.

72. *Réalités,* February 1955, 22–25.

73. Discours du Ministre des Finances, 29 June 1954, AEF Z 806.

74. Note des Inspecteurs Généraux des Finances sur le "Malaise fiscale et les remèdes actuellement proposés," 30 March 1955, AEF Z 805.

75. Faure, *Mémoires,* 2:129–130. See also Carl S. Shoup, "Some Distinguishing Characteristics of the British, French, and United States Public Finance Systems," *American Economic Review* 47, no. 2 (May 1957): 195.

76. Although the government raised the TVA rate to make it possible to eliminate the business transaction tax and the tax on services, some people suspected that it was also designed to compensate for reducing the burden on the income tax. See the transcript of the radio interview with M. Leguesne, a high-level civil servant at the Ministry of Finance, 13 May 1955, AEF Z 805.

77. *La vie économique*, 6 May 1955. For criticisms of higher TVA rates, see the transcript of the radio interview with Roger Millot, president of the Comité national de rénovation fiscale, 18 and 25 May 1955, AEF Z 805.

78. Souillac, *Le mouvement Poujade*, 168.

79. On the response of FO and CGT unions within the Ministry of Finance, see Bulletin du syndicat national des cadres des contributions directes et du cadastre, 6 April 1955, AEF Z 805; Note pour le Ministre, Mouvement de protestation des commerçants et artisans contre la fiscalité, 21 June 1954, AEF Z 806. See also the clippings in AMF Z 810, especially *Le Monde*, 21 April 55; *La Croix*, 23 March 1955; *Le Syndicaliste des Contributions Directes (CGT)*, 3 March 1955; and Edgar Faure, *Mémoires*, vol. 2 (Paris: Plon, 1984), 155. The Conseil d'administration of the tax administration considered the idea of having top tax officials meet directly with Pierre Poujade, but feared that doing so would outrage the already demoralized agents of the tax services. See Procès-verbaux, Conseil d'administration, Direction Générale des Impôts, 30 June 1955, AEF Z 827. On civil service unions, see André Tiano, *Les traitements des fonctionnaires et leur détermination (1930–1957)* (Paris: Éditions M.-Th. Génin, 1957).

80. Mémorandum du Secrétaire d'État aux Finances et aux Affaires Économiques à la Garde de Sceau, 27 mai 1955, dossier 5 A 54 F 52 (Bordeaux), AN BB18 4194; and mémorandum du Procureur de la République à Beaune au Procureur Général à Dijon, 21 mars 1955, dossier 5 A 55 F 16 (Dijon), AN BB18 4278.

81. Note pour le Ministre, Situation et perspectives du contrôle fiscal à la fin de mai 1956, AEF Z 806.

82. On resisting the temptation to step up repression and then observing the decline of the revolt in 1957, see Tristram, *Une fiscalité*, 420–422.

83. Note pour M. le Directeur Général, Suggestions Mendès France pour la réforme fiscale, 14 February 1958, AEF Z807.

84. Rioux, *The Fourth Republic*, 248.

85. On the importance of the partnership between the top tax experts and finance ministers and prime ministers, see Tristram, *Une fiscalité*, 355–356.

86. Discours du Ministre, 29 June 1954, AEF Z 806.

87. Ibid.

88. During the 1950s direct taxation grew at a somewhat faster rate than indirect taxation. (Nizet, *Fiscalité*, 90–91.) Even so, the French tax system during the Fifth Republic remained more weighted toward indirect taxes, and less dependent on the income tax, than elsewhere in Western Europe and in the United States. See Heidenheimer, Heclo, and Adams, *Comparative Public Policy*, 176–179.

89. Tristram, *Une fiscalité*, 363–423, 487–488.

90. Ibid., 545–550, 576–582.

91. Eric Kocher-Marboeuf, *Le patricien et le général: Jean-Marcel Jeanneney et Charles de Gaulle. 1958–1969*, vol. 1 (Paris: Comité pour l'histoire économique et financière de la France, 2003), 449.

92. Sylvie Guillaume, "Un syndicalisme des classes moyennes: La Confédération générale des petites et moyennes entreprises," *VS* 37 (January–March

1993): 105–114; Guillaume, *Le petit et moyen patronat dans la nation française de Pinay à Raffarin, 1944–2004* (Bordeaux: Presses universitaires de Bordeaux, 2005), 62–64.

93. Sylvie Guillaume, "Léon Gingembre, défenseur des PME," *VS* 15 (July–September 1987): 69–70.

94. Richard Vinen, "Faire pression sur les groupes de pression," in *Les groupes de pression dans la vie politique contemporaine en France et aux États-Unis de 1820 à nos jours,* ed. Jean Garrigues (Rennes: PUR, 2002), 157.

95. Ibid., 163.

96. André Viard, "Au siècle de l'atome, la fiscalité ne doit plus être une entreprise de mise à mort en règle," *La Volonté,* édition de Lille, May 1959.

97. Gustave Deleau, "Les raisons du mécontentement P.M.E.," *La Volonté,* édition de Lille, March 1960.

98. Léon Gingembre, "Franc de deuil ou franc d'espoir?" *La Volonté,* édition de Lille, January 1960.

99. Mayer, *La boutique contre la gauche,* 48.

100. Maurice Roy, *Les commerçants entre la révolte et la modernisation* (Paris: Éditions du Seuil, 1971), 76–78; Tristram, *Une fiscalité,* 550–554.

101. Suzanne Berger, "Regime and Interest Representation: The French Traditional Middle Classes," in *Organizing Interests in Western Europe: Pluralism, Corporatism, and the Transformation of Politics,* ed. Berger (Cambridge: Cambridge University Press, 1981), 91–92; Etienne Thil, *Combat pour la distribution: D'Edouard Leclerc aux supermarchés* (Paris: Arthaud, 1964), 108–120.

102. Victoria de Grazia, *Irresistible Empire: America's Advance through Twentieth-Century Europe* (Cambridge, MA: Harvard University Press, 2005), 398–401.

103. Lettre de Michel Debré à Léon Gingembre, 27 novembre 1961, Archives Michel Debré, 2 DE 100.

104. "Une interview de M. Joseph Fontanet," *Le Monde,* 5 August 1959.

105. Rapport sur les obstacles à l'expansion économique, présenté par le comité institué par le décret no. 59-1284 du 13 novembre 1959, Archives Michel Debré, 2 DE 37. See also *La Volonté,* September–October 1960.

106. *La Volonté,* November 1960.

107. See Jacquier-Bruère [pseudonyms for Michel Debré and Emmanuel Monick], *Refaire la France: L'effort d'une generation* (Paris: Plon, 1945).

108. Alfred Sauvy, cited in "Le possible et l'impossible dans la réforme du commerce," *L'Entreprise,* 6 August 1959.

109. Berger, "Regime and Interest Representation," 92.

110. Suzanne Berger, "D'une boutique à l'autre: Changes in the Organization of the Traditional Middle Classes from the Fourth to Fifth Republics," *Comparative Politics* 10, no. 1 (October 1977): 121–136; Berger, "The Traditional Sector in France and Italy," in *Dualism and Discontinuity in Industrial Societies,* ed. Suzanne Berger and Michael J. Piore (Cambridge: Cambridge University Press, 1980), 88–131; Delalande and Spire, *Histoire sociale de l'impôt,* 76–78.

4 · Family Matters

1. A vast literature explores the Great Depression and World War II as contexts for building European welfare states. See especially Tony Judt, *Postwar: A History of Europe since 1945* (New York: Penguin, 2005), 72–77; Alan Milward, *The European Rescue of the Nation-State* (Berkeley: University of California Press, 1992), 21–45; and Gøsta Esping-Andersen, *The Three Worlds of Welfare Capitalism* (Princeton: Princeton University Press, 1990).

2. The Left had largely opposed pronatalist policy in the 1920s, mostly on antimilitarist grounds. But in the Popular Front era even the Communist Party joined the emerging pronatalist consensus, a change in perspective abetted in part by the patriotic antifascism within the PCF, in part by a conservative sea change in family policy in the Soviet Union in the 1930s. See Susan Pedersen, *Family, Dependence, and the Origins of the Welfare State: Britain and France, 1914–1945* (Cambridge: Cambridge University Press, 1993), 368–369; Kristen Stromberg Childers, *Fathers, Families, and the State in France, 1914–1945* (Ithaca, NY: Cornell University Press, 2003), 33–34, 79; and Mary Louise Roberts, *Civilization without Sexes: Reconstructing Gender in Postwar France, 1917–1927* (Chicago: University of Chicago Press, 1994). On the Soviet Union, see Wendy Goldman, *Women, the State and Revolution: Soviet Family Policy and Social Life, 1917–1936* (Cambridge: Cambridge University Press, 1993).

3. *La protection sociale en France* (Paris: La Documentation française, 1995), 91; Antoine Prost, "L'évolution de la politique familiale en France de 1938 à 1981," *MS* 129 (October–December 1984): 7.

4. Robert Debré and Alfred Sauvy, *Des Français pour la France: Le problème de la population* (Paris: Gallimard, 1946), 9.

5. Claire Duchen, *Women's Rights and Women's Lives in France, 1944–1968* (London: Routledge, 1994), 105. The survey results were published in "Enquête sur l'information du public en matière démographique," *Population*, no. 4 (1947). Dominique Schnapper and her colleagues cite INED 1947 survey findings in greater detail: 64 percent of men and 61 percent of women surveyed approved of family allocations, another 24 percent and 21 percent approved of them with reservations, and only 9 percent and 13 percent disapproved of them. See Dominique Schnapper, Jeanne Brody, and Riva Kastoryano, "Les Français et la sécurité sociale," *VS* 10 (April 1986): 69.

6. Duchen, *Women's Rights*, 103. On broad support for family subsidies after the Liberation, see also Andrew Shennan, *Rethinking France: Plans for Renewal, 1940–1946* (Oxford: Clarendon Press, 1989), 208–209.

7. Prost, "L'évolution de la politique familiale." See also Rémi Lenoir, "Family Policy in France since 1938," in *The French Welfare State: Surviving Social and Ideological Change*, ed. John S. Ambler (New York: NYU Press, 1991), 159.

8. On early experiments with wage supplements, see Susan Pedersen, *Family, Dependence, and the Origins of the Welfare State: Britain and France,*

1914–1945 (Cambridge: Cambridge University Press, 1993), chap. 5; Laura Levine Frader, *Breadwinners and Citizens: Gender in the Making of the French Social Model* (Durham, NC: Duke University Press, 2008); and Paul Dreyfus, *Émile Romanet, père des allocations familiales* (Paris: Arthaud, 1964).

9. Farmers' wives were thought sufficiently capable of handling children and farmwork not to need financial incentives to expand their families. On family policy and pronatalism in the interwar years, see Pedersen, *Family*; Frader, *Breadwinners and Citizens*; Paul V. Dutton, *Origins of the French Welfare State: The Struggle for Social Reform in France, 1914–1947* (Cambridge: Cambridge University Press, 2002); Remi Lenoir, *Généalogie de la morale familiale* (Paris: Éditions du Seuil, 2003); Cheryl Ann Koos, "Engendering Reaction: The Politics of Pronatalism and the Family in France, 1919–1944" (PhD diss., University of Southern California, 1996); Richard Tomlinson, "The 'Disappearance' of France, 1896–1940: French Politics and the Birth Rate," *Historical Journal* 28, no. 2 (1985): 405–415; Karen Offen, "Body Politics: Women, Work and the Politics of Motherhood in France, 1920–1950," in *Maternity and Gender Policies: Women and the Rise of the European Welfare States, 1880s–1950s*, ed. Gisela Bock and Pat Thane (London: Routledge, 1991), 138–159; Andres Horacio Reggiani, "Procreating France: The Politics of Demography, 1919–1945," *FHS* 19, no. 3 (Spring 1996): 725–754; Marie-Monique Huss, "Pronatalism in the Inter-war Period in France," *Journal of Contemporary History* 25, no. 1 (January 1990): 39–68. On race and the colonial contexts of pronatalism, see Elisa Camiscioli, *Reproducing the French Race: Immigration, Intimacy, and Embodiment in the Early Twentieth Century* (Durham, NC: Duke University Press, 2009); and Margaret Cook Andersen, *French Pronatalists and Colonial Settlement in the Third Republic* (Lincoln: University of Nebraska Press, 2015).

10. Statistician and criminologist Jacques Bertillon founded the Alliance in 1896. Fernand Boverat served as its president in the interwar years. From the mid-1920s on, it claimed to have over 25,000 members. Pedersen, *Family*, 359; Camiscioli, *Reproducing the French Race*, 25.

11. Many people were both Catholic familialists and conservative republican pronatalists. On the relationship between these two movements, see Paul-André Rosental, *L'intelligence démographique: Sciences et politiques des populations en France (1930–1960)* (Paris: Éditions Odile Jacob, 2003), 56–60; Cheryl A. Koos, "Gender, Anti-Individualism, and Nationalism: The Alliance Nationale and the Pronatalist Backlash against the *Femmes modernes*, 1933–1940," *FHS* 19, no. 3 (Spring 1996): 701; and Childers, *Fathers*, 160–161.

12. Gérard Noiriel stresses continuities from the Third Republic to Vichy in *Les origines républicaines de Vichy* (Paris: Hachette, 1999). Most of the literature on Vichy and the family recognize continuities and ruptures but vary in emphasis. For continuity both from the Third Republic and going forward into the postwar era, see Aline Coutrot, "La politique familiale," in *Le gouvernement de Vichy, 1940–1942: Institutions et politiques*, ed. René

Rémond (Paris: Armand Colin, 1972); Philip G. Nord, *France's New Deal: From the Thirties to the Postwar Era* (Princeton: Princeton University Press, 2010); and Marc Boninchi, *Vichy et l'ordre moral*, preface by Gérard Noiriel (Paris: PUF, 2005). Ruptures take the foreground in Christophe Capuano, *Vichy et la famille: Réalités et faux-semblants d'une politique publique*, preface by Paul-André Rosental (Rennes: PUR, 2010); Rosental, *L'intelligence démographique*; Miranda Pollard, *Reign of Virtue: Mobilizing Gender in Vichy France* (Chicago: University of Chicago Press, 1998); Michèle Bordeaux, *La victoire de la famille dans la France défaite: Vichy, 1940–1944* (Paris: Flammarion, 2002); and Francine Muel-Dreyfus, *Vichy and the Eternal Feminine: A Contribution to a Political Sociology of Gender*, trans. Kathleen A. Johnson (Durham, NC: Duke University Press, 2001).

13. Jacques Doublet, "Family Allowances in France," *Population Studies* 2, no. 2 (September 1948): 222.

14. On extension of benefits beyond the restrictions of the Family Code, see Dominique Ceccaldi, *Histoire des prestations familiales en France*, preface by Pierre Laroque (Paris: Association pour l'étude de l'histoire de la Sécurité sociale, 2005), 88–90. On the single-wage allowance, see Bordeaux, *La victoire*, 85–95; Cecily Watson, "Population Policy in France: Family Allowances and Other Benefits," pt. 1, *Population Studies* 7, no. 3 (March 1954): 278–281; and Childers, *Fathers*, 174.

15. On continuity of personnel, see Nord, *France's New Deal*, 119; and Coutrot, "La politique familiale." On Laroque's work for the Vichy regime before his dismissal in December 1940, see Eric Jabbari, *Pierre Laroque and the Welfare State in Postwar France* (Oxford: Oxford University Press, 2012), 84–98.

16. Philippe Pétain, "Politique sociale de l'avenir," *Revue des Deux Mondes*, 15 September 1940, as quoted in Muel-Dreyfus, *Eternal Feminine*, 173.

17. On Pétain's self-presentation as father for the nation, see Childers, *Fathers*, 80–94.

18. *Almanac de la famille française* (published by the magazine *Foyers de France*, 1943), 26. See also Childers, *Fathers*, 94–95.

19. As quoted in Muel-Dreyfus, *Eternal Feminine*, 186.

20. Sarah Fishman, *We Will Wait: Wives of French Prisoners of War, 1940–1945* (New Haven, CT: Yale University Press, 1991), 36–39.

21. Bordeaux, *La victoire*, 142–153; Jacques Desmarest, *La politique de la main-d'oeuvre* (Paris: PUF, 1946), 131.

22. Capuano, *Vichy et la famille*, 248–250; Childers, *Fathers*, 106–107. On the continuation of Mother's Day after the Liberation, see Karen Adler, *Jews and Gender in Liberation France* (Cambridge: Cambridge University Press, 2003), 49–54.

23. Nord, *France's New Deal*, 124–130; Rosental, *L'intelligence démographique*, 169–76; Childers, *Fathers*, 125; Alain Drouard, *Une inconnue des sciences sociales: La Fondation Alexis Carrel, 1941–1945* (Paris: Éditions de la Maison des sciences de l'homme, 1992).

24. Philippe Renaudin as quoted in Muel-Dreyfus, *Eternal Feminine*, 196.

25. Muel-Dreyfus, *Eternal Feminine*, 191–192.

26. Nord, *France's New Deal*, 119–120.
27. On the Gounot law, see Capuano, *Vichy et la famille*, 83, 128–143; Pollard, *Reign of Virtue*, 112–113; and Muel-Dreyfus, *Eternal Feminine*, 194–199.
28. Though less conservative feminists regarded the family vote as a denial of women's citizenship. On the family vote, see Laura Downs, "La République garantit l'égalité des citoyen(ne)s," in *La République démystifiée*, ed. Marion Fontaine, Frédéric Monier, and Christophe Prochasson (Paris: La Découverte, 2013), 138–149; Jean-Yves Le Naour and Catherine Valenti, *La famille doit voter: Le suffrage familial contre le vote individuel* (Paris: Hachette, 2005); Reggiani, "Procreating France," 733; Pollard, *Reign of Virtue*, 16; Childers, *Fathers*, 49–55; and Adler, *Jews and Gender*, 81–82.
29. Pollard, *Reign of Virtue*, 113.
30. Capuano, *Vichy et la famille*, 132–138; Muel-Dreyfus, *Eternal Feminine*, 195–196; Childers, *Fathers*, 160–168.
31. Capuano, *Vichy et la famille*, 61–63, 311; Rosental, *L'intelligence démographique*, 62–64.
32. On the many disagreements family associations had with the government, see Capuano, *Vichy et la famille*, 149–175.
33. Ibid., 311–316; Fishman, *We Will Wait*, 44–45.
34. Dutton, *Origins*, 202; Shennan, *Rethinking France*, 215–217.
35. Nord, *France's New Deal*, 116.
36. On avoiding "family" as a label, see Rosental, *L'intelligence démographique*, 78–81; Capuano, *Vichy et la famille*, 276–277; Shennan, *Rethinking France*, 207–208.
37. Claire Andrieu, *Le programme commun de la Résistance: Des idées dans la guerre*, preface by René Rémond (Paris: Les Éditions de l'Érudit, 1984), 168–175.
38. On the difficulties of planning social policy within the Resistance, see Bruno Valat, "Résistance et sécurité sociale, 1941–1944," *Revue Historique* 592 (October–December 1994): 315–346; Shennan, *Rethinking France*, 213.
39. Dutton, *Origins*, 209–210; Pierre Laroque, *Au service de l'homme et du droit: Souvenirs et réflexions* (Paris: Association pour l'étude de l'histoire de la Sécurité sociale, 1993), 205. See also Eric Jabbari's analysis of Laroque's work in the 1930s, in *Pierre Laroque*, 26–28, 38–43, and 75–85.
40. Nord, *France's New Deal*, 43. On Laroque and corporatism, see Eric Jabbari, "Law and Politics in Interwar France: Pierre Laroque's Search for a Democratic Corporatism," *FPCS* 24, no. 1 (Spring 2006): 93–113; Jabbari, *Pierre Laroque*, chap. 2.
41. Conférence de Monsieur Laroque, 9 January 1946, Pierre Laroque Papers, CAC 20030430, art. 56, dossier 1946. See also Laroque, *Au service de l'homme*, 197.
42. Laroque, *Au service de l'homme*, 113–114.
43. Ibid., 113.
44. Ibid., 199.
45. On Laroque's plans and their modification, see Bruno Valat, *Histoire de la sécurité sociale (1945–1967)*, preface by André Guesline (Paris: Économica, 2001), 10–165; Bruno Palier, *Gouverner la sécurité sociale: Les réformes du*

système français de protection sociale depuis 1945 (Paris: PUF, 2002), 100–106; Dutton, *Origins*, 184–225; Jabbari, *Pierre Laroque*, chaps. 5 and 6; Shennan, *Rethinking France*, 210–223; Herrick Chapman, "French Democracy and the Welfare State," in *The Social Construction of Democracy, 1870–1990*, ed. George Reid Andrews and Herrick Chapman (New York: NYU Press, 1995), 291–314; Laroque, *Au service de l'homme*, 197–245; Henry C. Galant, *Histoire politique de la sécurité sociale française, 1945–1952* (Paris: Armand Colin, 1955); and Peter Baldwin, *The Politics of Social Solidarity: Class Bases of the European Welfare State, 1875–1975* (Cambridge: Cambridge University Press, 1990), 158–207.

46. Valat, *Histoire*, 85.

47. For Laroque's invocation of "revolution," see his "Sécurité sociale et assurances sociales," a lecture delivered at the École nationale d'organisation économique et sociale, 23 March 1945, Pierre Laroque Papers, CAC 20030430, art. 56, dossier 1945.

48. Ibid.

49. Except in Alsace and Lorraine, where Catholic unions (of the CFTC) were stronger.

50. Laroque, speech delivered in the British House of Commons, 31 March 1947, original in English, Laroque Papers, CAC 20030430, art. 56, dossier 1947.

51. Quoted in Valat, *Histoire*, 64.

52. Laroque, "L'évolution de la politique française des allocation familiales," lecture of 14 November 1949, 10, Pierre Laroque Papers, CAC 20030430, art. 56, dossier 1949.

53. Laroque, *Au service de l'homme*, 216.

54. Ibid.

55. Ibid., 214.

56. Douglas Ashford, "Advantages of Complexity: Social Insurance in France," in Ambler, *The French Welfare State*, 32–57; Valat, *Histoire*, 74. On the vote at the HCCPF, see Texte voté par sept voix contre deux, par la Haut Comité consultatif de la population et de la famille dans sa séance du 19 Juin 1945, à propos de l'organisation de la sécurité sociale, CAC 860269, art. 1.

57. A law of 21 February 1949 made the autonomy of the family allowance caisses permanent. Cisely Watson, "Population Policy in France: Family Allowances and Other Benefits," pt. 2, *Population Studies* 8, no. 1 (July 1954): 51.

58. Report of the Chambre de commerce de Paris, "L'organisation de la sécurité sociale," 17 June 1946, Paul Ramadier Papers, 55 J 44.

59. Gaston Tessier, "Devant la caisse unique," in *Faut-il bouleverser les assurances sociales?* (Paris: UNC Gas, 1945), 6, 12.

60. On politics within the ministry, see Virginie Bussat, "1945: Appropriation savante et inscription administrative des questions familiales," in *Les mouvements familiaux et leur institution en France: Anthologie historique et sociale*, ed. Michel Chauvière, with the collaboration of Pauline Kertudo (Paris: Comité d'histoire de la Sécurité sociale, 2006), 472–474; Rosental, *L'intelligence démographique*, 82–83.

61. Prigent as quoted in Valat, *Histoire*, 76.

62. Lenoir, *Généalogie*, 344; Capuano, *Vichy et la famille*, 297–299, 302. On Desmottes advising Prigent in the drafting of the 3 March 1945 law, see Bruno Béthouart, *Des syndicalistes chrétiens en politique (1944–1962): De la Libération à la Ve République* (Paris: Presses universitaires du Septentrion, 1999), 91.

63. Nord, *France's New Deal*, 188.

64. Capuano, *Vichy et la famille*, chap. 13.

65. Rosental, *L'intelligence démographique*, 83. For the membership estimate for 1946, see Rapport général de la Commission d'étude des problèmes de la famille, 1960, 22, Archives Michel Debré, 2 DE 50.

66. Michel Messu, *Les politiques familiales: Du natalisme à la solidarité* (Paris: Les Éditions Ouvrières, 1992), 56.

67. On Prigent, see Béthouart, *Des syndicalistes chrétiens*; Lenoir, *Généalogie*, 363; Bussant, "1945," 482; Chauvière, *Les mouvements familiaux*, 628–629.

68. Bethouart, *Des syndicalistes chrétiens*, 51.

69. Haut Comité consultatif de la population et de la famille, séance du 13 juin 1945, CAC 860269, art. 1. See also Adler, *Jews and Gender*, 81–82; Sylvie Chaperon, *Les années Beauvoir, 1945–1970* (Paris: Fayard, 2000), 39.

70. Valat, *Histoire*, 74; Ceccaldi, *Prestations familiales*, 108; and Galant, *Histoire politique*, 37.

71. For Laroque's respect for Croizat, see the compte rendu of the Commission supérieure des allocations familiales, 22 November 1947, p. 3, archives of the Commission supérieure des allocations familiales, CAC 760231, art. 35 (SS 935). Also Laroque, *Au service de l'homme*, 207–208.

72. On Croizat, see Bruno Béthouart, *Le ministère du travail et de la sécurité sociale: De la libération au début de la Ve République* (Rennes: PUR, 2006), 70–74.

73. Valat, *Histoire*, 179–180; Shennan, *Rethinking France*, 219.

74. Intervention of Amboise Croizat in the National Assembly, 6 August 1946, as quoted in Alain Barjot, *La sécurité sociale: Son histoire à travers les textes*, vol. 3 (Paris: Association pour l'études de l'histoire de la Sécurité sociale, 1997), 61.

75. Quoted in Michel Dreyfus, Michèle Ruffat, Vincent Viet, Danièle Voldman, with the collaboration of Bruno Valat, *Se protéger, être protégé: Une histoire des assurances sociales en France* (Rennes: PUR, 2006), 264.

76. Galant, *Histoire politique*, 99–102.

77. Jacques Doublet, "Family Allowances in France," *Population Studies* 2, no. 2 (September 1948): 227.

78. Duchen, *Women's Rights*, 102. On controversy over registering in the first three months, see Procès-verbal de la séance du 13 mai 1954, CAC 760231, art. 38 (SS 938).

79. Duchen, *Women's Rights*, 225–228; Pierre Laroque, *La politique familiale en France* (Paris: La Documentation française, 1985), 204–206; Galant, *Histoire politique*, 81–95.

80. On the tax incentives, see Jean-Yves Nizet, *Fiscalité, économie et politique: L'impôt en France, 1945–1990* (Paris: Librairie générale de droit et de jurisprudence, 1991), 60–64.

81. If the family allowance system became settled territory by early 1947, this was not true of the social security caisses, where several key occupational groups fought to maintain their own respective insurance funds. See Peter Baldwin, *The Politics of Social Solidarity: Class Bases of the European Welfare State, 1875–1975* (Cambridge: Cambridge University Press, 90), 163–186, 248–268.

82. Jacques Tessier, "Le syndicalisme chrétien, 1945–1956," in *La Quatrième République: Des témoins pour l'histoire, 1957–1997*, ed. Jean-Jacques Becker, Agnès Callu, and Patricia Gillet (Paris: Honoré Champion Éditeur, 1999), 77.

83. On the 1947 caisses elections, see Galant, *Histoire politique*, 123–129. In 1950 the CGT's share of the overall voting for caisse boards in social security slipped to 44 percent, with FO picking up 25 percent. See Valat, *Histoire*, 123.

84. Laroque later wrote in appreciation of Raynaud's alacrity in firing a CGT colleague whose incompetence as a regional caisse director Laroque had pointed out. Laroque, *Au service de l'homme*, 210, 227.

85. On the creation of the FNOSS and UNCAF, see Ceccaldi, *Prestations familiales*, 115–119; Galant, *Histoire politique*, 74–77; Valat, *Histoire*, 225–235.

86. Allocution prononcée par M. Laroque à l'Assemblée générale constitutive de l'Union Nationale des Caisses d'Allocations Familiales, 18 January 1947, Pierre Laroque Papers, CAC 20030430, art. 56, dossier 1945–1947.

87. Laroque, *Au service de l'homme*, 210. On Lebel, see Chauvière, *Les mouvements familiaux*, 629–631.

88. On new family associations after 1945, see Capuano, *Vichy et la famille*, 304–305.

89. Lenoir, *Généalogie*, 379–381.

90. Ibid., 381–382.

91. On masculinity in the Liberation era, see Michael Kelly, "The Reconstruction of Masculinity at the Liberation," in *The Liberation of France: Image and Event*, ed. H. R. Kedward and Nancy Wood (Oxford: Berg, 1995), 117–130; and Claire Duchen, "Opening Pandora's Box: The Case of *Femmes tondues*," in *Problems in French History*, ed. Martyn Cornick and Ceri Crossley (New York: Palgrave, 2000), 213–232. See also Luc Capdevila, "The Quest for Masculinity in a Defeated France, 1940–1945," *Contemporary European History* 10, no. 3 (November 2001): 423–446.

92. The defeat alone made roughly 900,000 married French men POWs in 1940. Fishman, *We Will Wait*, xii.

93. Duchen, *Women's Rights*, 26–27; Fishman, *We Will Wait*, 152–153; Rebecca Pulju, *Women and Mass Consumer Society in Postwar France* (Cambridge: Cambridge University Press, 2011), 106.

94. As Sarah Fishman points out, some of the rise in divorce after 1944 stemmed from the postponement of breakups during the war years. Fishman, *We Will Wait*, 159–163. See also Duchen, *Women's Rights*, 26–28.

95. Childers, *Fathers*, 177–181; Karen Offen, "Body Politics," 150.

96. On Prigent and Bouxom's concerns for fatherhood, see Arthur Plaza, "From Christian Militants to Republican Renovators: The Third *Ralliement* of Catholics in Postwar France, 1944–1965" (PhD diss., New York University, 208), 361–363. The proposal for the *prêt au marriage* did not win parliamentary approval.

97. Fishman, *We Will Wait,* 165–167; see also Plaza, "From Christian Militants," 361.

98. Pierre Laroque, "Aide aux familles et responsabilités familiales," text of a lecture in Brussels, 26 March 1950, Pierre Laroque papers, CAC 20040540, art. 56, dossier 1950.

99. Adler, *Jews and Gender,* 77–78.

100. Several Resistance heroines in the civil service broke through glass ceilings. Olga Raffalovich, for example, became Alexandre Parodi's chief of staff and then a director in the Ministry of Labor. Linda L. Clark, *The Rise of Professional Women in France: Gender and Public Administration since 1870* (Cambridge: Cambridge University Press, 2000), 268. On marriage loans, see also Duchen, *Women's Rights,* 30–31.

101. The women in Léon Blum's Popular Front government of 1936–1937— Cécile Brunschweig, Suzanne Lacore, and Irène Joliot-Curie—were undersecretaries.

102. Clark, *Professional Women,* 273.

103. Duchen, *Women's Rights,* 45; Sylvie Chaperon, " 'Feminism Is Dead. Long Live Feminism!' The Women's Movement in France at the Liberation, 1944–1946," in *When the War Was Over: Women, War and Peace in Europe, 1940–1956,* ed. Claire Duchen and Irene Bandhauer-Schöffmann (London: Leicester University Press, 2000), 155.

104. As Downs has shown, just how political the work could be in the parapolitical world of social service work varied a great deal. Laura Downs, "La République garantit l'égalité"; Downs, " 'Nous plantions les trois couleurs': Action sociale féminine et recomposition des politiques de la droite française; Le movement Croix-de-Feu et le Parti social français, 1934–1947," *Revue d'Histoire Moderne et Contemporaine* 58, no. 3 (July–September 2011):118–163; and Downs, " 'Each and Every One of You Must Become a Chef': Towards a Social Politics of Working-Class Childhood on the Extreme Right in France, 1930–1939," *JMH* 81, no. 1 (March 2009): 1–44.

105. Offen, "Body Politics," 144–145; Offen, "Defining Feminism: A Comparative Historical Approach," *Signs* 14, no. 1 (Autumn 1988): 119–157; Offen, "Depopulation, Nationalism, and Feminism in Fin-de-Siècle France," *AHR* 89, no. 3 (June 1984): 648–676; and Geneviève Dermenjian, introduction and "La conception de la femme et son évolution," in *Femmes, famille et action ouvrière: Pratiques et résponsabilités féminines dans les mouvements familiaux populaire (1935–1958),* ed. Dermenjian (Villeneuve d'Ascq: Groupement pour la recherche sur les mouvements familiaux, 1991), 15–16; Duchen, *Women's Rights,* 41.

106. On UFCS, see Chaperon, *Les années Beauvoir,* 55–64; Thérèse Doneaud and Christian Guérin, *Les femmes agissent, le monde change: Histoire*

inédite de l'Union féminine civique et sociale, preface by René Remond (Paris: Les Éditions du Cerf, 2005); Pedersen, *Family,* 392–410; and Pulju, *Women and Mass Consumer Society,* 43–44. On the LFAC, see Plaza, *From Christian Militants,* 307–308.

107. On the predominance of both the UFCS and the UFF, see Duchen, *Women's Rights,* 166. All but one in the UFF's top leadership group were PCF members. Renée Rousseau, *Les femmes rouges: Chronique des années Vermeersch* (Paris: Albin Michel, 1983), 43.

108. Duchen, *Women's Rights,* 43.

109. Fédération des Travailleurs de la Métallurgie, *Une tache importante du movement syndical: La Défense des revendications féminines.* Conférence nationale des femmes métallurgistes de 14 septembre 1946, Rapport de Henri Jourdain (Secrétaire de la FTM), Paris, 1946, 10–11.

110. Geneviève Dermenjian, "Les femmes dans les mouvements familiaux populaires de 1935 à l'après-guerre," in Dermenjian, *Femmes, famille et action ouvrière,* 37–46; Bruno Duriez, "Left-Wing Catholicism in France from Catholic Action to the Political Left: The *Mouvement populaire des familles,*" in *Left Catholicism: Catholics and Society in Western Europe at the Point of Liberation, 1943–1955,* ed. Gerd-Rainer Horn and Emmanuel Gerard (Leuven: Leuven University Press, 2001), 71–76. In "La maternité sociale et le Mouvement populaire des familles durant les Trente glorieuses," *Clio: Histoire, femmes et sociétés* 21 (2005): 91–105, Geneviève Dermenjian and Dominique Loiseau mention that in 1944–1945 about 200,000 POW wives were members of the MPF.

111. Pulju, *Women and Mass Consumer Society,* 167–169. Circulation of the MPF's weekly newspaper, *Monde Ouvrier,* rose to over 100,000, with an orbit of influence several times that number. See Duriez, "Left-Wing Catholicism," 76. A Gaullist newspaper reported, somewhat skeptically, that the MPF claimed to have about 400,000 members. *Le Rassemblement Ouvrier,* 5 November 1949.

112. Plaza, "From Christian Militants," 300–301. On Rollin, see Patricia E. Prestwich, "Modernizing Politics in the Fourth Republic: Women in the Mouvement républicain populaire, 1944–1958," in *Crisis and Renewal in France, 1918–1962,* ed. Kenneth Mouré and Martin S. Alexander (New York: Berghahn Books, 2002), 209–210.

113. Testimony of Françoise Villiers, in Dermenjian, *Femmes, famille et action ouvrière,* 61.

114. *Le Rassemblement Ouvrier,* 5 November 1949.

115. On the radicalization of the MPF and its schism into the MLP and MLO, see Duriez, "Left-Wing Catholicism in France," 76–90; Dermenjian, *Femmes, famille et action ouvrière,* 68, 70–72, 242, 263. On wanting to sing the Magnificat, see the testimony of Isabelle Brisset in Dermenjian, *Femmes, famille et action ouvrière,* 70.

116. As quoted in Yvonne Knibiehler, ed., *Germaine Poinso-Chapuis, femme d'État (1910–1981),* preface by René Rémond (Paris: Édisud, 1998), 96.

117. Prestwich, "Modernizing Politics," 209; Knibiehler, *Germaine Poinso-Chapuis,* 71–72.

118. "A propos du salaire unique," in *Pour l'Information Féminine* (March 1954), as quoted in Knibiehler, *Germaine Poinso-Chapuis*, 96. It is easy to see Poinso-Chapuis's critical stances toward the more conservative aspects of Catholic familialism early in her career. As a UFCS member and local Christian Democratic activist in Marseille in the 1930s, she had opposed the family vote and supported the rights of unwed mothers and illegitimate children. Chaperon, *Les années Beauvoir*, 61.

119. Robert Prigent, "Notion modern du couple humain uni par le mariage," in *Renouveau des idées sur la famille*, ed. Prigent, *Cahier de l'INED* 18 (Paris: PUF, 1952), 309, 315.

120. Duchen, *Women's Rights*, 177.

121. On the more radical feminism of the LFDF, the MJF, and other organizations, see Chaperon, *Les années Beauvoir*, 205, 214–216; and the *Dictionnaire biographique: Militer au XXe siècle: Femmes, féminismes, églises et société*, ed. Evelyne Diebolt (Paris: Michel Houdiard Éditeur, 2009).

122. Jane Jensen, "The Liberation and New Rights for French Women," in *Behind the Lines: Gender and the Two World Wars*, ed. Margaret Randolph Higonnet et al. (New Haven, CT: Yale University Press, 1987), 280. On the conventionality of Communist Party perspectives on the family, see also Gérard Vincent, "Communism as a Way of Life," in *A History of Private Life*, vol. 5: *Riddles of Identity in Modern Times*, ed. Antoine Prost and Gérard Vincent, trans. Arthur Goldhammer (Cambridge, MA: Harvard University Press, 1991), 330–336.

123. As quoted in Sandra Fayolle, "L'Union des femmes françaises et les sentiments supposés féminins," in *Émotions . . . Mobilisation!*, ed. Christophe Traïni (Paris: Presses de la FNPS, 2009), 170.

124. Chaperon, *Les années Beauvoir*, 113–114.

125. Fayolle, "L'Union des femmes françaises," 190–192; Chaperon, *Les années Beauvoir*, 148–149.

126. Germaine Guillé, "Nous les mamans . . . ," *La Revue des Travailleuses* (October–November 1952): 24–25; Fayolle, "L'Union des femmes françaises," 173, 177.

127. As quoted in Fayolle, "L'Union des femmes françaises," 178.

128. Éric Alary and Dominique Veillon, "L'après-guerre des femmes: 1947, un tournant?," in *L'Année 1947*, ed. Serge Berstein and Pierre Milza (Paris: Presses de Sciences Po, 2000), 508.

129. See Laure Adler's account of Duras's commitment to the Communist movement and her exclusion by the party. Laure Adler, *Marguerite Duras: A Life*, trans. Anne-Marie Glasheen (Chicago: University of Chicago Press, 1998), 150–179.

130. She was a secrétaire confédérale in the CGT from 1955 to 1969 and editor of *Antoinette* from 1955 to 1975. Madeleine Colin, *Traces d'une vie dans la mouvance du siècle* (Paris: Éditions Syllepse, 2007), 78. *Antoinette* began in 1952 as *La Revue des Travailleuses*.

131. Ibid., 89–100.

132. Ibid., 87.

133. As quoted in Chaperon, *Les années Beauvoir*, 248.

134. Ibid., 249–250. Renée Rousseau has also argued that party leaders regarded a ruckus over birth control as a welcome diversion from the upheaval and embarrassment that Khrushchev's speech brought to the party (*Femmes rouges*, 242–243). Alfred Sauvy had already observed in 1954 that the party's conservative stance on matters of family and sexuality paralleled an official affirmation of conventional notions of marriage and family in the Soviet Union (*Le Monde*, 12 May 1954).

135. On dissent in the party over birth control and abortion, see Rousseau, *Femmes rouges*, 232–234; Chaperon, *Les années Beauvoir*, 240–241.

136. Rosental, *L'intelligence démographique*, 164. On the importance of policy generalists, see Ezra N. Suleiman, *Politics, Power, and Bureaucracy in France: The Administrative Elite* (Princeton: Princeton University Press, 1974), 99.

137. Lenoir, *Généalogie*, 394.

138. Union internationale des organismes familiaux, Commission des niveaux de vie familiaux, "Dégradation du niveau de vie en function des dimensions de la famille: Principes de méthode" (1958), Pierre Laroque Papers, CAC 20030430, art. 159.

139. Ibid., 230–233.

140. Union internationale des organismes familiaux, Rapport général présenté au Congrès mondial de la famille, 15–23 June 1958, Paris, by Georges Desmottes, Directeur Adjoint chargés de la Famille au Ministère de la Santé Publique et de la Population, Pierre Laroque Papers, CAC 20030430, art. 159. See also Robert Boudet, "Union internationale des organismes familiaux," *Population* 4, no. 2 (1949): 406–408.

141. On Sauvy's involvement in the empire, see Matthew Connelly, *Fatal Misconception: The Struggle to Control World Population* (Cambridge, MA: Harvard University Press, 2008), 181–182. On Robert Debré and the CIE, see Jessica Pearson-Patel, "From the Civilizing Mission to International Development: France, the United Nations, and the Politics of Family Health in Postwar Africa, 1945–1960" (PhD diss., New York University, 2013), chap. 4.

142. On international and colonial networks of expertise, see Deborah J. Neill, *Networks of Tropical Medicine: Internationalism, Colonialism, and the Rise of a Medical Specialty, 1890–1930* (Stanford: Stanford University Press, 2012), 1–11.

143. Quoted in Galant, *Histoire politique*, 73–74.

144. Prestwich, "Modernizing Politics," 212–214; Knibiehler, *Germaine Poinso-Chapuis*, 65.

145. *Antoinette*, June–July 1953, 15–36.

146. Quoted in ibid., 17.

147. Chaperon, *Les années Beauvoir*, 251. Lamaze himself, ironically, supported the cause of birth control reform. For an insightful exploration of Lamaze, the popularity of his method, and the Cold War context in which it was received in France and the United States, see Paula A. Michaels, "Comrades in the Labor Room: The Lamaze Method of Childbirth Preparation and France's Cold War Home Front, 1951–1957," *AHR* 115, no. 4 (October 2010): 1031–1060.

148. As quoted in Yvonne Knibiehler, *La révolution maternelle: Femmes, maternité, citoyenneté depuis 1945* (Paris: Perrin, 1997), 141.

149. On Maternité heureuse, see ibid., 141–144; Chaperon, *Les années Beauvoir*, 238–243; Duchen, *Women's Rights*, 173–175.

150. Jackie Clarke, *France in the Age of Organization: Factory, Home, and Nation from the 1920s to Vichy* (New York: Berghahn, 2011), chap. 3.

151. Claire Duchen, "Occupation Housewife: The Domestic Ideal in 1950s France," *French Cultural Studies* 2, no.1 (1991): 5.

152. For a survey of a variety of forms of domestic science training programs, including the activities supported by the caisses, see the report of Mlle. Lomaze, "L'enseignement ménager et ses répercussions sur la santé familiale," n.d. (circa 1958), archives of the Ministère de la Santé et de la Population, Direction de l'action sociale, CAC 770393, art. 2, enseignement ménager familial (1943–1974). On the idea of making family assistance a national service obligation for young women, see *Temps Présent*, 2 August 1946. The newspaper solicited the views of a number of young women already serving as family aides, and though some liked the egalitarian implications of having young men and women both subject to national service (and one respondent even imagined the virtues of "deintellectualizing" well-off bourgeois young women by having them work for working-class families), most respondents apparently opposed making family assistance a service obligation. As for Michel Debré, he did not give up on the idea, and would return to it, again in vain, when he was minister of economy and finances in mid-1960s. Michel Debré, *Trois républiques*, vol. 3: *Gouverner, 1958–62* (Paris: Albin Michel, 1988), 97.

153. On *travailleuses familiales*, see Richard Ivan Jobs, *Riding the New Wave: Youth and the Representation of France after the Second World War* (Stanford: Stanford University Press, 2007), 71–83; Duchen, *Women's Rights*, 113–114. Family workers were not unique to France. For mention of how weak or robust the commitments to home assistance were in different countries, see the debate in the Conseil de la République (the Senate), 18 March 1958 (*JO*, Conseil de la République, séance de 18 March 1958), 539–541.

154. Ministère de la Santé Publique, *Définition de la travailleuse familiale et des taches qui lui incombent* (n.d., circa 1960), CAC 770393, art. 3.

155. "Témoignages," *Pages Sociales*, August–September 1945, 31, in Archives Départementales des Alpes Maritimes, 127 W 8.

156. Ministère de la Santé Publique, *Définition de la travailleuse familiale et des taches qui lui incombent* (n.d., circa 1960), CAC 770393, art. 3. The change in age requirements sparked controversy because young women aged 18 to 20 had been an important source of recruitment. See the debate in the Conseil de la République (the Senate), 18 March 1958 (*JO*, Conseil de la République, séance de 18 March 1958), 539–541.

157. On household advisers *(conseillères ménagères)*, see "Projet de programme de formation pour les conseillères ménagères," n.d.; Procès-verbal de la réunion du Conseil de perfectionnement de l'enseignement ménager familial, 29 April 1958, Ministère de l'Éducation Nationale, Direction de

l'enseignement technique; and Procès-verbal de la réunion du Conseil de perfectionnement de l'enseignement ménager familial, 28 June 1962, Ministère de l'Éducation Nationale, Direction générale de l'organisation et des programmes scolaires; Note à l'attention de Monsieur le Directeur-Général, Sous-Commission chargée de l'étude du projet relatif aux conseillères ménagères, réunion du 5 février 1954. In CAC 770393, art. 2, Enseignement ménager familial (1943–1974).

158. See, for example, articles in *La Croix* on marriage counseling that had emerged in the 1950s, some versions modeled on "Anglo-Saxon" experience. *La Croix*, 9 February 1951 and 9 August 1957. *Le Monde*, 7 April 1953, took a similar interest in professional efforts to tackle the rising divorce rate. On parental education for better child rearing, see, for example, *Le Monde*, 25 October 1955. The much-emphasized theme of maternal attachment figured prominently in the series "Pour une enfance heureuse" published by *Tribune du Peuple* (see 7 June 1958).

159. See Chapter 7 on linking services and policing. Clifford Rosenberg analyzes that linkage in the interwar years in *Policing Paris: The Origins of Modern Immigration Control between the Wars* (Ithaca, NY: Cornell University Press, 2006). As for the expansion for social work by the 1950s, see Pierre Laroque, "French Social Problems," a lecture given in English in 1952, p. 14, Pierre Laroque papers, CAC 20030430, art. 56, dossier 1952. René Mathevet, a CFTC specialist on social policy, argued that families ought to be able to choose their visiting social worker just like they chose their doctor or pharmacist. See Mathevet, "Action sociale et allocation familiale," *La Revue du Militant "Formation"* 12 (February 1949), in CFTC Archives, 5 H 83.

160. Compte rendu, Sous-Direction de la Coordination des Services Sociaux de la Seine, réunion de la Commission technique du 20 janvier 1954. Archives of the Groupement des industries métallurgiques et minières de la région parisienne, AN 39AS 385. For more on the tension between servicing and policing, see compte rendu, Sous-Direction de la Coordination des Services Sociaux de la Seine, réunion du Conseil de Surveillance du 20 décembre 1955. AN 39AS 385. Representatives from family-oriented associations were given three of the nine consumer seats on the commission. See Rapport general de la Commission d'étude des problèmes de la family, 1960 (hereafter cited as Prigent Report), 19, Archives Michel Debré, 2 DE 50.

161. Pulju, *Women and Mass Consumer Society*, 53–58; Rebecca Pulju, "Consumers for the Nation: Women, Politics, and Consumer Organization in France, 1944–1965,"*Journal of Women's History* 18, no. 3 (Fall 2006): 82–83.

162. On the apartment referendum of 1959, see Nicole Rudolph, " 'Who Should Be the Author of a Dwelling?' Architects versus Housewives in 1950s France," *Gender and History* 21, no. 3 (November 2009): 541–559; W. Brian Newsome, "The 'Apartment Referendum' of 1959: Toward Participatory Architectural and Urban Planning in Postwar France," *FHS* 28, no. 2 (Spring 2005): 329–358; and Pulju, *Women and Mass Consumer Society*, 202–209.

163. On the expansion of the state's role, see Lenoir, "Family Policy," 163–164.

164. Union internationale des organismes familiaux, Rapport général présenté au Congrès mondial de la famille, 15–23 June 1958, Paris, by Georges Desmottes, directeur Adjoint chargé de la Famille au Ministère de la Santé Publique et de la Population, Pierre Laroque Papers, CAC 20030430, art. 159 (see esp. p. 8).

165. Duchen, *Women's Rights,* 104; Prost, "La politique familiale," 15.

166. Alain Girard and Henri Bastide, "Une enquête sur l'efficacité de l'action sociale des caisses d'allocations familiales," *Population* 13, no. 1 (January–March 1958): 50–72.

167. Anne Revillard, "Work/Family Policy in France from State Familialism to State Feminism?," *International Journal of Law, Policy and the Family* 20 (2000): 138. Experts disagreed about how family benefits influenced fertility and to what degree.

168. The high percentage of families benefiting from the subsidy lent credence to this complaint. See "Rapport général de la commission de la main-d'oeuvre du Commissariat général du plan," *Revue Française du Travail* 12 (April–June 1958): 135. For business complaints, see the report of the CNPF's commission sociale, "Ce que nous demandons à la sécurité sociale," June 1950, in the archives of the Conseil national du patronat français, AN 72AS 480. The Paris Chamber of Commerce opposed extending the *salaire unique* to nonsalaried employees, on the grounds of both costs and the likelihood of fraud. Chambre de Commerce de Paris, Revalorisation des prestations familiailes, Projet de letter à M. le Président du conseil et adopté par la Chambre de Commerce de Paris, dans la séance générale du 19 Décembre 1957, AN 72AS 132.

169. Lenoir, "Family Policy," 162; Duchen, *Women's Rights,* 105. On FO's opposition to the *salaire unique,* see *Le Figaro,* 24 October 1955.

170. *Antoinette* (December 1960, January and February 1961). See also Chaperon, *Les années Beauvoir,* 287.

171. Lenoir, *Généalogie,* 347.

172. On Plan III and women's training, see the report of the working group on manpower, p. 8, in the archives of the Commissariat général du Plan, AN 80 AJ 145, also published in *Revue Française du Travail* 12 (April–June 1958).

173. Pierre Fougeyrollas, "Prédominance du mari ou de la femme dans le ménage: Une enquête sur la vie familiale," *Population* 6, no. 1 (January–March 1951): 83–101. The small but growing family planning movement of the 1950s called further attention to the value of women's autonomy within the couple. See Mathilde Dubesset, "Les figures du féminin à travers deux revues féminines, l'une catholique, l'autre proteste, *La Femme dans la Vie Sociale* et *Jeunes Femmes,* dans les années 1950–1960," *MS* 198 (January–March 2002): 31.

174. *Réalités* 114 (July 1955): 30–37, 81–85. See also Paul Chombart de Lauwe, "Que sera la famille de demain?,' *La Tribune du Peuple,* 30 May 1959; and Prost, "La politique familiale," 15–16; Claire Laubier, ed., *The Condition of Women in France, 1945 to the Present: A Documentary Anthology* (London: Routledge, 1990), 30.

175. Lenoir, "Family Policy," 162. In 1957 the UNCAF journal published an article on the economic value of housework: L. Vimeux, "La valeur économique du travail ménager," *Information Sociales* 11 (1957): 995–997. Rebecca Pulju also links this shift to growing recognition of women as consumers. Pulju, *Women and Mass Consumer Society*, 59.

176. *La Femme dans la Vie Sociale* 33 (October–December 1955): 4, 14–15.

177. "Faut-il supprimer l'allocation de salaire unique?," *Cahiers des Groupes Reconstruction* 13 (October 1954): 19–20, CFTC Archives, 3 F 8.

178. Dreyfus et al., *Se protéger, être protégé*, 305.

179. The Communist and CGT presence in family caisses diminished further after 1948. See Rapport général de la Commission d'étude des problèmes de la famille, 1960, Archives Michel Debré, 2 DE 50. On comparing social security and family caisses, see Antoinette Catrice-Lorey, *Dynamique interne de la sécurité sociale* (Paris: Économica, 1982), 140–155. Employers experienced the difference acutely. See Projet de circulaire aux fédérations sur la position du CNFP au regard des projets gouvernementaux connus sous le nom de "projet de budget social de la nation," 6 December 1952, AN 72AS 474, dossier on Réforme de l'oganisation de la sécurite sociale, 1951–1953.

180. Daniel Mayer, speaking in the National Assembly, 11 July 1949, as quoted in Dreyfus et al., *Se protéger, être protégé*, 302.

181. *Le Monde*, 30 July 1948.

182. Le Secrétariat d'État au travail et à la Sécurité sociale à M. le Directeur Régional de la Sécurité sociale de Lyon, 3 July 1957, CAC 800100, art. 6, dossier Lyon.

183. Études et documents du centre de recherches économiques et sociales, June 1954, AN 72AS 475, dossier on Réforme de l'organisation de la sécurité sociale, 1951–1955. On the 1952 turning point in transferring the surpluses, see Rapport général de la Commission d'étude des problèmes de la famille, 1960, Archives Michel Debré, 2 DE 50. Employer contributions to the family caisses were reduced 2.5 percent in recognition of the surplus, but the transfers still continued.

184. On cracking down on employers, see *Le Peuple*, 11–18 April 1951. On harmful bureaucratization, see the CGT's 1950 social security election leaflet, AN 39AS 994. The CGT's representative on the Labor Ministry's national standing committee on family allowances sought to protect the autonomy of the family caisses. Section permanente de la Commission supérieure des allocations familiales, procès-verbal de la séance du 4 janvier 1955, p. 4, CAC 760231, art. 38 (SS 938).

185. "Travail" 6 (October 1955), a campaign leaflet in 39 AS 994. On the Commission supérieure des allocations familiales in 1950, both FO's Lebel and the CGT's Mario had sought to limit the Administration's supervisory authority over the caisses. Commission supérieure des allocations familiales, Procès-verbal de la séance du 29 novembre 1950, CAC 760231, art. 36 (SS 936).

186. *Syndicalisme*, 11–17 March 1954.

187. Ibid., 25–31 March 1954 and 21–27 July 1955.

188. On the Rueff-Armand Report, see Lenoir, "La politique familiale," 166.

189. Prigent Report, 1960, 53, Michel Debré papers, 2 DE 50.

190. Prigent Report, 1960, 56. For Robert Debré as the "most natalist" member, see CNPF, Commission de sécurité sociale, Compte rendu de la réunion du 18 octobre 1960, AN 72AS 458.

191. *Combat*, 7 February 1959.

192. Prigent Report, 1960, 93–94.

193. Debré note to his ministers of interior, labor, agriculture, public health, finance, public works, industry, and domestic commerce, 17 July 1961, Archives Michel Debré, 2 DE 49.

194. For an example of questioning the taboo of means-testing family benefits, see the procès-verbaux of the Conseil Économique, Commission des Affaires Sociales, 27 November 1957, AN 72AS 492. On the Labor Ministry's antipathy toward the *salaire unique,* see Compte rendu de la réunion du mardi 13 décembre 1960, Commission de Sécurité Sociale, AN 72AS 533.

195. Note provisoire pour M. le Premier Ministre, 21 October 1961, Archives Michel Debré, 2 DE 49. For the contrasting perspectives of Debré's advisers, see also in this dossier the notes prepared for him dated 20 June; 20, 23, and 25 September; and 21, 23, 24, and 25 October, 1961.

196. Lenoir, "La politique familiale," 167.

197. See the 1962 election leaflets in AN 39AS 994.

198. Even by the late 1960s family supports still accounted for 4 to 5 percent of national income. Pierre Laroque, "Social Security in France," in *Social Security in International Perspective: Essays in Honor of Eveline M. Burns,* ed. Shirley Jenkins (New York: Columbia University Press, 1969), 181. On comparative old-age pensions as a percentage of national income in 1962, see Charles Mabit, Évolution des prestations sociales et financement de la sécurité sociale Conseil Économique et Social, 21 septembre 1962, AN 72AS 490.

199. Laroque, "Social Security in France," 182. Experts also debated the application and efficacy of family allowances in Algeria (discussed in Chapter 7, as is the inequity of family policies in the overseas *départements*).

200. On popular support for family benefits, see Jacques Doublet, "Observations sur le rapport de la Commission de la famille," Haut Comité consultatif de la population et de la famille (n.d., but likely 1961), CAC 860269, art. 1; Colin Dyer, *Population and Society in Twentieth-Century France* (New York: Holmes and Meier, 1978), 152–154.

201. On the next wave of innovation, see Anne Revillard, "Work/Family Policy," 133–150.

5 · Enterprise Politics

1. On the Constitution, see Dominique Borne, *Histoire de la société française depuis 1945* (Paris: Armand Colin, 1988), 21.

2. On women's rights in the Constitution, see Hanna Diamond, *Women and the Second World War in France, 1939–48: Choices and Constraints* (New York: Longman, 1999), 173.

3. Italians, including Communists, had little stomach for nationalizations and planning after fascism, and although the West Germans adopted co-management in enterprises, in 1945–1949 they lacked the state sovereignty to embark on nationalizations and planning. Britain had postwar nationalizations aplenty, but they were largely "technocratic," as Claire Andrieu argues: the unions and Labor Party did not regard public enterprises as places to challenge business hierarchies, nor did they endorse works councils, which on the basis of the World War I experience they regarded as threats to union power. If Austria adopted works councils and nationalizations, though not planning, it did so along conservative and nationalistic lines. See Claire Andrieu, "La France à gauche de l'Europe," *MS* 134 (January–March 1986):131–154. See also Adolf Sturmthal, "Nationalization and Workers' Control in Britain and France," *Journal of Political Economy* 61, no. 1 (February 1953): 43–79.

4. From 1948 to 1953, the EDF, GDF, Charbonnages de France, and SNCF received more than half of the money from the Fonds de modernization et d'équipement (FME), which was largely financed via the Marshall Plan. Laure Quennouëlle-Corre, *La direction du trésor, 1947–1967: L'État-banquier et la croissance* (Paris: Comité pour l'histoire économique et financière de la France, 2000), 217. The U.S. State Department overruled American expert and business objections to supporting nationalized firms in France. See Patrick Fridenson, "Réflexions sur les étapes de la nationalisation de l'électricité," in *La nationalisation de l'électricité: Nécessité technique ou logique politique?*, ed. Laurence Badel (Paris: Association pour l'histoire de l'électricité en France, 1996), 390–391. Nationalized firms absorbed more than half of domestic total investment during the Fourth Republic. Maurice Larkin, *France since the Popular Front: Government and People, 1936–1986* (Oxford: Oxford University Press, 1988), 189. See also Gérard Bossuat, "Les entreprises publiques dans le Plan Marshall," in Badel, *La nationalisation de l'électricité*, 343–370.

5. For an illuminating analysis of nationalizing Renault, see Patrick Fridenson, "Le périple de la nationalisation de Renault," *Renault Histoire* 33 (October 2014): 63–84. See also Fridenson, "Renault, une régie à la conquête de l'autonomie," in *Les nationalisations de la libération: De l'utopie au compromise*, ed. Claire Andrieu, Lucette Le Van, and Antoine Prost (Paris: Presses de la FNSP, 1987), 279–293; Fridenson, "La bataille de la 4 CV Renault," *L'Histoire* 9 (February 1979): 33–40; Cyrille Sardais, *Patron de Renault: Pierre Lefaucheux, 1944–1955* (Paris: Presses de Sciences Po, 2009); and Emmanuel Chadeau, *Louis Renault: Biographie* (Paris: Plon, 1998), 408–409.

6. F. Ridley and J. Blondel, *Public Administration in France*, with an introduction by Peter Campbell, 2nd ed. (London: Routledge and Kegan Paul, 1969), 236.

7. *JO, Débats de l'Assemblée Constituante*, 20 November 1945, *Année 1945*, 10.

8. Ibid.

9. On the waves of nationalization, see Antoine Prost, "Une pièce en trois actes," in Andrieu, Le Van, and Prost, *Les nationalisations de la libération*, 236–246; Michel Margairaz, "Companies under Public Control in France, 1900–1950," in *Governance, Industry and Labour Markets in Britain and France: The Modernising State in the Mid-Twentieth Century*, ed. Noel Whiteside and Robert Salais (London: Routledge, 1998); and Jean-Charles Asselain, "Les nationalisations, 1944–45," in *Études sur la France de 1939 à nos jours* (Paris: Éditions du Seuil, 1985), 180–207. On the comparison with Britain, see Adolf Sturmthal, "The Structure of Nationalized Enterprises in France," *Political Science Quarterly* 67 (1952): 357–377; Sturmthal, "Nationalization and Workers' Control"; Mario Einaudi, Maurice Byé, and Ernesto Rossi, *Nationalization in France and Italy* (Ithaca, NY: Cornell University Press, 1955), 33–44; and Ridley and Blondel, *Public Administration in France*, 233–255.

10. Darryl Holter, "Mineworkers and Nationalization in France: Insights in Concepts of State Theory," *Politics and Society* 11, no. 1 (1982): 32.

11. Margairaz, "Companies under Public Control," 38–39.

12. On the aircraft industry, see Herrick Chapman, *State Capitalism and Working-Class Radicalism in the French Aircraft Industry* (Berkeley: University of California Press, 1991); Emmanuel Chadeau, *L'industrie aéronautique en France, 1900–1950: De Blériot à Dassault* (Paris: Fayard, 1987); Claude d'Abzac-Epezy, "La reconstruction dans l'industrie aéronautique: L'exemple français, 1944–1946," *Histoire, Économie et Société* 18, no. 2 (1999): 435–449.

13. Ridley and Blondel, *Public Administration in France*, 235.

14. On Philip's plan, see Richard F. Kuisel, *Capitalism and the State in Modern France* (New York: Cambridge University Press, 1981),177–179.

15. René Courtin, *Rapport sur la politique économique d'après-guerre* (Algiers: Éditions "Combat", 1944), 17, 21.

16. Claire Andrieu, "Comment la nationalisation entra dans le programme du CNR?," in Andrieu, Le Van, and Prost, *Les nationalisations de la libération*, 58.

17. Claire Andrieu, "De Gaulle," in Andrieu, Le Van, and Prost, *Les nationalisations de la libération*, 233.

18. Ibid., 59–60.

19. *La Vie Française*, 24 November 1945.

20. Prost, "Une pièce en trois actes," 237.

21. Henri Morsel, "Paul Ramadier et l'électricité," in *Paul Ramadier, la République et le socialisme*, ed. Serge Berstein (Paris: Éditions Complexe, 1988), 327.

22. "Note de MM Billoux et Tillon sur les projets de nationalisations soumis par M le Ministre de l'Économie Nationale," 5 March 1945, Georges Bidault Papers, AN 457AP 141.

23. Quoted in Asselain, "Les nationalisations," 184.

24. Fridenson, "La puissance publique et les nationalisations," unpublished paper given at the colloque "La France en voie de modernization, 1944–52,"

4–5 December 1981, Fondation nationale des sciences politiques; Jean Bouvier, "Sur la politique économique en 1944–1946," in *La libération de la
France*, Actes du Colloque International tenu à Paris du 28 au 31 octobre
1974 (Paris: Édition du CNRS, 1976).

25. Andrew Shennan, *Rethinking France: Plans for Renewal, 1940–1946* (Oxford: Clarendon Press, 1989), 244.

26. Programme de travail du Ministère de l'Économie nationale, octobre
1944–décembre 1944. Exposé fait par le ministre de l'Économie nationale
au Conseil des ministres, 17 November 1944. Gaston Cusin Papers, AEF,
5 A 15.

27. Dominique Barjot and Henri Morsel, "La nationalisation de l'électricité:
Nécessité technique ou logique politique?," in Badel, *La nationalisation
de l'électricité*, 14–15. Deputies also debated how centralized (or regional-
ized) the new energy companies should be. See Réflexions préliminaires
sur une réorganisation de l'industrie électrique, 12 January 1945, Paul
Ramadier Papers, 52 J 42; and Fridenson, "Réflexions," 387–389.

28. For aircraft, see Chapman, *State Capitalism*; for coal, see Darryl Holter,
*The Battle for Coal: Miners and the Politics of Nationalization in
France, 1940–50* (DeKalb: Northern Illinois University Press, 1992); Ro-
lande Trempé, *Les trois batailles du charbon, 1936–1947* (Paris: Éditions
La Découverte, 1989); and Évelyne Desbois, Yves Jeanneau, and Bruno
Mattéi, *La foi des charbonniers: Les mineurs dans la Bataille du charbon,
1945–1947* (Paris: Éditions de la Maison des Sciences de l'Homme, 1986);
for the EDF, see Robert L. Frost, *Alternating Currents: Nationalized
Power in France, 1946–1970* (Ithaca, NY: Cornell University Press, 1991);
and Georges Malville, "La naissance de l'électricité de France," in *Histoire
de l'électricité en France*, vol. 3: *1946–1987*, ed. Henri Morsel (Paris: Fayard,
1996), 35–96.

29. Christian Chevandier and Georges Ribeill, "Louis Armand," in *Dictionnaire historique des patrons français*, ed. Jean-Claude Daumas (Paris:
Flammarion, 2010), 29–31.

30. Frost, *Alternating Currents*, 72. On workers' participation in management, see also Adam Steinhouse, *Workers' Participation in Post-Liberation
France* (Lanham, MD: Lexington Books, 2001).

31. Fridenson, "La puissance publique"; Fridenson, "Renault," 293; François
Bloch-Lainé and Jean Bouvier, *La France restaurée, 1944–1954: Dialogue
sur les choix d'une modernisation* (Paris: Fayard, 1986), 116.

32. See Union des Ingénieurs et Techniciens Français et le projet de nationalisation de l'électricité et du gaz, "Résolution," n.d., Paul Ramadier Papers,
52 J 42.

33. As quoted in Alain Beltran and Jean-François Picard, "EDF, pour la modernization," in Andrieu, Le Van, and Prost, *Les nationalisations de la
libération*, 336. On the labor statute in the EDF-GDF, see also Frost, *Alternating Currents*, 70–75; and Jeanne Siwek-Poudesseau, "L'élaboration
du statut du personnel," in Badel, *La nationalisation de l'électricité*,
413–423.

34. On shared power as a basis for postwar settlement, see Irwin Wall, "The French Social Contract: Conflict and Cooperation," *International Labor and Working-Class History* 50 (Fall 1996): 117.

35. This was the language in an unsigned note, "Nationalisations," dated 18 November 1947, archives of the Conseil national du patronat français, AN 72AS 90.

36. René Mayer, "Democratie et nationalisations," *France-Libre*, 14 May 1947.

37. François Lefrançois, "Le 'procès' des nationalisations," *Le Populaire*, 15 July 1949.

38. Pierre Commin, "Non M. Paul Reynaud!," *Le Populaire*, 9 June 1949.

39. *Le Peuple*, 28 October 1948.

40. "Les industries nationalisées à la recherché de leur structure définitive," *La Cote Desfossés*, 4 May 1948.

41. Claire Andrieu, Lucette Le Van, and Antoine Prost, "Des nationalisations de 1946 à celles de 1981," in Andrieu, Le Van, and Prost, *Les nationalisations de la libération*, 363.

42. On conflict in nationalized industry from 1947 to the early 1950s, see, on coal, Holter, *The Battle for Coal*, and Roland Trempé, "Les Charbonnages, un cas social," in Andrieu, Le Van, and Prost, *Les nationalisations de la libération*; on aviation, see Chapman, *State Capitalism*, 256–316; on the EDF, see Frost, *Alternating Currents*.

43. Unsigned article, "Les hauts fonctionnaires complices," *Le Peuple*, 15 September 1949.

44. "Les nationalisations vues par M. Léon Jouhaux," *La Croix*, 31 May 1951.

45. Raymond Aron, "Réforme des nationalisations?," *Gazette de Lausanne*, 9 June 1949.

46. Unsigned article, "Les nationalisations, bases de la dictature," *Le Bulletin de France Documents*,16 July 1948.

47. On "gravediggers," see *Revue Mensuelle*, special number, 13 April 1948 (publication of the Comité d'entreprise of SNECMA); on betrayal of national interest, see Commin, "Non M. Paul Reynaud!"

48. Antoine Prost, "Avant-propos," in Andrieu, Le Van, and Prost, *Les nationalisations de la libération*, 15.

49. Pierre Uri, "La querelle des nationalisations," *Le Temps Moderne* 45 (July 1949): 165–170.

50. On CNPF frustration over the channeling of Marshall Plan funds into public enterprises, see Compte rendu de la réunion tenue dans le Bureau de M. Dreyfus, directeur du cabinet de M. Lacoste, 25 March 1949, AN 72AS 218.

51. See the minutes of the meetings of the Commission des Investissements, created in 1948 to address the allocation of resources for industrial reconstruction and modernization. The committee continued until 1955. Many meetings included discussions of the steel industry. Minutes can be found in the archives of the Ministère des Finances, Direction du trésor, AEF, B 42268 and B 42269. On the steel industry in the first three plans, see Philippe Mioche, "Le plan et la sidérurgie: Du soutien mitigé l'effacement

possible (1946–1960)," in *De Monnet à Massé: Enjeux politiques et objectifs économiques dans le cadre des quatre premiers plans (1946–1965)*, ed. Henry Rousso (Paris: Éditions du CNRS, 1986), 127–137.

52. Socialist heavyweight Robert Lacoste made a point of emphasizing how private business had come to recognize that it benefited from the EDF, the GDF, the Charbonnages de France, and the state's leadership role in prospecting for oil resources. See Claude Delmas, "La 'débudgétisation' des investissments," *Combat*, 19 October 1953.

53. On the adaptation of private business to nationalization, see Henry Ehrmann, *Organized Business in France* (Princeton: Princeton University Press, 1943), 344–354; Chapman, *State Capitalism*, 289–294.

54. As quoted in Ehrman, *Organized Business in France*, 351.

55. On the mutually reinforcing effects of state intervention in industry and political radicalism in the workforce, see Chapman, *State Capitalism*, 299–316.

56. Fridenson, "Réflexions," 389–390

57. On investment planning, and lack of implementation, in the 1930s, see Margairaz, "Companies under Public Control," 40, 48.

58. EDF chief Pierre Simon got a rude reception at Société Générale when he tried to get financing in 1946–1947. See Martine Bungener, "L'électricité et les trois premiers plans: Une symbiose réussie," in Rousso, *De Monnet à Massé*, 111.

59. On Société Générale and bank nationalizations generally, see Lisa Maguire, "Contingent Obligations: Société Générale and the French State, 1945–1981" (PhD diss., New York University, 2003). The parapublic bank Crédit national was founded in 1919 to function as a private bank in the public interest, especially for channeling state funds to industry. See Patrice Baubeau, Arnaud Lavit d'Hautefort, and Michel Lescure, *Le Crédit national: Histoire publique d'une société privée* (Paris: Éditions Jean-Claude Lattès, 1994). Crédit agricole played a similar role for agriculture, as did Crédit foncier for housing, and Crédit hôtelier for tourism. The Caisse des dépôts et consignations was founded in 1816, after the Napoleonic wars, to safeguard public funds. By the 1940s it had become the state's largest financial institution, a veritable internal banking department for the Treasury.

60. "La nationalisation des banques a-t-elle échoué," *L'Observateur*, 5 October 1954.

61. Maguire, "Contingent Obligations," 187.

62. François Bloch-Lainé remarks on the restored self-confidence of the bankers in *Profession, Fonctionnaire: Entretiens avec Françoise Carrière* (Paris: Éditions du Seuil, 1976), 105. Also on bank nationalization, see Claire Andrieu, "Les banques, par fidélité au programme du CNR," in Andrieu, Le Van, and Prost, *Les nationalisations de la libération*, 310–326.

63. The only top bank executives purged at the Liberation were Henri Ardant, at Société Générale and a key architect of Vichy's bank regulation law of 1941, Yves Bréart de Boisanger at the Bank of France, and the latter's deputy, René Villard. Maguire, "Contingent Obligations," 111.

64. On investment for the modernization drive, see Michael Loriaux, "The French Developmental State as Myth and Moral Ambition," in *The Developmental State*, ed. Meredith Woo-Cumings (Ithaca, NY: Cornell University Press, 1999), 258–259; and Jean-Pierre Rioux, *The Fourth Republic, 1944–1958* (New York: Cambridge University Press, 1987), 175. For essential accounts of how Monnet, Bloch-Lainé, and others improvised to fund the Monnet Plan, see Michel Margairaz, *L'État, les finances et l'économie: Histoire d'une conversion, 1932–1952*, vol. 2 (Paris: Comité pour l'histoire économique et financière de la France, 1991), 1038–1047; Laure Quennouëlle-Corre, *La direction du trésor*, 89–131; Frances M. B. Lynch, *France and the International Economy: From Vichy to the Treaty of Rome* (London: Routledge, 1997), 72–102; and Richard F. Kuisel, *Capitalism and the State in Modern France: Renovation and Economic Management in the Twentieth Century* (New York: Cambridge University Press, 1981), 237–242.

65. On this method of securing participation by the big nationalized banks in the modernizing drive, see Bloch-Lainé, *Profession, Fonctionnaire*, 104–105; Maguire, "Contingent Obligations," 153–155, 218.

66. Bloch-Lainé and Bouvier, *La France restaurée*, 144–145.

67. "La nationalisation des banques a-t-elle échoué"; "Les hauts fonctionnaires complices," *Le Peuple*, 15 September 1949.

68. Frost, *Alternating Currents*, 32–33.

69. Michel Dreyfus, "Les activités sociales et culturelles à l'EDF-GDF," in Morsel, *Histoire de l'électricité de France*, 3:274.

70. On disciplining Marcel Paul, see Michel Dreyfus, "Les luttes sociales à l'EDF-GDF de la Libération à nos jours," in Morsel, *Histoire de l'électricité de France*, 3:225–227; and Val R. Lorwin, *The French Labor Movement* (Cambridge, MA: Harvard University Press, 1954), 165–166.

71. Dreyfus, "Les luttes sociales," 219–220.

72. On "mystique," see CFTC, Fédérations des cadres et du personnel des syndicats chrétiens des service publics et concédés, Rapport remis à chaque membre du Gouvernement le 8 décembre 1945, "Nationalisation des industries électriques et gazières," AEF, B 9810.

73. Gabrielle Hecht, *The Radiance of France: Nuclear Power and National Identity after World War II* (Cambridge, MA: MIT Press, 2009), chap. 4. On the EDF unions' embrace of technology, centralization, and expansion, see also Frost, *Alternating Currents*, 5, 85, 252.

74. See Martine Bungener, "Le role des pouvoirs publics: Une tutelle contraignante mais obligeante," in Morsel, *Histoire de l'électricité de France*, 3:315; Bungener, "L'électricité et les trois premiers plans," 112–114, 120; Michel Banal, "Le Plan Marshall et l'électricité," in *Le Plan Marshall et le relèvement économique de l'Europe* (Paris: Comité pour l'histoire économique et financière de la France, 1993), 251–264; Hubert Bonin, *Histoire économique de la IVe République* (Paris: Économica, 1987), 182. See also the minutes of meetings of the Commission des investissements, 27 October 1952, and 21 February 1953, AEF, B 42269. On hydroelectricity on the Rhône, see Sara B. Pritchard, *Confluence: The Nature of Technology*

and the Remaking of the Rhône (Cambridge, MA: Harvard University Press, 2011).

75. See Robert L. Frost, "The Flood of 'Progress': Technocrats and Peasants at Tignes (Savoy), 1946–1952," *FHS* 14, no. 1 (Spring 1985): 117–140. On the scarcity of locations, see Bungener, "L'électricité," 116.

76. For an instance of the latter, see Éric Kocher-Marboeuf, *Le patricien et le général: Jean-Marcel Jeanneney et Charles de Gaulle, 1958–1969*, vol. 1 (Paris: Comité pour l'histoire économique et financière de la France, 2003), 335.

77. *Force Ouvrière*, 9 February 1956.

78. Ibid., 17 January 1957.

79. Frost, *Alternating Currents*, 199–200; Hecht, *The Radiance of France*, 375–378.

80. Ridley and Blondel, *Public Administration in France*, 247–248.

81. Michel Dreyfus, "Marcel Paul et les origines du CCOS," in Badel, *La nationalisation de l'électricité*, 303–313.

82. The government also diluted CGT influence on the Conseil supérieur de l'électricité et du gaz by adding representatives from Algeria, from the non-nationalized branches of the industry, and from the minority unions at the EDF and GDF. Ministère de l'Industrie et de l'Énergie, Conseil supérieur de l'électricité et du gaz, Rapport, 1951, Projet de décret, portant réglement d'administration publique, modifiant le décret du 17 mai 1946 relatif à l'organisation du Conseil supérieur de l'électricité et du gaz, archives of the Direction du gaz, de l'électricité et du charbon, IND 22092.

83. Frost, *Alternating Currents*, 234–235.

84. Dreyfus, "Les activités," 313.

85. Price inflation for electricity was significantly lower than average for industrial goods. On this and on the growth of self-financed investment at the EDF, see *Le Monde*, 30 September 1959, and *La Vie Française*, 2 October 1959.

86. Bungener, "Le role des pouvoirs publics," 317.

87. On the complex history of CCOS, see Dreyfus, "Les activités." On the return of CGT representatives to the company board, see Henri Morsel, "Conclusion générale," in Morsel, *Histoire de l'électricité en France*, 3:1000.

88. On lagging wages, see the interview with Marcel Paul in *L'Humanité*, 10 October 1959. See also Éric Kocher-Marboeuf, "L'expansion industrielle au service de l'ambition nationale," in *Michel Debré, premier ministre, 1959–1962*, ed. Serge Berstein, Pierre Milza, and Jean-François Sirinelli (Paris: Presses de la FNSP, 2005), 321–322.

89. Premier Ministre, Cabinet, Note, "Rémunérations du Secteur Public," 28 October 1961, Archives Michel Debré, 2 DE 49.

90. On Jeanneney's views on "l'économie concertée," see Jean-Marcel Jeanneney, "Espoirs et difficultés d'une 'économie concertée,'" *Jeune Patron*, January 1961, 11–14.

91. On the wage struggle at EDF during the Debré government, see Kocher-Marboeuf, *Le patricien*, 297–312.

92. *L'Humanité*, 23 April 1953. See also Frost, *Alternating Currents*, 153.
93. After stepping down as directeur général, Gaspard stayed on for two years in the less important post of company president. Alain Beltran, "Dirigeants d'EDF," in Daumas, *Dictionnaire historique*, 265–268.
94. The CGT's influence on the administrative board of the Charbonnages extended beyond holding nearly all the employee seats. Mine union leader Léon Delfosse held one of the state's seats. Two CGT members (and one CFTC member) held seats assigned to consumers, of which there were six. See *Le Bulletin Économique de la Société d'Études Économiques et Documentaires*, 30 July 1946, AEF, B 9805.
95. Holter, *The Battle for Coal*, 96–98.
96. On the 1948 strike, see ibid., chap. 6; George Ross, *Workers and Communists in France: From Popular Front to Eurocommunism* (Berkeley: University of California Press, 1982), 55–58; and Xavier Vigna, *Histoire des ouvriers en France au XXe siècle* (Paris: Perrin, 2012), 177.
97. The nine regional units with the Charbonnages, in order of economic importance, were Nord and Pas-de-Calais, Lorraine, Loire, Cévennes, Acquitaine, Blanzy, Provence, Auvergne, and Dauphiné. Ridley and Blondel, *Public Administration in France*, 245.
98. Bernard Chenot, *Les entreprises nationalisées* (Paris: PUF, 1956), 41.
99. On America's role in the ECSC, see John Gillingham, *Coal, Steel, and the Rebirth of Europe, 1945–1955: The Germans and French from Ruhr Conflict to Economic Community* (Cambridge: Cambridge University Press, 1991); Gérard Bossuat, *La France, l'aide américaine et la construction européenne, 1944–1954*, 2 vols. (Paris: Comité pour l'histoire économique et financière de la France, 1992), chap. 20; and Michael Sutton, *France and the Construction of Europe, 1944–2007* (Oxford: Berghahn, 2007).
100. On tonnage, see Chenot, *Les entreprises nationalisées*, 44. On limiting French coal production within the ECSC, see Alan S. Milward, *The Reconstruction of Western Europe, 1945–51* (Berkeley: University of California Press, 1984), 410.
101. Productivity figures in Warren C. Baum, *The French Economy and the State* (Princeton: Princeton University Press, 1958), 195. On new equipment and investment, see Holter, *The Battle for Coal*, 186–187. On American aid for French coal, Jean-Paul Thuillier, "Les Charbonnages de France et le Plan Marshall," in *Le Plan Marshall et le relèvement économique de l'Europe*, ed. René Girault and Maurice Lévy-Leboyer (Paris: Comité pour l'histoire économique et financière de la France, 1993), 331–333.
102. Holter, *The Battle for Coal*, 190–191.
103. Bonin, *Histoire économique*, 331.
104. Donald Reid, *The Miners of Decazeville: A Genealogy of Deindustrialization* (Cambridge, MA: Harvard University Press, 1985), 190.
105. Ridley and Blondel, *Public Administration in France*, 246.
106. As quoted in Trempé, *Les trois batailles*, 235. In the 1950s officials disagreed over how much financial independence the Charbonnages should have from the ministries. See, for example, the discussion of the Commission des investissements on 21 February 1953, AEF, B 42269.

107. François Sellier, *La confrontation sociale en France, 1936–1981* (Paris: PUF, 1984), 164–166.

108. Reid, *The Miners of Decazeville*, 197.

109. Kocher-Marboeuf, *Le patricien*, 184; Reid, *The Miners of Decazeville*, 198.

110. As quoted in Reid, *The Miners of Decazeville*, 203.

111. Serge Berstein, *The Republic of de Gaulle, 1958–69*, trans. Peter Morris (Cambridge: Cambridge University Press, 1993), 139–140.

112. George Ross, *Workers and Communists*, 134.

113. Baum, *Les entreprises nationalisées*, 197; John Sheahan, *Promotion and Control of Industry in Postwar France* (Cambridge, MA: Harvard University Press, 1963), 191–192.

114. Quoted in Trempé, "Les Charbonnages," 309.

115. On the PCF's anti-ECSC position, see Kocher-Marboeuf, *Le patricien*, 125.

116. Chenot, *Les entreprises nationalisées*, 44.

117. Steinhouse, *Worker's Liberation*, 156. The CGT's railway union leader had been warning the SNCF about employee frustration with wage stagnation. See, for example, Procès-verbal, 5 February 1947, Conseil d'administration, SNCF, AN 14F 12865.

118. *La Vie Ouvrière*, 19 June 1947.

119. On the railroad strikes, Marie-Renée Valentin, "Les grèves des cheminots français au cours de l'année 1947," *MS* 130 (January–March 1985): 55–80; Christian Chevandier, *Cheminots en grève, ou, La construction d'une identité (1848–2001)* (Paris: Maissoneuve et Larose, 2002), 242–259; and Chevandier, "Le personnel des ateliers S.N.C.F. d'Oullin (1938–1948)," *Bulletin du Centre d'Histoire Économique et Sociale de la Région Lyonnaise* 1 (1987): 51–59. On the road lobby, see Georges Rebeill, "La SNCF au temps du Plan Marshall: Les années noires d'une entreprise publique," in Girault and Lévy-Leboyer, *Le Plan Marshall*, 326–327; and Joseph Jones, *The Politics of Transport in Twentieth-Century France* (Kingston: McGill-Queen's University Press, 1984), 181–182.

120. Three strikers died in Marseille at the hands of police, and another sixteen people perished in a train derailment near Arras thought to have been caused by a deliberate act of sabotage by strikers. Valentin, "Les grèves" 73–75. For a discussion of this incident, and of the CGT losing seats on the SNCF board, see Chevandier, *Cheminots en grève*, 254–259, 267.

121. SNCF, Rapport du Conseil d'administration sur l'exercice 1948, AEF, B 3331.

122. Chenot, *Les entreprises nationalisées*, 60–61; Chevandier, *Cheminots en grève*, 289.

123. "L'enthouiasme ou Louis Armand," *Réalités*, December 1956, 161.

124. These figures respectively from Jacob Meunier, "The Politics of High Speed Rail in France, 1944–1983" (PhD diss., Brandeis University, 2001); Jones, *The Politics of Transport*, 195–196; and Bonin, *Histoire économique*, 331.

125. Train engineers and many other workers retired at age 50, more sedentary employees at fifty-five. Baum, *The French Economy*, 203.

126. *La Vie Ouvrière*, 16 November 1950. Closing secondary rail lines triggered protest by unions defending jobs and by politicians protecting localities.

See *Le Bulletin Économique de la Société d'Études Économiquies et Docu-mentaires*, 29 March 1949, in AEF B 33507.

127. *Réalités*, February 1951, 58.

128. CNPF also lobbied in behalf of the private transport sector. See procès-verbal, CNPF, Comité Directeur, 19 December 1950, and 14 December 1954, AN 72AS 74; letter from Georges Villiers (president of the CNPF) to M. Chaban-Delmas, ministre des travaux publics, des transport et du tour-isme, 26 November 1954, AN 72AS 111.

129. Jones, *The Politics of Transport*, 188–193; Nicolas Neiertz, *La coordination des transports en France: De 1918 à nos jours* (Paris: Comité d'histoire économique et financières de la France, 1999), 356–358; "Les nationalisa-tions contre la nation," *Le Bulletin de France Documents*, 27 June 1947.

130. Neiertz, *La coordination des transports*, 356–357.

131. Common Market efforts to integrate transport networks, as well as Japan's breakthrough to high-speed rails, inspired further innovation at SNCF in the mid-1960s. See Meunier, "Politics of High Speed Rail," chap. 4; and Neiertz, *La coordination des transports*, 437–441. On Louis Armand and the Rueff-Armand Report, see Chevandier, *Cheminots en grève*, 267.

132. Ross, *Workers and Communists*, 111.

133. Text of the address, 12 June 1959, Archives Michel Debré, 2 DE 49.

134. Note pour M. le premier ministre, Renseignements concernant la grève des cheminots du mardi 16 juin 1959, Archives Michel Debré, 2 DE 49.

135. Penalties could include fines from 4,000 to 186,000 francs, temporary or permanent dismissal, and prison time of a month to a year. *Paris-Journal*, 13 June 1959. On the retreat of the railway unions, see Ross, *Workers and Communists*, 111–112.

136. Both quotations in Lorwin, *The French Labor Movement*, 199.

137. Philippe Brachet, *L'État-patron: Théories et réalités* (Paris: Syros, 1973), 215.

138. Ministère des Finances, Note pour le Directeur, Réunion de la Commis-sion de Coordination des Salaires, 2 September 1955, AEF B 124.

139. The Treasury and Budget departments also each developed special rela-tions with enterprises—the former, for example, with Renault, EDF, and Air France, the latter with the Charbonnages and the SNCF. Quennouëlle-Corre, *La direction du trésor*, 233, 480–485. On the challenge of intermin-isterial coordination, see also Baum, *The French Economy*, 185. Rivalry among "grands corps" in the state bureaucracy (such as the Inspection des finances, the Corps des mines, the Corps des comptes) could also have an impact. See Harvey B. Feigenbaum, *The Politics of Public Enterprise: Oil and the French State* (Princeton: Princeton University Press, 1985), 105–110; and Ezra Suleiman, *Elites in French Society* (Princeton: Princeton University Press, 1978), chap. 7.

140. In a letter from Debré to Bank of France chief, Wilfred Baumgartner. Quoted in Quennouëlle-Corre, *La direction du trésor*, 473, also 480–485 on his failure to streamline oversight authority.

141. Bloch-Lainé and Bouvier, *La France restaurée*, 199.

142. On nationalized firms as sites for risk taking and innovation, see Sheahan, *Promotion and Control*, 208; Kuisel, *Capitalism and the State*, 266–267;

Charles P. Kindleberger, *Economic Growth in France and Britain: 1851–1950* (New York: Simon and Schuster, 1964), 159–160. Warren Baum (*The French Economy*, 197) also argues that in coal mining, private firms would not have invested as much as the Charbonnages had. Thomas Marschak pointed out that "a majority of French economic theorists [were] associated in one capacity or another with the nationalized industries, some in the highest managerial posts" (Marschak, "Capital Budgeting and Pricing in the French Nationalized Industries," *Journal of Business* 33, no. 32 [April 1960]: 133).

143. J. M. Jeanneney, "Nationalization in France," in *Monopoly and Competition and Their Regulation*, ed. Edward H. Chamberlin (London: Macmillan, 1954), 487.

144. See, for example, Susanne Charpy, *Prendrons-nous des usines? Des comités d'entreprises à la gestion collective* (Paris: Idées et Combats, 1948); and Brachet, *L'État-patron*.

145. British governments did more to encourage self-financing. Margairaz, "Companies under Public Control," 46.

146. Chenot, *Les entreprises nationalisées*, 100. On Mayer's 1953 decree, see also *Le Monde*, 17 May 1953, as well as a critique by a former Charbonnages employee who felt the state already exerted too much control over the firm, in *Le Monde*, 26 May 1953.

147. *Le Monde*, 10 June 1953, as quoted in Holter, "Mineworkers and Nationalization," 48.

148. For the controversy over Mayer's decree, see Chenot, *Les entreprises nationalisées*, 98–105; Sturmthal, "Structure of Nationalized Enterprises," 373; Baum, *The French Economy*, 185.

149. On the contrast between an American focus on mass consumption in the postwar recovery and a French and West German emphasis on production and investment, see Monica Prasad, *The Land of Too Much: American Abundance and the Paradox of Poverty* (Cambridge, MA: Harvard University Press, 2012).

150. Left-leaning Gaullists and centrist liberals also took up an interest in reforming the social climate and governance in enterprises in the 1970s. See Alain Chatriot, "La réforme de l'entreprise: Du contrôle ouvrier à l'échec du projet modernisateur," *VS Siècle* 114 (April–June 2012): 183–197.

6 · Reformer Dilemmas

1. Éric Roussel, *Pierre Mendès France* (Paris: Gallimard, 2007), 34; and Alain Chatriot, *Pierre Mendès France: Pour une république moderne* (Paris: Armand Colin, 2015), 24–26.

2. Michel Winock, *Pierre Mendès France* (Paris: Bayard, 2005), 9–10. On the weakness of training in economics, see Michel Debré, *Les trois républiques pour une France*, vol. 1: *Combattre*, with the collaboration of Odile Rudelle (Paris: Albin Michel, 1984), 73.

3. Winock, *Pierre Mendès France*, 9–10.

4. Pierre Mendès France, *Oeuvres complètes*, vol. 1 (Paris: Gallimard, 1984), 47.

5. Jean Lacouture, *Pierre Mendès France,* trans. George Holoch (New York: Holmes and Meier, 1984), 69.

6. Mendès France, *Oeuvres complètes*, 1:94–95.

7. Ibid.

8. Pierre Mendès France, *La Banque internationale: Contribution à l'étude du problème des États-Unis d'Europe* (Paris: Librairie Valois, 1930), large portions of which are republished in Mendès France, *Oeuvres complètes*, vol. 1. On this book, see Jean-Louis Rizzo, *Mendès France ou la rénovation en politique* (Paris: Presses de la FNSP, 1993), 27.

9. Mendès France, *Oeuvre complètes*, 1:160.

10. Ibid., 161.

11. Ibid., 126.

12. Gilles Le Beguec, "Pierre Mendès France et la technocratie," *Matériaux pour l'Histoire de Notre Temps* 63–64 (July–December 2001): 116.

13. On the Toulouse speech, see Rizzo, *Mendès France*, 27.

14. Pierre Mendès France, "Les deux discours," *Le Journal du Neubourg*, 15 February 1933, as cited in Roussel, *Pierre Mendès France*, 79–80.

15. On Robert Debré, see *Hommage au professeur Robert Debré, 1882–1978* (Paris: Bernard Grasset, 1980); and Debré, *Trois républiques*, 1:27–40.

16. On Michel Debré's early life, see Patrick Samuel, *Michel Debré: L'architecte du général* (Paris: Arnaud Franel Éditions, 1999), 17–26; and Debré, *Trois républiques*, 1:27–40.

17. Michel Debré, "Le gouvernement des démocraties modernes," 13 leçons à l'École nationale d'administration, May–July 1947. In the Archives Michel Debré, 1 DE 31.

18. Michel Debré, *La mort de l'État républicain* (Paris: Gallimard, 1947), 38. See also his uses of medical metaphor in Debré, *Ces princes qui nous gouvernent: Lettre aux dirigeants de la nation* (Paris: Plon, 1957), 149–164.

19. Debré, *Trois républiques*, 1:32.

20. Quoted in Richard F. Kuisel, *Capitalism and the State in Modern France: Renovation and Economic Management in the Twentieth Century* (New York: Cambridge University Press, 1982), 127. From Michel Debré, "Pour une administration de l'économie française," *Sciences Politiques* 8 (June 1938): 262–263, 269.

21. Debré, *Trois républiques*, 1:91.

22. Ibid., 94–95.

23. Samuel, *Michel Debré*, 33–34.

24. Debré, *Trois républiques*, 1:164. On Debré's experience on Reynaud's staff, see Samuel, *Michel Debré*, 32–35; Debré, *Trois républiques*, 1:141–171; and Alfred Sauvy, *De Paul Reynaud à de Gaulle* (Paris: Casterman, 1972), 71–81.

25. Debré, *Trois républiques*, 1:168.

26. Ibid.

27. Mendès France, *Oeuvres complètes*, 822. See also Lacouture, *Pierre Mendès France*, 97; and Chatriot, *Pierre Mendès France*, 40.

28. Lacouture, *Pierre Mendès France*, 87–96; Roussel, *Pierre Mendès France*, 107; Mendès France, *Oeuvres complètes*, 1:798–821.

29. Olivier Feiertag, "Pierre Mendès France, acteur et témoin de la planification française, 1943–1962," in *Pierre Mendès France et l'économie: Pensée et action*, ed. Michel Margairaz (Paris: Éditions Odile Jacob, 1989), 367–369.

30. Eric Jabbari, "Law and Politics in Interwar France: Pierre Laroque's Search for a Democratic Corporatism," *FPCS* 24, no. 1 (Spring 2006): 93–113; and H. S. Jones, *The French State in Question* (Cambridge: Cambridge University Press, 1993).

31. On his resistance activity in 1940–1942, see Samuel, *Michel Debré*, 36–49; Debré, *Trois républiques*, 1:172–188; and transcripts from interviews with Debré in 1990, in Olivier Wieviorka, *Nous entrerons dans la carrière* (Paris: Éditions du Seuil, 1994), 105–136. On his interest in the Prussian reform, see Wieviorka, *Nous entrerons*, 111; and Debre, *Trois républiques*, 1:180.

32. The other members of the CGE were François de Menthon, Paul Bastid, Robert Lacoste, Alexandre Parodi, René Courtin, Pierre-Henri Teitgen, Jacques Charpentier, and Pierre Lefaucheux. See Kuisel, *Capitalism and the State*, 167.

33. Samuel, *Michel Debré*, 56. On the CGE, see Debré, *Trois républiques*, 1:189–228; and Samuel, *Michel Debré*, 52–58.

34. The book was finished by early 1944 but a copy was confiscated by the Gestapo. It was published after the Liberation under Debré and Monick's noms de guerre—Jacquier et Brière, *Refaire la France: Effort d'une génération* (Paris: Plon, 1945).

35. Ibid., 3. See also Andrew Shennan, *Rethinking France: Plans for Renewal, 1940–1946* (Oxford: Clarendon Press, 1989), 119–121.

36. Jacquier et Brière, *Refaire la France*, 12.

37. Nicholas Wahl, "The French Constitution of 1958: II. The Initial Draft and Its Origins," *American Political Science Review* 53, no. 2 (June 1959): 379.

38. Jacquier and Brière, *Refaire la France*, 123–124.

39. Wieviorka, *Nous entrerons*, 120.

40. Debré, *Trois républiques*, 1:295. Also quoted in Robert Gildea, *Marianne in Chains: Daily Life in the Heart of France during the German Occupation* (New York: Picador, 2002), 318.

41. Debré, *Trois républiques*, 1:326.

42. Ibid., 345.

43. Ibid., 367.

44. Michel Debré, *Réforme de la fonction publique* (Paris: Imprimerie Nationale, 1946), 24–25, as quoted and translated by Ezra Sulieman in *Elites in French Society: The Politics of Survival* (Princeton: Princeton University Press, 1978), 41. On the founding of ENA, see also Debré, *Trois républiques*, 1:366–374; Samuel, *Michel Debré*, 75–78; Jean-Michel Gaillard, *L'ENA:*

Miroir de l'État: De 1945 â nos jours (Brussels: Éditions Complexe, 1995); and Philip Nord, "Reform, Conservation, and Adaptation: Sciences-Po, from the Popular Front to the Liberation," in *The Jacobin Legacy in Modern France,* ed. Subhir Hazareesingh (Oxford: Oxford University Press, 2002), 138–139.

45. Samuel, *Michel Debré,* 19.

46. On the use of the ordinance in this case, see Ezra Suleiman, *Politics, Power and Bureaucracy in France: The Administrative Elite* (Princeton: Princeton University Press, 1974), 45–46. On Jean Zay's attempt to create an elite school of public administration, see Guy Thuillier, *L'ENA avant l'ENA* (Paris: PUF, 1983).

47. Interview with Debré by Nicholas Wahl, 13 September 1958, Papers of Nicholas Wahl, New York University Archives, Series I, Box 1.

48. Samuel, *Michel Debré,* 81.

49. On Mendès France's difficulties in 1944–1945, see Kuisel, *Capitalism and the State,* 187–202; Jean Bouvier, "Sur la politique économique en 1944–46," in *La libération de la France,* Comité d'histoire de la deuxième guerre mondiale, actes du colloque, octobre 1974 (Paris: Éditions du CNRS, 1976); for opposing views on the feasibility of Mendès France's monetary plan, see François Bloch-Lainé and Jean Bouvier, *La France restaurée, 1944–1954: Dialogue sur les choix d'une modernisation,* prologue by Jean-Pierre Rioux (Paris: Fayard, 1986), 84; and the interview with Jean-Marcel Jeanneny in Jean Daniel and Jean Lacouture, eds., *Le citoyen Mendès France* (Paris: Éditions du Seuil, 1992), 30–32.

50. As quoted in Lacouture, *Pierre Mendès France,* 161.

51. As quoted in ibid., 163.

52. Gérard Brun, "Pierre Mendès France, le technique et les technicians," in Margairaz, *Pierre Mendès France,* 225.

53. On Mendès France's relations to other experts, see Roussel, *Pierre Mendès France,* 182; Lacouture, *Pierre Mendès France,* 174, 180–181.

54. Mendès France, *Oeuvres complètes,* 2:75.

55. Ibid., 112–113.

56. Ibid., 86.

57. As quoted in Roussel, *Pierre Mendès France,* 172.

58. Le Beguec, "Pierre Mendès France et la technocratie," 117.

59. On Debré and Germany, see Samuel, *Michel Debré,* 86–94.

60. Quoted in Debré, *Ces princes qui nous gouvernent,* 126.

61. Interview with Debré by Nicholas Wahl, 13 September 1958, Papers of Nicholas Wahl, New York University Archives, Series I, Box 1.

62. Debré, *La mort de l'État républicain,* 32.

63. Samuel, *Michel Debré,* 96–97.

64. Ibid., 95–96.

65. Debré, *La mort de l'État républicain,* 32–33; Michel Debré took up this theme with renewed earnest in *Ces princes qui nous gouvernent.*

66. Michel Debré, "Les problèmes présents de l'administration française," second lesson on the problem of centralization and local administration, Archives Michel Debré, 1 DE 31.

67. Michel Debré, "Administration et liberté," a lecture given on 10 December 1948 to the students of the faculty of law and political economy at the Université de Groningue.

68. Ibid.

69. Debré, *La mort de l'État républicain*, esp. 38-42. See also Yves Mény, *Centralisation et décentralization dans le débat politique français (1945-1969)* (Paris: Libraire générale de droit et de jurisprudence, 1974), 158-159. On Debré's efforts to promote a local political strategy for the RPF, see Debré, *Trois républiques*, 2:133-134; Richard Vinen, *Bourgeois Politics in France, 1945-1951* (Cambridge: Cambridge University Press, 1995), 39, 230.

70. Interview with Debré by Nicholas Wahl, April 1958, Papers of Nicholas Wahl, New York University Archives, Series I, Box 1.

71. Debré, *La mort de l'État républicain*, 61; Mény, *Centralisation*, 160.

72. Feiertag, "Pierre Mendès France," 375-381.

73. Mendès France, *Oeuvres complètes*, 2:469-470.

74. On wanting a sense of war footing for national recovery, see Feiertag, "Pierre Mendès France," 382.

75. As quoted in Bloch-Lainé and Bouvier, *La France restaurée*, 248.

76. Mendès France, *Oeuvres complètes*, 2:432.

77. Ibid., 433.

78. Delphine Dulong, *Moderniser la politique: Aux origines de la Vème République* (Paris: L'Harmattan, 1997), 37-43, 160. On Mendès France and the rising cultural power of economics, see Matthew Watkins, " 'You've Got to Be Modernistic': The Myth of Pierre Mendès France and the Modernization of France" (PhD diss., New York University, 2014).

79. Delong, *Moderniser la politique*, 51; Patrick Rotman, "La diaspora mendésiste," *Pouvoirs* 27 (1983): 9; François Fourquet, *Les comptes de la puissance: Histoire de la comptabilité nationale et du Plan* (Fontenay-sous-Bois: Recherches, 1980), 211-214.

80. On using the first-person pronoun in his broadcasts, see Claude Marti, "Message et medias, Pierre Mendès France ou la communication en actes," in *Pierre Mendès France et l'esprit républicain* (Paris: Le Cherche Midi Éditeur, 1996), 80-81. On the radio chats, see also Léone Nora, "Un moyen d'expression moderne: Les causieres du samedi," *Matériaux pour l'Histoire de Notre Temps* 63-64 (July-December 2001): 109-111; Gérard Unger, "La communication de Pierre Mendès France," in *Pierre Mendès France et l'esprit républicain*, 230-254; and René Mouriaux and Annie Collovald, "Les conceptions syndicales de Pierre Mendès France et ses relations avec les syndicats ouvriers," in Margairaz, *Pierre Mendès France*, 290.

81. Jean-Pierre Azéma, "L'ambivalence," in *Pierre Mendès France et le mendésisme*, ed. François Bédarida and Jean-Pierre Rioux (Paris: Fayard, 1985), 106.

82. Michel Margairaz, "Pierre Mendès France, la gauche et les 'impératifs de l'efficacité économique,' " in Margairaz, *Pierre Mendès France*, 352. For an example of popularizing productivity, see Alfred Sauvy, *Le nouveau programme économique* (Paris: Éditions Françaises d'Informations, n.d.), in

the Pierre Mendès France Archives, Institut Pierre Mendès France, carton Économie I.

83. On Mendès France's response to Marxism, see Paul Thibaud, "La philosophie politique de Pierre Mendès France," in Bédarida and Rioux, *Pierre Mendès France et le mendésisme,* 51. On the economic and sociological vision of state planners as an alternative to Marxism, see Delphine Dulong, *Moderniser la politique,* 78–83.

84. Kuisel, *Capitalism and the State,* 269.

85. Jean Bouvier, "La modernité à l'épreuve du temps," in Bédarida and Rioux, *Pierre Mendès France et le mendésisme,* 365; and Bloch-Lainé and Bouvier, *La France restaurée,* 254–255; Jacques Wolff, "Pierre Mendès France: Une politique économique, 1953–1955," *Les Cahiers de l'IHTP* 1 (October 1985).

86. Margairaz, "Pierre Mendès France," 352–354; Feiertag, "Pierre Mendès France," 387–388.

87. Aude Terray, *Des francs-tireurs aux experts: L'organisation de la prévision économique au ministère des finances, 1948–1968* (Paris: Comité pour l'histoire économique et financière de la France, 2002), 115–119; Fourquet, *Les comptes de la puissance,* 214–216. On Nora's suggestion to take over the Finance Ministry, see his memorandum of 12 September 1954 in the Pierre Mendès France Archives, Institut Pierre Mendès France, carton Économie II.

88. Dulong, *Moderniser la politique,* 51–52.

89. On the "crise de la démocratie" speech at Evreux, see Rizzo, *Mendès France,* 52–54; Roussel, *Pierre Mendès France,* 393. For quotations from the speech itself, see Mendès France, *Oeuvres complètes,* 4:81–103.

90. Stanley Hoffmann, "Le confluent des modernités," *Pouvoirs* 27 (November 1983): 35.

91. On Mendès France and Algeria, see especially Irwin Wall, "Mendès France face au problème algérien: Une attitude moderne?," *Matériaux pour l'Histoire de Notre Temps* 63–64 (July–December 2001): 13–22; Pierre Guillen, "Pierre Mendès France et la décolonisation," in *Pierre Mendès France: La morale en politique* (Grenoble: Presses universitaires de Grenoble, 1990), 185–202; Seloua Boulbina, "Au confins de la République: L'Algérie," in *Pierre Mendès France et l'esprit républicain,* 106.

92. Written in February 1955 and quoted in François Bédarida, "Raison, modernité, progrès: L'appel de Pierre Mendès France," in Bédarida and Rioux, *Pierre Mendès France et le mendésisme,* 15–16.

93. On Debré's views of the Mendès France government of 1954–1955, see *Trois républiques,* 2:264–266.

94. Debré, *Ces princes qui nous gouvernent,* 197, also 183–185 on the likeness to Vichy.

95. Ibid., 175–176.

96. Ibid., 202.

97. Ibid., 199.

98. On the *Courrier de la République,* see Debré, *Trois républiques,* 2:281–287.

99. Lacouture, *Pierre Mendès France,* 375.

100. On similarities between Mendès France and de Gaulle, see Fourquet, *Les comptes de la puissance*, xxii–xxiii, 216–217; Rizzo, *Mendès France*, 232. On the John the Baptist analogy, coined by Maurice Duverger, see Bédarida, "Raison, modernité, progrès," 16.

101. Debré, *Trois républiques*, 2:292.

102. As quoted in Serge Berstein, *The Republic of de Gaulle, 1958–1969*, trans. Peter Morris (Cambridge: Cambridge University Press, 1993), 8.

103. Letter from Georges Boris to Pierre Mendès France, 22 May 1957, Pierre Mendès France Archives, Institute Pierre Mendès France, carton Correspondence 13. See also Lacouture, *Pierre Mendès France*, 374.

104. Chatriot, *Pierre Mendès France*, 164.

105. Raymond Aron, *Immuable et changeante: De la IVe à la Ve République* (Paris: Calmann Lévy, 1959), 16–17.

106. François Goguel, "The Evolution of the Institution of the French Presidency, 1959–1981," in *Constitutional Democracy: Essays in Comparative Politics*, ed. Fred Eidlin (Boulder, CO: Westview Press, 1983), 49.

107. Dulong, *Moderniser la politique*, 159–160.

108. On the impact of the Baumgartner appointment, see Dulong, *Moderniser la politique*, 165.

109. Frédérique Matonti, "Sur scène et en coulisses: Contribution à l'analyse du rôle du premier ministre sous la Ve République," in *Michel Debré, premier minister, 1959–1962*, ed. Serge Berstein, Pierre Milza, and Jean-François Sirinelli (Paris: PUF, 2005), 153; Dulong, *Moderniser la politique*, 212.

110. As quoted in Brigitte Gaïti, *De Gaulle, prophète de la Cinquième République (1946–1962)* (Paris: Presses de Sciences Po, 1998), 317.

111. Berstein, *The Republic of de Gaulle*, 5.

112. As quoted in Dulong, *Moderniser la politique*, 213.

113. Gaïti, *De Gaulle, prophète*, 306–307.

114. Brigitte Gaïta, "Décembre 1958 ou le temps de la révélation technocratique," in *La question technocratique: De l'invention d'une figure aux transformation de l'action publique*, ed. Vincent Dubois and Delphine Dulong (Strasbourg: Presses universitaires de Strasbourg, 1999), 145–147.

115. Berstein, *The Republic of de Gaulle*, 62; Frédéric Rouvillois, "Le constituant face à son oeuvre," in Berstein, Milza, and Sirinelli, *Michel Debré, premier ministre*, 35–36.

116. Goguel, "The Evolution," 54.

117. Berstein, *The Republic of de Gaulle*, 60; Rouvillois, "Le constituant," 30.

118. As quoted in Dulong, *Moderniser la politique*, 214.

119. Jean Lacouture, *De Gaulle*, vol. 2: *The Ruler, 1945–1970* (New York: Norton, 1993), 222.

120. As quoted in Laure Quennouëlle-Corre, *La direction du trésor, 1947–1967: L'État-banquier et la croissance* (Paris: Comité pour l'histoire économique et financière de la France, 2000), 331.

121. Rouvillois, "Le constituant," 30–33. See also Matonti, "Sur scène et en coulisses."

122. As quoted in Rouvillois, "Le constituant," 32.

123. As quoted in ibid., 48.

124. Gaïta, "Décembre 1958," 137–140.

125. Jacques Duclos, *Gaullisme, technocratie, corporatisme* (Paris: Éditions Sociales, 1963), 11.

126. These statements by deputies are quoted in Dulong, *Moderniser la politique,* 169–170.

127. As quoted in Lacouture, *Pierre Mendès France,* 378.

128. See, for example, Pierre Mendès France, *A Modern French Republic,* trans. Anne Carter (Westport, CT: Greenwood Press, 1963), 19.

129. Ibid., 51–52.

130. Ibid., 39.

131. Ibid., 161.

132. Ibid., 93.

133. On the statist and associationalist sides of the Radical tradition, see Sudhir Hazareesingh, *Political Traditions in Modern France* (Oxford: Oxford University Press, 1994), 209–226. On the Club Jean Moulin, see Claire Andrieu, *Pour l'amour de la République: Le Club Jean Moulin, 1958–1970* (Paris: Fayard, 2002).

134. Mendès France, *A Modern French Republic,* 98.

135. Ibid., 136–137.

136. Pierre Rosanvallon, "Pierre Mendès France et la démocratie," in *Pierre Mendès France et l'esprit républicain,* 130–134.

137. Gaïti, *De Gaulle, prophète,* 324.

138. Le Beguec, "Pierre Mendès France et la technocratie," 114.

139. Mendès France, *A Modern French Republic,* 98.

140. Paul Thebaud, "La philosophie politique de Pierre Mendès France," in Bédarida and Rioux, *Pierre Mendès France et le mendésisme,* 47–48.

141. Mendès France, *A Modern French Republic,* 149.

142. On Mendès France and labor, see especially Mouriaux and Collovald, "Les conceptions syndicales de Pierre Mendès France et ses relations avec les syndicates ouvriers," in Margairaz, *Pierre Mendès France,* 277–316.

143. Interview, Georges Rino with René Mouriaux, 12 June 1987, ibid., 308.

144. Interview, Jean Magniadas with René Mouriaux, 13 May 1987, ibid., 306.

145. Interview with Edmund Maire, in Jean Daniel and Jean Lacouture, *Le citoyen Mendès France* (Paris: Éditions du Seuil, 1992), 203–204.

146. On Mendès France's view of the direct election of the president as Bonapartist, see interview with Olivier Duhamel, in Daniel and Lacouture, *Le citoyen Mendès France,* 190. On Mendès France's pride as a source of his reluctance to accept the institutions of the Fifth Republic, see interview with Stanley Hoffmann, Cambridge, Mass., 13 January 2005.

147. Interview with François Mitterrand, in Daniel and Lacouture, *Le citoyen Mendès France,* 20.

148. As quoted in Dominique Franche and Yves Léonard, "Pierre Mendès France: Le pouvoir et l'influence," in *Pierre Mendès France et la démocratie locale,* Actes du colloque du conseil général de l'Eure, ed. Dominique Franche and Yves Léonard (Rennes: PUR, 2004), 14–15.

149. Debré, *Trois républiques,* 1:126.

150. On Debré's justification of state control over the media, see ibid., 127.
151. Michel Debré and Pierre Mendès France, *Le grand débat*, preface by Georges Altschuler (Paris: Éditions Gonthier, 1966), 193; Chatriot, *Pierre Mendès France*, 176–177.
152. Debré and Mendés France, *Le grand débat*, 192.
153. Ibid., 177.
154. Ibid., 200.
155. Ibid., 200–201.
156. See Nicholas Wahl's notes of his interview with Debré on 13 September 1958, Papers of Nicholas Wahl, New York University Archives, Series I, Box 1.
157. See "La 5e République et la haute administration ou le règne des 'jeunes messieurs,'" *Courrier de la République*, March 1965, 1–9. See also Le Beguec, "Pierre Mendès France et la technocratie," 115–116.
158. On Bloch-Lainé's view, see Brun, "Pierre Mendès France," 238; Lacouture, *Pierre Mendès France*, 444–445.
159. Interview with François Mitterrand, in Daniel and Lacouture, *Le citoyen Mendès France*, 13. For Rocard's views, see Rioux, "A la recherche du mendésisme," in Bédarida and Rioux, *Pierre Mendès France et le mendésisme*, 465.
160. See Roussel, *Pierre Mendès France*, 465.
161. After his dismissal in 1962, Debré remained loyal to de Gaulle and in 1963 ran successfully as a Gaullist for a National Assembly seat in the overseas department of La Réunion. There he pursued an integrationist approach to ethnic diversity, enhanced social welfare provisioning, suppressed the autonomist movement on the island, and promoted a (later much criticized) program relocating more than 1,600 children to the metropole. See Gilles Gauvin, *Michel Debré et l'Ile de la Réunion (1959–1967)* (Paris: L'Harmattan, 1996); Ivan Jablonka, *Enfants en exil: Transfer de pupilles réunionnais en métropole (19963–1982)* (Paris: Éditions du Seuil, 2007); and Héloise Finch-Boyer, "'The Idea of the Nation Was Superior to Race': Transforming Racial Contours and Social Attitudes and Decolonizing the French Empire from La Réunion, 1946–1973," *FHS* 36, no. 1 (Winter 2013): 109–140.
162. Berstein, *The Republic of de Gaulle*, 64.

7 · Algerian Anvil

1. French authorities retained the two-college system of representation, which preserved European settler political supremacy in Algeria. On liberalizing colonial rule, see Frederick Cooper, *Citizenship between Empire and Nation: Remaking France and French Africa, 1945–1960* (Princeton: Princeton University Press, 2014); and Todd Shepard, *The Invention of Decolonization: The Algerian War and the Remaking of France* (Ithaca, NY: Cornell University Press, 2006), 39–43.
2. René Gallisot, "La guerre et l'immigration algérienne en France," in *La guerre d'Algérie et les Français*, ed. Jean-Pierre Rioux (Paris: Fayard, 1990), 338. Statistics on migration flows between Algeria and the metropole were, by virtue of the lack of restrictions after 1947, unreliable and subject

to much debate. On this difficulty, see the discussion in the Commission de la Main-d'oeuvre of the Commissariat général du Plan, 24 July 1952, AN 80AJ 49, as well as Emmanuel Blanchard, *La police parisienne et les algériens (1944–1962)* (Paris: Le Grand Livre du Mois, 2011), 231–234; and Amelia Lyons, *The Civilizing Mission in the Metropole: Algerian Families and the French Welfare State during Decolonization* (Stanford: Stanford University Press, 2013), 68–69.

3. Compte rendu de la Commission Interministérielle de l'Immigration, 6 November 1946, archives of the Haut Comité consultatif de la population et de la famille, CAC 860269, art. 8.

4. On these pleas and the Population Ministry's response, see Compte rendu d'activité de la Direction générale de la main-d'oeuvre, 13–20 August 1945, Alexandre Parodi Papers, PA 16; and Compte rendu de la Commission nationale provisoire de la main-d'oeuvre, 13 December 1946.

5. For these ideas for discouraging migration, see Haut Comité consultatif de la population et de la famille, La migration des nord-africaines vers la France, 23 June 1948; Travaux du Haut Comité consultatif de la population et de la famille, année 1948, CAC 860269, art. 7; and Compte rendu de la Commission consultative nationale pour l'étude des questions nord-africaines, 13 February 1950, CFTC Archives, 4 H 143.

6. Fernand Boverat, Note pour la commission du bilan démographique, Haut Comité consultatif de la population et de la famille, pour la séance du mardi 10 juin 1952, CAC 860269, art. 1.

7. Alfred Sauvy, Rapport au Ministre de la santé publique et de la population sur l'évolution de la population de l'Afrique du Nord, circa 1950, CAC 860269, art. 7.

8. Rapport relatif aux possibilités d'utilisation de la main-d'oeuvre algérienne dans l'agriculture métropolitaine, Direction du travail et à la sécurité sociale, Gouvernment général de l'Algérie, 2 November 1954, archives of the Ministère de l'Intérieur, Administration Générale, AN F1a 5049. On rural resettlement, see AN F1a 5049 and AN F1a 5050.

9. Rod Kedward, *France and the French: A Modern History* (Woodstock, NY: Overlook Press, 2006), 338.

10. On the political insurgency in the metropole, and the rivalry between the MNA and FNL there, see Lina Amiri, *La bataille de France: La guerre d'Algérie en métropole* (Paris: Robert Laffont, 2004); M-Ali Haroun, *La 7e wilaya: La guerre du FLN en France, 1954–1962* (Paris: Éditions du Seuil, 1986); Benjamin Stora, *Ils venaient d'Algérie: L'immigration algérienne en France (1912–1992)* (Paris: Fayard, 1992); Rosemary Wakeman, *The Heroic City: Paris, 1945–1958* (Chicago: University of Chicago Press, 2009), 151–157; and Emmanuel Blanchard, *La police parisienne*, chap. 4.

11. On how Algerians became identified as key targets for housing, social services, and surveillance in Marseille by the late 1950s, see Minayo A. Nasiali, *Native to the Republic: Empire, Social Citizenship, and Everyday Life in Marseille since 1945* (Ithaca, NY: Cornell University Press, 2016).

12. See especially Lyons, *Civilizing Mission*; Blanchard, *La police parisienne*; Amit Prakash, "Colonial Techniques in the Imperial Capital: The

Prefecture of Police and the Surveillance of North Africans in Paris, 1925–circa 1970," *FHS* 36, no. 3 (Summer 2013): 479–510. For the interwar period, see Mary Dewhurst Lewis, *The Boundaries of the Republic: Migrant Rights and the Limits of Universalism in France, 1918–1940* (Stanford: Stanford University Press, 2007); and Clifford Rosenberg, *Policing Paris: The Origins of Modern Immigration Control between the Wars* (Ithaca, NY: Cornell University Press, 2006). For an important sociological study in the 1950s that noted the connection between services and policing, see Andrée Michel, *Les travailleurs algériens en France* (Paris: CNRS, 1956).

13. Rosenberg, *Policing Paris*, chap. 7.

14. Pierre Laroque and François Ollive, "Le problème de l'émigration en France des travailleurs nord-africains," March 1938, as quoted in Michel, *Les travailleurs algériens*, 68.

15. Lyons, *Civilizing Mission*, 65–66; Blanchard, *La police parisienne*, 85–92, 166–73; Prakash, "Colonial Techniques," 493–502. On policing after the disbanding of the North African Brigade, see the confidential note of 20 May 1947 in the Archives de la Prefecture de Paris, APP D/A 768.

16. Gallisot, "La guerre et l'immigration algérienne," 342.

17. Lyons, *Civilizing Mission*, 4–6; Sophie Lamri, "'Algériennes' et mères françaises exemplaires (1945–1982)," *MS* 199 (April–June 2002): 61–81.

18. Lamri, "'Algériennes' et mères françaises," 75–77.

19. Lyons, *Civilizing Mission*, 36.

20. Ibid., 62–63.

21. Alexis Spire, *Étrangers à la carte: L'administration de l'immigration en France (1945–1975)* (Paris: Grasset, 2005), 199–202.

22. Vincent Viet, "La cristallisation d'une politique sociale de l'immigration," in *Michel Debré, premier minister, 1959–1962*, ed. Serge Berstein, Pierre Milza, and Jean-François Sirinelli (Paris: PUF, 2005), 375.

23. On the CTAMs, see Françoise de Barros, "Contours d'un réseau administrative 'algérien' et construction d'une compétence en 'affaires musulmanes': Les conseillers techniques pour les affaires musulmanes en métropole (1952–1965)," *Politix* 19, no. 76 (2006): 97–117; Arthur Grosjean, "L'action des conseillers techniques aux affaires musulmanes: L'exemple de camp de Thiol," *Matériaux pour l'Histoire de Notre Temps* 92 (2008): 15–23; and Vincent Viet, *La France immigrée: Construction d'une politique, 1941–1997* (Paris: Fayard, 1998), 186–188.

24. See the several reports on Algerian students in agricultural schools, sent to the Ministère de l'Intérieur, Services des Affaires Musulmanes et de l'Action Sociales, in 1959 from Nice, Marseille, Versailles, and the prefecture of the Côte-d'Or, AN F1a 5050.

25. As quoted in Viet, *La France immigrée*, 187.

26. Ibid., 183.

27. Neil MacMaster, *Colonial Migrants and Racism: Algerians in France, 1900–62* (Houndmills, Basingstoke: Macmillan, 997), 194. Amelia Lyons (*Civilizing Mission*, 199) points out that, as late as 1972, 95 percent of housing directors in these residences had a military career in the colonies.

See also Marc Bernadot, "Une politique de logement: La SONACOTRA (1956–1992)" (PhD diss., Université de Paris I-Panthéon-Sorbonne, 1997).

28. Sous-Direction de la Coordination des services sociaux, Réunion de la Commission Technique, 20 January 1954, Archives of the Groupement des industries métallurgique et minière de la région parisienne, AN 39AS 385.

29. Sous-Direction de la Coordination des services sociaux, Union du Conseil de Surveillance, 20 December 1955, AN 39AS 385.

30. Lyons, *Civilizing Mission*, 4, 7, 66, 166–167.

31. Josée Bergeron, "La politique familiale française et l'identité nationale: Les famillles des DOM sont-elles françaises?," *FPCS* 17, nos. 3–4 (Summer–Fall 1999):101–116. See also Jacqueline Ancelin, *Histoire de l'action sociale familiale dans les départements d'outre-mer* (Paris: Association pour l'Étude de l'Histoire de la Sécurité Sociale, 2000); and Héloise Finch-Boyer, " 'The Idea of the Nation Was Superior to Race': Transforming Racial Contours and Social Attitudes and Decolonizing the French Empire from La Réunion, 1946–1973," *FHS* 36, no. 1 (Winter 2013): 109–140.

32. Frederick Cooper, *Decolonization and African Society: The Labor Question in French and British Africa* (Cambridge: Cambridge University Press, 1996), 281–283, 301–303, 314–322.

33. Margaret Cook Andersen, "The Office de la Famille Française: Family Policy and the National Revolution in 1940s Morocco," *FPCS* 34, no. 3 (Winter 2016): 44–62.

34. On the family allowance system for Algerian migrants, see Lyons, *Civilizing Mission*, 94–98; Michel, *Les travailleurs algériens*, 144–147; A. Chaulet, "Que peut-on faire pour les Nord-Africains en France?," *La Revue du Militant "Formation"* 20 (December 1949), in CFTC Archives, 4 H 143; and Antoine Math, "Les allocations familiales et l'Algérie colonial: A l'origine du FAS et de son financement par les régimes de prestations familiales," *Recherches et Prévisions* 53, no. 1 (1998): 35–44.

35. On the grievances over Italian immigrants' privilege and the discrimination against the self-employed, see Chaulet, "Que peut-on faire?." Pierre Laroque understood that Algerians would find it unfair to be deprived of the Italian arrangement. See compte rendu de la Commission nationale provisoire de la main-d'oeuvre, 13 December 1946, CAC 860269, art. 8.

36. Lyons, *Civilizing Mission*, 97–98.

37. Jim House and Neil MacMaster, *Paris 1961: Algerians, State Terror, and Memory* (Oxford: Oxford University Press, 2006), 61; Danièle Tartakowsky, *Les manifestations de rue en France, 1918–1968* (Paris: Publications de la Sorbonne, 1997), 649–650.

38. House and MacMaster, *Paris 1961*, 63.

39. Neil MacMaster, "Identifying 'Terrorists' in Paris: A Police Experiment with IBM Machines during the Algerian War," *FPCS* 28, no. 3 (Winter 2010): 23–45.

40. Prakash, "Colonial Techniques," 505.

41. Ibid.

42. On Papon's initiatives, see Blanchard, *La police parisienne*, 179–180, 316–335; House and MacMaster, *Paris 1961*, 33–35, 38–60, 67–80; Prakash,

"Colonial Techniques," 504–510; and Lyons, *Civilizing Mission*, 144–146. On beatings, torture, and internment, see especially Jean-Luc Einaudi, "Colonial Violence in the Metropole (1954–1961)," in *Colonial Culture in France since the Revolution*, ed. Pascal Blanchard, Sandrine Lemaire, Nicolas Bancal, and Dominic Thomas (Bloomington: Indiana University Press, 2014), 380–387; and House and MacMaster, *Paris 1961*, 80–87.

43. Viet, *La France immigrée*, 212.

44. Lyons, *Civilizing Mission*, 149.

45. Réunions de services, Conseillers techniques pour les affaires musulmanes, Carrefour sur quelques problèmes sociaux posés par la migration musulmane algérienne en métropole, 27 and 28 January 1959, Archives of the Ministère de la Santé et de la Population, Direction de la population et des migrations, CAC 760133, art. 17.

46. Quoted in Viet, *La France immigrée*, 216. For 17 October 1961, see especially House and MacMaster, *Paris 1961*; Blanchard, *La police parisienne*; Jean-Luc Einaudi, *Octobre 1961: Un massacre à Paris* (Paris: Fayard, 2001); Joshua Cole, "Remembering the Battle of Paris: 17 October 1961 in French and Algerian Memory," *FPCS* 21, no. 3 (Fall 2003): 21–50; and Jean-Paul Brunet, *Police contre FLN: Le drame d'octobre 1961* (Paris: Flammarion, 1999).

47. On *pieds noirs'* access to public housing, see Yann Scioldo-Zürcher, "Accueillir les Français rapatriés d'Algérie, histoire d'une régulation sociale par l'évitement des bidonvilles: L'exemple de Paris (1962–1969)," *FPCS* 31, no. 3 (Winter 2013): 45–64; and Lyons, *Civilizing Mission*, 191, 201–202.

48. On the starkly contrasting status and treatment of *pieds noirs* versus Harkis, see Todd Shepard, *The Invention of Decolonization*, chaps. 8 and 9; Chantal Morelle, "Les pouvoirs publics français et le rapatriement des Harkis en 1961–1962," in *La guerre d'indépendance des Algériens*, ed. Raphaëlle Branche (Paris: Perrin, 2009), 273–289. On Harkis in refugee camps, see Jeannette E. Miller, "A Camp for Foreigners and 'Aliens': The Harkis' Exil at the Rivesaltes Camp (1962–1964)," *FPCS* 31, no. 3 (Winter 2013): 21–44. On the problems Harkis faced in the Paris region, see the report of the Service d'Assistance Technique, Préfecture de Police, Des problèmes posés par l'accueil, la prise en charge et le reclassement des réfugiés musulmans algériens dans le département de la Seine, 25 June 1963, CAC 770391, art. 8.

49. Lyons, *Civilizing Mission*, 212.

50. Le Ministre de l'Intérieur, Service des affaires musulmane, à M. le Préfet de la Moselle, Inspecteur Général de l'Administration en Mission Extraordinaire, 4 January 1963, AN F1a 5048.

51. Ministère de l'Intérieur, Note sur les besoins en main d'oeuvre et le recrutement de travailleurs étrangers, 8 octobre 1963, CAC 760133, art. 16.

52. On the adaptation of the FAS and the social service network after 1962, see Viet, *La France immigrée*, 221–226; Lyons, *Civilizing Mission*, 209–219; Choukri Hmed, " 'Tenir ses hommes': La gestion des étrangers 'isolés' dans les foyers Sonacotra après la guerre d'Algérie," *Politix* 76 (2006): 11–30; Hmed, "L'encadrement des étrangers 'isolés' par le logement social (1950–

1980): Éléments pour une socio-histoire du travail des street-level bureaucrats," *Genèses* 72 (2009): 63–81; Nasiali, *Native to the Republic*; Melissa K. Byrnes, "Liberating the Land or Absorbing a Community: Managing North African Migration and the *Bidonvilles* in Paris's *Banlieues*," *FPCS* 31, no. 3 (Winter 2013): 1–20; Ed Naylor, "'Un âne dans l'ascenseur': Late Colonial Welfare Services and Social Housing in Marseille after Decolonization," *French History* 27, no. 3 (2015): 422–447; Emile Chabal, "Managing the Postcolony: Minority Politics in Montpellier, c. 1960–2010," *Contemporary European History* 23, no. 2 (2015): 237–258; and Jennifer E. Jenkins, "West Africans in Paris: An Assessment of French Immigration Policies in the 1960's and 1970's" (PhD diss., Brandeis University, 2007).

53. Gillian Glaes, "Policing the Post-Colonial Order: Surveillance and the African Immigrant Community in France, 1960–1979," *Historical Reflections* 36, no. 2 (Summer 2010): 108–126.

54. As quoted in Spire, *Étrangers à la carte*, 212.

55. Lyons, *Civilizing Mission*, 143.

56. Spire, *Étrangers à la carte*, 221–22; Prakash, "Colonial Techniques," 506–510; and Alexis Spire and Suzanne Thave, "Les acquisitions de nationalité depuis 1945: Regards sur l'immigration depuis 1945," *INSEE* (1999): 33–57, https://halshs.archives-ouvertes.fr/halshs-00721668.

57. On the Constantine Plan, see Daniel Lefeuvre, *Chère Algérie: Comptes et mécomptes de la tutelle coloniale, 1930–1962* (Saint-Denis: Société française d'histoire d'outre-mer, 1997), 283–326. On the indigenization of the civil service in Africa, see Michelle Pinto, "France and the Construction of the African Nation-State: Africanization in Postwar French Africa, 1946–1966" (PhD diss., New York University, 2013).

58. As quoted in Philip C. Naylor, *France and Algeria: A History of Decolonization and Transformation* (Gainesville: University Press of Florida, 2000), 21–22.

59. As quoted in John Talbott, *War without a Name: France in Algeria, 1954–1962* (New York: Knopf, 1980), 147.

60. Directive de Charles de Gaulle pour Paul Delouvrier, 18 December 1958, http://www.gaullisme.fr/2011/02/09/paul-delouvrier-un-grand-commis-de-letat/.

61. Quoted in Bernard Droz and Évelyne Lever, *Histoire de la guerre d'Algérie, 1954–1962* (Paris: Éditions du Seuil, 1982), 273.

62. On the Constantine Plan and French thinking about a Common Market Europe, see Muriam Davis, "Restaging *Mise en Valeur*: 'Postwar Imperialism' and the Constantine Plan," *Review of Middle East Studies* 44, no. 2 (Winter 2010): 176–186.

63. Quoted in Droz and Lever, *Histoire de la guerre d'Algérie*, 273.

64. Roselyne Chenu, *Paul Delouvrier ou la passion d'agir: Entretiens* (Paris: Éditions du Seuil, 1994), 313.

65. Naylor, *France and Algeria*, 22. Also, on the continuation of plan projects after independence, see Matthew Connelly, *A Diplomatic Revolution: Algeria's Fight for Independence and the Origins of the Post-War Era* (New York: Oxford University Press, 2002), 282–283.

66. Georges Boris, Note on Algeria, 20 February 1956, Institut Pierre Mendès France, Carton Algérie XI.

67. From a Delouvrier report on the Constantine Plan, as quoted in Hervé Lemoine, "Paul Delouvrier et l'Algérie: Comment servir et représenter l'État dans une guerre d'indépendance?," in *Paul Delouvrier, un grand commis de l'État*, ed. Sébastien Laurent and Jean-Eudes Roullier (Paris: Presses de Sciences Po, 2005), 49. On debate about the origins of the Algerian conflict, see the note, likely written by Michel Massenet, "De la promotion sociale en Algérie," ca. 1960, CAC 770391, art. 3.

68. Lefeuvre, *Chère Algerie*, 325–326.

69. Ibid., 307.

70. Extrait du compte rendu de la réunion de la commission "industrie" de la CGPA, 19 October 1959, Paul Delouvrier Papers, 1 DV 32. 307.

71. On business jitters, see the confidential memorandum (très secret) for Delouvrier from Lieutenant-Colonel Bourdonois, Note de renseignement, 15 December 1959, Paul Delouvrier Papers, 1 DV 32.

72. Daniel Lefeuvre, "L'échec du plan de Constantine," in Rioux, *La guerre d'Algérie*, 324–325.

73. Droz and Lever, *Histoire de la guerre d'Algérie*, 276.

74. Ibid.

75. Ibid.; Lyons, *Civilizing Mission*, 158–159.

76. Alistair Horne, *A Savage War of Peace: Algeria, 1954–1962* (New York: Penguin, 1979), 421.

77. For left-wing critiques of the plan, see André Gorz, "Gaullisme et néocolonialisme (à propos du Plan de Constantine)," *Les Temps Modernes* 170 (1961): 1150–1171; and the report of M. Nicollon to the politbureau of the French Communist Party, "Information sur l'industrialisation de l'Algérie," 2 May 1959, Maurice Thorez and Jeannette Vermeersch Papers, AN 626 AP 109.

78. Note sur le plan de Constantine et l'information, 12 August 1960, Paul Delouvrer Papers, 1 DV 32.

79. L'Union departmental CGT-FO d'Alger, réunie à l'occasion du passage de M. Ventejol désavoue le Plan de Constantine, 10 June 1960, Paul Delouvrier Papers, 1 DV 32. See also Allesandro Giacone, "Paul Delouvrier et le Plan de Constantine," in *Michel Debré et l'Algérie: Acte du colloque, Assemblée Nationale, 27 et 28 avril 2006* (Paris: Éditions Champs Elysées, 2007), 105.

80. Michel Massenet, Note sur les pratiques discriminatoires à l'égard des Français musulmans originaires d'Algérie et travaillant en Métropole, n.d. (most like early 1960), CAC 770391, art. 3.

81. Réunions de services, Conseillers techniques pour les affaires musulmanes, Carrefour sur quelques problèmes sociaux posés par la migration musulmane algérienne en métropole, 27 and 28 January 1959, CAC 760133, art. 17.

82. Massenet, Note sur les pratiques discriminatoires.

83. Le Ministre de l'Intérieur à Messieurs les Préfets (Métropole), Action à mener auprès des employeurs en faveur de la main-d'oeuvre de souche algérienne, 29 June 1960, CAC 770391, art. 3.

84. Algerians working at Renault nonetheless faced discrimination trying to advance in the firm. Laure Pitti, "Catégorisations ethniques au travail: Un instrument de gestion différenciée de la main-d'oeuvre," *Histoire et Mesure* 20, nos. 3–4 (2005): 69–101.

85. On Massenet's meetings with businesses, see Réunion relative à l'emploi des Français musulmans originaires d'Algérie dans le secteur des entreprises privées, 20 July 1960; and Réunion relative à l'emploi des Français musulmans originaires d'Algérie dans le secteur des entreprises nationalisées, 22 July 1960, CAC 770391, art. 3.

86. Lyons, *Civilizing Mission*, 156; Droz and Lever, *Histoire de la guerre d'Algérie*, 277.

87. Martin Evans, *Algeria, France's Undeclared War* (Oxford: Oxford University Press, 2012), 249.

88. On continuity from the Maspétiol Plan to the Constantine Plan, see Lefeuvre, *Chère Algérie*, 269–272, 283–285; Evans, *Algeria*, 241–243; Giacone, "Paul Delouvrier et le Plan de Constantine," 95–97.

89. On Delouvrier's work at the Planning Commission and Jean Monnet's influence on him, see Paul Delouvrier, "Quelques souvenirs sur Jean Monnet et le premier plan de modernisation et d'équipment," in *Modernisation ou décadence: Études, témoignages et documents sur la planification française*, ed. Bernard Cazes and Philippe Mioche (Aix-en-Provence: Publications de l'Université de Provence, 1990), 261–299; and Alessandro Giacone, *Paul Delouvrier: Un demi-siècle au service de la France et de l'Europe* (Paris: Descartes et Cie, 2004), 171–210.

90. A large literature now explores the emergence of the "development" paradigm. See especially Frederick Cooper and Randall Packard, eds., *International Development and the Social Sciences: Essays on the History and Politics of Knowledge* (Berkeley: University of California Press, 1997); Joseph M. Hodge, Gerald Hödl, and Martina Kopf, eds., *Developing Africa: Concepts and Practices in Twentieth-Century Colonialism* (Manchester: Manchester University Press, 2014); Marc Frey and Sönke Kunkel, "Writing the History of Development: A Review of the Recent Literature," *Contemporary European History* 20, no. 2 (May 2011): 215–232; and Colin Leys, *The Rise and Fall of Development Theory* (Bloomington: Indiana University Press, 1996).

91. See Giuliana Chamedes, "The Catholic Origins of 'Economic Development' after World War II," *FPCS* 33, no. 1 (Summer 2015): 55–75.

92. *L'aménagement de la région parisienne (1961–1969): Le témoignage de Paul Delouvrier* (Paris: Presses de l'école nationale des ponts et chaussées, 2003), 31. See also Sabine Effosse, "Paul Delouvrier et les villes nouvelles (1961–69)," in Laurent and Roullier, *Paul Delouvrier*, 75–86.

93. On how the Constantine Plan confirmed planners in their confidence in planning, see Stephen S. Cohen, *Modern Capitalist Planning: The French Model* (Berkeley: University of California Press, 1977), 47–48. On colonial architecture and urbanism as creating laboratories of modernity, see especially Gwen Wright, *The Politics of Design in French Colonial Urbanism* (Chicago: University of Chicago Press, 1991); Paul Rabinow, *French Modern:*

Norms and Forms of the Social Environment (Cambridge, MA: MIT Press, 1989). For criticisms that the metaphor was being carried too far, see Clifford Rosenberg, "The Colonial Politics of Health Care Provision in Interwar Paris," *FHS* 27, no. 2 (Summer 2004): 637–640.

94. On Plan IV's approach to the *pied noir* migration, see Shepard, *The Invention of Decolonization*, 221.

95. Lefeuvre, *Chère Algerie*, 280.

96. Jean Gravier, *Paris et le désert français* (Paris: Flammarion, 1947).

97. Sylvain Laurens, "La noblesse d'État à l'épreuve de 'l'Algérie' et de l'après 1962: Contribution à l'histoire d'une 'cohorte algérienne' sans communauté de destins," *Politix* 76 (2006): 82. For an assessment of the impact of colonial experience on prefects and other state officials when back in France, see Catherine Grémion, *Profession, décideurs: Pouvoir des hauts fonctionnaires et réforme de l'État* (Paris: Gauthier-Vilars, 1979), chaps. 12 and 13; and Matthew Wendeln, "Contested Territory: Regional Development in France, 1934–1968" (PhD diss., New York University, 2011), chap. 3.

98. As quoted in Tartakowsky, *Les manifestations de rue*, 680; see also Wendeln, "Contested Territory," 237–240.

99. Michel Debré, *Les trois républiques pour une France*, vol. 3: *Gouverner, 1958–1962* (Paris: Albin Michel, 1988), 69–70. See also Marc Olivier Baruch, "Les élites de l'État dans la modernisation," in *De Gaulle et les élites*, ed. Serge Berstein, Pierre Birnbaum, and Jean-Pierre Rioux (Paris: La Découverte, 2008), 99. For the speech, see http://fresques.ina.fr/de-gaulle/fiche-media/Gaulle00072/allocution-du-8-mai-1961.html.

100. Claire Andrieu, *Pour l'amour de la République: Le Club Jean Moulin, 1958–1970* (Paris: Fayard, 2002), 444.

101. Gérard Pogorel, "Le plan dans le débat politique français (1946–1965)," in *De Monnet à Massé: Enjeux politiques et objectifs économiques dans le cadre des quatre premiers Plans (1946–1965)*, ed. Henry Rousso (Paris: Éditions du CNRS, 1986), 183–195; Andrieu, *Pour l'amour de la République*, 44–50; Richard F. Kuisel, "La planification: Mythes, tendances, problèmes," in Cazes and Mioche, *Modernisation ou décadence*, 117–145.

102. Serge Berstein, *The Republic of de Gaulle, 1958–69* (Cambridge: Cambridge University Press, 1993), 8–11; Nicholas Wahl, *The Fifth Republic: France's New Political System* (New York: Random House, 1959), 39–44.

103. Irwin M. Wall argues persuasively that de Gaulle fought through at least the end of 1960 to keep Algeria tightly associated with France; see Wall, *France, the United States, and the Algerian War* (Berkeley: University of California Press, 2001), 192–201. Biographer Jean Lacouture takes de Gaulle's claims in his memoirs more at face value in arguing that de Gaulle understood years earlier that Algerian independence was inevitable; see Lacouture, *De Gaulle*, vol. 2: *The Ruler* (New York: Norton, 1992), 181.

104. Berstein, *The Republic of de Gaulle*, 50.

105. Ibid., 48, 55, 77: Michel Winock, "De Gaulle and the Algerian Crisis, 1958–1962," in *De Gaulle and Twentieth-Century France*, ed. Hugh Gough and John Horne (London: Edward Arnold, 1994), 80–82; Todd Shepard, *The Invention of Decolonization*, 248–259.

106. On de Gaulle, Debré, and the impact of the Algerian war on the prime ministership, see Jean Morin, "Les rapports entre Michel Debré et le Général de Gaulle concernant l'Algérie," in *Michel Debré et l'Algérie*, 257–271; Didier Maus, "La guerre d'Algérie et les institutions de la République," in Rioux, *La guerre d'Algérie*, 161–179; Danielle Bahu-Leyser, "Les voyages en province du Général de Gaulle," in Rioux, *La guerre d'Algérie*, 144–149; Berstein, *The Republic of de Gaulle*, 47; Chantal Morelle, "Debré et l'Algérie: Quelle Algérie française?," in Berstein, Milza, and Sirinelli, *Michel Debré, premier ministre*, 449–469; and Andrieu, *Pour l'amour de la République*, 392–393.

107. As quoted in John Talbott, *War without a Name* (New York: Knopf, 1980), 62.

108. On the state of emergency and special powers laws, see Sylvie Thénault, "L'état d'urgence (1955–2005): De l'Algérie colonial à la France contemporaine: Destin d'une loi," *MS* 218 (January–March 2007): 63–78. On parliamentary support for the special powers law, see Jean-Pierre Rioux, *The Fourth Republic, 1944–1958* (Cambridge: Cambridge University Press, 1989) 266.

109. Michel Pigenet, *Au coeur de l'activisme communiste des années de guerre froide: "La manifestation Ridgway"* (Paris: L'Harmattan, 1992), 25, 191, 163; Tartakowsky, *Les manifestations de rue*, 564–568; and Wakeman, *The Heroic City*, 124–126.

110. Wakeman, *The Heroic City*, 154–155.

111. Laure Pitti, "La 'forteresse ouvrière' à l'épreuve de la guerre d'Algérie," *VS* 83 (July–September 2004): 133–134.

112. "Des hommes sont parmi nous, que nous connaissons pas," *Monde Ouvrier*, 13 July 1957, CFTC Archives, 5 H 190.

113. See, for example, the concern of Malleret-Joinville, a member of the party's Central Committee, SN [Sécurité nationale], Paris, 19 May 1956, "Y-t-il des maquis de disponibles insoumis?," Archives Guy Mollet, AGM 88.

114. Wakeman, *The Heroic City*, 156. On the PCF and the war, see Irwin Wall, "The French Communists and the Algerian War," *Journal of Contemporary History* 12, no. 3 (July 1977): 521–543; Danièle Joly, *The French Communist Party and the Algerian War* (Houndsmills, Blasingstoke: Macmillan, 1991), 45–54; Xavier Vigna, *Histoire des ouvriers en France au XXe siècle* (Paris: Perrin, 2012), 243; Pitti, "La 'forteresse ouvrière.'"

115. On the reservists' revolt, see Jean-Charles Jauffret, "Le movement des rappelés en 1955–56," in *La guerre d'Algérie, 1954–2004: La fin de l'amnésie*, ed. Mohammed Harbi and Benjamin Stora (Paris: Robert Laffont, 2004), 133–160; Clément Grenier, "La protestation des rappelés en 1955, un movement d'indiscipline dans la guerre d'Algérie," *MS* 218 (January–March, 2007): 45–61; and Evans, *Algeria, France's Undeclared War*, 163–167.

116. On the antiwar movement, see Tramor Quemeneur, "Les oppositions françaises à la guerre d'indépendance," in *Histoire de l'Algérie à la period colonial, 1830–1962*, ed. Abderrahmane Bouchène, Jean-Pierre Peyroulou, Ouanassa Siari Tengour, and Sylvie Thénault (Paris: La Découverte, 2014),

595–601; Evans, *Algeria, France's Undeclared War*, 276–282. For intellectual dissent, see Jean-Pierre Rioux and Jean-François Sirinelli, eds., *La guerre d'Algérie et les intellectuels français* (Paris: Éditions Complexe, 1991).

117. On street demonstrations in shaping the New Left, see Tartakowsky, *Les manifestations de rue*, 692–693. On links between antiwar activism and May 1968 radicalism, see Kristin Ross, *May '68 and Its Afterlives* (Chicago: University of Chicago Press, 2002), 8, 26.

118. Alain Dewerpe, *Charonne, 8 février 1962: Anthropologie historique d'un massacre d'État* (Paris: Gallimard, 2006); Evans, *Algeria, France's Undeclared War*, 309–310.

119. Henry Rousso, *The Vichy Syndrome: History and Memory in France since 1944* (Cambridge, MA: Harvard University Press, 1991), 82–90.

Conclusion

1. Alexander Werth, *The De Gaulle Revolution* (London: Robert Hale, 1960), 396. For more on the notion that de Gaulle treated citizens as children, see Julian Jackson, "De Gaulle and May 1968," in *De Gaulle and Twentieth-Century France*, ed. Hugh Gough and John Horne (London: Edward Arnold, 1994), 140–141.

2. Laure Quennouëlle-Corre, "Le directeur du trésor et le financement des entreprises (1947–52)," in *François Bloch-Lainé, fonctionnaire, financier, citoyen*, ed. Michel Margairaz (Paris: Comité pour l'histoire économique et financière de la France, 2005), 99–100.

3. F. F. Ridley, "French Technocracy and Comparative Government," *Political Studies* 14, no. 1 (1966): 51.

4. As quoted in Pierre Rosanvallon, *L'État en France de 1789 à nos jours* (Paris: Éditions du Seuil, 1990), 257–258.

5. For GDP growth from 1946 to 1962, see J.-J. Carré, P. Dubois, and E. Malivaud, *French Economic Growth*, trans. John P Hatfield (Stanford: Stanford University Press, 1975), 24. For comparative annual growth rates in the 1960s, see Serge Berstein, *The Republic of de Gaulle, 1958–1969* (Cambridge: Cambridge University Press, 1993), 105.

6. Economists have debated whether success reflected state policy or the impact of the Common Market. William James Adams explains how it was both, in *Restructuring the French Economy: Government and the Rise of Market Competition since World War II* (Washington, DC: Brookings Institution, 1989).

7. Frances M. B. Lynch, *France and the International Economy: From Vichy to the Treaty of Rome* (London: Routledge, 1997), 206.

8. Monica Prasad, "Why Is France So French? Culture, Institutions, and Neoliberalism, 1974–1981," *American Journal of Sociology* 111, no. 7 (September 2005): 357–358.

9. On French influences on the European Community, see William Wallace and Julie Smith, "Democracy or Technocracy? European Integration and the Problem of Popular Consent," *West European Politics* 18, no. 3

(July 1995): 137–157; Larry Siedentop, *Democracy in Europe* (London: Allen Lane, 200); and Arthur Goldhammer, "The Old Continent Creaks," *Democracy Journal* 37 (Summer 2015).

10. Brigitte Gaïti, "Décembre 1958 ou le temps de révélation technocratique," in *La question technocratique: De l'invention d'une figure aux transformation de l'action publique,* ed. Vincent Dubois and Delphine Dulong (Strasbourg: Presses universitaires de Strasbourg, 1999), 137–153; and Delphine Dulong, *Moderniser la politique: Aux origines de la Ve République* (Paris: L'Harmattan, 1997), 159–176. For writings at the time, see, for example, the growing influence of Jacques Ellul, *The Technological Society* (New York: Vintage, 1964), first published in France in 1954 as *La Technique ou l'enjeu du siècle* (Paris: Armand Colin, 1954); Bernard Gournay, "Technocratie et administration," *Revue Française de Sciences Politiques* 10 (December 1960); Jean Meynaud, *Technocratie et politique* (Lausanne: R. Bellanger, 1960); and Meynaud, *Technocratie: Mythe et réalité* (Paris: Payot, 1964); and Philippe Bauchard, *Les technocrates et le pouvoir* (Paris: Arthaud, 1966). For intellectuals' views of technocracy, see Paul Gagnon, "French Responses to Technological Society," *Journal of European Studies* 6 (1976): 172–189; and Kristin Ross, *Fast Cars, Clean Bodies: Decolonization and the Reordering of French Culture* (Cambridge, MA: MIT Press, 1995), 176–180.

11. See the paper by François Garcia, "Le citoyen, le régime et la démocratie," written for the "Session nationale de formation politique" of the MRP, 5–10 April 1960, in the archives of the Fédération de la Seine du Mouvement républicain populaire, MRPS 25.

12. Todd Shepard, *The Invention of Decolonization: The Algerian War and the Remaking of France* (Ithaca, NY: Cornell University Press, 2006), 265; Berstein, *Republic of de Gaulle,* 72.

13. As quoted in Serge Berstein, "Pierre Mendès France et les institutions de la Ve République," *Matériaux pour l'Histoire de Notre Temps* 63–64 (July–December 2001): 85.

14. Ezra N. Suleiman, *Private Power and Centralization in France: The Notaires and the State* (Princeton: Princeton University Press, 1987). On the effect of parliamentary decline, see Henry W. Ehrmann, "Interest Groups and the Bureaucracy in Western Democracies," in *State and Society: A Reader in Comparative Political Sociology,* ed. Reinhard Bendix (Berkeley: University of California Press, 1968), 26–67.

15. Pierre Grémion, *Modernisation et progressisme: Fin d'une époque, 1968–1981* (Paris: Éditions Esprit, 2005).

16. Exceptional, but not unique. The social security caisses also played a similar role. For an illuminating exploration of how state elites can draw on the knowledge of local non-elites, see Chandra Mukerji, *Impossible Engineering: Technology and Territoriality on the Canal du Midi* (Princeton: Princeton University Press, 2009).

17. Martin A. Schain, *The Politics of Immigration in France, Britain, and the United States: A Comparative Study* (New York: Palgrave Macmillan, 2008), 106–109.

18. Charles de Gaulle, broadcast on French policy in war and peace, 2 February 1945, http//www.ibibilio.org/pha/policy/1945/450202a.html.

19. On the illusiveness of policy coherence, see Bruno Jobert and Pierre Muller, *L'État en action: Poliques publiques et corporatismes* (Paris: PUF, 1987); and Jobert, "Le ministère de l'industrie et la cohérence de la politique industrielle," *Revue Française de Science Politique* 23, no. 2 (April 1973): 321–329.

20. Michael Loriaux, "The French Developmental State as Myth and Moral Ambition," in *The Developmental State*, ed. Meredith Woo-Cumings (Ithaca, NY: Cornell University Press, 1999), 272–274. On de Gaulle's effort to harness science and industry to the creation of a nuclear strike force, see Dominique Pestre, "Scientists in Time of War: World War II, the Cold War, and Science in the United States and France," *FPCS* 24, no. 1 (Spring 2006): 36–37.

21. On this most corporatist of Fifth Republic policy domains, see John T. S. Keeler, "Situating France on the Pluralism-Corporatism Continuum: A Critique of and Alternative to the Wilson Perspective," *Comparative Politics* 17, no. 3 (January 1985): 229–249; and Keeler, *The Politics of Neocorporatism in France: Farmers, the State, and Agricultural Policy-Making in the Fifth Republic* (New York: Oxford University Press, 1987).

22. Henry W. Erhmann, "French Bureaucracy and Organized Interests," *Administrative Science Quarterly* 5, no. 1 (March 1961): 550–552.

Acknowledgments

THE AUTHOR OF A BOOK long in the making accumulates a mountain of personal and professional debt. I am delighted to acknowledge mine and express my gratitude to the many people and institutions that have helped me along the way. Several fellowships supported my research, including from the National Endowment of the Humanities, the German Marshall Fund of the United States, the Hoover Institution of War and Peace at Stanford University, Carnegie Mellon University, and the Remarque Institute at New York University. Above all, steady research support and regular sabbatical leaves from New York University made it possible to complete the archival work and write this book.

Wonderful faculty colleagues have helped me at every stage. I first began thinking about the project while teaching at Stanford, where James Sheehan, Paul Robinson, and Richard Roberts gave me sage advice about how to start. Then at Carnegie Mellon University, as I dug into the research, I benefited from working closely with Reid Andrews, Peter Stearns, and Lynn Eden on related projects, and from exchanges with Seymour Drescher, the late Samuel Hays, Mary Lindemann, Katherine Lynch, Dan Reznick, and Simon Reich. A long talk with the late Charles Tilly in New York helped me chart my way.

Thereafter, writing this book has been inseparable from my life at New York University. Any scholar in my field of modern French history knows how lucky I am to be a part of NYU's Institute of French Studies and Department of History—places of extraordinary intellectual vitality where I've drawn inspiration and advice from gifted colleagues and students. They have read my chapters or heard my presentations in workshops and colloquia. For their critical commentary and personal support, I am especially indebted to Edward Berenson, Jane Burbank, Fred Cooper, Stephane Gerson, Mary Nolan, Jerrold Seigel, Frédéric Viguier, and Larry Wolff. I also wish to thank Katherine Fleming, Yanni Kotsonis, Andrew Lee, and John Shovlin for their workshop feedback. I could single out many other past and present NYU colleagues for their ideas and support, but I wish especially to mention Agnès Antoine, Ruth Ben-Ghiat, Tom Bishop, Marie Desmartis, Yasmin Desouki, Wendy Diaz, Amy Farranto, Éric Fassin, Isabelle Genest, Stefanos Geroulanos, Francine Goldenhar, Françoise Gramet, Stephen Gross, Jennifer Hebert, Jair Kessler, Fabienne Moore, Guy Ortolano, Shanny Peer, Jacques Revel, Susan Rogers, Emmanuelle Saada, Martin Schain, Patrick Stancil, and Barbara Weinstein. Sadly, two of my close colleagues, Nicholas Wahl and Tony Judt, cannot share in the pleasure of seeing this book in print. They would be happy indeed.

I am also indebted to the many graduate students at NYU I have been fortunate to work with, many of whom have moved on into careers of their own. They will see their influence in these pages. For critical readings of chapters and research assistance, I am grateful to Marie Benedict, Elizabeth Campbell, Daniel Cohen, Kala DeStefano, Julie Fette, Marie Fortini, Jonathan Gosnell, Joshua Humphreys, Elizabeth Jelliffe, Mary Lewis, Gérarde Magloire, Jessica Pearson, William Poulin-Deltour, Nicole Rudolph, Michelle Pinto, Paul Sager, Andrew Seaton, Evan Spritzer, Sylvie Waskiewicz, Arlys Watkinson, Matthew Watkins, and Matthew Wendeln. Aro Velmet helped me a great deal with the photos. For newspaper research I also had help from Nicole Benhabib, then an undergraduate, and from Michel Goyer, then at MIT.

Several chapters of the book benefited from the generosity and insights of colleagues elsewhere who read drafts or were involved in editing articles from which chapters were later derived. My thanks to Martin Alexander, Lincoln Caplan, Judith Coffin, Valerie Deacon, Laura Downs, Andrew Knapp, Mary Lewis, and Kenneth Mouré. I am grateful, too, to Sarah Fishman, Brian Newsome, and Rebecca Pulju for advice on sources. Not least, I am deeply indebted to the two anonymous readers for the Press, who offered incisive advice.

I have had the opportunity to present portions of my work at conferences, invited lectures, and workshops. My thanks to the organizers and participants at sessions of the Society of French Historical Studies, the American Historical Association, the Conference of Europeanists of the Council of European Studies, the Twentieth-Century History Seminar at Columbia University, and at my presentations at Yale, Princeton, the CUNY Graduate Center, Georgetown, Cambridge University, and the American University of Beirut. In these venues I received valuable suggestions from Volker Berghahn, Joseph Bohling, Michael Bess, Ruth Harris, Jeff Horn, Gareth Stedman Jones, Richard Kuisel, Michael Miller, Philip Nord, Sara Pritchard, Judith Stein, Emmanuel Todd, Irwin Wall, Rachel White, Judith Wishnia, and Martin Woessner. My colleagues at the Minda de Gunzburg Center for European Studies at Harvard University, where I have been a local affiliate for two decades, have also responded to my work. My special thanks there go to James Cronin, Arthur Goldhammer, Laura Frader, Jim Kloppenberg, Michelle Lamont, Mary Lewis, Charles Maier, and the late Stanley Hoffmann.

Colleagues in France have helped me a great deal as well—above all, Patrick Fridenson, who has been giving me invaluable research advice, intellectual and practical, for as long as I have been doing research in France. For his steadfast advice and support, and his reading of portions of the work, I am grateful. My thanks, too, for readings or advice from Catherine Collomp, Brigitte Gaïti, Lucette Le Van-Lemesle, Michel Lescure, Catherine Omnès, Alexis Spire, Bruno Valat, Patrick Weil, Olivier Wieviorka, and Claire Zalc.

Many archivists in France have helped me find resources and get permission to read them. I especially wish to thank Dominique Parcollet at the Centre d'histoire contemporaines at Sciences Po in Paris, Erik Langlinay at the Institut Pierre Mendès France, Pascal Clerc at the archives of the Confédération française démocratique du travail, Gervaise Surzur at the Comité d'histoire de Sécurité sociale, Mme Dijoux at the Archives économiques et financières, Mme Petillat and Mme Lagrange at the Centre des archives contemporaines, and several archivists at the Archives nationales, including Jean Pouëssel, Yvonne Poulle, Chantal de Tourtier-Bonazzi, Mlle Grimaldi, and M. Guillot.

Chapters 1, 3, and 5 of this book explore themes that evolved from the following articles: "The Liberation of France as a Moment in State-Making," in *Crisis and Renewal in Twentieth-Century France*, ed. Martin S. Alexander and Kenneth Mouré (New York: Berghahn Books, 2002); "Réformateurs et contestataires de l'impôt après la seconde guerre mondiale," in *L'impôt en France aux XIXe et XXe siècles*, ed. Maurice Lévy-Leboyer, Michel Lescure, and Alain Plessis (Paris: Comité pour l'histoire économique et financière de la France, 2006); "Les petits commerçants et l'État de la révolte poujadiste au début de la Ve République," in *Les petites et moyennes entreprises de 1880 à nos jours: Pouvoirs, representation, action*, ed. Sylvie Guillaume and Michel Lescure (Brussels: Peter Lang, 2008); "France's Liberation Era, 1944–47: A Social and Economic Settlement?" in *Revisiting the Liberation*, ed. Andrew Knapp (New York: Palgrave, 2007).

I am especially grateful to Kathleen McDermott, my editor at Harvard University Press, for her support, insight, and guidance. For editing and other assistance in shepherding this book into print, I wish to thank Wendy Nelson, Stephanie Vyce, Katrina Vassallo, Mihaela Pacurar, and Brian Ostrander.

Finally, my debts to family, which are beyond reckoning. Liz Cohen and I have been sharing life and the love of writing history for a blessedly long time now. There's no appraising how much this book owes to her—the countless conversations, the close readings of drafts, the patience, the belief in it. No one is happier to see it out in the world than she, except perhaps our daughters, Julia and Natalie. As youngsters they first started coming to France on my research trips, and now with their husbands Paul and Nico they have made it a place of their own. Fine writers both, Julia and Natalie have inspired me to make the book better, with Julia even giving parts of it a last trenchant round of editing. This book is dedicated to the three women in my life for good reason. I owe them everything.

Index

Abbas, Ferhat, 281
Abortion, 113, 115, 117, 128, 140, 142
Administrative rule: as an approach
 to governance, 4–5; British versus
 French, 300; and democracy, 4–5,
 7–8. *See also* Technocracy
Agence France-Presse, 168
Aircraft industry, 46, 166, 168; cutbacks
 at, 180–181; expertise in, 204–206;
 labor relations in, 168, 171–172,
 175, 177, 204, 305–306; production
 committees in, 178. *See also* Strikes;
 Tillon, Charles
Algerians: and CGT, 295; discrimination against, 270–272, 282–283, 295;
 as migrants, 69–70, 73–74, 261–264,
 267–278; navigating social services
 and surveillance, 277–278; in protest, 274–275, 294–298; as outsiders
 in their policy domain, 308; and
 pronatalist policy, 271; as wartime
 laborers, 45. *See also* FLN (Front
 de libération nationale); Mouvement pour le triomphe des libertés
 démocratiques (MTLD)
Algerian war, 15; as context for French
 reconstruction, 7, 14–15, 260–261,
 297–298; and founding of the Fifth
 Republic, 261; impact on economic
 and social planning, 278–289; impact
 on migration policy, 264–266; impact
 on policing, 266–278; impact on
 social services, 266–278; impact on

state authority, 7–8, 245, 290–298,
 308; inspiring protest, 294–298
Algiers, 95, 125; and Algerian migrants,
 69; during Algerian war, 241, 245,
 261, 290–291; Constantine Plan and,
 278, 282, 287; and the Resistance, 3,
 18, 21–23
Alliance nationale contre la dépopula-
 tion, 113, 131
Allix, Pierre, 90–92, 98–101, 108
Andrieu, Claire, 165
Anti-Semitism, 44, 59; toward Mendès
 France, 97, 239, 252; and Poujade,
 102, 239; and the Vichy regime,
 114–115
Ardant, Gabriel, 227, 251
Armand, Louis, 176, 183, 200, 202–203
Armengaud, André, 182, 242
Aron, Raymond, 182
Attlee, Clement, 167
Aubert-Picard, Jeanne, 152
Aubrac, Raymond, 31–33, 37
Auffray, Bernard, 65, 70
Austria, 15

Bacon, Paul, 125, 159
Banatais, 68
Bank for International Settlements
 (BIS), 212–214, 256
Bank of France, 186, 218, 244
Banks and banking, 80, 106, 281; Bank
 of France, 218, 244; banking law of
 1941, 169, 185; in Britain, 179;